I0127036

Debt Relief and Beyond

Debt Relief and Beyond

Lessons Learned and
Challenges Ahead

Edited by

Carlos A. Primo Braga

Dörte Dömeland

THE WORLD BANK
Washington, D.C.

© 2009 The International Bank for Reconstruction and Development / The World Bank
1818 H Street, NW
Washington, DC 20433
Telephone: 202-473-1000
Internet: www.worldbank.org
E-mail: feedback@worldbank.org

All rights reserved
1 2 3 4 12 11 10 09

This volume is a product of the staff of the International Bank for Reconstruction and Development / The World Bank. The findings, interpretations, and conclusions expressed in this volume do not necessarily reflect the views of the Executive Directors of The World Bank or the governments they represent.

The World Bank does not guarantee the accuracy of the data included in this work. The boundaries, colors, denominations, and other information shown on any map in this work do not imply any judgement on the part of The World Bank concerning the legal status of any territory or the endorsement or acceptance of such boundaries.

Rights and Permissions
The material in this publication is copyrighted. Copying and/or transmitting portions or all of this work without permission may be a violation of applicable law. The International Bank for Reconstruction and Development / The World Bank encourages dissemination of its work and will normally grant permission to reproduce portions of the work promptly.

For permission to photocopy or reprint any part of this work, please send a request with complete information to the Copyright Clearance Center Inc., 222 Rosewood Drive, Danvers, MA 01923, USA; telephone: 978-750-8400; fax: 978-750-4470; Internet: www.copyright .com.

All other queries on rights and licenses, including subsidiary rights, should be addressed to the Office of the Publisher, The World Bank, 1818 H Street, NW, Washington, DC 20433, USA; fax: 202-522-2422; e-mail: pubrights@worldbank.org.

ISBN: 978-0-8213-7874-8
eISBN: 978-0-8213-7875-5
DOI: 10.1596/978-0-8213-7874-8

Cover design: Edelman Design Communications
Cover photo: © Manuel Ribeiro

Library of Congress Cataloging-in-Publication Data
Debt relief and beyond: lessons learned and challenges ahead / Carlos A. Primo Braga and Dörte Dömeland (editors).
    p. cm.
Includes bibliographical references and index.
ISBN 978-0-8213-7874-8 — ISBN 978-0-8213-7875-5 (electronic)
    1. Debt relief—Developing countries. I. Braga, Carlos Alberto Primo, 1954- II. Dömeland, Dörte, 1971- III. World Bank.

HJ8899.D4383 2009
336.3'435091724—dc22

2009020887

Contents

Tables

Preface

This book is the outcome of a conference titled "Debt Relief and Beyond: A World Bank Conference on Debt and Development," held in October 2008 at the World Bank in Washington, DC. The conference brought together more than 200 participants, many of them from developing countries—including policy makers, debt managers, researchers, and representatives of civil society international organizations and the private sector, as well as donors—to draw lessons, learn, and discuss the challenges that developing countries, particularly low-income countries, face after 12 years of debt relief under the Heavily Indebted Poor Countries (HIPC) Initiative.

This volume presents the background papers that were prepared for the conference. They are grouped into four main topics: debt relief, debt sustainability, odious debt, and debt management. Some of the papers are impressionistic, offering the benefit of the authors' years of experience in the field. Others are highly analytical, oriented toward economists and other social scientists.

The book is intended for members of the development community—government officials, development professionals from donor countries, capital market professionals, representatives from civil society organizations, and researchers—interested in debt relief and development. It provides practical approaches that must be taken in going *beyond* debt relief.

Acknowledgments

Many people helped to create this volume. We especially thank Danny Leipziger, who was vice president and head of the Poverty Reduction and Economic Management Network (PRM) at the World Bank at the time of the conference, for his support of this book and the conference ("Debt Relief and Beyond: A World Bank Conference on Debt and Development") upon which it is based. We are very grateful to the Norwegian Ministry of Foreign Affairs for a generous grant that made both the conference and this book possible. We also want to express our appreciation to conference presenters, panelists, and attendees for their contributions to the refinements of the background papers. In particular, we thank our commentators—Werner Baer, Jesús Crespo Cuaresma, Mansoor Dailami, Abraham Nwankwo, M. Govinda Rao, and Sudhir Shetty—for their insightful comments, and we thank Dana Weist for intellectual guidance.

In addition, the authors received valuable comments from a number of reviewers. These include Charles Abrahams, Myrvin Anthony, Nancy Birdsall, Stephania Bonilla, Lee Buchheit, Robert Cocker, Larry J. Forgy, Tomislav Galac, Karina Garcia-Casalderrey, Herve Joly, Jürgen Kaiser, Homi Kharas, Yan Liu, Thomas Inge Magnusson, Perry Perone, Brian Pinto, Mona Prasad, Maurizio Ragazzi, P. S. Rao, Rubens Ricupero, Juan Pedro Schmid, Stefan Talmon, Eduardo Valencia Ospina, Paul Williams, and John Williamson. Galina Hale and Carlos Arteta shared their data set for chapter 7. The authors also thank Detre Bradley, Shannon Mockler, Emeka Osakwe, and support staff in the Economic Policy and Debt Department of PRM for excellent research assistance.

Contributors

Phillip Anderson is a senior manager in the Banking and Debt Management Department of the Office of the Vice President and Treasurer at the World Bank.

Luca Bandiera is an economist in the Economic Policy and Debt Department of the Poverty Reduction and Economic Management Network at the World Bank.

Christian Beddies is a senior economist in the Strategy, Policy, and Review Department at the International Monetary Fund.

Nina Budina is a senior economist in the Fiscal Affairs Department at the International Monetary Fund.

Jesús Crespo Cuaresma is a professor of economics at the University of Innsbruck, Austria.

Udaibir S. Das is the chief of the Exchange Regime and Debt & Reserve Management Division at the International Monetary Fund.

Dörte Dömeland is an economist in the Economic Policy and Debt Department of the Poverty Reduction and Economic Management Network at the World Bank.

Boris Gamarra is a senior economist in the Economic Policy and Debt Department of the Poverty Reduction and Economic Management Network at the World Bank.

Frederico Gil Sander is in the Young Professionals Program working in the Poverty Reduction and Economic Management Unit in the East Asia and Pacific Region at the World Bank.

Leonardo Hernández is a lead economist in the Economic Policy and Debt Department of the Poverty Reduction and Economic Management Network at the World Bank.

Homi Kharas is a senior fellow at the Wolfensohn Center for Development at the Brookings Institution, Washington, DC.

Marie-Hélène Le Manchec is a consultant in the Economic Policy and Debt Department of the Poverty Reduction and Economic Management Network at the World Bank. When writing the chapter, she was a senior economist with the Strategy, Policy, and Review Department at the International Monetary Fund.

Ying Li is a consultant to the Economic Policy and Debt Department of the Poverty Reduction and Economic Management Network at the World Bank.

Lili Liu is a lead economist in the Economic Policy and Debt Department of the Poverty Reduction and Economic Management Network at the World Bank.

Henry Mooney is a consultant in the Economic Policy and Debt Department of the Poverty Reduction and Economic Management Network at the World Bank.

Vikram Nehru is the director of the Poverty Reduction and Economic Management Network and of the Private and Financial Sector Department of the East Asia and Pacific Region at the World Bank.

Michael G. Papaioannou is a senior economist in the Monetary and Capital Markets Department of the Sovereign Asset and Liability Management Division at the International Monetary Fund.

Brian Pinto is an adviser to the managing director at the World Bank.

Magdalena Polan is an economist in the Capital Markets Department of the Sovereign Asset and Liability Management Division at the International Monetary Fund.

Malvina Pollock retired as a lead financial specialist in the Credit Risk Department at the World Bank and the Bank's representative to the Paris Club and the Berne Union of Credit and Investment Insurers.

Abha Prasad is a senior debt specialist in the Economic Policy and Debt Department of the Poverty Reduction and Economic Management Network at the World Bank.

Mona Prasad is a consultant in the Economic Policy and Debt Department of the Poverty Reduction and Economic Management Network at the World Bank.

Carlos A. Primo Braga is the director of the Economic Policy and Debt Department in the Poverty Reduction and Economic Management Network at the World Bank.

Francis Rowe is a senior country economist in the Economic Policy and Debt Department in the South Asia Region of the World Bank.

Juan Pedro Schmid is a junior professional officer in the Economic Policy and Debt Department of the Poverty Reduction and Economic Management Network at the World Bank.

Mark Thomas is the lead economist in the Poverty Reduction and Economic Management Network in the Europe and Central Asia Region at the World Bank.

Eriko Togo is a senior economist in the Economic Policy and Debt Department of the Poverty Reduction and Economic Management Network at the World Bank.

Christoph Trebesch is a PhD candidate in economics at the Free University of Berlin.

Sweder van Wijnbergen is a professor of economics at the University of Amsterdam.

Gallina Andronova Vincelette is an economist in the Economic Policy and Debt Department of the Poverty Reduction and Economic Management Network at the World Bank.

Signe Zeikate is a consultant in the Economic Policy and Debt Department of the Poverty Reduction and Economic Management Network at the World Bank.

Abbreviations

$	All dollar amounts are U.S. dollars.
ASEAN	Association of Southeast Asian Nations
BIC	Bayesian information criterion
BMA	Bayesian model averaging
CPA	country programmable aid
CPI	consumer price index
CPIA	Country Policy and Institutional Assessment
CRF	common reduction factor
DAC	Development Assistance Committee
DeMPA	Debt Management Performance Assessment
DHS	demographic and health survey
DRF	Debt Reduction Facility
DSA	debt sustainability analysis
DSF	Debt Sustainability Framework
EAI	Enterprise for the Americas Initiative
EMBI	Emerging Markets Bond Index
ESAF	Enhanced Structural Adjustment Facility
FDI	foreign direct investment
GAVI	Global Alliance for Vaccines and Immunisation
GDP	gross domestic product
GNI	gross national income
HIPC	heavily indebted poor countries
IBRD	International Bank for Reconstruction and Development
ICRG	*International Country Risk Guide*
IDA	International Development Association
IDB	Inter-American Development Bank
IFS	*International Financial Statistics*
IIR	Institutional Investor Rating
IMF	International Monetary Fund
IMR	infant mortality rate
MDG	Millennium Development Goal
MDRI	Multilateral Debt Relief Initiative
MTDS	medium-term debt-management strategy
NGO	nongovernmental organization

ODA	official development assistance
OECD	Organisation for Economic Co-operation and Development
PRGF	Poverty Reduction and Growth Facility
PRS	poverty reduction strategy
PRSP	Poverty Reduction Strategy Paper
S&P	Standard & Poor's
SAF	Structural Adjustment Facility
SPA	Special Program of Assistance (to Low-Income, Debt-Distressed Countries in Sub-Saharan Africa)
StAR	Stolen Assets Recovery
UNCTAD	United Nations Conference on Trade and Development

Introduction

Dörte Dömeland and Carlos A. Primo Braga

Heavily indebted low-income countries benefited from significant debt relief over the past decade. Under the Heavily Indebted Poor Countries (HIPC) Initiative and the Multilateral Debt Relief Initiative (MDRI), assistance of about $117 billion in nominal terms had been committed to 35 HIPCs as of end-April 2009. This debt relief represents about half of the 2007 GDP of these countries, whose debt burden is expected to drop by more than 80 percent once full debt relief is granted. As a result of relief already provided, debt-service payments have plummeted and expenditures on pro-poor growth programs increased.

These debt-relief initiatives have provided HIPCs with the opportunity for a fresh start. But many of the fundamentals that led to the accumulation of unsustainable debt burdens—narrow production and export bases, vulnerability to exogenous shocks, capacity and institutional constraints—remain, raising questions about how the benefits from debt relief can be preserved. This issue is critical, especially as debt relief is generally designed as a one-time intervention (to avoid moral hazard issues). Locking in the benefits of debt relief requires a complex set of incentives, policy and institutional arrangements, and intertemporal policy choices designed to pave the way to debt sustainability.

In October 2008, the World Bank hosted "Debt Relief and Beyond: A World Bank Conference on Debt and Development." The conference brought together more than 200 policy makers: debt managers from developing countries; donors; researchers; and representatives of civil society, international organizations, and the private sector to confer on the challenges developing countries, particularly low-income countries, face after 12 years of debt relief under the HIPC Initiative.[1] This book builds upon the background papers prepared for the conference.

The book is divided into four parts. Part I examines the design of debt-relief initiatives and provides evidence of its effect on education, health, and economic growth. Part II describes the risks and opportunities developing countries face following debt relief. It identifies how they can safeguard debt sustainability; describes the role of sovereign risk for private sector access to capital; and draws lessons from the experience of market-access countries on the links between sovereign debt and development. Part III examines the concept and various policy proposals of dealing with "odious" debt (defined broadly as loans made to sovereign borrowers that are not used in the interest of the people). Part IV looks at debt management, debt restructuring, and the interplay between debt and fiscal policies. It provides guidance on debut sovereign bond issues; examines the issuance and management of subnational debt; describes the challenges of crafting fiscal policy and managing debt and oil revenues in a (temporarily) oil-rich country (the Republic of Congo); and draws lessons from Chile's experiences using debt swaps in the 1980s.

Part I: Debt Relief

The history of debt-relief initiatives goes back several decades. Over the past half century, 52 low-income countries that have been unable to service their external debt have requested debt relief from their creditors. Countries currently considered HIPCs are estimated to have received at least $30 billion (in end-1997 net present value terms) in debt relief from Paris Club creditors through agreements signed between 1988 and 1998. Since 1989, low-income countries were able to extinguish about $10 billion of commercial external debt through operations supported under the International Development Association's Debt Reduction Facility (DRF). Moreover, since 1996, 35 countries have qualified for an estimated debt relief of $57 billion (in end-2008 net present value terms) under the HIPC Initiative. In addition, the 26 HIPCs that had reached the completion point as of June 2009 will receive $29 billion (in end-2008 net present value terms) in debt relief under the MDRI.

Chapter 1 (by Boris Gamarra, Malvina Pollock, and Carlos A. Primo Braga) reviews the history of debt restructuring and debt relief to low-income countries and explains the rationale underlying the adoption of increasingly concessional terms. It traces the progression of debt relief from short-term debt-restructuring operations to outright debt forgiveness under the HIPC Initiative and the MDRI, describes the range of debt-relief measures adopted by creditors, and analyzes the extent to which debt relief has alleviated the debt burden of low-income countries.

Debt-relief initiatives have never been only about reducing debt. They have been used as leverage to move the indebted country into a new mode of operations to ensure that resources freed up through debt relief are used to reduce poverty or increase growth. In the context of the HIPC Initiative, this commitment to reform is, among other things, translated into the requirement to implement a government-owned poverty reduction strategy. Chapter 2 (by Jesús Crespo Cuaresma and Gallina Andronova Vincelette) and chapter 3 (by Juan Pedro Schmid) look at the impact of

HIPC Initiative debt relief on education and health, respectively, two cornerstones of such strategies. Both chapters provide evidence that several social outcome indicators improved as countries moved through the HIPC Initiative process.

Tracing the effects of debt relief on social outcomes is difficult, however. Debt relief frees up resources that would otherwise have been used for debt service. Through the conditionalities associated with HIPC relief, it also fosters improved policies and institutions that allow more efficient and equitable use of those resources. Both chapters 2 and 3 conclude that although the reduction in debt-service payment undoubtedly contributed to improved social indicators, it may not have been the primary vehicle through which improvements materialized.

The important effect of improvements in institutional quality on successful debt-relief outcome hints at the fact that implementation of debt relief may face particular challenges in fragile states (defined as states with particularly weak policies and institutions). Fragile states that are also heavily indebted start from a worse position than either nonfragile HIPCs or fragile non–HIPCs. For example, fragile HIPCs experienced much slower growth in per capita income over the past decade than nonfragile completion point HIPCs, and their average social indicators are lower across the board. This difference between fragile and nonfragile completion point HIPCs has triggered a debate over whether the HIPC process should be better tailored to the needs of fragile HIPCs to enable them to complete the HIPC process more quickly. Chapter 4 (by Luca Bandiera, Jesús Crespo Cuaresma, and Gallina Andronova Vincelette) shows that although fragility has slowed progress under the HIPC Initiative, the slowdown does not seem to have exacerbated countries' fragility. Fragile states that improved the quality of their policies and institutions and maintained macroeconomic stability throughout the HIPC process seem to have enjoyed stronger economic growth.

Part II: Debt Sustainability

As more and more countries graduate from the HIPC Initiative and the MDRI, the question of how these countries can maintain their debt at sustainable levels has become preeminent. In 2005, the joint World Bank–International Monetary Fund (IMF) Debt Sustainability Framework (DSF) was put in place to monitor and analyze the sustainability of debt in low-income countries. The DSF aims to help guide the borrowing decisions of low-income countries and the lending and grant-allocation decisions of creditors in a way that aligns these countries' financing needs with their repayment capacity.

Chapter 5 (by Christian Beddies, Dörte Dömeland, Marie-Hélène Le Manchec, and Henry Mooney) outlines the DSF and provides an overview of debt sustainability in low-income countries. It shows that although debt relief has given many of these countries a chance for a fresh start, an array of challenges remains. Low-income countries tend to have relatively weak institutions, are highly exposed to external shocks, and struggle with large financing needs. As debt relief has created new borrowing space, the menu of financing options to low-income countries has expanded. These new options provide welcome additional resources for development—but they also raise the risk of new debt sustainability problems if borrowing options are not managed carefully.

Chapter 6 (by Dörte Dömeland and Homi Kharas) uses new fiscal data to show that debt dynamics in low-income countries have improved not only as a result of debt relief and the accompanying improvement in policies but also because of higher growth. It shows that the improved debt sustainability outlook—accompanied by an enhanced security situation, better macroeconomic performance, and higher commodity prices—has led to increased interest by foreign investors and nontraditional creditors, especially in Sub-Saharan Africa. It has also improved access to finance by the domestic private sector, as discussed in chapter 7 (by Udaibir S. Das, Michael G. Papaioannou, and Christoph Trebesch), which analyzes how sovereign default risk affects private sector access to international capital markets, in the form of external credit (loans and bond issuances) and equity issuances

Chapter 8 (by Brian Pinto and Mona Prasad) draws on the experience of market-access countries to gain insights about which macroeconomic policies low-income countries should follow as they eye market-access status. After the 1990s, a successful strategy of market-access countries was to reduce indebtedness; shift prudently toward domestic debt; focus on the government's intertemporal budget constraint instead of short-term fiscal deficits; run high primary surpluses; build up reserves; and, in many cases, strengthen financial and fiscal systems. The experience of these countries suggests that low-income countries may benefit from focusing first on aligning fiscal policy and growth, rather than resuming high-level borrowing immediately in their pursuit of market-access status.

Part III: Odious Debt

The concept of odious debt has been a subject of debate for decades. Although the understanding of what constitutes odious debt has evolved, no agreement has been reached regarding a workable definition. This may explain why the concept has very rarely been invoked in law to justify nonpayment of sovereign debts. Chapter 9 (by Vikram Nehru and Mark Thomas) summarizes the evolution of the concept of odious debt over time and proposes that better borrowing and lending practices could go a long way toward ensuring that sovereign loans are used for the benefit of the population.

As the concept of odious debt has evolved, several policy proposals have been put forward to protect countries from servicing odious loans. Chapter 10 (by Frederico Gil Sander) uses a simple political agency model to analyze three proposed frameworks and their effects on commercial lenders and sovereign borrowers. It finds that none of these frameworks produces unambiguous welfare improvements to the populations living under repressive regimes.

Chapter 11 (by Dörte Dömeland, Frederico Gil Sander, and Carlos A. Primo Braga) analyzes whether the proposed frameworks would make it less costly for borrowers to repudiate loans deemed odious. Like chapter 10, it concludes that all odious debt policy proposals entail nontrivial costs. Using different approaches, both chapters conclude that ex ante frameworks appear superior to ex post ones, because they minimize the cost associated with default.

Part IV: Debt Management

As the complexity of debt instruments available to low-income countries increases, strengthening their debt-management capacity has become particularly important. Chapter 12 (by Phillip Anderson and Eriko Togo) describes how government debt-management practices evolved in more advanced countries and draws lessons for low-income countries. It highlights the importance of maintaining macroeconomic stability and reliable and timely databases as preconditions for developing a medium-term debt-management strategy underpinned by a quantitative assessment of the cost and risk consequences of alternative debt-management strategies. It also notes that given the volatility of donor aid, developing the domestic debt market is another path worth exploring to ensure that the government has access to additional sources of financing over the medium term.

Chapter 13 (by Udaibir S. Das, Michael G. Papaioannou, and Magdalena Polan) examines some of the advantages and disadvantages of international debut bonds. It outlines key preconditions, discusses strategic considerations, and presents some empirical evidence on the determinants of the size and cost of debut issues. It also discusses some typical pitfalls in accessing international capital markets.

Chapter 14 (by Lili Liu, Abha Prasad, Francis Rowe, and Signe Zeikate) shows that although decentralized financial planning can help governments identify infrastructure needs and allocate resources, it also creates significant risks. Subnational governments have an incentive not to repay their loans if they believe the central government will bail them out if necessary. A soft budget constraint undermines the sustainability of subnational fiscal policy and may lead to contingent liabilities for the central government. The chapter identifies components of a regulatory framework that can reduce these problems and examines the impact of the ongoing global financial crisis on the management of subnational debt.

Using the example of the Republic of Congo, chapter 15 (by Nina Budina, Sweder van Wijnbergen, and Ying Li) illustrates the difficulty of managing debt in a country whose wealth comes primarily from one key commodity. Analyzing the effects of uncertainty through stochastic analysis, it shows that oil-rich countries face major challenges in managing gains and losses from the oil windfall in a way that ensures fiscal sustainability. The variance of future debt outcomes can be greatly reduced if fiscal policy is tightened when negative debt shocks occur.

Good debt-management practices not only can prevent the accumulation of unsustainable debt but also can support innovative approaches to debt restructuring, as illustrated by the use of debt-swap mechanisms in Chile during the 1980s, described in chapter 16 (by Leonardo Hernández). A recession and high indebtedness had left Chile without access to international capital markets and, consequently, a shortage of foreign exchange. The government created two programs that allowed residents and foreigners to swap foreign debt for domestic debt or equity, converting 35 percent of its foreign debt over the course of six years. Chapter 16 analyzes the advantages and disadvantages of these two mechanisms. It concludes that before adopting a similar program, a country must first establish a strong legal, regulatory, and supervisory framework; adopt a strict adjustment program for macro stability and growth; demonstrate a commitment to equitable outcomes; and create a sufficiently deep domestic capital market.

The Road Ahead

Debt relief has provided low-income countries with new opportunities, but formidable challenges remain. Broadening the production and export bases of these economies remains a challenge, particularly given the current global financial and economic crisis, which is likely to put additional pressure on debt-burden indicators in many low-income countries. Declines in commodity prices and plummeting capital inflows, combined with limited tools with which to address the economic downturn, are fostering liquidity problems and are likely to raise the probability of debt distress in many of these countries if the effects of the financial crisis persist. What can be to done to dampen the impact of the financial crisis on low-income countries and ensure that the benefits from HIPC Initiative and MDRI debt relief are not reversed in the years to come?

Most low-income countries and emerging economies perform better now than in the past on key dimensions the literature identifies as relevant to the risk of sovereign defaults. On average, for example, Latin American countries and emerging markets in Asia have significantly reduced the ratio of external debt to GDP in recent years. Only Eastern European countries had higher external debt levels in 2008 than they did in 2000 (the result of increases in private sector external debt). Accordingly, a wave of sovereign defaults seems less likely than in previous global economic crises.

That said, the impact of the current crisis is just beginning to reach low-income countries, as the spillover of the slowdown in richer economies and the resulting decline in external demand for commodity exporters affects their trade flows. A reversal in financial flows, particularly private capital flows, could lead to a strong decline in capital formation and eventually to liquidity problems. Before the boom in private sector flows, low-income countries had limited or no access to private foreign capital, even in good times. As global credit conditions tighten and investors' risk aversion increases, credit has once again become more limited. As a result, investment flows are moving to higher-quality and more liquid assets. After peaking in the second quarter of 2007, for example, portfolio flows to African markets decreased substantially, leaving countries that had begun to integrate into global financial markets particularly vulnerable. Given the dependence of many low-income countries, especially African countries, on primary exports and the bleak near-term prospects of substantial private capital inflows, a shortfall in aid could be an additional harmful side effect of the global crisis.

Implementation of the joint World Bank–IMF Debt Sustainability Framework can play a role in helping countries manage the impact of the financial crisis. By enabling better monitoring of the debt sustainability outlook, increasing coordination among creditors, and raising the amount of grant financing, especially to countries with elevated levels of risk distress, the DSF partly offsets the negative impact of the financial crisis on debt sustainability prospects. The DSF suffers, however, from the still limited understanding of the complex link between debt and economic growth, especially in low-income countries, which lies at the heart of debt sustainability. More analytical work in this area is therefore needed.

The global financial crisis also underscores the importance of strengthening public debt-management capacity and institutions. Better debt management not only can improve the quality and comprehensiveness of debt data and information systems and increase the coordination with fiscal policies, but also may enable low-income countries to develop a sound and efficient domestic debt market, which could provide governments with a stable alternative source of financing. These efforts take time to bear fruit, however; in the interim, continuing donor support and creditor coordination will be essential to maintain the momentum gained to date.

The road ahead remains extremely challenging. Translating debt relief into sustainable growth requires low-income countries to invest in building strong and accountable institutions and avoiding the temptation to overborrow. In the absence of such efforts, debt relief is unlikely to have a lasting impact.

Note

1. Information about the conference, including comments by discussants, is available at http://www1.worldbank.org/economicpolicy/debtconf08/DebtConferenceHome.asp.

Part I

Debt Relief

1

Debt Relief to Low-Income Countries: A Retrospective

Boris Gamarra, Malvina Pollock, and Carlos A. Primo Braga

The machinery for sovereign debt workouts has been evolving since the United Nations Monetary and Financial Conference at Bretton Woods in 1944. Over the past half century, 85 developing countries, including 52 low-income countries, have been unable to service their external debt and requested debt relief from their creditors.

This chapter provides a retrospective on how debt relief has been granted to low-income countries since Bretton Woods.[1] It traces the evolution of debt relief from short-term debt-restructuring operations to outright debt forgiveness, describes the range of debt-relief measures adopted by creditors, and analyzes the extent to which debt relief has alleviated the debt burden of low-income countries.

Debt Relief: A Brief History

During the first 25 years after World War II, few countries requested debt relief. By the end of the 1970s, serious balance of payments problems and high levels of external debt caused many countries to do so. Since the late 1970s, creditor countries have repeatedly modified debt-relief efforts, making them increasingly generous.

Debt Relief before 1972

In the years after World War II, most lending to developing countries was provided through new programs of official development assistance or in the form of insured private credit to support export-related lending. Before the quadrupling of oil prices in 1973, requests for debt relief from developing countries were limited: from the time the World Bank opened its doors (in 1946) until 1972, only nine countries (Argentina, Brazil, Chile, Ghana, India, Indonesia, Pakistan, Peru, and Turkey) sought relief on their external obligations. Their experiences are instructive, because many of the principles and procedures that still govern debt restructuring were formulated at that time.

Creditors' initial motivation in helping debtor countries over periods of payment difficulties was to increase the likelihood of collecting on the claims they held. This was accompanied by a desire to treat all creditors equally and to see debtor countries make the maximum effort to redress their economic problems. Creditors quickly determined that these objectives could best be met by restructuring their claims on sovereign governments in a concerted framework. The Paris Club has provided such a framework since the mid-1950s (box 1.1). (For analyses of Paris Club activities, see Rieffel 2003 and Cosio-Pascal 2008.)

Not all of the negotiations for the nine countries took place within the Paris Club forum: restructuring with Turkey (1955–70) was conducted under the auspices of the Organisation for Economic Co-operation and Development (OECD), and debt relief for India (1968–76) and Pakistan (following the separation of Bangladesh in 1971) was arranged through aid consortium meetings organized and chaired by the World Bank.[2] Still, in all cases the negotiations followed the format developed in the Paris Club, in both the nature of the agreement and the rescheduling terms granted.

The debt relief granted was aimed at helping the debtor country avoid "imminent default." A common guiding principle was that the period of debt relief should be short. One year was the typical consolidation period granted. During this period, creditors could reassess the debtor country's

---

Box 1.1 The Paris Club

In 1956, the French Treasury hosted a group of creditor countries in Paris to renegotiate supplier and buyer credits to Argentina. The group, an informal group of official creditors dedicated to finding "coordinated and sustainable solutions to the payment difficulties experienced by debtor countries," came to be known as the Paris Club. It remains a voluntary group of creditor countries that makes decisions by consensus. Since its inception, it has helped 85 debtor countries restructure debt totaling $513 billion.

Source: www.clubdeparis.org.

need for further relief; its economic performance, which was subsequently linked to its ability to maintain eligibility for International Monetary Fund (IMF) upper-tranche resources; and the debtor country's success in renegotiating debts to other creditors on terms comparable to those extended by Paris Club creditors. The possibility of additional debt relief was often embodied in a goodwill clause—an implicit recognition that the initial debt-relief arrangements might prove inadequate.

For the first nine countries with which agreements were concluded, Paris Club creditors restructured $6.9 billion of principal and interest in 35 separate agreements. From the perspective of this chapter, the agreements with Ghana and Indonesia are the most interesting, because they are the first instances in which the importance of debt sustainability for low-income countries was addressed in the restructuring process.

Both countries approached their Paris Club creditors in 1966 for debt relief to help restructure their economies, following programs of vast, unproductive public sector expenditures by recently overthrown governments. In the first round of negotiations, creditors tried to impose the type of terms established with the Latin American countries to help overcome liquidity crises. In the face of the unsustainable levels of external debt accumulated by both countries, creditors were forced to modify their approach, in the end extending highly concessional terms.

Under the agreement concluded with Indonesia in 1970, the entire stock of debt owed to Paris Club creditors was consolidated and paid over 30 years, interest free. There was no grace period, but the agreement had a "bisque" clause (the right to unilaterally suspend or defer payments) that allowed 50 percent of payments during the first six years to be deferred, at an interest rate of 4 percent, and repaid at the end of the 30-year term.

After prolonged negotiations, the outcome for Ghana was comparable. Under the agreement concluded in 1974, the entire stock of debt was consolidated and paid over 28 years, with 11 years of grace at an interest rate of 2.5 percent.

Debt Relief 1973–86

The shock of the fourfold rise in petroleum prices at the end of 1973 and the simultaneous rise in the prices of primary commodities generated economic winners and losers in Sub-Saharan Africa. But as commodity prices collapsed following a global recession in the mid-1970s and oil prices rose in 1979, many of these countries ran into serious balance of payments problems. Their problems were compounded by high levels of external debt, built up as the result of massive public sector spending during the commodity price boom.

By the end of the 1970s, requests from African countries for debt relief from Paris Club creditors were pouring in. Countries leading the way included the Central African Republic, the Democratic Republic of Congo,

Liberia, Senegal, Sierra Leone, Sudan, Togo, and Uganda, all subsequently classified as heavily indebted poor countries (HIPCs).

Paris Club creditors responded to this avalanche of requests by building on their earlier experiences with the middle-income countries of Latin America. The accepted wisdom of the day was that the low-income countries were confronting short-term liquidity crises and that rescheduling of debt service would provide sufficient breathing space and debt relief to enable them to get back on an even keel and grow out of their debt problems. The agreements with Ghana and Indonesia were set aside as "exceptional," and the lesson of the importance of debt sustainability in the restructuring process was lost. This proved to be a costly mistake for debtor countries and creditors alike.

The modus operandi adopted by creditors was to determine the minimum amount of relief to be granted to allow debtors to pay their remaining debt service without recourse to further debt relief. Emphasis was put on the need for adjustment by the debtor country. Paris Club agreements in the 1970s and much of the 1980s (as well as those concluded with commercial creditors under the auspices of the London Club, described below) were on nonconcessional "classic" terms, with relatively short maturities of 8–10 years. Market-related interest rates were also retained. The creditors' position was that the interest rate charged on rescheduled debt (the so-called moratorium interest) must be equal to the cost of borrowing for the export credit agencies that had extended or guaranteed the debt.

Despite these efforts, the nature of the debt problem in Sub-Saharan Africa (which was magnified by political shocks, such as wars and social strife) and the persistent tendency of creditors to underestimate the amount of debt relief needed led to a continued buildup of debt stocks and repetitive debt rescheduling. By the end of 1986, the Paris Club had restructured the debt of 22 Sub-Saharan African countries in 55 agreements. Between 1973 and 1986, 14 African countries went to the Paris Club more than once, and 9 went three times or more. The principle that debts once rescheduled were not to be rescheduled proved unworkable. In almost half of the 55 agreements signed with African countries during this period, creditors were forced to restructure previously rescheduled claims.

Debt Relief 1987–96: A Coordinated Policy Response

The turning point came in 1987, at a time when growth prospects for developing countries continued to be adversely affected by persistent weakness in commodity prices, modest growth in industrial countries, and increasing protectionism. It became clear that for the poorest, most indebted countries in Sub-Saharan Africa, faced with unsustainable debt burdens and inadequate external financing, something more radical had to be done. The focus of the debt restructuring efforts moved from cash flow considerations to an attempt to deal with the unsustainable buildup of debt stocks (see Daseking and Powell 1999).

The Special Program of Assistance (SPA) to Low-Income, Debt-Distressed Countries in Sub-Saharan Africa was launched in September 1987 at the annual meetings of the IMF and the World Bank. The program was significant because it marked the international community's first coordinated framework in response to the widespread debt and development crisis on the African continent. Geared toward the resumption of economic growth, the program was essentially a commitment by donors to provide balance of payments support, including debt relief, to eligible African countries with credible and sustained economic reform programs in place. Three criteria were established for eligibility for debt relief. Countries had to be low income, defined as eligible for (concessional) loans from the World Bank's International Development Association (IDA); debt distressed, defined as having a debt-service-to-export ratio of 30 percent or more; and engaged in adjustment, defined as implementing a program supported by the IMF and IDA.

The SPA framework identified six channels through which donors' resources could be delivered. Four of them—IDA adjustment credits, the IMF Structural Adjustment Facility (SAF) and the Enhanced Structural Adjustment Facility (ESAF), bilateral and other multilateral adjustment financing, and debt relief by bilateral donors—involved adjustment financing. The other two were supplemental financing to offset debt service owed to the International Bank for Reconstruction and Development (IBRD) (known as the Fifth Dimension) and funding for commercial debt reduction through the IDA Debt Reduction Facility (known as the Sixth Dimension).

Between 1988 and 1996, 17 donors, including IDA and the IMF, disbursed more than $27.7 billion in adjustment support. These resources accounted for almost half of total concessional assistance to SPA–eligible countries over this period. Among the 31 countries eligible for SPA assistance, Tanzania ($1.8 billion), Mozambique ($1.6 billion), and Zambia ($1.4 billion) received the most adjustment assistance. They were followed by Côte d'Ivoire, Ghana, Kenya, Senegal, and Uganda, each of which received $0.8–$1.1 billion. Over the same period, Paris Club creditors rescheduled or cancelled $28.2 billion in claims on SPA countries.

From Debt Relief to Debt Reduction

The first tentative move toward incorporating an element of debt reduction (or forgiveness) of nonconcessional debt by Paris Club creditors followed the G-7 Venice summit meeting, in June 1987. In their communiqué, leaders of the major industrial countries recommended that for low-income African countries undertaking adjustment efforts, "consideration should be given to the possibility of applying lower interest rates on their existing debt and agreement should be reached, especially in the Paris Club, on longer repayment and grace periods to ease the debt burden." Following this communiqué, the Paris Club quickly declared Mauritania, Mozambique, Somalia, and Uganda eligible for special treatment in view of their large debt-service obligations, poor balance of payments prospects, and low per capita income. Agreements signed with these countries extended the repayment term for rescheduled nonconcessional debt to 20 years, with a 10-year grace period.

A year later, at the Toronto economic summit, in June 1988, G-7 leaders went a step further. Consistent with the framework of the SPA, they agreed that the nonconcessional, bilateral official debt and guaranteed commercial debt of low-income (defined as IDA–only) African countries could be reduced by up to 33 percent in net present value terms. A menu of restructuring options for creditors was introduced. Creditors could choose to deliver debt reduction through outright cancellation of their claims or by setting the interest rate on restructured claims at below-market rates. The repayment period for restructured claims was also greatly extended (to 23 years). In 1990, Toronto terms were extended to IDA–only countries outside Africa.

Between October 1988 and September 1990, Paris Club creditors restructured their claims on Toronto terms with 19 countries, including 2 outside Sub-Saharan Africa (Bolivia and Guyana), in 26 agreements. These agreements consolidated $5.8 billion in arrears and debt-service payments falling due and reduced the present value of the debt of the recipient countries by more than $800 million. Seven African countries (the Central African Republic, Madagascar, Mali, Niger, Senegal, Tanzania, and Togo) concluded more than one agreement on Toronto terms during this period.

Although Toronto terms had some beneficial effect on the debt situation of recipient countries, it did not take long for the international community to recognize that most low-income countries were going to need more far-reaching concessions to achieve a sustained improvement in their external debt situation. Moreover, there was growing recognition that a change in approach was needed: experience had demonstrated that the long-standing practice of Paris Club creditors to restructure only debt-service payments falling due during a limited consolidation period was simply setting the stage for a successive round of rescheduling agreements. For example, between 1976 and 1990, nine Paris Club agreements were concluded with the Democratic Republic of Congo and with Senegal, and seven Paris Club agreements were concluded with Madagascar.

The starting point for discussions on more far-reaching debt relief for low-income countries was the United Kingdom's Trinidad terms proposal of September 1990. In the spring of 1991, political expedience led Paris Club creditors to restructure the entire stock of debt of two middle-income countries (the Arab Republic of Egypt and Poland) on highly concessional terms. Both agreements reduced the net present value of all future debt-service payments by 50 percent. Subsequently, some of the innovative features of these two agreements were incorporated into the menu of enhanced concessions for low-income countries (the Enhanced Toronto terms) that the Paris Club creditors agreed to in December 1991.

The enhanced menu increased the reduction in nonconcessional, bilateral official debt and guaranteed commercial debt to 50 percent in net present value terms. It contained several innovative features. The most important was the two-step approach to debt restructuring, which combined the flexibility of the flow approach (that is, restructuring debt-service payments falling due in a defined consolidation period) with the possibility of a later stock-of-debt operation to allow the debtor country to "exit" the rescheduling process. Another innovation was the introduction of a graduated repayment schedule for debt service due on restructured claims, which rose by an annual rate of about 3 percent in nominal terms. With exports projected to increase at a faster rate, the debt-service burden on restructured debt was expected to decline over time.

Once again, however, resolution of the debt problems of the poorest countries proved elusive. By the mid-1990s, it became clear that resolving the structural problems inherent in the debt problems of the most severely indebted countries would require even deeper concessions. Following the G-7 summit in Naples, in 1994, Paris Club creditors agreed that, where necessary, concessionality could be increased to 67 percent on debt eligible for restructuring.

The Naples terms built on the Enhanced Toronto terms menu, but it extended those terms significantly in several respects. In addition to the increase in the level of concessionality, creditors also agreed that for debtor countries with good track records (under an IMF–supported program and prior rescheduling agreements), a concessional rescheduling of the entire stock of eligible debt could be implemented. The Naples terms also allowed more flexibility on the coverage of debt to be rescheduled. In particular, debt rescheduled on concessional (Toronto or Enhanced Toronto) terms could be rescheduled again and the level of concessionality increased (or topped up) to the new level of 67 percent.

Uganda was the first country to receive an exit rescheduling agreement on Naples terms. The February 1995 agreement provided a massive reduction in debt contracted before July 1, 1981 (the cutoff date), excluding debt previously rescheduled in February 1992 on Enhanced Toronto terms (which had already received a 50 percent net present value reduction). Debt rescheduled in 1989 on Toronto terms, including arrears and late interest, was increased (topped up) to 67 percent in net present value (from the 33 percent net present value reduction granted in the earlier agreement). In the first half of 1995, 10 other low-income countries concluded agreements on Naples terms, consolidating about $2.7 billion of debt.

Naples terms were heralded as an exit strategy from the rescheduling process. The expectation was that in the context of sound economic policies of adjustment and reform, these terms would bring debt to sustainable levels in most low-income countries and permit a sustainable "exit."

This hope was based on an overestimation of the impact of the reforms on the economies in question. Of the 37 low-income countries that concluded agreements on Naples terms between 1995 and 2008, only two (Cambodia and Yemen) had their external debt reduced to sustainable levels and exited from the rescheduling process.[3] All of the other countries were declared eligible for debt reduction under the Heavily Indebted Poor Countries (HIPC) Initiative, launched in 1996.

As the HIPC Initiative got under way, creditors increased the level of debt forgiveness. In November 1996, they agreed to increase the present value reduction to up to 80 percent (Lyon terms); in June 1999, they agreed to reduce debt relief to 90 percent (Cologne terms). Such operations could be in the form of flow restructuring or stock-of-debt reductions.

Complementary Measures

Some Paris Club creditors took important complementary measures. These measures included forgiveness of official development assistance (ODA) loans (using the Development Assistance Committee [DAC] of the OECD as a platform to coordinate these efforts) and debt-conversion arrangements under Paris Club auspices and through special initiatives such as the U.S. Enterprise for the Americas Initiative and the Swiss Debt Reduction Facility.

Forgiveness of Official Development Assistance Debt

An important component of debt reduction is the forgiveness by bilateral donors of their ODA loans. Many middle-income countries and virtually every low-income country have benefited from the forgiveness of at least part of these loans.

Forgiveness of ODA loans, like forgiveness of aid more generally, has always been considered a strictly bilateral issue between individual donor and debtor countries. Periodically, however, there have been rounds of concerted action by donors, often in the face of global crises. In the late 1970s, in response to the burgeoning debt crisis and the 1978 resolution of the United Nations Conference on Trade and Development (UNCTAD), most DAC member countries cancelled all or part of their ODA loans to a group of low-income countries considered less developed. In tandem, they began to provide all new bilateral aid flows to this group of countries in the form of grants. Between 1978 and 1986, 15 DAC member countries granted about $3 billion in debt forgiveness under this initiative. More than two-thirds of this debt forgiveness related to debt owed by developing countries in Sub-Saharan Africa. Beneficiary countries included both those that had rescheduled debt and those that had avoided debt difficulties.

DAC member countries launched a second concerted round of ODA debt forgiveness in 1988, as part of the coordinated program of assistance to Africa and in parallel with the decision by governments represented at the Paris Club to provide partial debt reduction on nonconcessional claims rescheduled within the Paris Club. In keeping with the framework of the SPA, ODA debt forgiveness was focused primarily on the heavily indebted low-income countries of Sub-Saharan Africa. It was also increasingly linked directly to policy performance by the debtor country. However, some countries that had avoided debt difficulties were again the beneficiaries of debt forgiveness.

In 1989 alone, donors announced ODA debt cancellation of more than $6 billion. This included $3.1 billion by France for ODA loans contracted by 35 low-income African countries before end-1988, $1.4 billion by Germany for ODA loans to least developed countries, and $330 million by Belgium for ODA loans to several African countries. In July 1989, the United States announced its intention to forgive $500 million in ODA loans to certain low-income countries of Sub-Saharan Africa and to provide future aid to these countries as grants. The forgiveness was delivered in tranches, conditional upon satisfactory implementation of structural adjustment programs supported by the IMF and the World Bank. Later in the year, Canada canceled $570 million of ODA loans to 13 Sub-Saharan African countries and pledged to provide future aid as grants.

Debt Swaps and Debt Conversion

A swap arrangement transforms one type of asset into another with different characteristics. The most common type of swap arrangements are debt for equity, debt for development, debt for investment in environmental conservation projects, debt for debt, and debt for local currency. The market for these types of operations evolved in the context of the market-based debt reduction schemes that emerged to deal with the commercial debt crises of the 1980s in middle-income countries. Swap arrangements involving bilateral creditors emerged in the 1990s as another instrument in the ongoing effort to reduce the external debt burden of low-income countries.

The first of these arrangements was the U.S. Enterprise for the Americas Initiative (EAI), announced in June 1990. Its aim was to enhance development prospects through action in the areas of trade, investment, and debt. For eligible countries in Central and Latin America, debt owed to the United States could be reduced provided the country was undertaking macroeconomic and structural reforms, was liberalizing its investment regime, and had concluded a debt restructuring agreement with its commercial bank creditors. Under EAI, bilateral concessional loans extended by the U.S. Agency for International Development or the U.S. Department of Agriculture under the food aid program governed by Public Law 480 could be reduced and interest payments made in local currency provided these resources were committed to environmental or child development projects. In addition, a portion of nonconcessional loans extended by the Export-Import Bank of the United States or the Commodity Credit Corporation could be bought back by the debtor to facilitate debt-for-nature, debt-for-development, or debt-for-equity swaps. Bolivia was the only low-income country to qualify for this initiative.

The Swiss Debt Reduction facility, which became operational in January 1991, was aimed at highly indebted low-income countries. Access was limited to countries with a strong track record of reform, acceptable conditions of governance, and adequate debt management systems that were implementing structural reform programs supported by the IMF and the World Bank. The 45 countries eligible for the facility included low-income countries the United Nations considered to be least developed (a definition that takes into account per capita income, the stock of human assets, and economic vulnerability) and other developing countries that had either rescheduled with Paris Club creditors on enhanced concessional terms or were recipients of Swiss ODA. The resources of the facility could be used for a wide range of measures, including buyback of officially insured Swiss export credits and commercial noninsured debt and contributions to clearing arrears and financing debt-serviced payments owed to multilateral institutions. Debt cancellation could also be linked to creation by the debtor government of a local currency counterpart fund to be used to finance development projects. An estimated $1.8 billion of outstanding claims was eliminated through this facility.

Other bilateral initiatives for debt forgiveness included France's Libreville Debt Initiative, announced at the Franco-African summit in 1992, and the U.S. Tropical Forest Conservation Act of 1998. Under the Libreville Debt Initiative, France committed to set up a FF 4 billion (about $800 million) fund to cancel or convert ODA loans to four African countries (Cameroon, the Republic of Congo, Côte d'Ivoire, and Gabon) in conjunction with specific development projects approved by the Agence Française de Développement.

The Tropical Forest Conservation Act established a facility that allowed low- and middle-income countries with tropical forests to finance debt buybacks with concessional debt owed to the United States provided the debtor country had a bilateral investment treaty with the United States and an ongoing investment reform program supported by the World Bank or the Inter-American Development Bank. Five low-income countries (Bolivia, Côte d'Ivoire, Guyana, Liberia, and Madagascar) were eligible for this facility.

Debt conversions for lower-middle-income countries under Paris Club agreements were first introduced in September 1990. A provision allowed creditors to swap a limited amount of their ODA claims and 10 percent of their guaranteed commercial claims (on a purely voluntary and bilateral basis) in the form of debt for aid, debt for equity, debt for nature, and debt for local currency. In December 1991, these provisions were extended to low-income countries.

Between 2002 and 2007, Paris Club creditors concluded more than 376 operations that extinguished $8.3 billion in claims. Sixty percent of the total amount swapped was in the form of debt for aid; 31 percent was in the form of debt-for-equity swaps. Five creditors (France, Germany, Italy, Spain, and Switzerland) accounted for 80 percent of the total volume of debt swapped. The largest beneficiaries of debt swaps were Côte d'Ivoire, Egypt, Honduras, Jordan, Morocco, and Peru, which together accounted for 60 percent of all debt swapped by Paris Club creditors.

Twenty HIPCs have concluded debt-swap operations with Paris Club creditors, primarily in the form of debt-for-aid swaps. These operations have extinguished almost $2 billion of these countries' external debt.

Debt Relief by Non–Paris Club Creditors

Many countries have debt-service obligations to official bilateral creditors that do not participate in Paris Club rescheduling or other established institutional forums for negotiation. Individual creditor countries not participating in the Paris Club have developed various approaches, which have been adapted to the individual circumstances of each debtor country. Most non–Paris Club bilateral creditors have agreed to a rescheduling of obligations, although in some cases debt buybacks involving substantial discounts have been implemented. In some instances, claims have been forgiven: in 1991, the Gulf countries (principally Kuwait and Saudi Arabia) forgave $6 billion of their claims on Egypt and more than $2 billion of their claims on Morocco.

As a condition of debt rescheduling, Paris Club creditors require that debtor countries seek debt relief on terms comparable to those of other creditors. Because of the ad hoc and bilateral nature of negotiations with non–Paris Club bilateral creditors, comprehensive information on the terms of agreements concluded and the volume of claims restructured is not generally available. However, in the context of the HIPC Initiative, debt relief by non–Paris Club bilateral creditors is monitored in parallel with debt relief provided by all other categories of creditors.

About 13 percent of total debt is owed by HIPCs to non–Paris Club bilateral creditors. Of the 51 non–Paris Club bilateral creditors with claims on HIPCs, only 8 (Egypt, Hungary, Jamaica, the Republic of Korea, Morocco, Rwanda, South Africa, and Trinidad and Tobago) have provided full relief. Another 22 creditors have provided partial relief.

Twenty-one creditors have not yet delivered any HIPC Initiative debt relief, although some, including Colombia and Kuwait, are making efforts to modify their national laws so that they no longer hinder their delivery of such relief.

For individual HIPCs, the relief delivered by non–Paris Club bilateral creditors varies significantly. Four HIPCs (Honduras, Madagascar, São Tomé and Principe, and Zambia) have received less than 15 percent of their expected debt relief from non–Paris club creditors. Others (Benin, Cameroon, Ghana, and Sierra Leone) have received more than 75 percent of the expected debt relief.

Debt Relief by Commercial Creditors

The debt crisis that engulfed low-income countries in the 1970s and 1980s also led to restructuring with commercial creditors. These agreements evolved from ad hoc arrangements by individual creditors to a more coordinated restructuring through commercial bank advisory committees, often referred to as the London Club.

Unlike the Paris Club, the London Club held no regular group meetings with debtors: a special advisory committee, representing the major creditor banks, was formed for each negotiation (meetings did not always take place in London). Membership in the advisory committee was based on the size of individual banks' exposure and the need to spread representation among key creditor countries. Normally, only principal payments were rescheduled, and arrears were expected to be paid at the time the restructuring agreement went into effect. In addition to restructuring outstanding loan maturities, commercial bank creditors sometimes provided new money (normally extended in proportion to existing exposure) and maintained or extended short-term credit facilities.

The process followed by the London Club required the advisory committee and the debtor government to first reach an agreement in principle for a restructuring. That agreement was then signed by all creditor banks. The agreement became effective when a specified proportion of creditors signed the agreement and other conditions (such as payment of arrears) were met.

In an effort to eliminate uncertainties, in some cases commercial banks concluded multiyear agreements that consolidated principal payments over a three- to five-year period. Formal arrangements to monitor economic performance were an essential element of multiyear agreements, for which the debtor country was required to have an upper-credit tranche agreement in place with the IMF.

Between 1980 and end-1988, 20 low-income countries restructured their commercial bank debt one or more times.[4] During this period, $18.7 billion of commercial bank debt owed by low-income countries was restructured. Five countries (the Democratic Republic of Congo,

Côte d'Ivoire, Nicaragua, Nigeria, and Sudan) accounted for 85 percent of this amount.

By the mid-1980s, it had become evident that the debt crisis in low-income countries was too deep-rooted to be resolved through rescheduling of principal payments owed to commercial creditors, and participation in concerted lending was becoming increasingly difficult to arrange. Creditor banks began to recognize that some form of debt cancellation was essential to a viable debt-relief package.

In March 1989, the creditor community established a mechanism to support voluntary debt and debt-service reduction operations based on a plan by then U.S. Treasury Secretary Nicholas Brady. The Brady Plan was designed to provide the debtor country with a reduction in the stock of debt or future debt service as well as new money, with support from international financial institutions and bilateral donors, notably Japan. Commercial lenders found the plan attractive, because it provided a menu of instruments from which they could choose depending on their balance sheet needs. The main instruments were buybacks and discounted exchanges for debt-stock reduction, par exchanges at reduced interest rates for debt-service reduction, and a new money option for debt not subject to debt or debt-service reduction.

The Brady Plan was aimed primarily at middle-income countries. Brady operations were concluded with only two low-income countries, Nigeria in 1992 and Côte d'Ivoire in 1997. The agreement with Nigeria restructured $5.4 billion through a cash buyback of $3.3 billion at 40 cents per dollar and an exchange of $2.1 billion for collateralized 30-year bullet-maturity par bonds with reduced interest rates. A recovery value provision allowed bondholders to recapture part of the discount if the international price of oil rose above an agreed reference price. The total cost of the operation ($1.7 billion) was paid from Nigeria's own resources.

The agreement with Côte d'Ivoire was something of a hybrid: in essence a Brady operation but with a portion of the costs provided by the Debt Reduction Facility for IDA–only countries (described below). In total, $6.5 billion was restructured, and debt owed to commercial creditors was reduced by $4.1 billion in nominal terms, equivalent to a reduction of just under 80 percent in net present value terms. Of the $2.3 billion of eligible principal, $0.7 billion was bought back at 24 cents per dollar, $0.2 billion was exchanged for 50 percent discount bonds, and $1.4 billion was exchanged for front-loaded interest reduction bonds. Of the $4.2 billion of past-due interest, $0.9 billion was exchanged for past-due interest bonds, $30 million was paid in cash at closing, and $3.3 billion was written off. The principal component of the discount bond was collateralized with 30-year U.S. Treasury or French Treasury zero-coupon bonds, delivered at closing. The total cost of the operation was $226 million, of which $19 million came from Côte d'Ivoire's own resources and $207 million was funded with external loans and grants ($70 million from the IMF, $52 million from France, $50 million from IDA, and $35 million from the Debt Reduction Facility, supported by $15 million in grants from the Netherlands and Switzerland).

The Debt Reduction Facility

Created in July 1989, the IDA Debt Reduction Facility (DRF) was designed to address the commercial debt problems of low-income countries. Its objective is to help reforming, heavily indebted, IDA–only countries reduce their sovereign commercial external debt as part of a broader debt-resolution program, and thereby to contribute to growth, poverty reduction, and debt sustainability.

Under a typical DRF–supported operation, a government buys back its public and publicly guaranteed debts from external commercial creditors for cash at a deep discount.[5] The DRF provides grants for both the preparation and the implementation of commercial debt–reduction operations. The preparation grants support eligible governments in retaining the services needed to prepare such operations. The implementation grants finance the costs of debt buybacks as part of the implementation of commercial debt–reduction operations. In April 2008, the policies and practices of the DRF were modified to enhance its effectiveness (by, for example, allowing it to provide more rapid support for the preparation of commercial debt–reduction operations) and better align it with the HIPC Initiative framework.

Since its inception, the DRF has helped extinguish about $10 billion of external commercial debt and become one of the key instruments used to promote commercial creditor participation under the HIPC Initiative. As such, it helps reduce the risk of these creditors taking advantage of debt relief provided by other creditors. By settling commercial claims, which are generally in arrears, the DRF may also help improve the climate for foreign direct investment and trade. In addition, the DRF enables countries to manage their debts and reserves in a more cost-effective way, by reducing the likelihood that their debts will be sold to aggressive distressed debt funds and by avoiding litigation and attempted attachment of assets. In some cases, the DRF can help HIPCs extinguish court judgments, even after awards have been distributed.[6]

The DRF is financed mainly from transfers from IBRD, grant contributions from other donors, and investment income earned on such contributions. As of March 2009, the DRF had received $350 million in transfers from IBRD's net income. In addition, bilateral donors, including Canada, Finland, France, Germany, Norway, the Netherlands, the Russian Federation, Sweden, Switzerland, the United Kingdom, and the United States, had contributed grants to support commercial debt–reduction operations. The European Commission, France, Germany, Japan, Switzerland, and the United States have made grants directly to debtor governments in support of DRF–sponsored operations. Debtor governments' own financing has also been contributed to DRF–supported operations.

Debt-Relief Initiatives by Multilateral Creditors

Three initiatives—the Fifth Dimension of the SPA, the HIPC Initiative, and the Multilateral Debt Relief Initiative (MDRI)—provide debt relief. Each is described below.

The Fifth Dimension. The Fifth Dimension of the SPA was aimed explicitly at IDA–only countries with outstanding obligations on IBRD loans. These loans were contracted when the debtor country had access to IBRD and other market-based financing. Initially, concessional bilateral assistance, mainly from the Nordic countries, was provided to help finance debt-service payments to IBRD. Subsequently, IDA introduced supplemental (Fifth Dimension) credits to offset interest payments to IBRD.

Financed with IDA reflows, the supplemental credits were allocated to eligible countries on an annual basis, in proportion to the interest payments due on their IBRD loans. In order to receive supplemental IDA credits, the debtor country had to be current with its debt-service payments to IBRD and IDA and have an ongoing adjustment program supported by IDA. In total, IDA provided about $1 billion in supplemental IDA credits to SPA countries to offset debt-service payments to IBRD; donors contributed another $0.2 billion.

The HIPC Initiative. After a difficult period at the onset of the debt crisis of the 1980s, the debt situation of most middle-income countries improved substantially, thanks to the support provided by the international financial community. A number of low-income countries, however, most of them in Sub-Saharan Africa, continued to bear heavy external debt burdens. This burden reflected several factors, including imprudent external debt management, deficiencies in macroeconomic management, adverse developments in the terms of trade, and poor governance. By the mid-1990s, with an increasing share of debt owed to multilateral creditors, it became clear that further action from the international community was needed to help these countries overcome their external debt difficulties.[7]

In February 1996, the Executive Boards of the World Bank and the IMF discussed two papers that set out the scope and nature of the debt problems of the HIPCs (World Bank and IMF 1996a, 1996b). The analyses concluded that the debt burden of about half of the countries studied was likely to remain above manageable levels in the medium to long term, even with strong policy performance and full use of existing debt-relief mechanisms. During the discussion, there was a widespread sense that the initiatives to assist such countries in dealing with their debt problems needed to be supplemented with new strategies and instruments. As a result, a new debt-relief initiative was called for at the G-7 summit in Lyon.

In response to that call, in September 1996 the World Bank and IMF launched the HIPC Initiative (World Bank and IMF 1996c). The key objective of the initiative was to ensure that adjustment and reform efforts were not put at risk by continued high debt and debt-service burdens. The initiative aimed to reduce the debt burden of eligible countries to predetermined levels, provided they adopted and carried out strong programs of macroeconomic adjustment and structural reforms (box 1.2). Its launch represented a major departure from past practice, in that, for the first time, debt relief was offered on multilateral debt.

Box 1.2 Key Features of the HIPC Initiative

To be considered for HIPC Initiative debt relief, a country must be IDA only and eligible for a Poverty Reduction and Growth Facility (PRFG); have debt burden indicators above the HIPC Initiative thresholds after full use of traditional debt-relief mechanisms; establish a track record of policies and reform through IMF– and IDA–supported programs; and have developed a Poverty Reduction Strategy Paper (PRSP) through a broad-based participatory process.

Once a country has met or made sufficient progress in meeting these criteria, the World Bank and the IMF decide on its eligibility for debt relief. This decision is called the HIPC Initiative decision point. At the decision point, the World Bank and the IMF decide how much debt reduction a country will receive in the context of the HIPC Initiative. The World Bank and the IMF also come to agreement with authorities from debtor countries on the requirements that need to be fulfilled (the so-called completion point triggers) for the country to receive irrevocable debt relief. Once a country reaches its decision point, it may immediately begin receiving interim relief from some creditors on its debt service falling due. (For a list of countries that have reached the decision point, see http://go.worldbank.org/4IMVXTQ090.)

In order to receive irrevocable debt relief under the HIPC Initiative, a country must meet the completion point triggers. Once it does, it can reach the HIPC Initiative completion point, at which time lenders are expected to provide the full debt relief committed at the decision point. This amount is equal to the reduction needed to bring down the country's debt to the relevant HIPC Initiative threshold (150 percent for the net present value of the debt-to-exports ratio or 250 percent of the net present value of the debt-to-revenue ratio).

The initiative was based on six guiding principles:

- Overall debt sustainability should be assessed on a case-by-case basis that focuses on the totality of a country's debt.
- Action should be taken only when a debtor has shown the ability to put the debt relief provided to good use.
- Existing debt-relief mechanisms should be built on.
- The provision of debt relief should be coordinated by all creditors, with broad and equitable participation.
- The delivery of debt relief by multilateral creditors should preserve the financial integrity of the institutions and their preferred creditor status.
- New external financing to beneficiary countries should be provided on appropriate concessional terms.

At the onset of the initiative, a two-year limit was established, at the end of which a comprehensive review would be conducted to decide whether to continue the program. The 1998 review of the initiative acknowledged that, while the initiative had accomplished significant results over its first two years, more needed to be done (IDA and IMF 1998). To make the initiative as effective as possible, the Executive Boards of the World Bank and the IMF called for a comprehensive review of the initiative's framework.

The review of the initiative's framework was informed by a two-stage consultation process.[8] The first phase, finalized in mid-March 1999, addressed concerns about, and possible modifications to, the initiative's framework, including debt-relief targets, timing of decision and completion points, and performance under economic and social reform programs (see IDA and IMF 1999a). The second phase, finalized in mid-June 1999, focused on the link between debt relief and social development.

Three clear messages emerged from the consultation process. First, there was general acknowledgment that the initiative was a positive step forward toward solving the debt problems of HIPCs. Second, there was disappointment with the depth of debt relief and the pace of implementation (often expressed as "too little, too late"). Third, there was a clear desire for a more direct link between debt-relief and poverty reduction measures. Proposals for modifying the HIPC Initiative framework ranged from building on the existing framework (by, for example, making changes to timing, conditionality, debt ratios, and targets) to adopting a completely different approach for debt relief (by, for example, adopting the human development approach or introducing international insolvency procedures).

In April 1999, the president of the World Bank and the managing director of the IMF outlined a set of guiding principles for modifying the HIPC Initiative framework. The proposed principles stated that debt relief should

- reinforce the wider tools of the international community to promote sustainable development and poverty reduction
- strengthen the incentives for debtor countries to adopt strong programs of adjustment and reform
- focus on the poorer countries, for whom excessive debt can be an obstacle to development that is particularly difficult to overcome
- remove the debt overhang and provide an appropriate cushion against exogenous shocks
- be provided to all countries, including those that have already reached decision and completion points under the initiative, provided that they qualify under any revised thresholds
- be provided in a simplified framework
- be accompanied by proposals for financing the cost to multilateral institutions.

In line with these principles, the president of the World Bank and the managing director of the IMF proposed a number of specific modifications. They included more debt relief to a broader group of countries by a reduction in the initiative's debt-burden thresholds and the calculation of assistance based on actual data at the decision point rather than projected data for the completion point (as under the original framework). They also proposed providing faster debt relief, by delivering interim debt relief on a voluntary basis and front-loading debt relief after the completion point. In addition, they proposed the introduction of "floating" completion points, contingent on an outcome-based assessment of country performance rather than a fixed track record (as under the original framework). These changes aimed to provide incentives to implement reforms quickly, speed up the delivery of debt relief, and develop country ownership of reforms.

At the G-7 Summit in Cologne, in June 1999, government leaders endorsed a number of specific suggestions of their finance ministers to provide "faster, deeper and broader debt relief for the poorest countries that demonstrate a commitment to reform and poverty alleviation" (G-7 Finance Ministers 1999, p. 1). In response, the World Bank and IMF enhanced the HIPC Initiative framework per the approach proposed in April 1999 (IDA and IMF 1999b). At the same time, the HIPC Initiative process was linked to progress in preparing and implementing Poverty Reduction Strategies (PRSs), which were designed to be country driven and developed with the broad participation of civil society. The framework was adapted to provide an adequate cushion against exogenous shocks: under the revised framework, additional debt relief ("topping up") can be provided if, by the time a HIPC reaches the completion point, its debt burden indicators have deteriorated because of factors beyond its control.

The flexibility of the Enhanced Framework has facilitated HIPCs' access to debt relief while preserving the initiative's principles. (For a detailed discussion of the flexibility of the Framework, see IDA and IMF 2008.) In particular, as the universe of countries in need of debt relief changed, operational modalities were adapted to fit their challenging circumstances better. Flexibility has been exercise with respect to three features:

- the eligibility criteria, which were reviewed to ensure that no country with debt burdens in excess of the HIPC Initiative's thresholds would be left without a comprehensive framework to address its debt problems
- the definition of a satisfactory track record of policy performance
- the preparation and implementation of poverty reduction strategies.

The Multilateral Debt Relief Initiative. The HIPC Initiative was followed by the MDRI. This initiative, called for at the 2005 G-8 Summit, at Gleneagles, Scotland, seeks to achieve two objectives: (a) deepen debt relief to HIPCs to support their progress toward the Millennium Development Goals while safeguarding the long-term financial capacity of the international financial institutions and (b) encouraging the best use of additional donor resources for development by allocating them to low-income countries on the basis of policy performance (box 1.3).

The MDRI entails the cancellation of all eligible debts owed to IDA, the IMF, and the African Development Fund for countries reaching the HIPC

Box 1.3 Key Features of the Multilateral Debt Relief Initiative

Unlike the HIPC Initiative, the MDRI is not comprehensive in its creditor coverage; it does not involve participation by official bilateral or commercial creditors or multilateral creditors other than IDA, the IMF, the African Development Fund (administered by the African Development Bank), and the Inter-American Development Bank (IDB). (The IDB in 2007 also decided to cancel eligible debts of the five HIPCs in the Western Hemisphere in an initiative similar to the MDRI.) While the MDRI is an initiative common to the four institutions, their implementation modalities vary.

The initiative covers all countries that reached the HIPC completion point. Debt relief covers all debt disbursed by the IMF, the African Development Fund, and the IDB by end-December 2004 and all debt disbursed by IDA by end-December 2003 and still outstanding at the time of qualification (after HIPC Initiative debt relief).

Source: IDA and IMF 2006.

Figure 1.1 Debt Stock of Post–Decision Point HIPCs at Different Stages of Debt Relief

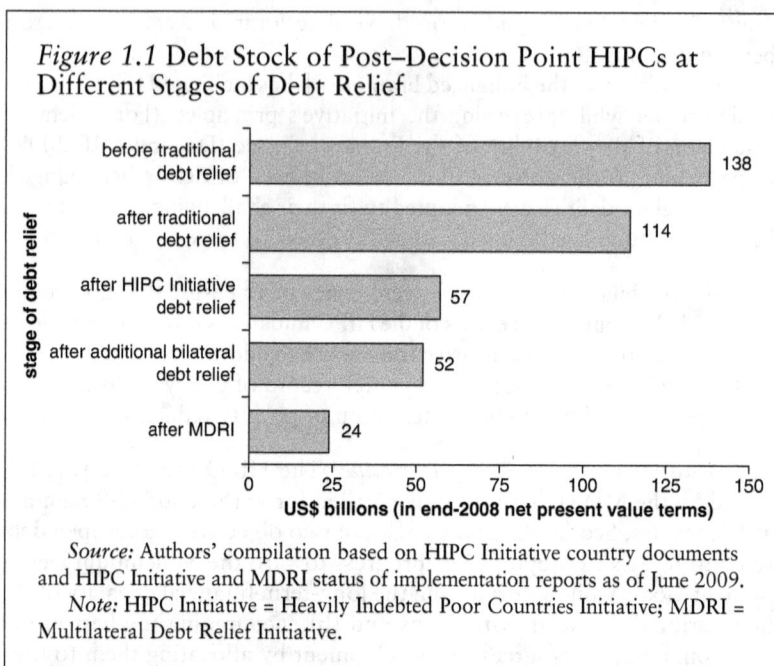

Source: Authors' compilation based on HIPC Initiative country documents and HIPC Initiative and MDRI status of implementation reports as of June 2009.
Note: HIPC Initiative = Heavily Indebted Poor Countries Initiative; MDRI = Multilateral Debt Relief Initiative.

completion point. In 2007, the Inter-American Development Bank agreed to cancel eligible debts to HIPCs through an initiative similar to the MDRI.

Substantial progress has been made in implementing the HIPC Initiative and the MDRI. As of end-April 2009, more than three-quarters of eligible countries (35 out of 40) had passed the decision point and qualified for assistance. Twenty-six of these countries have reached the completion point (by June 30, 2009), qualifying for irrevocable debt relief under the HIPC Initiative and the MDRI. Overall assistance committed to the 35 post–decision point HIPCs amounts to $117 billion (in nominal terms), including $45 billion under the MDRI. As a result of this debt relief, as well as relief under traditional mechanisms and additional relief from some creditors, the debt burden of the 35 post–decision point HIPCs is expected to be reduced by more than 80 percent relative to their pre–decision point debt stock (figure 1.1).

Conclusions

Debt relief provided to low-income countries has significantly reduced their debt burden. Countries currently considered HIPCs are estimated to have received at least $30 billion (in end-1997 net present value terms) in debt relief from Paris Club creditors through agreements signed between 1988 and 1998. Since then, substantial progress has been made in the implementation of the HIPC Initiative and the MDRI: 26 HIPCs have reached the completion point and qualified for irrevocable debt relief under the HIPC Initiative and $29 billion (in end-2008 net present value terms) of additional debt relief in the context of the MDRI.

As a result of the debt relief provided under the HIPC Initiative and the MDRI, as well as relief under traditional mechanisms and additional relief from some creditors, the debt stock of the 35 post–decision point HIPCs is expected to fall by over 80 percent. This reduction has been accompanied by an increase in poverty-reducing spending in HIPCs of about 2 percent of GDP since the late 1990s.

Despite significant debt reduction, long-term debt sustainability remains a concern, even for some of the 26 post–completion point HIPCs. Debt sustainability analyses performed using the joint World Bank/IMF Debt Sustainability Framework for low-income countries confirm that these HIPCs are in a better situation than other HIPCs and other low-income countries that are not HIPCs. Nevertheless, as of 2008, only about 40 percent of post–completion point HIPCs had been assessed as having a low risk of debt distress (World Bank and IMF 2008). Four of these countries were assessed as being at high risk of debt distress, because of structural weaknesses in their economies or weak macroeconomic management. The debt outlook in post–completion point countries is also very sensitive to export shocks and the terms of new financing, highlighting the need for countries to implement sound borrowing policies and strengthen their capacity to manage public debt.

A country's debt sustainability depends on implementing sound growth-enhancing policies, which boost its repayment capacity. This is particularly relevant for post–completion point countries, given their increased attractiveness for private and nontraditional official creditors. In that regard, it is critical for low-income countries to reflect on the middle-income countries' experience regarding the links between debt sustainability and growth.

Notes

1. Debt relief covered in this chapter includes rescheduling of principal and interest payments by Paris Club creditors; forgiveness of official development assistance loans by bilateral creditors; debt restructuring and debt forgiveness by non–Paris Club creditors; reduction of commercial debt, including through the International Development Association (IDA) Debt Reduction Facility; special programs to help debtors meet obligations to multilateral creditors, including the World Bank's Fifth Dimension program and the International Monetary Fund's Rights Accumulation program; debt swaps; the Heavily Indebted Poor Countries (HIPC) Initiative; and the Multilateral Debt Relief Initiative (MDRI).

2. Since 1971, no debt relief has been arranged through aid consortia.

3. Vietnam exited the rescheduling process following a debt restructuring on Enhanced Toronto terms (50 percent net present value reduction) in 1993.

4. The low-income countries involved were Bolivia, the Democratic Republic of Congo, the Republic of Congo, Côte d'Ivoire, The Gambia, Guinea, Guyana, Honduras, Liberia, Madagascar, Malawi, Mozambique, Nicaragua, Niger, Nigeria, Senegal, Sierra Leone, Sudan, Togo, and Zambia

5. Other modalities have also occasionally been used. They include debt swaps (which have been part of operations in Albania, Bolivia, Niger, Senegal, Tanzania, and Zambia) and debt restructurings (used in Vietnam and for a substantial part of the debt reduction in Côte d'Ivoire).

6. A significant number of litigating creditors participated in the recent DRF–supported buyback operations in Liberia and Nicaragua. These arrangements extinguished almost half of the overall value of reported court judgments against post–decision point HIPCs.

7. During the debt crisis, most low-income countries continued to receive positive net transfers from the international community. This contrasts with the negative net transfers to the heavily indebted middle-income countries in the mid-1980s. The positive net transfers resulted mainly from increased grants from official bilateral creditors; bilateral debt forgiveness/restructuring; and increased loans from multilateral institutions, mostly on highly concessional terms.

8. A request for comments and proposals was posted on the World Bank and IMF Web sites, and staff from both institutions attended seminars and conferences in Africa, Europe, Latin America, and the United States. As of end-March 1999, 65 written comments and proposals for improvement of the HIPC Initiative framework had been received.

References

Cosio-Pascal, Enrique. 2008 "The Emerging of a Multilateral Forum for Debt Restructuring: The Paris Club." UNCTAD Discussion Paper 192, United Nations Conference on Trade and Development, Geneva.

Daseking, Christina, and Robert Powell. 1999. "From Toronto Terms to the HIPC Initiative: A Brief History of Debt Relief for Low-Income Countries." IMF Working Paper WP/99/142, International Monetary Fund, Washington, DC.

G-7 Finance Ministers. 1999. Report of the G-7 Finance Ministers on the Köln Debt Initiative. Köln Economic Summit, Cologne, June 18–20.

IDA (International Development Association) and IMF (International Monetary Fund). 1998. "The Initiative for Heavily Indebted Poor Countries: Review and Outlook." IDA/SecM98-480, August 25, Washington, DC.

———. 1999a. "Heavily Indebted Poor Countries (HIPC) Initiative: Perspectives on the Current Framework and Options for Change." IDA/SecM99-155, Washington, DC.

———. 1999b. "Modifications to the Heavily Indebted Poor Countries (HIPC) Initiative." IDA/SecM99-475, September 17, Washington, DC.

———. 2006. "Heavily Indebted Poor Countries (HIPC) Initiative and Multilateral Debt Relief Initiative (MDRI): Status of Implementation." IDA/SecM2006-0455, August 25, Washington, DC.

————. 2008. "Heavily Indebted Poor Countries (HIPC) Initiative and Multilateral Debt Relief Initiative (MDRI): Status of Implementation." IDA/SecM2008-0561, September 12, Washington, DC.

Rieffel, Lex. 2003. *Restructuring Sovereign Debt: The Case for Ad Hoc Machinery.* Washington, DC: Brookings Institution Press.

World Bank. 1989. "Operational Guidelines and Procedures for the Use of Resources of the Debt Reduction Facility for IDA–Only Countries." R89-156, IDA/R89-103, July 13, Washington, DC.

World Bank and IMF (International Monetary Fund). 1996a. *Analytical Aspects of the Debt Problems of Heavily Indebted Poor Countries.* Washington, DC.

————. 1996b. "Debt Sustainability Analysis for the Heavily Indebted Poor Countries." SecM96-94, January 31, Washington, DC.

————. 1996c. "The Heavily Indebted Poor Countries (HIPC) Debt Initiative: A Program for Action." Report of the President of the World Bank and the Managing Director of the IMF, SecM96-975/1, September 20, Washington, DC.

2

Debt Relief and Education in Heavily Indebted Poor Countries

Jesús Crespo Cuaresma and
Gallina Andronova Vincelette

With the launch of the Heavily Indebted Poor Countries (HIPC) Initiative in 1996, debt-relief efforts by a wide range of creditors (multilateral, bilateral, and commercial) were directed specifically toward poor countries struggling to cope with their external debt that constrained export earnings or fiscal revenues. Modifications to the initiative in 1999 provided faster, broader, and deeper debt relief (see chapter 1).

In 2005, the HIPC Initiative was supplemented by the Multilateral Debt Relief Initiative (MDRI) to help accelerate countries' progress toward the United Nations Millennium Development Goals (MDGs).[1] As of November 2008, debt-relief assistance of $117 billion had been committed to the 33 countries that had reached the decision point under the two initiatives. These two major international efforts have helped significantly reduce the external debt burden of HIPCs (IDA and IMF 2007, 2008).

What are the links between the fiscal space created by the two intiatives and the incentives to use freed-up resources for human capital accumulation in these countries? Debt relief might be expected to have an effect on human capital accumulation, particularly educational outcomes, but no convincing empirical evidence exists for such effects. The economic rationale behind the prediction that debt relief could have positive effects on education is straightforward: to the extent that debt relief frees up resources in indebted countries, those resources can be channeled toward alternative uses. The framework of debt relief may provide incentives to investment in human capital accumulation as a potential strategy for achieving high and sustainable rates of economic growth.

The absence of comparable data (see Chauvin and Kraay 2005, 2007) on the present value of external debt for developing countries partly explains the relatively late birth of the study of the economic effects of debt relief. It may also explain the disappointing macroeconomic results of such aid strategies.

Chauvin and Kraay (2005) investigate the effects of debt relief on expenditures on health and education, without finding a significant relationship with the reduction in debt stocks. Thomas (2006) uses data on more than 100 countries to assess a number of factors in addition to debt relief that may affect social expenditure (defined as expenditure on health and education). Among these factors are foreign aid, output per capita, urbanization, and the literacy rate. Thomas's results suggest that a decline in debt-service costs significantly raises expenditures on health and education in low-income countries, with a 1 percent decline in debt service increasing these expenditures by 0.35 percent of output in the long run.

The literature cites the opportunity debt relief creates to build human capital, particularly through education. In some contributions, the freeing up of resources that is inherent to debt relief is associated with educational attainment levels in developing countries. Nafula (2002), for instance, stresses the fact that, as long as it frees up resources for education provision, debt relief may be an important instrument for reaching the MDG of universal primary education. Easterly's (2002) results hinge on the potential effects debt relief have on the discount factor of governments. To the extent that debt-relief programs are successful in inducing a reduction in the discount factor (and thus in the optimal tax rate) in developing countries, human capital accumulation may be directly affected by the decision to extend debt relief.[2]

This chapter presents an overview of the effects of debt relief on human capital accumulation in HIPCs. It is structured as follows. The next section presents descriptive statistics on educational attainment variables before and after debt relief. It concentrates on the recent experience of HIPCs to draw conclusions about the likely effects of debt relief on education. The following section examines the analytics of debt relief. The third section outlines key challenges HIPCs face with respect to sustaining gains achieved during the HIPC process in the area of education. The last section draws some conclusions.

Debt Relief and Educational Outcomes: The Facts

The significance of a HIPC's reaching its decision point lies in the commitment to pursue a set of agreed-on floating completion point triggers. This commitment to reform is usually translated into implementation of a government-owned poverty reduction strategy (PRS), the maintenance of macroeconomic stability, and other areas. Reforms in the health and education sectors have become cornerstones of PRSs.

Triggers on education were included in all 23 post–completion point countries. Examples of triggers in post–completion point countries can be found in table 2.1. Such triggers are also prominent in interim countries.

The strategies concerning the composition of public expenditures on education emphasized by national Poverty Reduction Strategy Papers (PRSPs) and the HIPC Initiative completion point triggers differ across countries, reflecting country-specific needs. Descriptive statistics are presented on various educational measures for the full group of HIPCs at each stage of the process (pre–decision point, interim, and post–completion point) (table 2.2 and figure 2.1).[3] The statistics refer to yearly data on the following educational variables: primary school dropout rates; secondary school repetition rates; student-teacher ratio; public expenditure on education as percentage of total government expenditure; public expenditure on education as percentage of GDP; and public expenditure on primary/secondary/tertiary education as percentage of public expenditure on education.

The standard deviations and the difference between maximum and minimum values of the education variables reveal considerable heterogeneity in the sample of HIPCs. Just two variables behave in a monotonic fashion during all three stages of the HIPC Initiative process: on average, educational expenditures as a percentage of GDP systematically rise, and the secondary school repetition rate systematically declines.

Table 2.1 Examples of HIPC Completion Point Triggers on Education

Type of trigger	Countries
Higher expenditure on education	Benin, Bolivia, Mali, Mozambique, Zambia
Higher primary school enrollment rates	Cameroon, Ethiopia, Mozambique, Niger
Lower dropout or repetition rates	Benin, Burkina Faso, Ethiopia, Madagascar, Mozambique, Niger, Zambia
Better access to schools by area or gender	Bolivia, Cameroon, Ethiopia
Lower student-teacher ratios	Burkina Faso, Malawi, Mozambique, Senegal, Sierra Leone

Source: Authors' compilation based on data from HIPCs' completion point documents.

Table 2.2 Descriptive Statistics for Various Measures of Education in HIPCs at Each Stage of the HIPC Initiative Process, 1998–2005

Variable	Mean	Standard deviation	Minimum	Maximum
Pre-decision point HIPCs				
Primary school dropout rate (percent)	36.4	16.4	4.7	71.8
Secondary school repetition rate (percent)	18.9	8.6	2.2	31.2
Student-teacher ratio in secondary school (percent)	28.3	10.8	11.3	54.1
Public education expenditures as percentage of total government expenditures	16.6	5.4	6.4	26.2
Public education expenditures as percentage of GDP	3.6	1.3	1.0	8.8
Public expenditures on primary education as percentage of total public education expenditures	44.6	9.4	23.1	63.2
Public expenditures on secondary education as percentage of total public education expenditures	29.3	6.8	7.8	41.2
Public expenditures on tertiary education as percentage of total public education expenditures	20.0	7.0	3.3	32.9
Interim HIPCs				
Primary school dropout rate (percent)	42.8	15.2	12.5	72.8
Secondary school repetition rate (percent)	17.3	8.4	1.6	36.1
Student-teacher ratio in secondary school (percent)	29.4	8.6	14.4	54.3
Public education expenditures as percentage of total government expenditures	15.4	3.8	8.9	25.6

Public education expenditures as percentage of GDP	3.7	1.7	1.8	8.6
Public expenditures on primary education as percentage of total public education expenditures	50.5	6.0	40.5	63.9
Public expenditures on secondary education as percentage of total public education expenditures	24.2	5.3	13.3	37.3
Public expenditures on tertiary education as percentage of total public education expenditures	16.6	6.9	4.9	34.7
Post–completion point HIPCs				
Primary school dropout rate (percent)	33.8	18.1	5.5	69.2
Secondary school repetition rate (percent)	11.3	7.7	1.4	30.0
Student-teacher ratio in secondary school (percent)	26.5	10.3	16.5	54.3
Public education expenditures as percentage of total government expenditures	18.5	0.7	18.1	19.7
Public education expenditures as percentage of GDP	4.7	1.5	2.3	7.0
Public expenditures on primary education as percentage of total public education expenditures	41.3	9.6	31.2	61.2
Public expenditures on secondary education as percentage of total public education expenditures	24.8	6.9	17.3	38.7
Public expenditures on tertiary education as percentage of total public education expenditures	19.1	7.4	6.2	26.6

Source: Authors' compilation based on World Bank data.
Note: Sample includes the 34 countries listed in note 3.

Figure 2.1 Average Educational Variables in HIPCs at Each
Stage of the HIPC Initiative Process

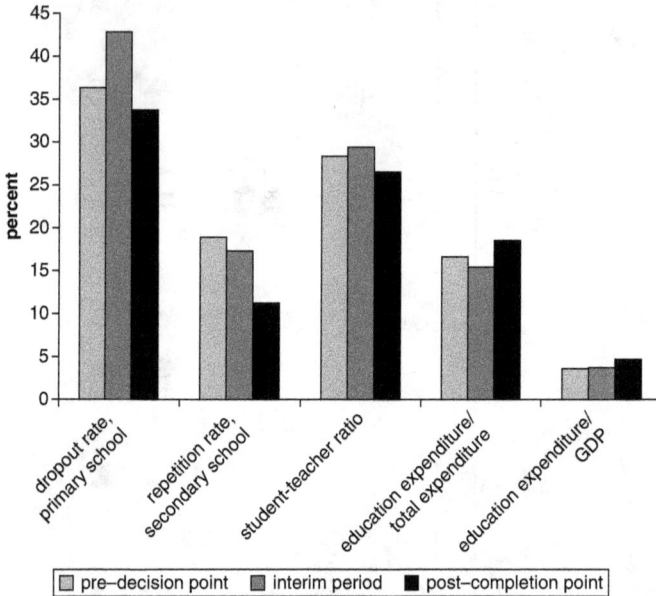

Source: Authors' compilation based on World Bank data.
Note: Sample in all figures includes the 34 countries listed in note 3.

The descriptive statistics suggest that on average, countries that have
reached the HIPC Initiative decision point (that is, interim and post–
completion point HIPCs) have significantly higher educational expenditures than do pre–decision point countries. As a share of GDP, education expenditures in post–decision point countries are more than 0.33
percentage point higher than the 4 percent average in pre–decision point
countries. More important, in the post–completion point group, the
share of educational expenditure in total public expenditures is largest
and spending much more homogeneous than in the other two groups.
On average, post–completion point countries spend 5 percent of output
on education, almost 30 percent (1 percentage point of GDP) more than
interim and pre–decision point HIPCs.

Post–completion point HIPCs also display lower dropout and repetition rates than do other HIPCs. Dropout rates in these countries are on

average 27 percent (nearly 10 percentage points) lower and repetition rates about 54 percent (more than 6 percentage points) lower than HIPCs receiving interim assistance (figures 2.2 and 2.3). The decrease in dropout rates is steep when the completion point is reached. Although the trend of decline in repetition rates is not strongly affected, it is not interrupted after the completion point is reached.

On average, post–completion point HIPCs allocate a larger share of total government expenditure to education than do other HIPCs. Average educational expenditures are about 18.5 percent of total government expenditures in countries that have graduated from the HIPC Initiative—some 2–3 percentage points higher than other HIPCs. Notwithstanding individual country variations, the distribution of expenditures within the education category is similar across groups, with close to half of all expenditure on education directed toward primary schooling (figure 2.4). Homogeneous increases in the share of educational expenditures for a schooling level within country groups should manifest themselves in rightward shifts in the distribution function of interest. For each value of the expenditure variable (x axis), figure 2.5 shows the proportion of observations below the value on the y axis. For no expenditure type is a systematic reduction

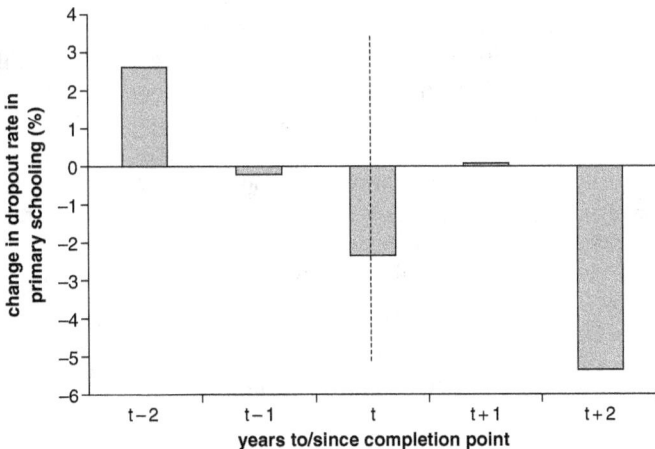

Figure 2.2 Primary School Dropout Rates in Post–Completion Point HIPCs before and after Reaching the Completion Point

Source: Authors' compilation based on World Bank data.

Figure 2.3 Secondary School Repetition Rates in
Post–Completion Point HIPCs before and after Reaching
the Completion Point

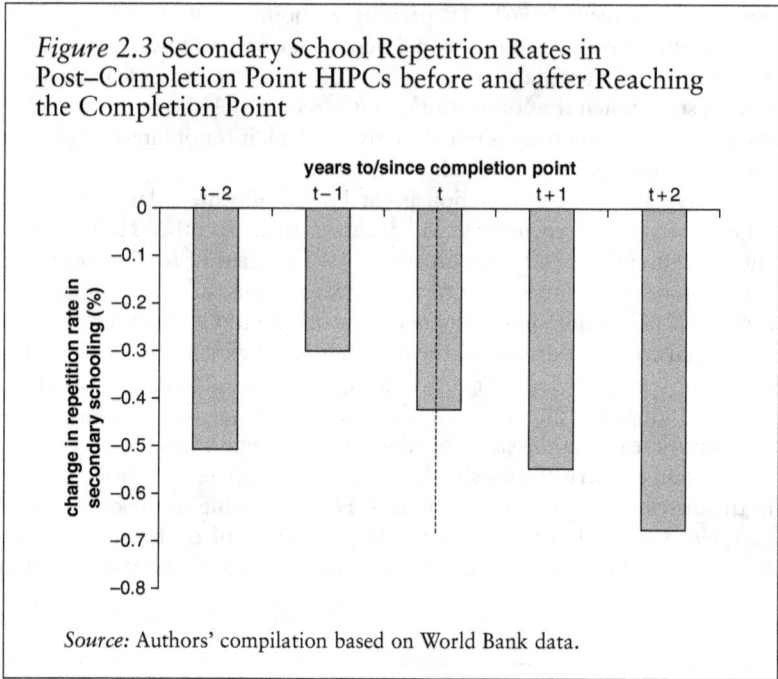

Source: Authors' compilation based on World Bank data.

in the frequency of low values coupled with an increase in high values that
corresponds to the different stages of HIPC Initiative observed.

Convergence across HIPCs in the share of educational expenditures in
total public expenditures has occurred as they go through the different
stages of the initiative. In contrast, the allocation across levels of education
(primary, secondary, and tertiary) varies widely among post–completion
point HIPCs. Countries in the interim period allocate the largest share
of their education budgets to primary schooling. While this development
may have been partly responsible for the decrease in dropout rates, the
proportion of educational expenditures dedicated to primary schooling
does not remain systematically high for the whole group of HIPCs once
the completion point is reached.

Debt Relief and Educational Outcomes: The Analytics

While the trends discussed above suggest a plausible association between
the HIPC Initiative process and the achievement of educational outcomes,
relying solely on descriptive statistics provides insufficient robustness.
Standard statistical tests based on differences across groupings may be

Figure 2.4 Distribution of Education Expenditures in
Pre–Decision Point, Interim, and Post–Completion
Point HIPCs

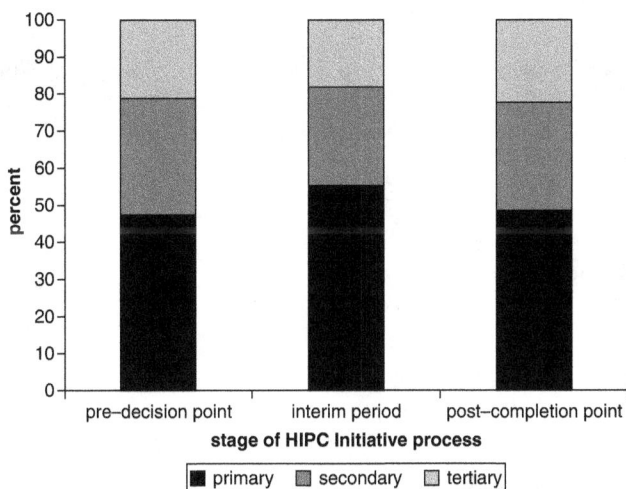

Source: Authors' compilation based on World Bank data.

flawed, in the sense that belonging to each one of the stages of the HIPC
Initiative is not a randomized experiment. To the extent that observed
and unobserved country characteristics affect both the stage of the HIPC
Initiative of a country and the process of human capital accumulation or
education policy measures, the effects implied by statistical tests will not
necessarily capture a causal effect of debt relief on educational variables.

To address these issues, Crespo Cuaresma and Vincelette (2008a) estimate the effects on the change in educational variables of HIPCs reaching
the decision or completion point, after controlling for selection factors,
such as the quality of democratic institutions, inflation, armed conflicts, net
aid transfers, per capita income, GDP growth rate, and country size, among
others. They use estimation procedures based on propensity score matching
methods and Heckman's (1979) sample selection estimator. Their results
imply that countries that reach the completion point exhibit declines in primary school dropout rates that are about 5–9 percentage points lower than
those in interim countries, where the average dropout rate is 43 percent.
Less robust results are found for changes in repetition rates, educational
expenditures, and student-teacher ratios, although several specifications
point toward a positive effect of debt relief on these variables.

Figure 2.5 Composition of Expenditures on Primary, Secondary, and Tertiary Education in HIPCs as a Percentage of Total Education Expenditures: Empirical Distribution Functions
(percent)

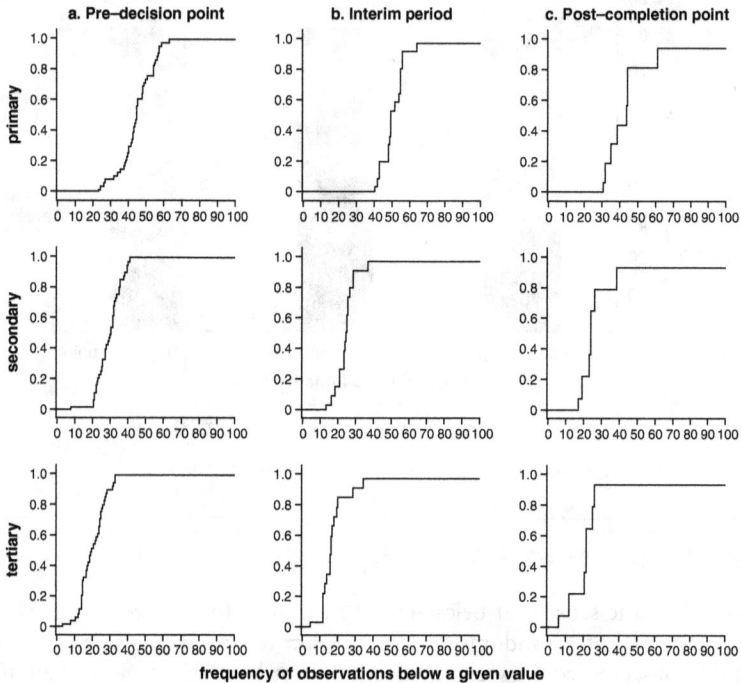

a. Pre–decision point   b. Interim period   c. Post–completion point

frequency of observations below a given value

Source: Authors' compilation based on World Bank data.

The results of Crespo Cuaresma and Vincelette (2008a) provide insight into the determinants of reaching the decision and completion points. Although they present empirical evidence that reaching the HIPC Initiative decision point does not significantly affect human capital accumulation, they show that HIPCs with higher levels of net aid inflows and the absence of armed conflict are more likely to reach the decision point. They suggest that price stability may be marginally significant but that neither the quality of governance nor civil liberties has played a significant role in moving countries toward the decision point. These results reinforce those of Freytag and Pehnelt (2009), who show that the quality of governance did not play a significant role in the process of reaching the decision point.

The discussion has referred primarily to two types of educational out-comes: policy decisions on the size and composition of expenditure on education and variables that affect the flow of children into and out of school. The ultimate interest, however, lies in the effects of debt relief on school enrollment and overall years of schooling, particularly because the direct effects of human capital on economic growth have usually been tested using these measures. The lack or poor quality of data tends to be a binding constraint in measuring these effects, however, particularly if one wants to evaluate the demographic distribution of such educational outcomes by concentrating on young age groups.

Recently, new efforts have been invested in obtaining data on the demo-graphic distribution of educational attainment. These data will prove especially important for evaluating policy measures in a wide sample of countries, including HIPCs. The International Institute for Applied Sys-tems Analysis-Vienna Institute of Demography (IIASA–VID) data set (see Lutz and others 2007; Lutz, Crespo Cuaresma, and Sanderson 2008) includes data on educational attainment by five-year age groups for more than 100 countries since 1970, at five-year intervals.[4]

Crespo Cuaresma and Vincelette (2008b) use this new source of data to evaluate whether the HIPC Initiative has affected the dynamics of edu-cational attainment in developing countries. Their results indicate that the proportion of young people who have completed primary school tends to increase in countries that have reached the decision point. Combining this evidence with the results on primary school dropout rates reported above allows us to obtain a first general picture of the qualitative and quantita-tive effects of debt relief on human capital accumulation.

Debt Relief and Educational Outcomes: The Challenges

The empirical evidence reported in the previous section suggests that the HIPC Initiative is positively associated with human capital accumulation in HIPCs. However, important challenges remain with respect to the frame-work in which poverty-reducing policies can create incentives for human capital accumulation under and beyond the HIPC Initiative process.

Before the launch of the HIPC Initiative, average spending on debt ser-vice was slightly higher than spending on health and education combined in eligible countries. Since then, HIPCs have markedly increased their expenditures not only on education but also on health and other social services. On average, such combined spending has been about six times the amount of debt-service payments.

While undoubtedly contributing, the spending channel may not have been the primary vehicle through which improvements in educational variables, or more broadly, human capital accumulation, materialized. HIPCs will need to continue to address the issue of efficiency of their social expenditure. Further research examining the effects of different educational policy strategies (by composition of educational expenditures across schooling levels, for example, or by refining educational policy measures) is needed to assess the relative success of PRS implementation and completion point triggers during the interim period. Such assessment could provide information that might be very useful in designing optimal educational policies in the context of PRSs and the framework of the HIPC Initiative, particularly as there is no clear evidence that increases in educational expenditures have systematically translated into improvements in human capital accumulation for countries participating in the HIPC Initiative.

While there is evidence associating educational outcomes with the HIPC Initiative process, improvements across the educational variables after HIPCs pass the completion point are not universal. A shift toward long-term strategies is key for designing educational policies that capitalize the dividend of human capital accumulation in terms of future economic growth. This is particularly important for policies affecting education, the benefits of which may take years to appear. Lutz, Crespo Cuaresma, and Sanderson (2008) report on the particular importance of secondary schooling as a driver of economic growth in developing countries. Improvements in primary school enrollment should thus be considered more of a necessary condition than a sufficient one for sustainable economic growth.

The implementation of institutional frameworks that guarantee that the returns to education in HIPCs can be appropriated is also critical. The alleviation of credit constraints has been one of the aims of many policy measures implemented in the interim period. Political stability and the absence of conflict are also crucial to reduce the adverse effects of brain drain in HIPCs.

Conclusion

This chapter examines the incentives debt relief may provide to investment in human capital accumulation as a key precondition for high and sustainable rates of economic growth in HIPCs. It reviews the descriptive statistics on the effects on educational variables of reaching the decision and completion points under the HIPC Initiative. It provides evidence of significant changes in the size of educational expenditures, dropout rates in primary schooling, repetition rates in secondary schooling, and student-teacher ratios. Crespo Cuaresma and Vincelette (2008a) present strong and statistically significant evidence that primary school dropout rates fall after a HIPC has reached its completion point. While not universally robust, decreases in repetition rates, increases in educational expenditures, and declines in student-teacher ratios appear to be associated to different degrees with the HIPC Initiative process.

These results shed light on the factor accumulation mechanisms triggered by debt relief in HIPCs. By focusing on the change in the human capital stock, Crespo Cuaresma and Vincelette (2008b) analyze the effects of debt relief for young cohorts. They find a statistically significant increase in the proportion of young people with primary schooling in countries that have reached the decision point under the HIPC Initiative. They also report some significant effects on the dynamics of the proportion of people without formal education, which falls after the decision point.

The results on educational outcomes achieved under the HIPC process are encouraging. They suggest that the initiative is indeed associated with positive benefits on human capital accumulation. Sustaining and broadening these achievements remains challenging, however. Appropriate investment by HIPC governments is needed to attain these positive results post–debt relief. Doing so is key to long-run prosperity in these countries.

Notes

1. The MDRI allows for a cancellation of eligible debts by the International Monetary Fund (IMF), the International Development Association (IDA) of the World Bank, and the African Development Fund (AfDF) for countries reaching completion point under the HIPC Initiative process. In 2007, the Inter-American Development Bank also decided to cancel eligible debts of the five HIPCs in the Western Hemisphere in an initiative similar to the MDRI.

2. See King and Rebelo (1990) for an economic growth model with taxation and human capital accumulation.

3. The data set is not balanced, and the number of missing observations varies across countries and variables. The following countries are included in the sample: Benin, Bolivia, Burkina Faso, Burundi, Cameroon, Central African Republic, Chad, Comoros, the Democratic Republic of Congo, the Republic of Congo, Côte d'Ivoire, Eritrea, Ethiopia, The Gambia, Ghana, Guinea, Guinea-Bissau, Guyana, Madagascar, Malawi, Mali, Mauritania, Mozambique, Nepal, Nicaragua, Niger, Rwanda, São Tomé and Principe, Senegal, Sudan, Tanzania, Togo, Uganda, and Zambia.

4. Not all HIPCs are represented in the data set.

References

Chauvin, N. D., and A. Kraay. 2005. "What Has 100 Billion Dollars Worth of Debt Relief Done for Low-Income Countries?" *International Finance (EconWPA)* 0510001.

———. 2007. "Who Gets Debt Relief?" *Journal of the European Economic Association* 5 (2–3): 333–42.

Crespo Cuaresma, J., and G. A. Vincelette. 2008a. "Debt Relief and Education in HIPCs." University of Innsbruck, Department of Economics, and World Bank, Economic Policy and Debt Department.

————. 2008b. "Debt Relief and Human Capital Accumulation of Young Cohorts."
     University of Innsbruck, Department of Economics, and World Bank, Economic
     Policy and Debt Department.

Easterly, W. 2002. "How Did the Heavily Indebted Poor Countries Become Heavily
     Indebted? Reviewing Two Decades of Debt Relief." *World Development* 30 (10):
     1677–96.

Freytag, A., and G. Pehnelt. 2009. "Debt Relief and Governance Quality in Devel-
     oping Countries." *World Development* 27 (1): 62–80.

Heckman, J. J. 1979. "Sample Selection Bias as a Specification Error." *Econometrica*
     47 (1): 153–61.

IDA (International Development Association) and IMF (International Monetary
     Fund). 2007. "The HIPC Initiative and the MDRI: Status of Implementation
     Report." Washington, DC.

————. 2008. "Heavily Indebted Poor Countries (HIPC) Initiative and Multilateral
     Debt Relief Initiative: Status of Implementation Report." IDA/Sec m2008=0561,
     September 12. Washington, DC.

King, R., and S. Rebelo. 1990. "Public Policy and Economic Growth: Developing
     Neoclassical Implications." *Journal of Political Economy* 98 (5): 126–50.

Lutz, W., J. Crespo Cuaresma, and W. Sanderson. 2008. "The Demography
     of Educational Attainment and Economic Growth." *Science* 319 (5866):
     1047–48.

Lutz, W., A. Goujon, K. C. Samir, and W. Sanderson. 2007. "Reconstruction of
     Populations by Age, Sex and Level of Educational Attainment for 120 Countries
     for 1970–2000." In *Vienna Yearbook of Population Research 2007*, 193–223.
     Vienna: Austrian Academy of Sciences.

Nafula, N. N. 2002. *Achieving Sustainable Universal Primary Education through
     Debt Relief: The Case of Kenya.* WIDER Discussion Paper 2002/66, World
     Institute for Development Economics Research, Helsinki.

Thomas, A. 2006. "Do Debt-Service Savings and Grants Boost Social Expenditures?"
     IMF Working Paper 06/180, International Monetary Fund, Washington, DC.

3

Is Debt Relief Good for the Poor? The Effects of the HIPC Initiative on Infant Mortality

Juan Pedro Schmid

How much does debt relief contribute to economic development in poor countries? Massive investments have been made to remove the heavy debt burdens on some low-income countries: committed debt relief to the 40 countries eligible under the Heavily Indebted Poor Countries (HIPC) Initiative and the MDRI (Multilateral Debt Relief Initiative) amounted to almost $100 billion in net present value terms as of end-2007 (IDA and IMF 2008).

Empirical evidence of the impact of debt relief under the HIPC Initiative on economic and human development is scarce. Some recent studies indicate that the HIPC Initiative had beneficial effects on education (Crespo Cuaresma and Vincelette 2008) and the earning prospects of companies operating in HIPCs (Raddatz 2009). Other studies find no effect on economic development and question the effectiveness of channeling funds through multilateral debt-relief initiatives (Easterly 2002; Arslanalp and Henry 2004; Chauvin and Kraay 2005).

Although it is possible that high levels of debt constrain economic development, it is equally likely that the same factors that lead to poverty (weak governance, armed conflicts) are responsible for high levels of debt. The question then becomes whether debt relief, or the conditionality embedded in the debt-relief process, will remove these underlying constraints for development. The empirical challenge is to separate the effects of debt relief, which may work through indirect channels and can have lags of unknown length, from other potential factors. The analysis is further complicated by the lack of annual development indicators other than GDP in many countries and the fact that it is still too early to examine the long-term effects of the initiative.

This chapter focuses on the effects on development of the HIPC Initiative. It tracks annual mortality data from a cross-country household panel data set around the HIPC Initiative decision point. The decision point is important, because it marks the initiation of economic and political reforms that must be satisfactorily implemented before reaching the completion point, the point at which debt relief is irrevocably granted.

A number of empirical studies analyze the effects of high indebtedness and debt relief on economic growth (see, for example, Chauvin and Kraay 2005; Raddatz 2009). This chapter focuses instead on the effects on the infant mortality rate (IMR). The IMR is a good proxy for the well-being of the poor, because it is highly sensitive to changes in socio-political conditions and has been used to study the impact of policies and socioeconomic conditions on human development (see, for example, Kudamatsu 2006 on democracy; Bhalotra 2007 on health expenditure; Bhalotra forthcoming on business cycles). In addition, the IMR is a good indicator of whether the HIPC Initiative affects the poor, because high mortality is strongly concentrated among poor regions and households (Bhalotra 2007).

The analysis presented here shows that the IMR decreases in countries that pass the decision point of the HIPC Initiative. In these countries, the decrease is positively related to the amount of debt-service reduction, improvements in the quality of institutions and policies, increases in aid flows, and increased immunization coverage and negatively related to the incidence of armed conflict. These factors alone, however, cannot completely explain the effect of the HIPC Initiative on the IMR, which suggests that countries experience pro-poor improvements in socioeconomic conditions that go beyond the indicators used in the analysis.

The chapter is organized as follows. The first section overviews possible channels between debt relief under the HIPC Initiative and economic development. The following section compares the development of health services that are related to infant mortality in HIPCs and low-income non–HIPCs. The third section presents the empirical framework, the data used, and the econometric results and explores whether the HIPC Initiative had an effect on health expenditures and immunization. The last section draws some conclusions.

Debt Relief, the HIPC Initiative, and Development

Debt relief can affect a country's development through various channels. A number of studies examine whether high indebtedness negatively affects incentives for investment, a phenomenon known as "debt overhang" (Krugman 1988; Sachs 1989). Empirical studies on the debt overhang hypothesis are mixed (see, for example, Loko and others 2003; Clements, Bhattacharya, and Nguyen 2005; Imbs and Ranciere 2005), and it is not clear whether debt overhang is important for low-income countries. Arslanalp and Henry (2004), for instance, find no effect of the HIPC Initiative on growth. They argue that the key constraint to development in HIPCs is not debt overhang but the lack of basic economic institutions. Other studies find that high debt levels and the resulting debt service can have a negative impact on growth and investment, especially in low-income countries and countries that are eligible for the HIPC Initiative (Clements, Bhattacharya, and Nguyen 2005; Presbitero 2005).

High indebtedness can negatively affect the development of a country if the debt service leads to a strain on public funds for economic and social services. Debt relief would then positively affect development by freeing up funds for public services and infrastructure that would otherwise have been used to service debt. Serieux and Samy (2001) point out that indebtedness does not constrain investment because of debt overhang but because the government revenue used to service debt decreases the volume and productivity of public and private investment.

Increased funds for basic health and education services as a result of debt relief could have an important impact in poor countries in which the population relies on public provision of social services. The empirical evidence on this effect is not conclusive, however, and depends on the period and countries chosen. Lora and Olivera (2006) find that higher debt levels reduce social expenditures in an unbalanced panel of 50 middle- and low-income countries. Similarly, Cassimon and Van Campenhout (2007) find that debt relief has desirable effects on both recurrent and capital spending. Conversely, Chauvin and Kraay (2005) find no evidence of a causal relationship between debt relief and pro-poor spending. Dessy and Vencatachellum (2007) find that debt relief to African countries increased expenditure on health and education only in countries that had improved institutional quality. A 2008 report by the International Development Association (IDA) and the International Monetary Fund (IMF) shows that debt service decreases and poverty-reducing expenditure increases in countries that pass the decision point of the HIPC Initiative (IDA and IMF 2008).

An additional effect could come from the impetus to adopt economic and political reforms that benefit the poor or improve growth. Debt relief under the HIPC Initiative entails conditionality in the form of completion-point triggers. These triggers are conditions for economic and political reforms that must be fulfilled before a country reaches the completion point. As outlined in chapter 2, some of the triggers under the enhanced HIPC Initiative target basic social services, which benefit the poor. The focus of the enhanced HIPC Initiative on poverty reduction is illustrated by the fact that all countries in the sample used in this chapter have completion point triggers on health.[1]

The evidence on a casual relation between debt relief on the one hand and improvements in public service delivery and governance on the other is mixed. Chauvin and Kraay (2005) find no evidence that debt relief influences governance indicators. Conversely, completion point documents provide evidence of improvements in areas such as public financial management, regulation and procurement, and education and health indicators, all of which are completion point triggers.

Some studies find positive effects from debt relief on economic development, but data problems usually require a number of caveats to be made. Loko and others (2003) study the effect of external indebtedness on measures of human development using a panel of 67 low-income countries. They find that external debt indicators are negatively related to life expectancy and infant mortality, but their results are not very strong and depend on the specification. Crespo Cuaresma and Vincelette (2008) use an approach similar to the one used here to test whether the HIPC Initiative had an effect on educational attainment and education expenditure. They find that the primary school completion rate increases in countries that have passed the decision point, a finding they attribute to decreases in dropout rates. They do not find an increase in education expenditure.

The HIPC Initiative and Health Services

Low-income countries are characterized by a tragic combination of insufficient basic public service provision (in terms of quality and access) and vulnerable populations who depend on public provision. Although health services in these countries remain inadequate, they have improved over time, as indicated by data on births attended by skilled health staff, diphtheria-pertussis-tetanus (DPT) immunization coverage, and access to improved water and sanitation.

Attendance at birth is an important indicator, because in addition to making deliveries much safer, it proxies for the treatment mothers receive before and after giving birth. Attendance at birth is low for all countries, and the median values hide substantial variation within groups, as indicated by the standard deviations. Countries that participated in the HIPC Initiative experienced the largest improvement in attended births between 1995–2000 and 2003–07 (figure 3.1). Attendance at birth in pre–decision point countries and non–HIPCs started substantially higher but increased only slightly. These two groups also display substantial within-group variation.

Many children in developing countries die from diseases that could be avoided with vaccinations, making immunization a simple and cost-effective way to prevent unnecessary infant and child death. Data for 2000 (the year when most of the countries in the sample reached the decision point) reveal that immunization coverage is relatively high and

Figure 3.1 Median Births Attended by Skilled Health Staff in Low-Income Countries at Different Stages of the HIPC Initiative, 1995–2000 and 2003–07
(percentage of total)

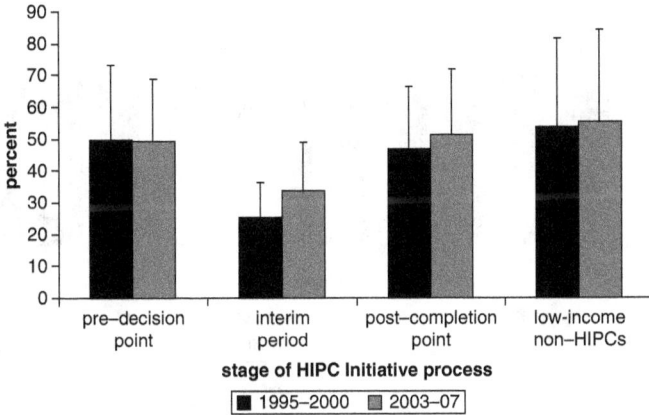

Source: Author's calculations based on data from World Bank 2009.
Note: The rules above the bars represent standard deviations. HIPC = Heavily Indebted Poor Countries.

has increased substantially, especially for countries that had passed the decision point. Immunization is at similar levels for the three groups of countries (pre–HIPC Initiative, post–HIPC Initiative, and low-income non–HIPC) five years after the decision point (figure 3.2).

Diarrhea, caused by lack of clean water and sanitation, is an important cause of death for infants and children in poor countries (Gamper-Rabindran, Shakeeb, and Timmins 2008). Progress in access to improved sanitation facilities in rural areas remains slow, and the level of access remains very low (figure 3.3). Reaching the completion point seems to be unrelated to changes in access to clean water and sanitation: the countries with the greatest progress after 2000 are interim countries or non–HIPCs.

All indicators increased substantially between the second half of the 1990s and the first half of the 2000s, in both countries that participated in the HIPC Initiative and countries that did not. At the same time, the median values remain at low levels and hide substantial variation within the different groups. The exception is the rate of immunization, which is close to 80 percent in all groups by 2005. In general, interim and post–completion point countries experienced the highest increase,

Figure 3.2 Median Immunization Coverage of DPT in Low-Income Countries around Decision Point at Different Stages of the HIPC Initiative
(percentage of children ages 12–23 months)

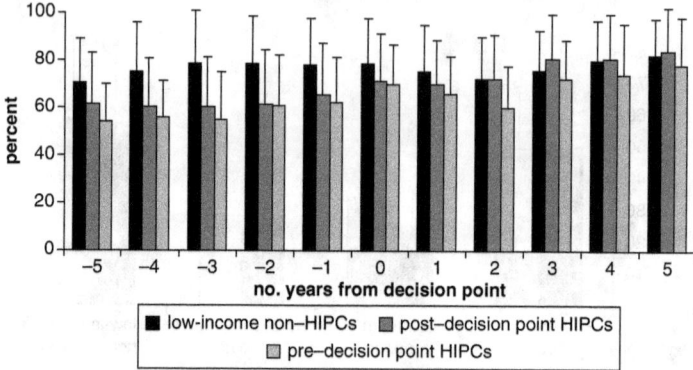

Source: Author's calculations based on data from World Bank 2009.
Note: Zero represents the decision point year for HIPCs and the year 2000 for low-income non–HIPCs. The rules above the bars represent standard deviations. HIPC = Heavily Indebted Poor Countries. DPT = diphtheria, pertussis, and tetanus.

Figure 3.3 Median Access to Improved Sanitation Facilities in Rural Areas in Low-Income Countries at Different Stages of the HIPC Initiative, 1995, 2000, and 2006
(percentage of rural population with access)

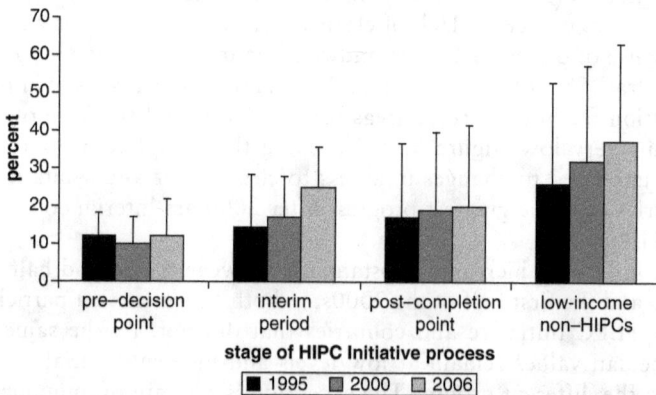

Source: Author's calculations based on data from World Bank 2009.
Note: The rules above the bars represent standard deviations.

and pre–decision point countries fared worst. As a group, low-income non–HIPC countries started with the highest level, but the other groups are catching up.

Empirical Analysis

This section presents the methodology, data, and econometric results of this study. It tries to explain the decline in the IMR and to show how the HIPC Initiative affected health expenditures and immunization rates.

Methodology and Data

To analyze the impact of the enhanced HIPC Initiative on infant mortality, I use the following model:

$$Mct = b\mathbf{HIPC} + q' \mathbf{X}ct + hs + cc + tcc + est, \tag{3.1}$$

where M is the share of children born in year t in country c who died by the age of 12 months; $\mathbf{HIPC}$ is a vector for the different stages in the HIPC process; $\mathbf{X}$ is a vector of socioeconomic country-specific controls; cc are country fixed effects; and tcc are country-specific trends.

I use a yearly panel of the IMR, constructed by collapsing retrospective surveys to the country/year level. I then estimate equation (3.1) using a panel fixed-effects model. Standard errors are robust and clustered at the state level to allow for serial correlation within countries.

The decision point is the starting point for the economic and political reforms that must be implemented to achieve the completion point and the point at which debt relief starts, through the delivery of interim debt relief. I isolate it by including control variables for passing the decision point and control variables for the two years just before the decision point. I include the measures for the years before the decision point, because countries have to be on track with World Bank and IMF–monitored programs to reach the decision point. These programs themselves could affect the IMR. Using both sets of measures helps address possible endogeneity of the decision point. One could see a spurious effect of the HIPC Initiative if countries reach the decision point during a period of declining trends in mortality, especially if the control variable that measures whether countries have a lower IMR two years before the decision point is significant.

Two factors have proven very important when modeling infant mortality: female education and average income of the country (see Filmer, Jeffrey, and Lant 1998). In addition to these two variables, I include the distribution of the age ranges of the mothers and the share of the rural population.

I also include a full set of country dummies and country-specific time trends to account for omitted differences in mortality across countries and over time. The country dummies control for constant differences in mortality levels across countries; the country-specific time trends pick up the fact that, in general, the IMR falls over time as a result of unobserved changes (such as improvements in health technology). The way I control for these changes assumes that the IMR decreases linearly over time at a country-specific rate. An alternative way to control for time effects is to include time dummies, assuming that all countries are affected by omitted common shocks. I prefer country-specific trends, because the countries in the sample are very diverse and therefore less likely to experience common shocks to mortality, but I also test specifications with additional year dummies.

The country-specific socioeconomic controls, X, also include variables that could explain the mechanism through which the HIPC Initiative affects the IMR. These are the World Bank's Country Policy and Institutional Assessment (CPIA) Indicator[2]; debt service; health expenditure; a dummy that measures whether the country is experiencing an armed conflict; immunization rates; and net aid transfers. HIPC conditionality also includes macroeconomic stability, which can have effects on poverty and mortality. I control for this variable by including inflation and GDP in the model.

Data

The data on infant mortality are obtained from the demographic and health surveys (DHSs), conducted by ORC Macro in various developing countries. Part of the DHS questionnaire consists of a survey of women of childbearing age (15–49 years), which includes the complete birth history for both children who were still alive and children who had died by the time of the interview. The retrospective nature of the data allows the construction of a panel of yearly mortality statistics over a long time period that is comparable across countries.

The surveys are not available for all low-income countries. To investigate the effect of the HIPC Initiative on the IMR, I select all the DHSs for low-income countries and lower-middle-income countries completed after 1999. This gives 31 countries, 23 of which are eligible for debt relief under the HIPC Initiative (see annex table 3A.1).[3] Many of the countries have multiple surveys, which I include to obtain more reliable estimates for early years. I drop all births in the year of or before the interview, because these children might die before reaching the age of one even if they were alive at the time of the interview.

In addition to the data from the DHS, I use a panel of aggregate country-level data, constructed from different sources. The data on net aid transfers are based on Roodman (2005). In addition, I use health expenditure data collected by the IMF from country reports, which

I updated using later country reports. All economic control variables are from the *World Development Indicators* and *Global Development Finance* (World Bank various years). All the information on the HIPC process is taken from the decision point and completion point documents of specific countries.

Results

How do IMRs in low-income HIPCs and non–HIPCs compare around the decision point? In order to control for time and country effects, I display the conditional IMR, which is the residual in a regression of the IMR on country dummies and country-specific time trends (figure 3.4). The values show the deviation of the IMR from a country-specific linear trend. In HIPCs, the IMR deviates positively from the linear trend until the decision point year, after which it becomes negative. The residual follows a similar pattern in low-income non–HIPCs, but the variation of the residual is greater and the residual becomes strongly negative in 2002.

Figure 3.4 Infant Mortality Rates in Low-Income Countries at Different Stages of the HIPC Initiative

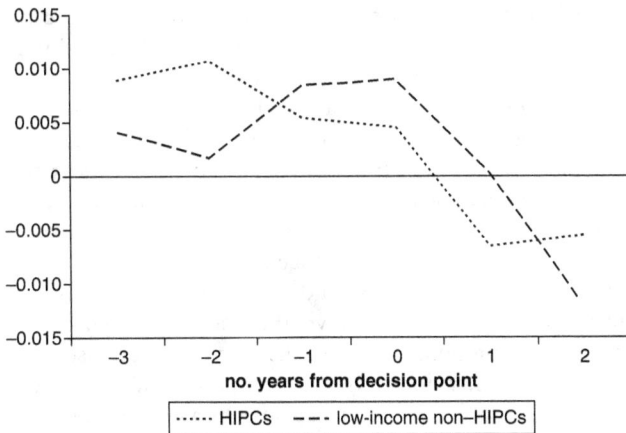

Source: Author's calculation based on Macro International Inc. Demographic and Health Surveys, various years.

Note: Zero represents the decision point year for HIPCs and the year 2000 for low-income non–HIPCs. The values represent the conditional average to control for time and country effects.

It is not evident from figure 3.4 that the HIPC Initiative has an effect on the IMR: the development of the IMR follows a very similar pattern in both HIPCs and non–HIPCs. However, changes over time in socioeconomic conditions, which are related to the IMR, were not the same in the two groups of countries, as the summary statistics in table 3.1 indicate. Countries that are eligible for debt relief under the HIPC Initiative are generally worse off than low-income non–HIPCs. They have lower GDP, CPIA scores, per capita health expenditure, immunization rates, and access to improved water and sanitation, all of which result in higher IMRs. In addition, they have higher debt-service-to-GDP ratios but receive more net aid transfers. The differences are substantial in both periods, albeit less pronounced after 2000. It is notable that immunization rates rise substantially for HIPCs between the two periods and that the CPIA score of HIPCs catches up.

Econometric Analysis

Table 3.2 presents the results for the basic econometric model. As the estimates include country dummies and country-specific time trends to control for unobservable country- and time-specific effects, the model tests whether the covariates can explain a deviation in the IMR from a country-specific trend. The model also includes a set of socioeconomic controls discussed above. Error terms are robust and clustered to control for serial correlation within countries.

The econometric analysis explores whether the IMR is different for countries in the interim period (the period between the decision point and the completion point). For this purpose, I include variables that split the timing of the HIPC Initiative into a pre–decision point period, an interim period, and a post–completion point period, using dummies for the two years preceding the decision point, dummies for the years in the interim period, and a dummy for post–completion point countries. The completion point can be reached only after fulfilling the completion point triggers. It is therefore likely to be endogenous to improvements in health. However, not controlling for it would lead to biased estimates.

Column 1 in table 3.2 explores whether the IMR decreases once countries pass the decision point. It shows that the IMR decreases in a statistically significant manner during the interim period, declining even farther during the post–completion point period. On average, the IMR falls by half a percentage point for every year after the decision point. This effect is quite substantial, as the yearly average decline in the period 1992–2005 is only 0.2 percentage point.

The second column includes dummies for each year a country is in the interim period. The effects are statistically significant for the years that follow the decision point year and increase over time by a similar amount, with the F-test rejecting the null hypothesis that the coefficients for the

Table 3.1 Descriptive Statistics for Control Variables in HIPCs and Low-Income Non–HIPCs, 1996–99 and 2002–07

Period/country type	Debt service/ GDP	Per capita GDP	Net aid transfers/ GDP	Health expenditure/ GDP	CPIA	Immunization	Water and sanitation
Average 1996–99							
Low-income non–HIPC	0.04	464.01	0.07	5.87	3.30	71.61	43.75
	(0.03)	(210.93)	(0.06)	(1.22)	(0.66)	(19.93)	(24.15)
HIPC	0.05	352.80	0.14	5.82	3.12	58.17	26.46
	(0.06)	(256.41)	(0.13)	(0.88)	(0.84)	(21.5)	(16.61)
Average 2002–07							
Low-income non–HIPC	0.04	511.49	0.10	6.31	3.23	77.89	53.60
	(0.04)	(186.14)	(0.17)	(0.64)	(0.48)	(15.47)	(22.78)
HIPC	0.03	383.82	0.14	5.93	3.24	73.34	30.35
	(0.03)	(277.72)	(0.11)	(0.84)	(0.45)	(18.77)	(17.05)

Source: Author's calculation based on data from World Bank 2009.
Note: Standard deviations are in parentheses.

Table 3.2 Regression Results on the Effect of the HIPC Initiative on Infant Mortality Rates

Variable	(1)	(2)	(3)	(4)	(5)	(6)	(7)	(8)	(9)	(10)	(11)	(12)	(13)	(14)	(15)	(16)	(17)
Years in interim period (before completion point)	-0.006 (2.84)**																
Decision point year		-0.006 (1.32)	-0.007 (1.42)	-0.006 (1.38)	-0.005 (1.10)		-0.005 (0.97)	-0.006 (1.22)	-0.007 (1.42)	0.002 (0.35)	0.001 (0.19)	-0.005 (1.01)	-0.006 (1.35)	-0.006 (1.22)	-0.006 (1.08)	-0.006 (1.06)	-0.012 (1.84)
One year after decision point		-0.013 (2.62)*	-0.014 (2.71)*	-0.014 (2.69)*	-0.012 (2.41)*		-0.012 (2.05)	-0.013 (2.65)*	-0.014 (2.69)*	-0.003 (0.41)	-0.004 (0.54)	-0.013 (2.45)*	-0.012 (2.12)*	-0.013 (2.49)*	-0.013 (2.39)*	-0.013 (2.33)*	-0.012 (1.76)
Two years after decision point		-0.018 (2.68)*	-0.019 (2.75)*	-0.019 (2.74)*	-0.017 (2.53)*		-0.017 (2.11)*	-0.017 (2.53)*	-0.018 (2.70)*	-0.004 (0.42)	-0.005 (0.55)	-0.017 (2.55)*	-0.016 (2.23)*	-0.017 (2.58)*	-0.017 (2.54)*	-0.017 (2.40)*	-0.016 (1.95)
Three years after decision point		-0.020 (2.26)*	-0.021 (2.36)*	-0.021 (2.32)*	-0.018 (2.03)		-0.020 (1.81)	-0.020 (2.23)*	-0.021 (2.31)*	-0.009 (0.75)	-0.011 (0.86)	-0.017 (2.03)	-0.018 (1.95)	-0.018 (2.11)*	-0.016 (1.98)	-0.016 (1.90)	-0.024 (2.48)*
Country passed completion point	-0.014 (3.06)**	-0.015 (2.83)**	-0.016 (2.94)**	-0.015 (2.91)**	-0.013 (2.52)*	-0.012 (2.71)*	-0.015 (2.61)*	-0.014 (2.74)*	-0.015 (2.88)**	-0.001 (0.18)	-0.002 (0.28)	-0.015 (2.73)*	-0.013 (2.31)*	-0.013 (2.38)*	-0.014 (2.50)*	-0.014 (2.41)*	-0.015 (1.96)
Two years before decision point	0.001 (0.34)	0.001 (0.20)	0.000 (0.13)	0.000 (0.14)	0.002 (0.52)	0.002 (0.68)	0.001 (0.27)	0.001 (0.19)	-0.000 (0.06)	0.002 (0.70)	0.002 (0.59)	-0.000 (0.04)	0.000 (0.15)	0.000 (0.07)	-0.001 (0.18)	-0.001 (0.18)	-0.005 (0.95)
One year before decision point	-0.006 (1.65)	-0.006 (1.56)	-0.007 (1.65)	-0.006 (1.61)	-0.005 (1.23)	-0.004 (1.10)	-0.007 (1.64)	-0.006 (1.59)	-0.007 (1.74)	0.000 (0.04)	-0.000 (0.05)	-0.006 (1.48)	-0.006 (1.58)	-0.006 (1.63)	-0.007 (1.72)	-0.007 (1.71)	-0.011 (2.27)*
Lag log GDP per capita (in constant US$)	-0.009 (1.84)	-0.009 (1.79)		-0.009 (1.79)	-0.008 (1.26)	-0.009 (1.77)	-0.011 (0.71)	-0.011 (2.34)*	-0.020 (3.35)**	0.001 (0.05)	-0.004 (0.25)	-0.011 (2.31)*	-0.008 (1.54)	-0.012 (0.86)	-0.011 (0.67)	-0.011 (0.66)	-0.003 (0.13)
Total debt service/GDP				-0.011 (0.66)													
Lag CPIA					-0.002 (1.71)										-0.002 (1.09)	-0.002 (1.10)	-0.003 (1.50)
Common reduction factor						-0.010 (2.61)*											

	(1)	(2)	(3)	(4)	(5)	(6)	(7)	(8)	(9)	(10)	(11)	(12)	(13)	(14)	(15)	(16)	(17)
Lag inflation, consumer prices (annual percent)							0.000 (0.71)										0.001 (0.29)
Lag log per capita net aid transfers								-0.003 (1.21)							-0.012 (1.25)	-0.012 (1.22)	
Lag Net aid transfers/GDP									-0.020 (2.50)*								
Lag per capita health expenditure										-0.004 (1.19)							
Lag health expenditure/GDP											-0.002 (0.73)						
Lag armed conflict dummy												0.009 (3.90)**			0.008 (3.13)**	0.008 (3.08)**	0.007 (2.41)*
Lag GAVI DPT campaign in place													-0.003 (1.03)				0.001 (0.22)
Percentage of DPT immunization 12–23 months														-0.000 (2.25)*	-0.000 (1.22)	-0.000 (1.18)	-0.000 (1.18)
Lag infant																0.002 (0.04)	
Constant	2.340 (1.89)	2.194 (1.62)	2.421 (1.83)	2.176 (1.60)	1.144 (0.90)	2.661 (2.13)*	1.640 (1.18)	2.521 (1.76)	2.305 (1.67)	4.998 (2.67)*	-3.991 (0.86)	2.265 (1.56)	1.990 (1.49)	1.352 (1.01)	2.186 (1.49)	2.184 (1.50)	5.283 (1.61)
Number of observations	352	352	352	352	349	352	300	351	352	211	211	352	352	344	341	341	340
Number of countries	31	31	31	31	31	31	29	31	31	25	25	31	31	31	31	31	31
R-squared	0.69	0.69	0.69	0.69	0.68	0.69	0.69	0.69	0.69	0.72	0.72	0.71	0.69	0.67	0.69	0.69	0.71

Source: Author.

Note: All estimates include the socioeconomic controls described in the text as well as country dummies and country-specific time trends. CPIA = country political and institutional assessment; DPT = diphtheria, pertussis, and tetanus; GAVI = Global Alliance for Vaccines and Immunisation; NAT = net aid transfers; TDS = total debt service. Robust *t*-statistics are in parentheses.

** Significant at the 1 percent level; * significant at the 5 percent level.

different years are the same. The dummies for the two years before the decision point are not statistically significant, indicating that the IMR decreases only after the decision point is reached.

The analysis that follows adds variables that proxy for likely channels through which the HIPC Initiative could affect the IMR. Passing the decision point is likely to trigger a wide variety of changes, making the covariates at least partly collinear. For this reason, I include the variables individually in the baseline regression.

What Caused the Decline in the Infant Mortality Rate? A very important determinant of the IMR is the income level of the country. The HIPC Initiative is most likely beneficial for the poor if it has a positive effect on economic growth. However, the main question posed in this chapter is whether the HIPC Initiative has a direct effect on the lives of the poor, or at least an effect other than through changes in GDP. Therefore, I ignore this effect and control for GDP in the baseline regression.

A simple test to explore the indirect effect of HIPC on mortality through its effects on GDP consists of estimating the baseline model without GDP (see column 3). The coefficients and the *t*-values on the HIPC dummies and the dummy for passing the completion point remain very similar if GDP is excluded. Although the relation between the HIPC Initiative and GDP growth would have to be studied in detail, changes in the IMR after the decision point are not related to changes in GDP in my specification.

Columns 4–12 extend the baseline regression by total debt service to GDP, the CPIA indicator, the amount of debt service reduction (the common reduction factor [CRF][4]), inflation, net aid transfers, health expenditure, a dummy for armed conflicts, a dummy that is 1 if the Global Alliance for Vaccines and Immunisation (GAVI) was disbursing funds, and the percentage of children ages 12–23 months who received vaccinations for DPT.[5] All of these variables proxy for factors that may explain the effect of the decision point on the IMR. The last column includes the variables that were statistically significant when added individually.

Only a few explanatory variables are significant. These are the CRF, net aid transfers as a share of GDP, the dummy for armed conflicts, and the share of children immunized against DPT. In addition, the coefficient for the overall CPIA is not strongly rejected.

Only countries in the interim period have a CRF, which is the reason why I include the CRF interacted with the years in the interim period in the regression. However, I cannot add the years in the interim period, because the two variables are to some extent collinear, making it difficult to interpret whether the coefficient on the CRF measures the impact of the extent of debt service reduction or acts as a dummy for the interim period. The coefficient on the interaction is larger than the coefficient for the years in the interim period alone (in column 1), indicating that, in addition to being in the interim period, the degree of debt service reduction could play a role.

Net aid transfers increase on average after the decision point. The results in column 9 indicate that net aid transfers as a share of GDP but not net aid transfers per capita have a desirable effect on the IMR. On average, the CPIA also increases after the decision point, but the effect on the IMR is not statistically significant.

Armed conflict increases the IMR. Immunization coverage reduces the IMR, although the effect is not very strong: a 1 percentage point increase in DPT immunization coverage leads to a statistically significant reduction of 0.02 percent in the IMR. I include the involvement of GAVI to test whether the IMR is lower after the decision point because nongovernmental organizations (NGOs) target more help to these countries. The coefficient is not statistically significant.

Health expenditure (measured per capita or as a share of GDP) does not affect the IMR. The result may reflect the short time series for health expenditure, which is also the reason why the HIPC measures loose significance,[6] but it is in line with evidence that the overall amount of health expenditure is only weakly related to health outcomes (see, for example, Filmer, Jeffrey, and Lant 1998). Other variables that are not statistically significant are per capita net aid transfers, total debt service, the dummy for the GAVI campaigns, and inflation.

The estimate in column 15 combines the variables that were statistically significant (or close to being so) in the individual estimates. The measures for the HIPC Initiative remain statistically significant even in this specification. Of all the additional explanatory variables, only the coefficient on armed conflicts remains statistically significant in this specification.

The last two columns make some specification changes, using the extended model to test for the robustness of the results. Column 14 includes the lagged dependent variable, to check whether the results are driven by consistency in the series.[7] The lagged variable is not significant, and the level and significance levels on the HIPC coefficients remain very similar.

In long panels with substantial variance, it is important to make sure that the results are not driven by the way in which the omitted time trend is accounted for or the period chosen.[8] The model in column 15 includes both country-specific time trends and year dummies. It therefore represents the most conservative way of controlling for omitted time effects: regressing the IMR on country dummies, year dummies and country-specific trends already explain 64 percent of its variance. The coefficients on the HIPC timing loose significance (to 10 percent) but remain otherwise similar. However, the coefficient on the year before the decision point becomes statistically significant.

An important result is that the decision point measures remain significant in most specifications. Although the results indicate that some of the controls included in the model played a role in reducing the IMR, omitted factors related to the HIPC Initiative influence the IMR. The fact that the dummy for the year preceding the decision point is statistically significant in some specification implies that it is not completely clear whether the IMR decreases only once the country passes the decision point or the year before. Further analysis (not shown here) reveals that the variable for the year before the decision point is also sensitive to the years included; the variable for two years before the decision point is strongly rejected in all specifications.

A likely explanation for this effect is that the dummy for the year before the decision point picks up the effects of programs by the IMF and the World Bank that have to be achieved before reaching the decision point. Another explanation would be that the dummy picks up an existing downward trend in mortality that would have happened anyway.

The decision point coefficients remain significant even after controlling for all likely channels, suggesting that poor people experience improvements in socioeconomic conditions that go beyond what the indicators used in the analysis measure. The strong effect of DPT immunizations shows that the public health provision can improve independent of increases in aid, health expenditure, or the CPIA.

Health Expenditures, Immunization, and the HIPC Initiative. Immunization is especially important for this study, because its absence is a main cause of infant and child mortality and because all the HIPCs in the sample have completion point triggers on health that are related to immunization targets. The period of debt relief under the HIPC Initiative coincides with a strong focus on immunization campaigns by NGOs and donors, including GAVI, which offers health system support with a strong focus on immunizations.

The first column in table 3.3 indicates that immunization and the HIPC Initiative are indeed related. Passing the HIPC decision and completion points has a strong, statistically significant effect on immunization. Immunization increases only once countries pass the decision point: neither dummy for the two years before the decision point is statistically significant. The variable GAVI explores whether interventions under GAVI were related to the increase in immunization. Involvement of GAVI had a strong effect, but the coefficient is not statistically significant. Conversely, the HIPC Initiative affects neither per capita health expenditure nor health expenditure as a share of GDP.

Similar analysis (not shown here) indicates that the HIPC Initiative had no effect on attendance at birth, availability of water and sanitation, or the share of women who received prenatal care. The analysis is restricted by the long spells between observations for all the outcome variables other than immunization, but the results indicate that HIPCs did not experience a surge in provision of health-related services.

Table 3.3 Estimation Results on Immunization and Health Expenditures

Variable	DPT immunization (percentage of children ages 12–23 months)	Per capita health expenditure (constant US$)	Health expenditure (percentage of GDP)
Country participated in GAVI	2.946 (1.64)		
Years since decision point	2.626 (2.31)*	0.026 (0.37)	−0.079 (0.51)
Country passed completion point	12.727 (2.28)*	0.007 (0.04)	−0.375 (0.84)
Country is two years before decision point	1.925 (1.00)	0.038 (0.38)	−0.123 (0.57)
Country is one year before decision point	1.181 (0.57)	0.135 (1.56)	0.042 (0.23)
Number of observations	716	324	335
R-squared	0.92	0.91	0.89

Source: Author.

Note: Robust *t*-statistics are in parentheses. All estimates include country dummies and country-specific time trends. Column 1 also includes year dummies. GAVI = Global Alliance for Vaccines and Immunisation.

* Significant at the 5 percent level.

Conclusions and Discussion

The results presented in this chapter provide strong evidence that the IMR decreases once countries pass the decision point of the HIPC Initiative. The results are robust and not affected by changes in the specification or by inclusion of additional explanatory variables. Part of the decrease in the IMR is related to increases in aid flows; to the lower risk of armed conflict; and, possibly, to the amount of debt relief. The coefficient for the quality of policies and institutions could not be rejected strongly. However, even conditional on all these factors, the IMR decreases in HIPCs after the decision point, suggesting that poor people experience improvements in the socio-economic conditions that go beyond the indicators used in the analysis.

As the control variables could not fully explain the effect of the HIPC Initiative on the IMR, it is likely that the effectiveness of debt relief depends on whether it leads to economic and political reforms that improve service delivery. The conditionality built into the HIPC process aims to strengthen the link between debt relief, poverty reduction, and social services, so that countries experience improvements in basic service provision that go beyond higher expenditure. An additional benefit is that other donors and NGOs might be encouraged by the decision point to increase their involvement in HIPCs—for instance, in programs that focus directly on health, such as vaccination campaigns.

The conditionality incorporated into the HIPC process can also have a positive influence on macroeconomic stability and growth, both of which affect poverty and health. Macroeconomic stability is one of the conditions stipulated for both the decision point and the completion point. In my specifications, changes in GDP were not related to the IMR, but the exact interaction between HIPC, GDP growth, and human development needs to be studied in detail.

Because infant mortality is concentrated among poor regions and households, the evidence that the HIPC Initiative is associated with a decline in infant mortality suggests that the same effect is likely to be found for other measures of well-being of the poorest segments of the population. The effect is partly explained by increases in aid, as measured by net aid transfers, but there is more to the story. Likely explanations, which require further research, are improvements in public service delivery and macroeconomic stability caused by the conditionality integral to the HIPC Initiative.

For all these reasons, conditional debt relief as a complement to more traditional forms of aid can play an important role in helping countries achieve sustainable development and improving the lives of the poor. It is probably preferable to unconditional debt relief. The HIPC Initiative gave countries a unique window of opportunity to lock in policies and reforms with benefits that can go beyond the short-term fiscal benefits from debt relief alone.

Annex: Countries Included in the Sample

Table 3A.1 Countries Included in Sample

Country	Decision point	Completion point	Last year for which data are available
Bangladesh	n.a.	n.a.	2002
Benin	2000	2003	2004
Bolivia	2000	2001	2001
Burkina Faso	2000	2002	2001
Cambodia	n.a.	n.a.	2003
Cameroon	2000	2006	2002
Chad	2001	n.a.	2002

Table 3A.1 (continued)

Country	Decision point	Completion point	Last year for which data are available
Congo, Dem. Rep. of	2003	n.a.	2005
Congo, Rep. of	2006	n.a.	2003
Ethiopia	2001	2004	2003
Ghana	2002	2004	2001
Guinea	2000	n.a.	2003
Haiti	2006	n.a.	2003
Honduras	2000	2005	2003
Kenya	n.a.	n.a.	2001
Lesotho	n.a.	n.a.	2002
Liberia	2007	n.a.	2004
Madagascar	2000	2004	2001
Malawi	2000	2006	2002
Mali	2000	2003	2004
Mozambique	2000	2001	2001
Nepal	n.a.	n.a.	2004
Niger	2000	2004	2004
Nigeria	n.a.	n.a.	2001
Philippines	n.a.	n.a.	2001
Rwanda	2000	2005	2003
Senegal	2000	2004	2003
Tanzania	2000	2001	2002
Uganda	2000	2000	2004
Zambia	2000	2005	1999
Zimbabwe	n.a.	n.a.	2003

Source: Author.

Note: n.a. Not applicable.

Notes

1. The focus on social sectors is an important difference between the original HIPC Initiative and the Enhanced Initiative. Mozambique is the only country that reached the completion point under the original HIPC Initiative for which the completion point document notes satisfactory progress in health. The completion-point documents for the Plurinational State of Bolivia, Burkina Faso, and Mali indicate mixed or limited progress in the health sector; the sector is not specifically mentioned in the completion point documents for Guyana or Uganda.

2. The CPIA index groups 20 indicators into 4 broad categories: economic management, structural policies, policies for social inclusion and equity, and public sector management and institutions. Countries are rated on their current status in each of these performance criteria, with scores from 1 (lowest) to 6 (highest). This index is updated annually.

3. In analysis not shown here, I use other data sources to explore whether the results are driven by the selection of the countries with DHSs, but this is not the case.

4. The CRF—the percentage decrease in the net present value of debt needed to achieve the debt threshold of the HIPC Initiative—is a measure of the debt service reduction a country will receive.

5. A child is considered adequately immunized against diphtheria, pertussis (whooping cough), and tetanus (DPT) after receiving three doses of vaccine.

6. The results remain the same when the regression is rerun excluding health expenditure for the same observations. Conversely, if the state-specific time trends are replaced by a common time trend, the HIPC measures become statistically significant but the health expenditure coefficient remains not statistically significant.

7. The coefficient on the dependant variable in dynamic panel models is biased, but the bias becomes insignificant in long panels like the one used here (Roodman 2007).

8. The results did not change when a shorter time period was used (analysis not shown here).

References

Arslanalp, S., and P. B. Henry. 2004. "Helping the Poor to Help Themselves: Debt Relief or Aid." NBER Working Paper 10230, National Bureau of Economic Research, Cambridge, MA.

Bhalotra, S. 2007. "Spending to Save? State Health Expenditure and Infant Mortality in India." *Health Economics* 16(9): 911–28.

———. Forthcoming. "Fatal Fluctuations? Cyclicality in Infant Mortality in India." *Journal of Development Economics.*

Cassimon, D., and B. Van Campenhout. 2007. "Aid Effectiveness, Debt Relief and Public Finance Response: Evidence from a Panel of HIPC." *Review of World Economics* 143 (4): 742–63.

Chauvin, N. D., and A. Kraay. 2005. "What Has 100 Billion Dollars Worth of Debt Relief Done for Low-Income Countries?" *International Finance (Econ-WPA)* 0510001.

Clements, B., R. Bhattacharya, and T. Q. Nguyen. 2005. "Can Debt Relief Boost Growth in Poor Countries." *Economic Issues* 34, International Monetary Fund, Washington, DC. http://www.imf.org/external/pubs/ft/issues/issues34/index.htm.

Crespo Cuaresma, J., and G. Vincelette. 2008. "Debt Relief and Education in HIPCs." University of Innsbruck, Economics Department, and World Bank, Economic Policy and Debt Department.

Dessy, S. E., and D. Vencatachellum. 2007. "Debt Relief and Social Services Expenditure: The African Experience 1989–2003." *African Development Review* 19 (1): 200–16.

Easterly, W. 2002. "How Did Heavily Indebted Poor Countries Become Heavily Indebted? Reviewing Two Decades of Debt Relief." *World Development* 30 (1): 1677–96.

Filmer, D., S. H. Jeffrey, and H. P. Lant. 1998. "Health Policy in Poor Countries: Weak Links in the Chain 1." Policy Research Working Paper 1874, World Bank, Washington, DC.

Gamper-Rabindran, S., K. Shakeeb, and C. Timmins. 2008. "The Impact of Piped Water Provision on Infant Mortality in Brazil: A Quantile Panel Data Approach." NBER Working Paper 14365, National Bureau of Economic Research, Cambridge, MA.

IDA (International Development Association) and IMF (International Monetary Fund). 2008. "Heavily Indebted Poor Countries (HIPC) Initiative and Multilateral Debt Relief Initiative (MDRI): Status of Implementation." Washington, DC.

Imbs, J., and R. Ranciere. 2005. "The Overhang Hangover." Policy Research Working Paper 3673, World Bank, Washington, DC.

Krugman, P. 1988. "Financing versus Forgiving a Debt Overhang." *Journal of Development Economics* 29 (3): 253–68.

Kudamatsu, M. 2006. *Has Democratization Reduced Infant Mortality in Sub-Saharan Africa? Evidence from Micro Data.* ISER Discussion Paper 685, Institute for Social and Economic Research, University of Essex, United Kingdom.

Loko, B., M. Mlachila, R. Nallari, and K. Kalonji. 2003. "The Impact of External Indebtedness on Poverty in Low-Income Countries." IMF Working Paper 3, International Monetary Fund, Washington, DC.

Lora, E., and M. Olivera. 2006. "Public Debt and Social Expenditure: Friends or Foes." Research Department Working Paper 563, Inter-American Development Bank, Washington, DC.

Macro International Inc. 2009. "Measure DHS: Demographic and Health Surveys." Calverton, MD.

Presbitero, A. 2005. "The Debt-Growth Nexus: A Dynamic Panel Data Estimation." Working Paper 243, Università Politecnica delle Marche, Ancona, Italy.

Raddatz, C. 2009. "Multilateral Debt Relief through the Eyes of Financial Markets." Policy Research Working Paper 4872, World Bank, Washington, DC.

Roodman, D. 2005. "An Index of Donor Performance." Working Paper 67, Center for Global Development, Washington, DC.

———. 2007. "A Note on the Theme of Too Many Instruments." Center for Global Development Working Paper 125, Washington, DC.

Sachs, J., 1989. "The Debt Overhang of Developing Countries." In *Debt, Stabilization and Development: Essays in Memory of Carlos Diaz-Alejandro,* ed. G. Calvo, R. Findlay, P. Kouri, and J. Braga De Macedo, 80–102. Oxford, U.K.: Basil Blackwell.

Serieux, John, and Yiagadeesen Samy. 2001. "The Debt Service Burden and Growth: Evidence from Low-Income Countries." North-South Institute Working Paper, Ottawa, Ontario, Canada.

World Bank. 2009. *Global Development Finance.* Washington, DC: World Bank.

4

Drivers of Growth in Fragile States: Has the HIPC Process Helped Fragile Countries Grow?

Luca Bandiera, Jesús Crespo Cuaresma, and Gallina Andronova Vincelette

F ragile states are a group of low-income countries that share certain common characteristics, such as a poor record of economic growth, predominantly young populations, and rapid rates of population growth.[1] These countries are home to more than 300 million poor people living on less than a $1 a day—more than a third of the world's extreme poor. They have the highest concentration of extreme poverty and are farthest away from reaching the United Nations' Millennium Development Goals. Most fragile states have been affected by wars in recent years, and many remain at a high risk of conflict or political instability. All fragile states have suffered periods of prolonged contraction, usually around the time of conflict and political instability.

For the purpose of this chapter, we define fragile states as low-income countries with a score of less than 3.2 on the World Bank Country Policy and Institutional Assessment (CPIA) rating. According to this method, 34 states and territories are classified as fragile. Twenty of these fragile states are also heavily indebted (figure 4.1).

The Heavily Indebted Poor Countries (HIPC) Initiative and the Multilateral Debt Relief Initiative (MDRI) have helped qualifying countries reduce extreme external debt burdens and contributed to creating fiscal space for channeling resources into poverty-reducing activities and economic development. Per capita income in fragile HIPCs is less than half that of fragile non–HIPCs, and their social indicators across the board are,

Figure 4.1 Groups of Fragile States and HIPCs

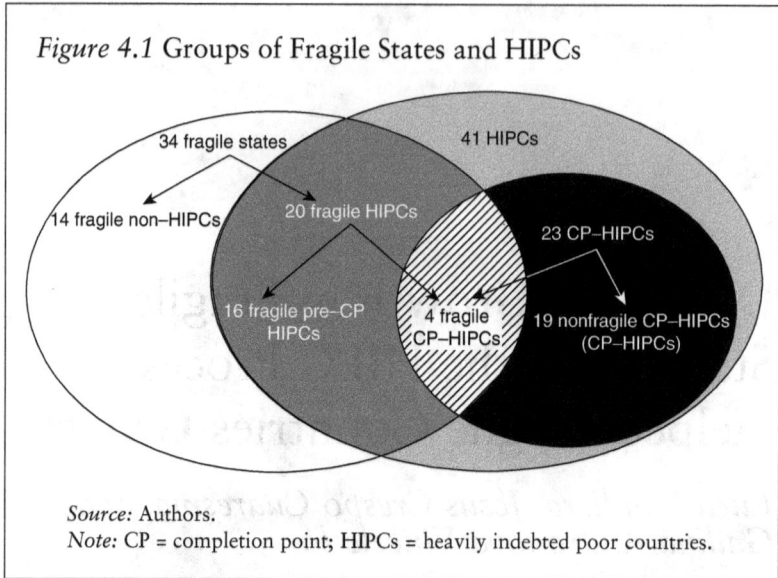

34 fragile states

41 HIPCs

14 fragile non–HIPCs

20 fragile HIPCs

23 CP–HIPCs

16 fragile pre–CP HIPCs

4 fragile CP–HIPCs

19 nonfragile CP–HIPCs (CP–HIPCs)

Source: Authors.
Note: CP = completion point; HIPCs = heavily indebted poor countries.

on average, lower. Their annual economic growth rates remained negative until the mid-1990s, significantly lower than those of fragile non–HIPCs. Total investment growth in fragile HIPCs has been substantially lower and real exchange rate volatility higher than in fragile non–HIPCs.

Apart from being consistently at the bottom of the fragile states group, the 20 fragile HIPCs are not homogeneous. They are at different stages of the HIPC Initiative. At end-2008, four countries (The Gambia, Mauritania, São Tomé and Principe, and Sierra Leone) had reached the completion point and received irrevocable HIPC Initiative and MDRI debt relief. Ten countries (Afghanistan, Burundi, the Central African Republic, Chad, the Democratic Republic of Congo, the Republic of Congo, Guinea, Guinea-Bissau, Haiti, and Liberia) had reached the decision point and started to receive interim assistance. Another six (the Comoros, Côte d'Ivoire, Eritrea, Somalia, Sudan, and Togo) had yet to reach the decision point. In addition, three HIPCs that were fragile states according to the CPIA–based definition (Cameroon, Ethiopia, and Niger) when they reached the HIPC Initiative decision point lost their fragile-state status in the following years.

This chapter explains the economic growth differentials in fragile states and analyzes variables that appear to be robust determinants of economic growth in these countries. Do the differences across groups of fragile states suggest that there are fundamental differences in the drivers of economic prosperity in these countries? If so, has the HIPC Initiative process helped countries improve their prospects for growth?

A large body of literature supports the possibility that countries in different states of the world do not follow a homogeneous growth process (see Begun 2008). In this sense, the literature has traditionally considered parameter heterogeneity based on initial income levels (see Brock and Durlauf 2001) and, in a parallel branch of literature, model uncertainty concerning the choice of variables in the specification. (An exception, in which both issues are treated simultaneously, is Crespo Cuaresma and Doppelhofer 2007.)

This study uses Bayesian model averaging (BMA) to assess and identify economic growth determinants in low-income countries in the presence of both model and parameter uncertainty. It explores the factors affecting the growth of fragile HIPCs and compares them with the robust determinants of income growth in both nonfragile HIPCs and in fragile non–HIPCs. This technique recognizes that the "true" underlying growth model is not known and assesses the relevance of a broad set of covariates for groups of countries differing in their initial characteristics.

The chapter is structured as follows. In the next section, we present some descriptive statistics with which we assess the proposition that the very dimension of large debt stock and its macroeconomic consequences makes the group of fragile HIPCs significantly worse off in terms of economic growth prospects than other fragile states. In the following section, we present the methodology used to address the issue of relevant determinants to growth in these countries. In the third section, we report the results of the BMA analysis for the various groups of countries considered. The last section summarizes the chapter's main conclusions.

Characteristics of Fragile States

Stark differences are evident across subgroups of fragile states. Fragile HIPCs are worse off in economic and social aspects of development than both other fragile states and other HIPCs. Average per capita income in fragile HIPCs was half that of fragile non–HIPCs between 1990 and 2006. Fragile HIPCs also exhibit much lower per capita income growth than do nonfragile post–completion point HIPCs (henceforth, CP–HIPCs) and fragile non–HIPCs.[2] The gap has widened in recent years: fragile non–HIPCs, with an average level of per capita income of $1,079, were almost three times richer than their HIPC counterparts in 2006.

For the period 1990–2006, the average headcount ratio (the poor as a share of the population) was 20 percentage points higher in fragile HIPCs than in fragile non–HIPCs (56 percent versus 35 percent). Persistent poverty is also revealed in aspects of human development such as health and education. Although under-five mortality declined in all fragile states between 1990 and 2006, it was 41 percent higher in fragile HIPCs than in other fragile states. Primary school completion rates were about 37 percent lower in fragile HIPCs than in other fragile states (40 percent versus 70 percent). Primary school enrollment in fragile states over the same period was 58 percent in HIPCs and 77 percent in non–HIPCs. Such differences remain over time. Along a variety of human development indicators, the group of fragile HIPCs underperforms the group of CP–HIPCs (table 4.1).

Important differences along human development indicators distinguish the CP–HIPCs from other fragile states, partly explaining their gains on the development front. HIPC debt relief, especially the cancellation of debt stocks under the MDRI, aims to increase the fiscal space for the beneficiary government and allow it to direct expenditures into poverty-reducing activities. Indeed, the HIPC Initiative frequently includes education or health completion point triggers, negotiated at the decision point. The CP–HIPCs exhibit the largest drop in poverty rates and significant advances

Table 4.1 Human Development Indicators in Fragile HIPCs, Fragile Non–HIPCs, and Nonfragile Completion Point HIPCs

Period/indicator	Fragile HIPCs	Fragile non–HIPCs	Nonfragile CP–HIPCs
Average 1990–2006			
Poverty headcount ratio at national poverty line (percentage of population)	56.4	35.9	50.7
Net primary school enrollment (percent)	57.6	76.7	65.4
Total primary completion rate (percentage of relevant age group)	40.0	69.6	47.1
Life expectancy at birth (years)	23.3	26.9	25.2
Under-five mortality rate (per 1,000)	158.3	112.3	147.4
Last available year			
Poverty headcount ratio at national poverty line (percentage of population)	70.2	35.0	28.5
Net primary school enrollment (percent)	60.6	81.1	77.6
Total primary completion rate (percentage of relevant age group)	54.9	82.1	59.8
Life expectancy at birth (years)	50.8	58.4	55.6
Under-five mortality rate (per 1,000)	146.8	96.3	130.7

Source: World Bank World Development Indicators (WDI) database.
Note: CP = completion point; HIPCs = heavily indebted poor countries.

in school enrollment (and even greater gains may be expected with a few years' lag). Primary school drop-out rates decrease significantly in CP–HIPCs as well (Crespo Cuaresma and Vincelette 2008). Gains are less pronounced in other areas of human development.

Macroeconomic indicators are also weaker in fragile HIPCs (figure 4.2), and growth rates of fragile states are much more volatile than those of CP–HIPCs (figure 4.3). Half of the fragile HIPCs experienced negative growth until the mid-1990s. All fragile states have undergone periods of prolonged contraction, usually around the time of conflict and political instability. Moreover, the average growth rate of income in countries that have gone through the HIPC Initiative has been higher than that of fragile states, especially given the lower dependence on resource exports in CP–HIPCs. Resource-rich primary commodity exporters have bene-fited from high commodity prices, fueling their output growth. Similarly, total investment as a share of output has been roughly 50 percent lower in fragile HIPCs than in other fragile countries and CP–HIPCs.

Fragile non–HIPCs have demonstrated stronger improvement of their institutional environment than have fragile HIPCs, whose average CPIA rating remained unchanged in the past 25 years. This rating has stayed well below that of CP–HIPCs.

The quality of governance institutions is also lower in fragile HIPCs than in other fragile states (figure 4.4). On average, along all six dimen-sions of the World Bank governance indicators, fragile non–HIPCs fare better than fragile HIPCs. The largest differences (also carrying statistical significance) are on the indicators of political stability and government effectiveness. No significant differences are found on the dimension of control of corruption, hinting at the complexity of removing patronage and vested interests of groups frequently linked to lucrative opportunities in the extractive industry.

Although governance quality in HIPCs did not play a significant role in the decision of creditor countries to forgive debt in the 1990s, CP–HIPCs had notably better governance than any either group of fragile states (Freytag and Pehnelt 2009). This suggests that the presence of fragility is associated with lower-quality governance and that alleviation of the debt burden in poor developing countries has been associated with improving not only the availability of financial resources of these countries but also the quality of their governance institutions.

Data and Methodology

To ascertain if the determinants of income growth differ in HIPCs, frag-ile non–HIPCs, and CP–HIPCs, we collected data for the period 1984–2004 and used panel data for the five resulting four-year nonoverlapping subperiods. Growth rates are therefore defined as averages over these

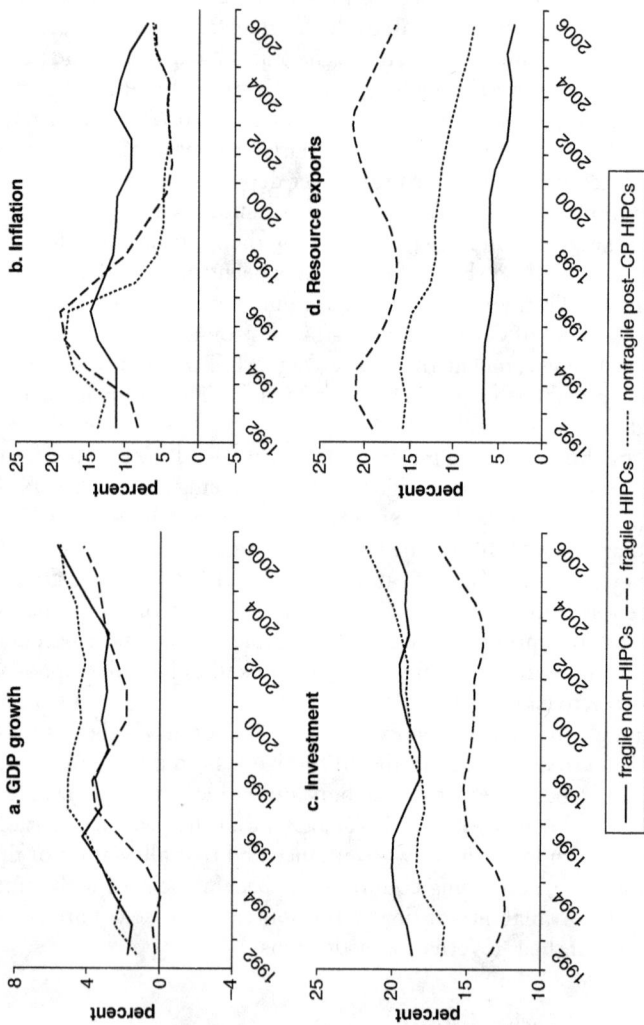

Figure 4.2 Selected Macroeconomic Indicators in Fragile States and HIPCs, 1992–2006
(three-year moving average of annual median)

a. GDP growth

b. Inflation

c. Investment

d. Resource exports

———— fragile non-HIPCs   – – – fragile HIPCs   ········ nonfragile post-CP HIPCs

Source: World Bank WDI database and UN Comtrade Statistics.
Note: CP = completion point; HIPCs = heavily indebted poor countries.

76

Figure 4.3 Annual Growth of per Capita Income in Fragile States and HIPCs, 1992–2006

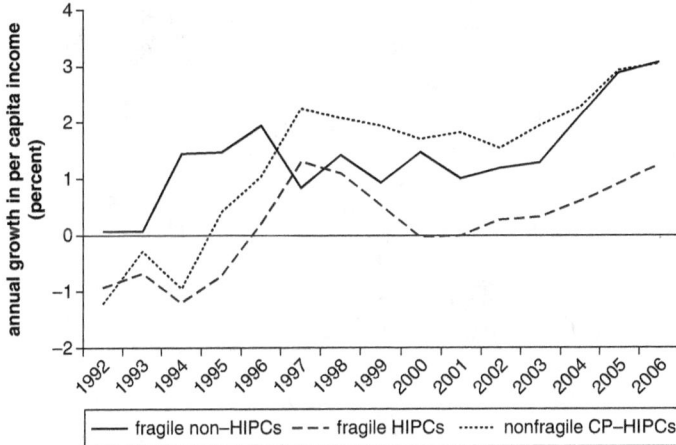

Source: World Bank WDI database.
Note: CP = completion point; HIPCs = heavily indebted poor countries.

four-year subperiods. Variables are evaluated at the beginning of each four-year period to address eventual endogeneity problems.

We consider a variety of potential growth determinants in the analysis. They include some standard determinants implied by neoclassical growth theory (such as the initial level of per capita GDP and the physical capital investment rates), as well as other variables deemed important economic growth covariates for developing countries (such as the private-credit-to-GDP ratio, life expectancy, and openness and macroeconomic stability, among others). Given the presence of high levels of external debt burden in HIPCs, we also include the present value of the debt-to-output ratio as a covariate in the growth regression.

We assess two situations. The first is whether a reduction in the external debt burden enhances growth in HIPCs despite their fragility status; the second is whether with improvement in policies and institutions only, a lower debt burden positively contributes to growth. In the first case, we can infer that fragile HIPCs would benefit from an up-front debt reduction. In the second case, we suggest that the two-step HIPC process (which requires countries to implement structural reforms, maintain macroeconomic stability, and implement a country-owned poverty reduction strategy) is important for debt relief to be beneficial for growth and that the HIPC process helps countries shed their fragility status.

Figure 4.4 CPIA and Governance in Fragile HIPCs and Non–HIPCs

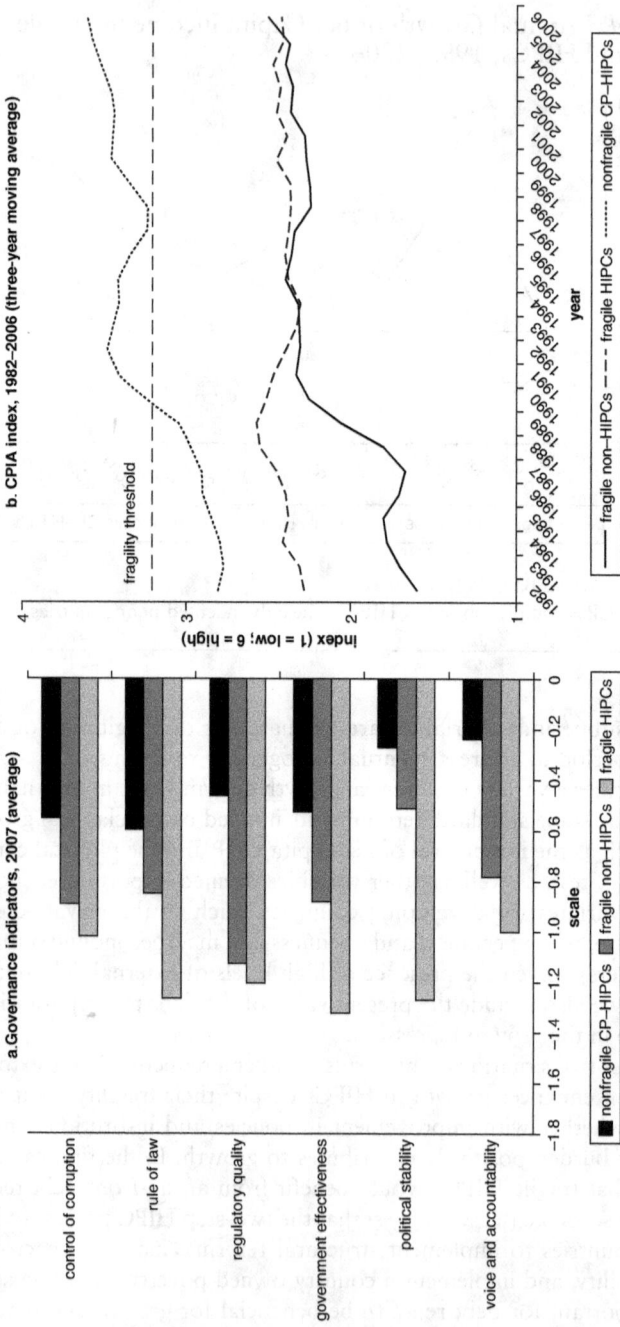

a.Governance indicators, 2007 (average)

b. CPIA index, 1982–2006 (three-year moving average)

Source: World Bank Governance Indicators.

Note: The six governance indicators are measured on a scale of –2.5 to 2.5, with higher values corresponding to better governance outcomes. The CPIA Index ranks countries from 1 to 6, with higher values corresponding to better-quality policies and institutions. CP = completion point; CPIA = Country Policy and Institutional Assessment (World Bank); HIPCs = heavily indebted poor countries.

We first analyze which variables appear to be robust determinants of economic growth in different groups of developing countries using BMA techniques, which have recently become a workhorse of empirical economic growth research. (For two of the most influential contributions in this branch of the literature, see Fernández, Ley, and Steel 2001 and Sala-i-Martin, Doppelhofer, and Miller 2004). BMA aims to assess explicitly the issue of model uncertainty when estimating parameters of a model whose specification is not perfectly known. This is usually the setting in empirical economic growth research, where many (partly complementary) theories lead to different variable choices for the model specification. BMA is used to estimate the parameters of interest in our model as weighted averages of parameter estimates from individual models, where the weights are obtained as the posterior probability of the corresponding models being the true specification.

Consider a model relating the growth rate of per capita GDP (y) to some covariates

$$y = \alpha + X_k \beta + \varepsilon, \tag{4.1}$$

where $X_k = (x_1 x_2 \ldots x_k)$ is a subset formed by K variables corresponding to elements of $X_K = (x_1 x_2 \ldots x_K)$, which contains all possible regressors (K of them); $\beta = (\beta_1 \ldots \beta_k)$ is a vector of parameters; and ε is a vector of independently and normally distributed error terms with constant variance. We can assess the issue of model uncertainty by averaging over all the alternative models implied by the combinations of variables among those in the set of K covariates. Given a prior structure on model size and the model parameters, Bayes factors (the ratio of marginal likelihoods of two competing models) can be used to compare models with different variables.[3] Inference about a quantity of interest, γ, can then be based on its posterior distribution, taking into account model uncertainty through the use of posterior model probabilities as weights

$$P(\gamma \mid X) = \sum_{m=1}^{2^K} P(y \mid X, M_m) P(M_m \mid X), \tag{4.2}$$

where X is a given set of data and a model M_m is defined by the choice of independent variables. The posterior model probabilities, $P(M_s \mid X)$, are given by

$$P(M_s \mid X) = \frac{P(X \mid M_s) P(M_s)}{\sum_{m=1}^{2^K} P(X \mid M_m) P(M_m)}, \tag{4.3}$$

which is, in turn, the normalized product of the integrated likelihood for each model $P(X \mid M_k)$ and the prior probability of the model $P(M_k)$. This implies that, for a given prior on the model space, the posterior distribution of y can be obtained as a weighted average of the model-specific estimates using posterior probability of the respective models as weights. We can simplify this expression by using the Bayesian information criterion (BIC) approximation (Leamer 1978; Schwarz 1978).

$$P(M_s \mid X) = \frac{\exp\left(-\frac{1}{2}BIC(M_s)\right)P(M_s)}{\sum_{m=1}^{2^K}\exp\left(-\frac{1}{2}BIC(M_m)\right)P(M_m)}. \tag{4.4}$$

where the BIC is given by BIC $(M_k) = -2\log (Likelihood \mid M_k) + k \log (N)$, *Likelihood* is the value of the likelihood function evaluated at its maximum, k is the number of estimated parameters, and N is the sample size. If the cardinality of the model space is computationally tractable, these expressions can be obtained directly.[4] The posterior mean and variance of the parameters of interest can be used to make inference on the quantitative effect of changes in the covariates on economic growth explicitly taking into account the existence of model uncertainty. In the same fashion, we can evaluate posterior inclusion probabilities for the different variables proposed, which we obtain by summing the posterior probability of models containing each individual variable (or groups of it). This measure captures the relative importance of the different covariates as determinants of economic growth. It can be interpreted as the probability that a given variable belongs to the true specification.

Results

For the BMA estimation, we assume a uniform prior over the model space, which results in a 0.5 prior inclusion probability for each potential explanatory variable. The results are based on averaging over models that, in all cases, include fixed country effects as well as global subperiod fixed effects common to all countries in the sample. This implies that we obtain our estimates by extracting information from the variation within rather than between countries. We describe the variables used for the BMA analysis in table 4.2.

The analysis is presented for three partially overlapping groups: the full set of fragile states, the entire group of HIPCs, and the group of fragile HIPCs (table 4.3). The posterior inclusion probabilities for the full set of fragile states reveal great heterogeneity across these countries with respect to their determinants of economic growth. For only two variables—the initial level of income and physical capital formation—is the probability that they actually belong to the model greater after observing the data

Table 4.2 Variables Used in Bayesian Model Averaging Estimates

Variable	Observations per country	All countries		Fragile countries		HIPCs		Fragile HIPCs		Nonfragile CP–HIPCs	
		Average	Standard deviation	Average	Standard deviation	Average	Standard deviation	Average	Standard deviation	Average	Standard deviation
Annual growth rate of GDP per capita (percent)[a]	25	0.3	6.3	0.2	6.9	0.0	6.6	-0.4	7.8	0.4	5.2
Initial level of GDP per capita (log)[a]	25	5.9	0.7	6.0	0.7	5.7	0.6	5.7	0.6	5.8	0.7
Gross fixed capital formation as percentage of GDP[a]	22	17.8	7.5	17.6	8.7	17.4	7.6	16.7	9.4	18.0	5.8
Trade as percentage of GDP[a]	25	67.5	35.9	74.2	34.3	61.8	34.5	65.6	32.1	58.8	36.1
Domestic credit to private sector as percentage of GDP[a]	24	14.7	14.7	13.5	15.4	14.1	14.3	11.5	14.9	16.4	13.4
Annual population growth (percent)[a]	27	2.5	1.2	2.4	1.2	2.5	1.3	2.5	1.2	2.5	1.3
Annual inflation rate (percent)[b]	21	55.0	734.7	67.0	859.5	56.4	822.0	77.6	1,072.6	37.3	496.5

(continued)

Table 4.2 (continued)

Variable	Observations per country	All countries		Fragile countries		HIPCs		Fragile HIPCs		Nonfragile CP-HIPCs	
		Average	Standard deviation	Average	Standard deviation	Average	Standard deviation	Average	Standard deviation	Average	Standard deviation
Agricultural output as percentage of total value added[a]	23	29.1	17.8	27.1	19.5	31.2	16.9	30.1	19.4	32.1	14.4
Life expectancy (years)[a]	12	24.0	27.3	23.4	27.1	23.5	26.7	22.0	25.7	24.9	27.5
Mineral exports as percentage of total exports[c]	21	30.2	79.6	40.1	104.6	30.0	82.7	42.9	115.9	17.9	19.7
Years of armed conflict[d]	28	0.2	0.4	0.2	0.4	0.2	0.4	0.2	0.4	0.2	0.4
Net ODA as percentage of GDP[a]	22	14.4	12.4	15.1	14.4	15.1	12.6	16.8	15.2	13.6	9.6
Number of countries		51		32		40		22		19	

Source: Authors' compilation based on sources shown below.
Note: Data cover the period 1980–2006. Figures exclude data for the Republic of Kosovo, Somalia, and Timor Leste. CP = completion point; HIPCs = heavily indebted poor countries; ODA = official development assistance.
a. World Development Indicators database.
b. International Financial Statistics database.
c. UN Comtrade statistics.
d. UCDP/PRIO Armed Conflict Dataset (Uppsala Conflict Data Program/Peace Research Institute, Oslo).

Table 4.3 Bayesian Model Averaging Results: Pooled Data with Country Fixed Effects

Variable	All fragile states			All HIPCs			All fragile HIPCs		
	Posterior inclusion probability	Posterior mean, E(b)	Posterior standard deviation, SD(b)	Posterior inclusion probability	Posterior mean, E(b)	Posterior standard deviation, SD(b)	Posterior inclusion probability	Posterior E(b)	Posterior SD(b)
Initial income	**0.9846**	**-0.1163**	**0.0420**	0.3786	-0.0149	0.0243	0.3879	-0.0260	0.0442
Gross fixed capital formation	**0.9914**	**0.4121**	**0.1360**	0.1314	0.0090	0.0405	0.4444	0.1058	0.1581
Openness	0.2749	-0.0169	0.0389	0.1535	-0.0041	0.0146	0.2395	-0.0147	0.0398
Agricultural value added	0.1138	0.0001	0.0369	0.0964	0.0021	0.0159	0.1535	0.0097	0.0618
Inflation	0.4491	-0.0071	0.0104	0.0975	0.0000	0.0001	0.1783	-0.0014	0.0055
Life expectancy	0.4430	0.0012	0.0017	0.1439	0.0002	0.0006	0.1370	0.0001	0.0012
Mineral exports	0.2102	-0.2360	0.7213	0.0997	0.0299	0.2467	0.1692	-0.1312	0.6033
Conflict	0.1368	-0.0019	0.0108	**0.9899**	**-0.0459**	**0.0147**	**0.5186**	**-0.0227**	**0.0290**
Present value of debt over GDP	0.1235	-0.0003	0.0094	0.2037	-0.0034	0.0092	0.1440	-0.0017	0.0111
CPIA	0.1693	-0.0012	0.0047	0.0860	0.0000	0.0015	0.1270	-0.0001	0.0035
Number of observations	66			123			53		

Source: Authors.

Note: Numbers in bold have posterior inclusion probabilities larger than their 50 percent prior probability of model inclusion. CPIA = Country Policy and Institutional Assessment (World Bank); HIPCs = heavily indebted poor countries.

than the prior inclusion probabilities. These results indicate that along with convergence dynamics, it is the differences in the levels of physical capital investment that matter most when explaining the growth experience of fragile states in the past two decades. The estimated coefficient for investment in physical capital in the group of fragile states is about 0.26, relatively close to the standard value of 1/3 that tends to be assumed in Cobb-Douglas specifications based on aggregate data for the share of income paid to capital.

In all HIPCs and in fragile HIPCs, economic growth does not seem responsive to investment in physical capital. Only the recurrence of armed conflict robustly explains growth differences within the HIPCs, including fragile HIPCs. Given the ambiguity of such results, concentrating on more homogenous subgroups of countries is warranted.

To account for some of the heterogeneity that appears to be driving the results for the broad groups of fragile states and the HIPCs, we reassess the robustness of economic growth determinants, focusing on subsamples of fragile states and HIPCs with debt-to-GDP ratios below the median for each of the evaluated groups. We label each of these subgroups as countries with (relatively) low debt burdens. The results yield estimates for the full set of fragile states and for the entire group of HIPCs (table 4.4). The analysis based on within-country variation and period effects identifies a broader set of robust growth covariates in these three low–debt burden subgroups of countries.

For fragile states with low debt burdens (below the median value of the present value of the debt-to-GDP ratio), economic growth responds robustly to investment in physical capital. In fact, the estimated coefficient of the elasticity of the growth-to-investment ratio appears high in this group of countries, where debt stocks are low relative to output, supporting the debt overhang theory. The convergence speed to the country-specific equilibrium income level is also notably faster than that in the entire group of both HIPCs and fragile states. In addition, the results reveal the importance of health improvements (measured through changes in life expectancy) and positive changes in the share of mineral exports to GDP and agricultural value added as variables contributing to economic growth in the low-debt fragile states.

Table 4.4 also presents the results for the subgroups of HIPCs with relatively low debt burdens. The findings for low-debt HIPCs are similar to those for low-debt fragile states. Growth in low-debt HIPCs seems to be responsive to improvements in health, investment, inflation, and mineral exports. The speed of convergence to the country-specific equilibrium level of income also seems similar to that in low-debt fragile states. The results for low-debt HIPCs point also to the importance of macroeconomic stability (as captured in the inflation rate) as an extra driver of economic growth. Interestingly, however, the (negative) effect of armed conflict on economic growth loses its robustness as a driver of

Table 4.4 Bayesian Model Averaging Results: Pooled Data with Country Fixed Effects for Countries with Low Present Value of Debt

Variable	All fragile states			All HIPCs		
	Posterior inclusion probability	Posterior mean, E(b)	Posterior standard deviation, SD(b)	Posterior inclusion probability	Posterior mean, E(b)	Posterior standard deviation, SD(b)
Initial income	**1.0000**	**−0.2800**	**0.0646**	**1.0000**	**−0.2552**	**0.0469**
Gross fixed capital formation	**1.0000**	**0.8766**	**0.1606**	**0.9819**	**0.5041**	**0.1615**
Openness	**0.8103**	**−0.1019**	**0.0863**	0.1959	0.0188	0.0647
Agricultural value added	**0.6133**	**0.1307**	**0.1662**	0.1567	−0.0113	0.0586
Inflation	0.2071	−0.0092	0.0607	**0.9274**	**−0.0504**	**0.0272**
Life expectancy	**0.9301**	**0.0039**	**0.0022**	**0.9758**	**0.0062**	**0.0022**
Mineral exports	**0.9740**	**4.1919**	**1.9270**	**0.9408**	**3.4151**	**1.5887**
Conflict	0.1850	0.0013	0.0188	0.1605	−0.0023	0.0110
Present value of debt over GDP	0.2714	−0.0157	0.0493	0.1150	−0.0002	0.0183
CPIA	0.1711	−0.0003	0.0095	0.1383	−0.0001	0.0038
Number of observations	33			61		

Source: Authors.
Note: Numbers in bold have posterior inclusion probabilities larger than their 50 percent prior probability of model inclusion. CPIA = Country Policy and Institutional Assessment (World Bank); HIPCs = heavily indebted poor countries.

growth for this subgroup of HIPCs. This finding implies (by inference) that the negative effect of armed conflict for the full set of HIPCs is strongly driven by the effect of wars and political instability for the economic prosperity of HIPCs with relatively high levels of debt. For these countries, none of the variables that were considered as potential growth covariates appears robustly related to growth. In particular, there is no robust link between economic growth and physical capital accumulation, further supporting the debt overhang hypothesis. Put differently, high debt burdens decrease the quantity or efficiency of investment in this group of countries.

As an extra robustness check, we also include net official development assistance (ODA) as a repressor in the BMA estimates. The results do not yield robust effects from this variable but enforce the findings reported above.

Has fragility negatively affected economic growth in HIPCs? To address this issue, we exploit determinants of growth in CP–HIPCs. Although it would be valuable to reveal the determinants of growth in the subgroup of fragile HIPCs that have reached the completion point under the HIPC Initiative, the small number of observations (only four countries) does not allow us to run a full-fledged analysis on this subgroup. The posterior inclusion probabilities reveal that as a broad group, CP–HIPCs (including the four fragile countries) are not generally different from the entire group of HIPCs, with the notable exception that they experience a more rapid convergence to their country-specific steady-state level of income (table 4.5). In nonfragile CP–HIPCs, convergence is faster, conflict reduces growth marginally less, and mineral exports contribute significantly to growth. Decreases in the present value of debt stock to GDP tend to be associated with higher economic growth in CP–HIPCs than in the group of all HIPCs that reached the completion point, including the four fragile countries, and the entire group of HIPCs.

These results are further reinforced in the group of CP–HIPCs with relatively low debt burdens. In these countries, the relatively low level of debt, coupled with stronger policies and institutions, positively contributes to growth as well as to macroeconomic stability, investment, agricultural value added, mineral exports, and health improvements. This finding suggests that fragility does hinder progress under the HIPC Initiative, because countries failing to improve the quality of their policies and institutions and to reach the completion point do not benefit from the extra growth bonus that seems to be associated with reducing debt levels.

We next substitute the fixed time effects with a step dummy to control for the effect of launching the HIPC process in 1996. The results indicate that nonfragile HIPCs grew more rapidly after 1996. This result engenders two hypotheses: (a) the HIPC Initiative process has successfully facilitated economic development in nonfragile HIPCs, and (b) the best performers were selected and completed the HIPC Initiative process. Although we

Table 4.5 Bayesian Model Averaging Results: Pooled Data with Country Fixed Effects for Completion Point HIPCs

Variable	All CP-HIPCs			Nonfragile CP-HIPCs			CP-HIPCs with low present value of debt		
	Posterior inclusion probability	Posterior mean, E(b)	Posterior standard deviation, SD(b)	Posterior inclusion probability	Posterior mean, E(b)	Posterior standard deviation, SD(b)	Posterior inclusion probability	Posterior mean, E(b)	Posterior standard deviation, SD(b)
Initial income	**0.7652**	−0.0424	0.0322	**0.9751**	−0.0860	0.0339	**1.0000**	−0.2022	0.0500
Gross fixed capital formation	0.1186	−0.0018	0.0365	0.1377	0.0056	0.0407	**0.9815**	0.2617	0.1218
Openness	0.1252	0.0009	0.0109	0.1445	0.0018	0.0130	0.3888	0.0295	0.0637
Agricultural value added	0.1839	0.0074	0.0245	0.2335	0.0109	0.0297	**0.9931**	0.3147	0.1379
Inflation	0.1118	0.0000	0.0001	0.1176	0.0000	0.0001	**0.9982**	−0.0523	0.0164
Life expectancy	0.1032	0.0000	0.0004	0.1411	0.0001	0.0005	**0.9997**	0.0085	0.0017
Mineral exports	0.5059	0.7612	0.9764	**0.7960**	1.4988	1.0864	**0.9887**	3.5910	1.4015
Conflict	**1.0000**	−0.0754	0.0179	**0.9905**	−0.0660	0.0215	0.1617	0.0011	0.0148
Present value of debt over GDP	0.3796	−0.0096	0.0161	**0.8137**	−0.0290	0.0200	**0.9184**	−0.0683	0.0461
CPIA	0.1551	−0.0006	0.0025	0.1245	0.0001	0.0020	0.1591	0.0000	0.0035
Number of observations	77			65			37		

Source: Authors.

Note: Numbers in bold have posterior inclusion probabilities larger than their 50 percent prior probability of model inclusion. CP = completion point; CPIA = Country Policy and Institutional Assessment (World Bank); HIPCs = heavily indebted poor countries.

cannot infer causality, we can state that the HIPC Initiative process and economic development in nonfragile HIPCs have gone hand in hand.

Conclusions

Interpreting the growth experience of the 54 developing countries falling into the group of fragile states or HIPCs in the 20-year period under consideration is not straightforward. Overall, the analysis reveals that the drivers of growth are widely heterogeneous and that a great deal of model uncertainty plagues the econometric analysis. Economic growth responds to the differences in the initial level of physical capital investment and the initial level of income in fragile states. However, economic growth in HIPCs, including fragile HIPCs, seems to respond robustly only to the recurrence of armed conflict. None of the other factors is systematically helpful in explaining economic growth differences.

To overcome the issue of heterogeneity, we split the groups and look at countries with debt-to-GDP ratios below and above the median for HIPCs. For countries with relatively low debt burdens, economic growth is more responsive to improvements in health, investment, and primary exports. The speed of convergence to country-specific equilibrium levels of income in each of the two groups also appears similar. The results for relatively low-debt HIPCs suggest the importance of macroeconomic stability as an extra driver of economic growth.

The results on the determinants of the economic growth process in fragile states yield an important insight into the HIPC process. Fragile HIPCs suffer from the largest reduction in economic growth as a result of armed conflict, have the lowest volume of investment and returns to investment, converge to their long-run equilibrium level less rapidly, and depend more on mineral exports than do nonfragile HIPCs. Moreover, convergence is faster, conflict hurts growth marginally less, and mineral exports contribute significantly more to growth in nonfragile CP–HIPCs than in either group of fragile states, especially fragile HIPCs. CP–HIPCs are less dependent on mineral resources than are the other two groups of countries, although mineral exports tend to contribute positively and strongly to economic growth in these countries.

We find evidence of decreases in the overall level of the debt-stock-to-GDP ratio associated with higher economic growth in nonfragile CP-HIPCs. As debt overhang theory would imply, investment is positively associated with growth in the presence of a lower debt burden. As expected, this link appears to be strongest in lower-debt (mainly post–CP) HIPCs, where the quality of policies and institution is, on average, the highest.

Fragility appears to have hindered progress under the HIPC Initiative, and the staggered debt-relief structure of the HIPC process does not seem to have exacerbated fragility. For the broad group of fragile states (that is, countries with poor-quality policies and institutions), there seems to be no link between debt burden and growth. Most standard growth covariates do not contribute to economic prosperity in the presence of fragility, independent of the level of debt. Countries that benefited from debt relief while improving the quality of their policies and institutions seem to have enjoyed more rapid economic growth after receiving debt relief.

Notes

1. For a comprehensive review of characteristics and economic policies in fragile states, see Favaro (2008) and Lluch (2008).
2. The list of nonfragile CP–HIPCs includes Benin, Bolivia, Burkina Faso, Cameroon, Ethiopia, Ghana, Guyana, Honduras, Madagascar, Malawi, Mali, Mozambique, Nicaragua, Niger, Rwanda, Senegal, Tanzania, Uganda, and Zambia.
3. See Hoeting and others (1999) for a formal treatment of the BAM technique.
4. Several methods have been proposed for approximating the posterior model probability when the cardinality of the model space makes the problem intractable. Raftery (1995) proposes the use of a leaps and bounds algorithm. Fernández, Ley, and Steel (2001) use a simple Markov chain Monte Carlo model composite algorithm to evaluate the posterior distribution, based on the work of Madigan and York (1995). Sala-i-Martin, Doppelhofer, and Miller (2004) use a particular type of importance sampler.

References

Begun, J. 2008. "Initial Conditions and Heterogeneity in Cross-Country Growth: An Iterative Bayesian Model Averaging (IBMA) Analysis." Department of Economics, University of Washington, Seattle.

Brock, W. A., and S. N. Durlauf. 2001. "What Have We Learned From a Decade of Empirical Research on Growth? Growth Empirics and Reality." *World Bank Economic Review* 15 (2): 229–72.

Crespo Cuaresma, J., and G. Doppelhofer. 2007. "Nonlinearities in Cross-Country Growth Regressions: A Bayesian Averaging of Thresholds (BAT) Approach." *Journal of Macroeconomics* 29 (3): 541–54.

Crespo Cuaresma, J., and G. A. Vincelette. 2008. "Debt Relief and Education in HIPCs." University of Innsbruck, Department of Economics, Austria, and World Bank Economic Policy and Debt Department, Washington, DC.

Favaro, E. 2008. "Fragility and Beyond: The World Bank Economic Growth Agenda in Fragile States." World Bank, Washington, DC.

Fernández, C., E. Ley, and M. Steel. 2001. "Model Uncertainty in Cross-Country Growth Regressions." *Journal of Applied Econometrics* 16 (5): 563–76.

Freytag, A., and G. Pehnelt. 2009. "Debt Relief and Governance Quality in Developing Countries." *World Development* 27 (1): 62–80.

Hoeting, J., D. Madigan, A. Raftery, and C. Volinsky. 1999. "Bayesian Model Averaging." *Statistical Science* 14 (4): 382–401.

International Monetary Fund International Financial Statistics at http://www.imf .org/external/data.htm

Leamer, E. E. 1978. *Specification Searches*. New York: John Wiley & Sons.

Lluch, C. 2008. "Economic Policy Issues in Fragile States: Where Does the Bank Stand?" World Bank, Washington, DC.

Madigan, D., and J. York. 1995. "Bayesian Graphical Models for Discrete Data." *International Statistical Review* 63 (1): 215–32.

Raftery, A. E. 1995. "Bayesian Model Selection in Social Research (with Discussion)." *Sociological Methodology* 25 (1): 111–96.

Sala-i-Martin, X., G. Doppelhofer, and R. I. Miller. 2004. "Determinants of Long-Term Growth: A Bayesian Averaging of Classical Estimates (BACE) Approach." *American Economic Review* 94 (4): 813–35.

Schwarz, G. 1978. "Estimating the Dimension of a Model." *Annals of Statistics* 6 (2): 461–64.

United Nations (UN) Comtrade Statistics at http://comtrade.un.org.

World Bank Governance Indicators at http://www.worldbank.org/wbi/governance.

World Bank World Development Indicators (WDI) database at http://www .worldbank.org/data/onlinedatabases/onlinedatabases.html.

Part II

Debt Sustainability

5

Debt Sustainability in Low-Income Countries: Recent Experience and Challenges Ahead

Christian Beddies, Dörte Dömeland,
Marie-Hélène Le Manchec, and Henry Mooney

L ow-income countries continue to face significant challenges in meeting their vast development needs while maintaining sustainable debt positions.[1] These countries have a number of macroeconomic and financial features that can complicate their capacity to generate sufficient revenues to repay the debt incurred and expose them to greater solvency and liquidity risks. These features include narrower production bases and export structures, shallower financial markets, less efficient tax systems, higher dependence on aid, and weaker policies and institutions.

Although debt relief through the Heavily Indebted Poor Countries (HIPC) Initiative and the Multilateral Debt Relief Initiative (MDRI) have charted a course toward restoring debt sustainability, these initiatives cannot preclude the rapid buildup of new debt and a new round of debt difficulties. The combination of low debt and new financing opportunities will allow low-income countries to make important strides toward achieving their economic goals, but they could also pose risks for new debt distress if not managed carefully. The implementation of policies and reforms geared toward entrenching macroeconomic stability and strengthening the resilience of the economy is thus critical in safeguarding debt sustainability.

Against this backdrop, the International Monetary Fund (IMF) and the World Bank have been intensifying their efforts to help low-income countries avoid new rounds of debt distress while meeting their development agendas. An analytical framework, the Debt Sustainability Framework

(DSF) for low-income countries, was introduced in 2005 to help monitor and analyze the sustainability of external and public debt in low-income countries. The objective of the Framework is to guide lending for creditors and borrowing decisions for policy makers based on regularly updated debt sustainability analyses (DSAs). Major multilateral institutions, such as the International Development Association (IDA) and the African Development Bank, use the DSA's classification of the risk of external debt distress as the main criterion for determining the grant-loan mix low-income countries receive.

Still, challenges remain. Long-term debt sustainability requires adequate policies from borrowers and lenders. Sustained efforts from the international community are critical to support low-income countries in achieving and maintaining debt sustainability. An analysis of DSAs over the past three years shows that achieving and maintaining debt sustainability hinges on export diversification; the provision of new financing primarily on concessional terms; and, for many low-income countries, a strengthening of the quality of their policies and institutions.

This chapter is organized as follows. The next section summarizes the main features of the DSF. The second section takes stock of the current debt-sustainability situation in low-income countries, identifies patterns, and highlights existing vulnerabilities. The third section discusses the challenges surrounding the conduct of DSAs, highlighting areas in which further work may be needed. The last section summarizes the chapter's conclusions.

The Debt Sustainability Framework

Maintaining debt sustainability should be a central objective for all countries. Low-income countries have characteristics that make doing so a challenge.[2] These countries face large financing needs to meet their development objectives. They depend heavily on aid flows, which tend to be difficult to predict. Their production and export structures are often concentrated in a few raw commodities, for which prices are determined in world markets. Low-income countries are also more prone to weather vagaries, which often engender large, unexpected reconstruction costs. Their policies and institutions are also weaker, including in the areas of project and debt management, complicating the implementation of sustainable macroeconomic policies, impairing investor confidence, and increasing the chances that scarce public resources are diverted toward unproductive uses. These features contribute to these countries' sensitivity to external and domestic shocks and lower-than-expected returns on public investments.

To assist low-income countries in maintaining debt sustainability, in 2005 the World Bank and the IMF introduced the DSF. It builds on the DSA framework for middle-income countries introduced by the IMF in 2002, taking into account the specific characteristics of low-income countries.

The Framework should be seen as a tool to help policy makers strike a balance between achieving development objectives and maintaining macroeconomic stability. It can also guide lenders in aligning their aid policies and helping prevent the reemergence of debt distress.

The design and objectives of the DSF differ in several important ways from those of the DSAs carried out under the HIPC Initiative; the two exercises should not be confused.[3] The DSF has become a critical instrument for analyzing a country's capacity to finance its policy objectives and service the ensuing debt without unduly large adjustments.

The main objectives of the DSF are to

- guide the borrowing decisions of low-income countries in ways that match their financing needs with their current and prospective repayment ability, taking into account each country's circumstances;
- provide guidance for creditors' lending and grant-allocation decisions to ensure that resources are provided to low-income countries on terms that are consistent with both progress toward their development goals and long-term debt sustainability;
- improve World Bank and IMF assessments and policy advice in these areas; and
- help detect potential debt crises early, so that preventive action can be taken.

Under the DSF, a DSA consists of the following elements:

- An analysis of a country's projected external and public sector–debt burden and its vulnerability to external and policy shocks (baseline and shock scenarios are calculated), with a focus on the present value of debt obligations. The trajectories of debt ratios are analyzed over 20 years, because loans to low-income countries are primarily concessional and therefore carry long maturities.
- An assessment of the risk of debt distress based on indicative external debt–burden thresholds that depend on the quality of the country's policies and institutions.
- Recommendations for a borrowing (and lending) strategy that limits the risk of debt distress.

The risk of external debt distress is assessed by comparing external debt–burden indicators with policy-dependent debt-burden thresholds (table 5.1). The thresholds reflect the empirical finding that the debt levels that low-income countries can sustain are affected by the quality of their policies and institutions. Low-income countries with weaker policies and institutions tend to face repayment problems at lower levels of debt.

The indicative thresholds should not be seen as rigid ceilings—there may be cases in which a mechanistic approach would imply an unreasonable

Table 5.1 External Public Debt–Burden Thresholds under the Debt Sustainability Framework

	Present value of debt as percentage of			Debt service as percentage of	
Policy	Exports	GDP	Revenue	Exports	Revenue
Weak	100	30	200	15	25
Medium	150	40	250	20	30
Strong	200	50	300	25	35

Source: World Bank and IMF 2008.

rating. The thresholds constitute guideposts for informing the assessment of debt sustainability and the risk of debt distress.

There are four ratings of external debt distress. They are the following:

- Low risk—all debt-burden indicators are well below thresholds
- Moderate risk—debt-burden indicators are below the thresholds in the baseline scenario, but stress tests indicate that the thresholds are breached if there are external shocks or abrupt changes in macroeconomic policies
- High risk—one or more debt-burden indicators breach the thresholds under the baseline scenario
- Debt distress—the country is already having repayment difficulties.

The quality of policies and institutions is measured by the Country Policy and Institutional Assessment (CPIA) index, compiled annually by the World Bank. The DSF divides countries into three performance categories: strong, medium, and poor. To reduce uncertainty regarding the country's financing terms from IDA (and possibly other donors) from annual fluctuations in the CPIA, the DSF includes the three-year moving average CPIA score. The DSF takes into account the risks posed by the accumulation of domestic debt and acknowledges the different nature of these risks (see Kraay and Nehru 2006; World Bank and IMF 2006).

Public DSAs are now a key part of the DSF. Their interpretation poses challenges, because there are no accepted thresholds for the risk of total public debt distress. Moreover, external and domestic debt are qualitatively different concepts, making it difficult to simply add them. These risks are different because governments often resort to seigniorage or financial repression, rather than default, in response to pressures from domestic debt. The use of domestic debt is not limited to budget financing but also serves other policy objectives, such as the conduct of monetary policy. The financial terms of domestic debt, including its maturity profile, are significantly different from those of external debt, leading to a different set of risks.

The effectiveness of the DSF depends on its broad use by borrowers, donors, and lenders. It helps inform borrowers about the amount and terms of financing that are consistent with long-term debt sustainability and progress toward achieving their development objectives. It also provides guidance to donors and lenders on lending and grant-allocation decisions that are consistent with these goals. The DSF can thus help reduce the risk of debt crises and promote the use of scarce concessional resources by the countries that need them most. Its effectiveness in achieving these objectives increases with the number of borrowers, donors, and lenders using it.

The DSF has improved access to and the timeliness, comparability, and quality of information on the debt situation of low-income countries. Country-specific information on debt sustainability is easily accessible, improving the capacity of borrowers, donors, and lenders to make informed decisions. The IMF and the World Bank have established dedicated pages on their external Web sites that give the general public easy access to information on their work on debt-related issues in low-income countries.[4]

Effective information sharing hinges on additional efforts by borrowers, donors, and lenders. Debtor-reported information, the main source of data for DSAs, still suffers from weaknesses in many low-income countries, such as lack of reliability, comprehensiveness, and timeliness.

Borrowers

The DSF can help borrowers identify debt-related vulnerabilities so that they adequately take them into account when formulating their policies. It is a tool for assessing the risks associated with a country's current debt situation and evaluating the potential implications for medium- and long-term sustainability of different policy choices, such as front-loading or back-loading some key public investment projects or spending of scaled-up aid (see Barkbu, Beddies, and Le Manchec 2008 for an example of alternative scaling-up scenarios). It can also help identify policies that are consistent with maintaining or achieving debt sustainability, such as determining the appropriate terms for new financing.[5] In particular, the DSF can help determine an appropriate pace of debt reaccumulation for countries that have received debt relief and are faced with increased borrowing space. Governments can also use it in their communications with donors, lenders, and other stakeholders, including in discussions of countries' poverty reduction strategies.

The DSF provides a platform for developing a medium-term debt-management strategy (MTDS). The MTDS should seek to address the vulnerabilities uncovered in the DSA. It should help operationalize a country's debt-management objectives by outlining cost-risk trade-offs in meeting the government's financing needs and payment obligations.

Lenders

The lack of comprehensive information from low-income countries and their pervasive institutional weaknesses require a proactive approach by lenders. Unlike middle-income countries, low-income countries tend to produce poor data, and their overall domestic capacity is limited. Implementation of sustainable lending practices is therefore critical to safeguard their debt sustainability. In practice, such lending should follow a number of broad principles: it should foster development, preserve debt sustainability, and support good governance and transparency. Although debt relief has significantly reduced debt ratios in many low-income countries, maintaining debt sustainability may prove challenging in a volatile macroeconomic and weak policy environment.

Increased creditor coordination can facilitate sustainable lending practices. Coordination gives confidence to creditors that other creditors will not provide financing on terms that jeopardize debt sustainability and hence, undercut their own efforts to prevent payment difficulties. Although the DSF can help promote these good practices, donors and lenders face operational difficulties in implementing information sharing and coordination in practice. They must also take into consideration other constraints when making financing decisions.

An increasing number of creditors are using the DSF. Multilateral creditors represent a large share of external financing to low-income country governments. IDA began using DSAs' rating of the risk of debt distress as a criterion for grant eligibility in mid-2005. Regional development banks, such as the Asian Development Bank, the African Development Bank, the Inter-American Development Bank, and the International Fund for Agricultural Development, have adopted similar systems for grant and lending decisions.

Bilateral official creditors also use the DSF as an input for financing decisions, but coordination by these creditors faces challenges. Bilateral official creditors include a diverse group of creditors with respect to coordination, policy objectives, and investment strategies. Some initiatives for coordination have, however, succeeded. In January 2008, member countries of the Organisation for Economic Co-operation and Development (OECD) adopted a set of principles and guidelines that adhere to IDA and IMF concessionality requirements and refer explicitly to the DSF (OECD 2008). These principles, designed to ensure that loans supported by export credit agencies are in line with sustainable development objectives, have been officially endorsed by European Union countries.

To reinforce the effectiveness of the DSF, the Bank and the IMF have increased their outreach efforts on the DSF with nearly all major multilateral and bilateral creditors to low-income countries. Outreach opportunities to commercial creditors have been pursued as well. Both institutions have set up mailboxes (LendingToLICS@worldbank.org and

LendingToLICS@imf.org) to which specific questions on DSF issues can be sent. As noted earlier, an increasing number of creditors are referring to the DSF to make their financing decisions, but broader coordination and information sharing will require additional outreach efforts from interested parties, including the IMF and the World Bank.

The Debt Sustainability Outlook in Low-Income Countries

DSAs conducted under the DSF provide a comprehensive view of the debt outlook of low-income countries.[6] Since the implementation of the DSF (in 2005), 181 DSAs have been completed, covering 70 low-income countries (90 percent of countries that are eligible for a poverty reduction and growth facility).[7] Using data from those DSAs, this section looks at how debt relief has affected the prospects of low-income countries and highlights key debt-related vulnerabilities in both HIPCs and non–HIPC low-income countries.

Debt Sustainability in Post–Completion Point Countries

DSAs confirm that (unsurprisingly) post–completion point countries are in a better debt situation than other HIPCs.[8] At end-2007, the present value of the debt-to-export ratio averaged 61 percent for post–completion point HIPCs and 234 percent for pre–completion point HIPCs.[9] The average in post–completion point countries masks large discrepancies, however: the present value of the debt-to-exports ratio was just 14 percent in Zambia and 138 percent in Mauritania. The present value of the external-debt-to-export ratio was below its relevant threshold at end-2007 in all but two countries.

The risks of debt distress are also lower for post–completion point countries than for other HIPCs. Under recent DSAs, most post–completion point countries have received a low or moderate risk rating (figure 5.1). The better rating distribution reflects both lower debt ratios—a direct outcome of debt relief—and the fact that on average, post–completion point countries tend to have better policies and institutions than other HIPCs (figure 5.2).[10] Average export growth was stronger in pre–completion point countries (12 percent versus 10 percent), but this difference reflects the impact of oil-exporting countries (table 5.2). Excluding oil exporters, the average export growth rate was stronger in post–completion point countries by about 2.5 percentage points.

Long-term debt sustainability remains a challenge. Despite the significant decline in debt burdens thanks to debt relief, less than half of the post–completion point HIPCs have a low risk of debt distress, according to the most recent DSAs. Furthermore, there is evidence of deterioration in the distribution of ratings, with the number of countries with high risk

Figure 5.1 Risk of Debt Distress in HIPCs

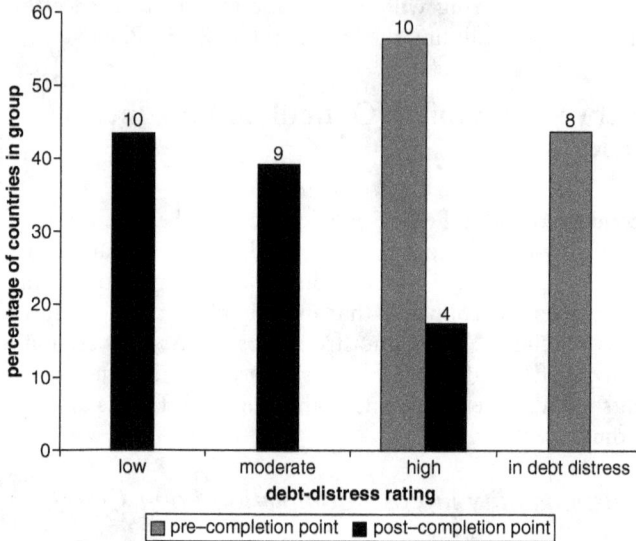

Source: World Bank–IMF debt sustainability analyses for HIPCs available as of August 2008.

Note: The numbers above the bars represent the number of countries within each risk rating.

ratings increasing from two to four between 2007 and 2008 (figure 5.3). In addition to Rwanda (for which the latest DSA confirmed the earlier high risk rating) and The Gambia (which, despite its access to full debt relief at the completion point, was assessed to be at high risk in December 2007), Burkina Faso and São Tomé and Principe recently joined the group of high debt-distress countries.

The four countries rated as high risk share a number of vulnerabilities. These include a higher concentration of key raw commodities in total exports relative to other post–completion point countries; a poor or deteriorating quality of policies and institutions, as measured by the CPIA index; and, in Rwanda and São Tomé and Principe, a lower export base, which renders them highly susceptible and sensitive to shocks such as droughts and price volatility (see IDA and IMF 2008).[11]

Post–completion point HIPCs with a low or moderate risk of debt distress also exhibit, to various extents, a vulnerability to export shocks. The debt-ratio trajectories under the most extreme stress test—often

Figure 5.2 Distribution of Present Value of Debt-to-Exports Ratio in HIPCs, end-2007

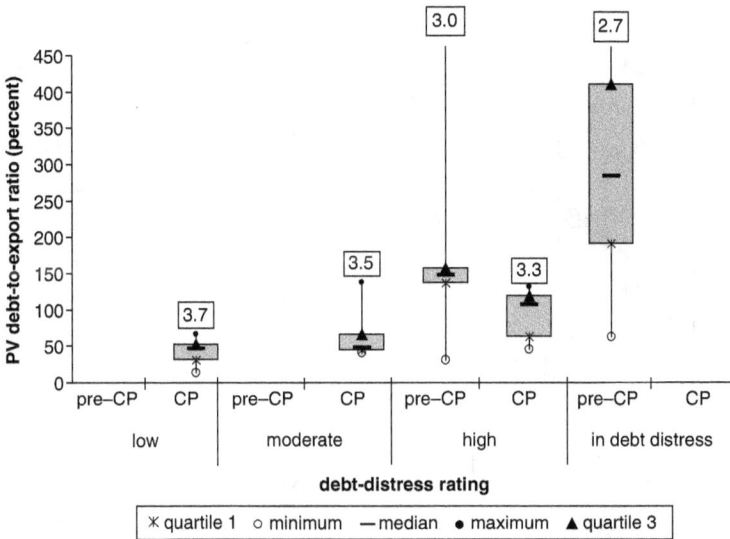

Source: World Bank–IMF debt sustainability analyses for HIPCs available as of August 2008.

Note: The figure is based on the baseline scenario. The numbers in boxes above the bars show the average Country Policy and Institutional Assessment (CPIA) index for each group and the risk of debt distress. No pre–completion point (pre-CP) countries have low or moderate risk of debt distress. No completion point (CP) countries are in debt distress.

reflecting a shock to exports—increase significantly after 10 years in each DSA (figure 5.4).[12] In low-risk countries, which on average have lower initial debt ratios and a higher capacity to carry debt thanks to better policies and institutions, the external debt ratio remains at manageable, albeit much higher, levels after the shock. The increase is much larger for moderate-risk countries, whose average deviation from the baseline scenario is 76 percentage points, than for low-risk countries, whose average deviation is 54 percentage points. The dispersion of outcomes also appears larger than for low-risk countries.

DSAs also reveal that the debt outlook of post–completion point HIPCs is highly sensitive to the terms of new financing. The DSF includes a standard alternative scenario that models the impact of a 2 percent increase in the interest rate for new borrowing. Despite its mildness, this assumption

Table 5.2 Real GDP Growth, Export Growth, and Net FDI in Pre–Completion Point and Completion Point HIPCs, 1998–2007

Country type	Real GDP growth (percent)		Export growth (percent)		Net FDI (percentage of GDP)	
	Average	Standard deviation	Average	Standard deviation	Average	Standard deviation
Pre-completion point HIPCs	3.7	4.1	12.1	24.2	4.2	3.6
Excluding hydrocarbon-rich or potentially hydrocarbon-rich countries (Chad, Republic of Congo, and Sudan)	3.0	3.8	7.8	17.7	2.7	2.7
Debt-distress rating						
High	4.1	3.8	11.4	25.2	4.1	3.3
In debt distress	3.1	4.5	12.9	23.0	4.3	4.0
Completion point HIPCs	5.2	3.6	10.2	16.1	3.9	2.8
Excluding hydrocarbon-rich or potentially hydrocarbon-rich HIPCs (Bolivia, Cameroon, Mauritania, and São Tomé and Principe)	5.2	3.7	10.2	14.5	3.6	2.1
Debt-distress rating						
Low and moderate	4.9	3.6	11.0	15.9	3.6	2.1
High	6.4	3.7	6.4	17.1	5.5	6.4

Source: World Bank–IMF debt sustainability analyses for HIPCs available as of August 2008; IMF 2007.
Note: FDI = foreign direct investment.

Figure 5.3 Risk of Debt Distress in Post–Completion Point HIPCs, 2005/06 and 2007/08

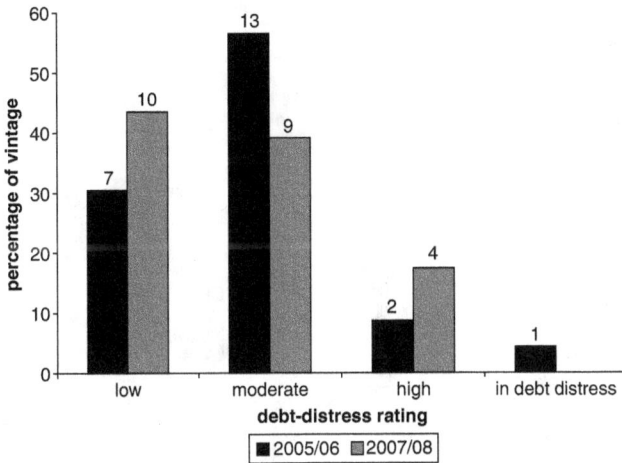

Source: World Bank–IMF debt sustainability analyses for post–completion point HIPCs available as of August 2008.

Note: The numbers above the bars represent the number of countries within each risk rating.

of less favorable terms leads to a breach of the present value of the external-debt-to-exports ratio in about 60 percent of post–completion point HIPCs. This result confirms that these countries should continue to borrow on concessional terms (even when the borrowing space is large) and approach nonconcessional financing with caution.

Debt Sustainability in Low-Income Non–HIPCs

Debt ratios in low-income non–HIPCs are higher than those of post–completion point countries. At end-2007, the present value of the debt-to-exports ratio for low-income non–HIPCs averaged 80 percent—much higher than the 61 percent for post–completion point HIPCs.[13] Moreover, the dispersion of the ratios across countries is wider, ranging from 8 percent in Nigeria to 231 percent in Grenada, and the standard deviation of the debt ratio is 36 percentage points higher than in post–completion point HIPCs. At end-2007, the present value of the debt-to-exports ratio was below its relevant threshold in all but four countries.

The risks of debt distress also tend to be higher than in post–completion point countries. Debt sustainability is a concern in more than one-third

Figure 5.4 Distribution of Present Value of Debt-to-Exports Ratio in HIPCs, 2007 and 2017

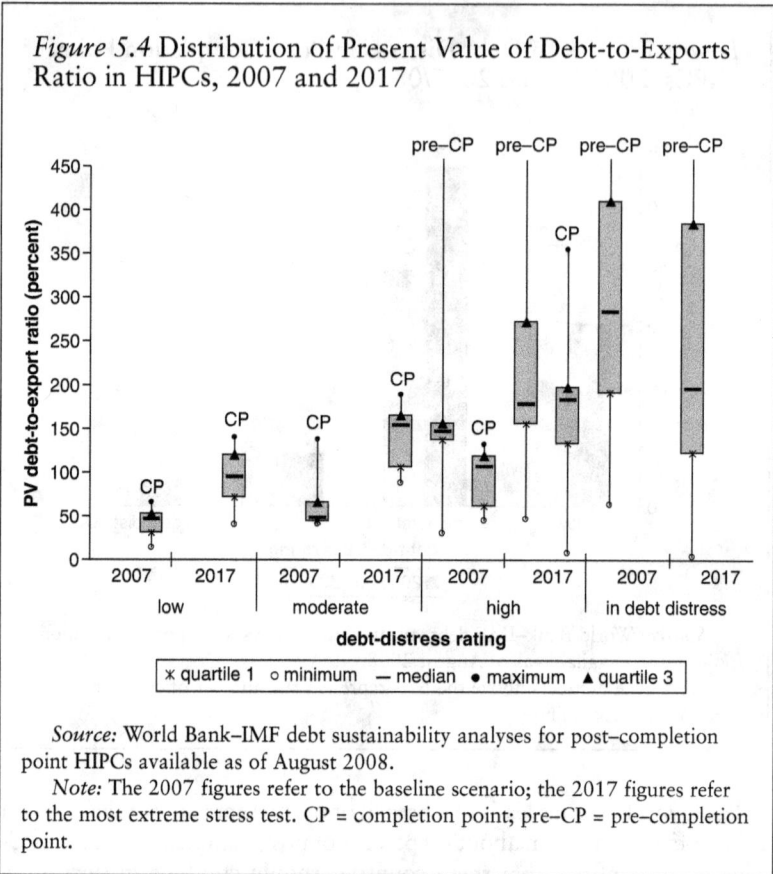

Source: World Bank–IMF debt sustainability analyses for post–completion point HIPCs available as of August 2008.

Note: The 2007 figures refer to the baseline scenario; the 2017 figures refer to the most extreme stress test. CP = completion point; pre–CP = pre–completion point.

of low-income non–HIPCs and less than one-fifth of post–completion point HIPCs. Of these countries, two are in debt distress (Myanmar and Zimbabwe), and the remainder are rated at high risk of debt distress (figures 5.5 and 5.6). This weaker performance reflects higher initial debt ratios and, to a lesser extent, weaker policies and institutions. Both factors overcome the positive impact of slightly higher export growth rates (a 10-year average of 11 percent in low-income non–HIPCs compared with 10 percent in post–completion point HIPCs) (table 5.3).

However, low-income non–HIPCs appear to be more resilient to exogenous shocks. Although the average present value of the debt-to-exports ratio under the most extreme stress test increases by 42 percentage points after 10 years, the increase is still less than in post–completion point countries, in which it rises by 68 percentage points. This outcome partly reflects the higher 10-year historical average export growth.

Figure 5.5 Risk of Debt Distress in Post–Completion Point HIPCs and Low-Income Non–HIPCs

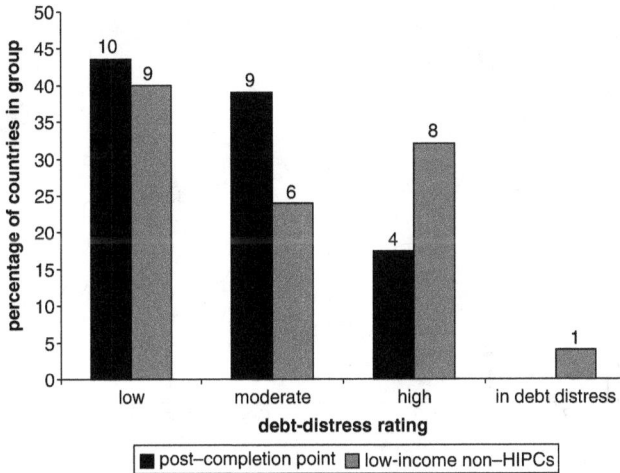

Source: World Bank–IMF debt sustainability analyses for low-income countries available as of August 2008.

Note: The numbers above the bars represent the number of countries within each risk rating. No completion point countries are in debt distress.

Looking at individual country categories, note that low-income non–HIPCs rated as having low and moderate risk exhibit stronger resilience to shocks (figure 5.7).

Comparison

Debt sustainability has improved for most post–completion point countries, but vulnerabilities persist. Adequate policies, including prudent borrowing policies and reforms in debt management, are critical to maintain debt sustainability. Such policies are also needed in countries at low risk of debt distress whose strengthened macroeconomic fundamentals are attracting a new range of investors and creditors and a larger spectrum of financial instruments, exposing their economies to new vulnerabilities.

Low-income non–HIPCs appear to be more indebted than post–completion point countries, but they are more resilient to shocks. Although

Figure 5.6 Distribution of Present Value of Debt-to-Exports Ratio in Completion Point HIPCs and Low-Income Non–HIPCs, end-2007

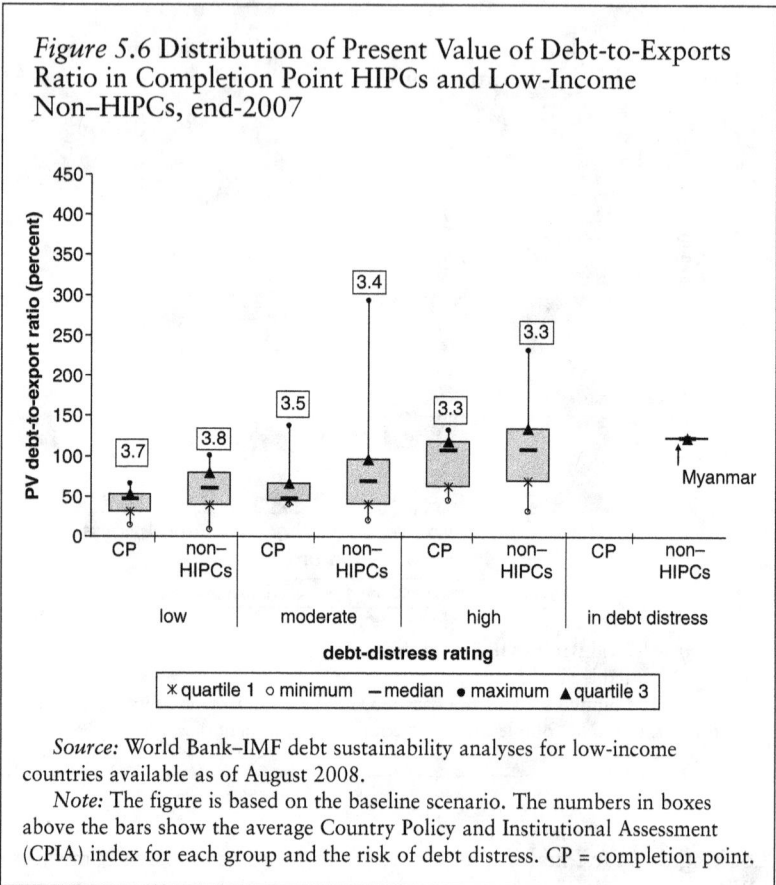

Source: World Bank–IMF debt sustainability analyses for low-income countries available as of August 2008.
Note: The figure is based on the baseline scenario. The numbers in boxes above the bars show the average Country Policy and Institutional Assessment (CPIA) index for each group and the risk of debt distress. CP = completion point.

the present value of their debt-to-exports ratio was, on average, one-third higher than in post–completion point countries at end-2007, these countries appear to be in a better position to cope with the associated vulnerabilities. Nonetheless, the distribution of debt-distress ratings, which is skewed toward the high debt-distress category, highlights that these countries should continue to implement policies that will reduce the risks posed by debt, including continued efforts to mobilize concessional resources and ensure the productive use of external financing.

There are some indications that post–completion point countries are converging toward low-income non–HIPCs. With debt relief, these countries' debt burdens have declined significantly, eliminating the sizable debt overhang and paving the way for better macroeconomic performance. Their average growth rates of real GDP and exports and their inflows of foreign direct investment (FDI) are now

Table 5.3 Real GDP Growth, Export Growth, and Net FDI in Completion Point HIPCs and Low-Income Non–HIPCs, 1998–2007

Country type	Real GDP growth (percent)		Export growth (percent)		Net FDI (percentage of GDP)	
	Average	Standard deviation	Average	Standard deviation	Average	Standard deviation
Completion point HIPCs	5.2	3.6	10.2	16.1	3.9	2.8
Excluding hydrocarbon-rich or potentially hydrocarbon-rich countries (Bolivia, Cameroon, Mauritania, and São Tomé and Príncipe)	5.2	3.7	10.2	14.5	3.6	2.1
Debt-distress rating						
Low and moderate	4.9	3.6	11.0	15.9	3.6	2.1
High	6.4	3.7	6.4	17.1	5.5	6.4
Low-income non–HIPCs	5.0	3.2	11.3	15.9	4.6	3.6
Excluding hydrocarbon-rich or potentially hydrocarbon-rich countries (Angola, Nigeria, Vietnam, and Yemen)	4.5	3.1	9.8	14.4	4.8	3.4
Debt-distress rating						
Low and moderate	5.8	3.4	14.6	16.3	3.7	3.0
High and in debt distress	3.9	3.0	7.2	15.4	5.7	4.5

Source: World Bank–IMF debt sustainability analyses for low-income countries available as of August 2008; IMF 2007.
Note: FDI = foreign direct investment.

Figure 5.7 Distribution of Present Value of the
Debt-to-Exports Ratio in HIPCs

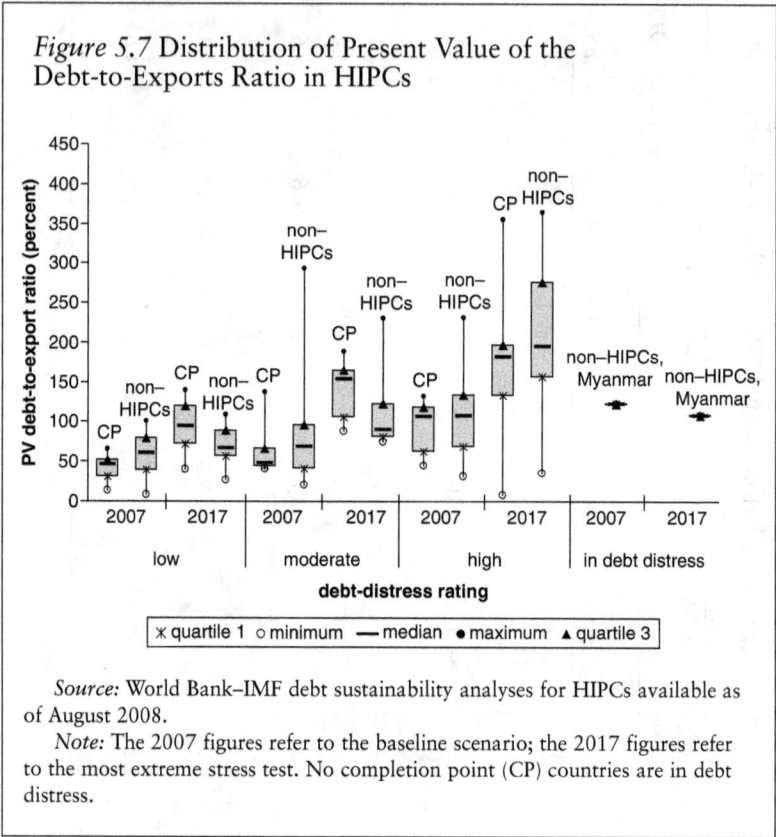

Source: World Bank–IMF debt sustainability analyses for HIPCs available as of August 2008.

Note: The 2007 figures refer to the baseline scenario; the 2017 figures refer to the most extreme stress test. No completion point (CP) countries are in debt distress.

more similar to those of low-income non–HIPCs than to those of pre–completion point countries (table 5.4). Their performance improved markedly in 2006–07 following the provision of MDRI debt relief. Economic volatility tends to be less pronounced in post–completion point countries and low-income non–HIPCs than in pre–completion point countries.

Overall, low-income countries remain vulnerable to debt distress, regardless of the category into which they fall. Therefore, it is important that borrowers and lenders continue to monitor debt sustainability. Measures geared toward entrenching macroeconomic stability, diversifying their export bases, and increasing the overall quality of policies and institutions could help these countries expand their borrowing in a sustainable manner. Strengthening of domestic capacity—by implementing an MTDS or other measures in the area of public financial management, for example—is also key for informed policy decisions

Table 5.4 Real GDP Growth, Export Growth, and Net FDI in Pre–Completion Point and Completion Point HIPCs and Low-Income Non–HIPCs

Country type	Real GDP growth (percent)		Export growth (percent)		Net FDI (percentage of GDP)	
	1998–2005	2006–07	1998–2005	2006–07	1998–2005	2006–07
Pre–completion point HIPCs	3.5	4.6	13.5	9.0	3.4	6.9
Excluding hydrocarbon-rich or potentially hydrocarbon-rich countries (Chad, Republic of Congo, and Sudan)	2.7	4.1	8.3	8.7	1.8	6.2
Debt-distress rating						
High	4.2	4.1	11.7	11.7	4.0	4.3
In debt distress	2.5	5.2	15.9	5.6	2.8	10.2
Completion point HIPCs	4.9	6.4	8.9	15.3	3.6	5.4
Excluding hydrocarbon-rich or potentially hydrocarbon-rich countries (Bolivia, Cameroon, Mauritania, and São Tomé and Principe)	5.0	6.0	9.2	13.8	3.3	4.9
Debt-distress rating						
Low and moderate	4.5	6.5	9.5	17.2	3.6	3.8
High	6.5	5.9	6.5	6.4	3.5	13.2

(continued)

Table 5.4 *(continued)*

Country type	Real GDP growth (percent)		Export growth (percent)		Net FDI (percentage of GDP)	
	1998–2005	2006–07	1998–2005	2006–07	1998–2005	2006–07
Low-income non–HIPCs	4.6	6.2	10.6	14.3	4.1	6.4
Excluding hydrocarbon-rich or potentially hydrocarbon-rich countries (Angola, Nigeria, Vietnam, and Yemen)	4.3	5.5	8.7	14.2	4.2	7.1
Debt-distress rating						
Low and moderate	5.3	7.8	14.2	16.8	3.4	4.7
High and in debt distress	3.8	4.2	6.2	11.3	4.9	8.6

Source: World Bank–IMF debt sustainability analyses for low-income countries; IMF 2007.
Note: FDI = foreign direct investment.

(including the level of sustainable borrowing) and improved communications with creditors.

Challenges Going Forward and Issues for Discussion

The financial landscape in low-income countries has changed markedly in the past few years, creating new challenges. In some low-income countries, debt relief, stronger macroeconomic fundamentals, and rising commodity prices have led to increased interest by new creditors, including domestic ones. New types of financing offer countries the opportunity to step up development, but they also create significant analytical difficulties, raise new policy questions, and increase risk.

Although low-income countries recognize the importance of mobilizing resources in a sustainable manner, many of them have voiced concerns that the DSF—and the concessionality policies of the IMF and World Bank—unduly constrain financing for development, particularly to develop infrastructure. The following elements, voiced, for example, at the 2008 African Caucus meeting in Nouakchott, are sources of particular concern:

- *Economic assumptions.* Baseline scenarios are often criticized for being too conservative. In fact, the evidence suggests that projections tend to be too optimistic. According to a report by the IMF's Independent Evaluation Office (IEO 2003), in the 159 IMF programs considered, actual GDP growth outcomes fell short of projected growth by an average 1.5 percentage points during the various two-year periods studied.[14] A report by the World Bank's Independent Evaluation Group (IEG 2006) finds that the projected average growth rates of GDP and exports for 2005–10 were more than twice their 1990–2000 averages and 2.5 times their 1980–2001 averages. The report also concludes that this optimism appears to have diminished in recent years.[15] This issue will need to be revisited once more vintages of DSAs are available to assess whether new projections have been adjusted to take into account past forecasting errors.
- *Investment and growth.* Stepped-up investment in infrastructure is critical to supporting long-term growth in many low-income countries. However, the links between higher investment and growth are difficult to quantify, especially as economic growth and debt sustainability depend on many other factors, such as the strength of macroeconomic and structural policies, the quality of institutions and decision-making processes, and the management of exogenous shocks. Further work in this area, which goes well beyond the DSF itself, may be needed.

- *Assumptions about the quality of policies and institutions.* The DSF uses the World Bank's CPIA to measure the quality of a country's policies and institutions. The CPIA is a diagnostic tool that provides results that are comparable across countries. Since June 2006, its numerical ratings have been disclosed and detailed information about the exercise made public. Some low-income countries have suggested a switch to a system for evaluating country policies that is more transparent and country led (see, for example, the HIPC Finance Minister's Communiqué, October 10, 2008[16]).

- *Domestic debt.* Domestic debt undoubtedly matters for the assessment of overall fiscal sustainability. Although thresholds for overall public debt would allow a more systematic integration of domestic debt into the DSF, their design poses conceptual and practical challenges. Moreover, the distinction between domestic and external debt has become increasingly blurred with the participation of foreign entities in secondary market trading. Additional work is needed to more systematically conceptualize the impact of domestic debt on total debt sustainability.

- *Private creditors.* Foreign investors are increasingly entering domestic markets for equities and domestic debt. With these new opportunities, many low-income countries, in particular those that have large fiscal space as a result of the provision of debt relief, wish to accelerate borrowing to address their development needs.[17] The menu of financing instruments is also expanding, with the possible use of public-private partnership arrangements, for example. The DSF was strengthened in 2006 to address these new developments, but additional work may be required to provide more specific guidance on how to monitor and contain these new risks.

- *Capacity constraints in low-income countries.* Capacity constraints in low-income countries hamper the effective use of the DSF by borrowing countries. The World Bank and the IMF have put forward several initiatives to strengthen domestic capacity, including through the provision of technical assistance in debt management and DSF training workshops. These efforts need to be intensified. Continued collaboration between donors and creditors and stepped-up and well-targeted technical assistance is critical in building low-income countries' capacity to monitor debt and improve debt sustainability.

The DSF is a tool for assessing debt sustainability prospects in varying circumstances. As such, it must be flexible enough to adapt to changes in the financial environment as well as advances in the understanding of macroeconomic linkages. The current version of the DSF crystallizes the current state of knowledge and thus represents the best instrument currently available for analyzing debt sustainability in low-income countries. It is not a static tool: continuous work—nourished with inputs from a broad range of users—is needed to deepen its analytical foundations and improve its relevance and effectiveness.

Conclusions

Low-income countries have often struggled with large external debts and destabilizing macroeconomic outcomes, which constrain development. Although debt relief has given many low-income countries a chance for a fresh start, these countries continue to face an array of challenges. The financial landscape has changed and will continue to change. Debt relief has created significant borrowing space that will need to be filled very cautiously. The menu of financing options is expanding and its composition changing. The increased availability of resources for growth-enhancing investment from nontraditional creditors is a welcome development, but additional financing needs to be managed carefully to avoid excessive debt accumulation and a return of the debt problems of the past. Domestic market development provides new opportunities for additional financing but also poses risks.

The DSF can help address these challenges by guiding borrowing decisions of low-income countries in ways that match their financing needs with their current and prospective repayment ability. It also provides guidance for creditors' lending and grant-allocation decisions to ensure that resources are provided on terms that are consistent with both progress toward development goals and long-term debt sustainability; improves World Bank and IMF assessments and policy advice in these areas; and helps detect potential crises early so that preventive action can be taken.

The introduction of the DSF has also improved access to information and the emphasis on the debt situation in low-income countries, thereby increasing the capacity of borrowers, donors, and lenders to make informed decisions, which reduces the risk of renewed episodes of debt distress. For most low-income countries, concessional flows will remain the most appropriate source of external financing for some time. But some low-income countries will develop more quickly and become more mature market economies. Nonconcessional financing will then play a more prominent role, given the scarcity of concessional resources and countries' desire to tap international capital markets. The DSF is well placed to guide such decisions by showing the impact of such borrowing on overall debt sustainability.

Significant challenges remain. The IMF and the Bank have worked to take into account more fully the growth potential offered by increased infrastructure and other investment in the DSF. However, the links between higher infrastructure investment and growth are difficult to quantify. Moreover, integrating domestic debt and private sector flows has proven difficult. More work in these areas, which would go well beyond the DSF itself, may be needed.

Notes

Christian Beddies and Marie-Hélène Le Manchec are staff members of the International Monetary Fund (IMF). The views expressed in this chapter are those of the authors and do not necessarily reflect the views of national authorities, the IMF, or IMF Executive Directors. The authors are indebted to Shannon Mockler, of the IMF, for excellent research assistance.

1. Throughout this chapter, the term *low-income countries* refers to PRGF-eligible, IDA-only countries (where PRGF = Poverty Reduction and Growth Facility and IDA = International Development Association).

2. This section draws on Barkbu, Beddies, and Le Manchec (2008).

3. DSAs for HIPCs, called Debt Relief Analyses (DRA), were first requested by the Executive Boards of the World Bank and the IMF in spring 1995, in the context of discussions on means to alleviate high debt burdens. When the HIPC Initiative was adopted, in 1996, the HIPC DRA became the key tool for determining a country's eligibility for, and the amount of, assistance under the initiative, based on current levels of debt. DSAs for low-income countries under the DSF are forward looking, with a view to assessing the risks associated with future debt accumulation.

4. Web sites: http://www.imf.org/concessionality and http://www.worldbank.org/debt.

5. Many outlays related to achieving development objectives do not, by nature, generate sufficient cash flow to the government in the near term to service nonconcessional debt.

6. This section draws on IDA and IMF (2008). The analysis in this section was drafted in September 2008 based on data as of end-August 2008.

7. Middle-income country DSAs are conducted for some countries with market access that are eligible for poverty reduction and growth facilities (for example, India and Pakistan).

8. The analysis here focuses on the present value of the external debt-to-exports ratio, which was found to be the indicator most often breaching its indicative threshold and therefore most likely to drive the risk rating.

9. For HIPCs in the interim period, debt ratios incorporate only the impact of interim debt relief.

10. Better policies and institutions lead to a higher capacity to carry debt. Under the DSF, they translate into higher indicative thresholds.

11. For detailed information about the CPIA, visit go.worldbank.org/74EDY81YU0.

12. The DSF includes a standardized shock to exports and a shock to exports combined with a shock to GDP and nondebt-creating flows.

13. Low-income non–HIPCs include 24 countries for which data were available.

14. The report considers the experiences of countries under various IMF programs, including the enhanced structural adjustment facility, the poverty reduction and growth facility, and stand-by arrangements.

15. The study finds that real GDP growth and growth projections from completion point HIPC DSAs for the period 2000–10 were, on average, 0.42 and 0.11 percentage points, respectively, lower than those for the same period included in earlier decision point DSAs.

16. Web site: http://www.hipc-cbp.org/files/en/open/Advocacy/MM15_Declaration_EN.pdf.

17. The current financial crisis could reduce investor appetite, as many potential lenders are squeezed for liquidity.

References

Barkbu, B., C. Beddies, and M. Le Manchec. 2008. "The Debt Sustainability Framework for Low-Income Countries." Occasional Paper 266, International Monetary Fund, Washington, DC.

IDA (International Development Association) and IMF (International Monetary Fund). 2008. "Heavily Indebted Poor Countries (HIPC) Initiative and Multi-lateral Debt Relief Initiative (MDRI): Status of Implementation." Washington, DC. http://www.imf.org/external/np/pp/eng/2008/091208.pdf.

IEG (Independent Evaluation Group). 2006. "Debt Relief for the Poorest: An Evaluation Update of the HIPC Initiative." World Bank, Washington, DC.

IEO (Independent Evaluation Office). 2003. "Fiscal Adjustment in IMF–Supported Programs." International Monetary Fund, Washington, DC. http://www.imf.org/External/NP/ieo/2003/fis/.

IMF (International Monetary Fund). 2007. *Guide on Resource Revenue Transparency.* Washington, DC: IMF.

Kraay, A., and V. Nehru. 2006. "When Is External Debt Sustainable?" *World Bank Economic Review* 20 (3): 341–65.

OECD (Organisation for Economic Co-operation and Development). 2008. "Principles and Guidelines to Promote Sustainable Lending Practices in the Provision of Official Exports Credits to Low-Income Countries." Working Party on Export Credits and Guarantees, TAD/ECG/2008(1), Paris. http://www.olis.oecd.org/olis/2008doc.nsf/LinkTo/NT00000962/$FILE/JT03238627.PDF.

World Bank and IMF (International Monetary Fund). 2006. "Applying the Debt Sustainability Framework for Low-Income Countries Post Debt Relief." Washington, DC. http://www.imf.org/external/pp/longres.aspx?id=3959.

———. 2008. "Staff Guidance Note on the Application of the Joint Fund-Bank Debt Sustainability Framework for Low-Income Countries (LICs)." Washington, DC. http://www.imf.org/external/np/pp/eng/2008/070308.pdf.

6

Debt Relief and Sustainable Financing to Meet the MDGs

Dörte Dömeland and Homi Kharas

In its mid-term assessment of progress toward meeting the Millennium Development Goals (MDGs), the World Bank concluded that "at the country level, on current trends, most countries are off track to meet most MDGs" (World Bank 2008, p. 22). This assessment—mirroring the "development emergency" declared by world leaders at Davos, Switzerland, in January 2008 in issuing the MDG Call to Action—highlights the need to accelerate progress across the developing world.

In June 2008, a high-level panel, the MDG Steering Group for Africa— the region that has made the least progress toward achieving the MDGs— costed out the requirements to meet the MDGs (MDG Africa Steering Group 2008). The total public external financing needed from all sources was estimated at $72 billion by 2010, $62 billion of which was requested in the form of official development assistance (ODA). The remaining $10 billion could come from donors that do not belong to the Development Assistance Committee of the Organisation for Economic Co-operation and Development (OECD), such as China and India, and from private aid.

Financing at such levels represents a significant increase over the current amounts of ODA being provided. In 2006, net ODA to Sub-Saharan Africa was about $40 billion, of which $13 billion was debt relief and $15.5 billion was in the form of development projects and programs being implemented in the country.[1] With debt relief providing such a substantial portion of external assistance, it is natural to ask what contributions the debt-relief program has made in accelerating development.

Debt relief can affect development through several channels. First, by reducing interest and principal payments, it can free up domestic resources for spending on development programs.[2] For a given path of future revenues, one would expect to see countries that receive debt relief running significantly higher primary deficits on their budgets than countries that still must service their debt. Of course, increasing expenditures is not the only option that governments are facing. Instead of increasing expenditures, a government could reduce taxes or the rate of public debt accumulation. Given the link between the enhanced Heavily Indebted Poor Countries (HIPC) Initiative and poverty reduction and the small tax basis, however, it seems unlikely that HIPC Initiative resources are used to cut taxes.[3]

The evidence on the effect of the HIPC Initiative on poverty-reducing expenditures is mixed. Dessy and Vencatachellum (2007) find that debt relief provided to African countries between 1989 and 1993 increased expenditures on public education and health in countries that had improved their institutions. In contrast, Chauvin and Kraay (2005) find no significant effect of debt relief on expenditure on health and education, and Crespo Cuaresma and Vincelette (2008) conclude that the effect of debt relief on educational expenditure is not statistically significant.[4]

Second, debt relief eliminates a significant "overhang" from countries' balance sheets. Previous literature, mostly associated with commercial borrowing in the 1970s, suggests that countries with high debt levels experience lower investment, because private businesses face greater uncertainty over future tax increases that could be required to service public debt (see, for example, Cohen and Sachs 1986; Krugman 1988). In these circumstances, debt relief can have an indirect benefit on growth by inducing more private investment. Public investment can also be negatively affected if the returns go largely to repay foreign creditors.

Arslanalp and Henry (2005, 2006) find that, unlike the Brady Plan, debt relief provided under the HIPC Initiative had little impact on either investment or growth. They argue that the key constraint to investment in HIPCs is not tax uncertainty but the absence of functional economic institutions that provide the foundation for a profitable private sector. Raddatz (2009) provides evidence that the market values of firms operating in countries that benefited from debt relief under the Multilateral Debt Relief Initiative increased when that initiative was launched. Using vector autoregressive techniques, Cassimon and Van Compenhout (2006) find a positive effect of debt relief on overall investment spending in African HIPCs.

Third, debt relief can open the way for additional borrowing to generate resources for MDG–related programs. There is considerable controversy about this channel. On the one hand, the objective of debt relief is to make countries creditworthy, but doing so has value only if countries borrow and spend more. On the other hand, if countries end up overborrowing— and the fact that they got into debt problems in the first place suggests that there is a proclivity to do so or at least an absence of institutional checks to prevent overborrowing from occurring—then the benefits of debt relief can be quickly eroded.[5] If those benefits result from the removal of the debt overhang, as suggested above, then new borrowing will quickly eliminate the investors' confidence in a stable future tax regime.

Fourth, debt relief has been provided in a structured way, focusing on countries that adopt specific programs of reform designed to improve their development prospects and governance capabilities. Even absent new resources, such reforms could generate significant benefits for growth and poverty reduction. From this perspective, debt relief serves as the grease to move the internal political economy of a recipient country toward more liberal reform. The impact therefore depends on whether the reform program is appropriately designed and implemented. Debt relief could also have a negative effect on reform if, for example, the softening of the budget constraint provided an opportunity to relax tax collection efforts (as discussed above, this scenario is unlikely).

This chapter first examines comprehensive international agreements for debt relief. It then reviews the four channels through which debt relief can have an impact on poverty reduction and growth. Specifically, it asks whether countries receiving debt relief have had larger flows of net ODA than countries that did not receive debt relief; whether debt dynamics improved significantly in these countries; whether debt relief affected HIPCs' access to finance; and whether reforms were implemented more rapidly as a result of programs that are part of the debt-relief package. The analysis is based on new data on the budgets of debt-relief countries, published in annual debt sustainability analyses.[6]

Providing Funds through Debt Relief: Comprehensive International Agreements

After almost two decades of repeated debt reschedulings for low-income countries, it was clear that debt problems needed to be resolved in a comprehensive way. Therefore, in 1996, the HIPC Initiative was launched. It differed from previous debt-relief initiatives, providing deeper debt relief than did traditional mechanisms and involving debt relief from multilateral financial institutions for the first time.[7] It was thus the first (and to date, remains the only) internationally agreed-on framework for providing comprehensive debt relief to low-income countries. Although the HIPC Initiative is based on the principle of equal burden-sharing, participation in the initiative is voluntary. While some creditors provide debt relief beyond what is required under the initiative, participation of some creditor groups is limited.

In 1999, the HIPC Initiative was enhanced to provide faster, deeper, and broader debt relief to eligible countries. Debt relief was front-loaded, and the amount to be provided was increased. Moreover, debt relief to countries would only become irrevocable once they implemented satisfactory policy reform programs that would demonstrate their ability to put the resources freed up through debt relief to good use.[8]

By 2005, it was evident that countries could not expand development programs fast enough to meet the MDGs. The Multilateral Debt Relief Initiative (MDRI) was introduced to reduce further the debts of HIPCs. Under the MDRI, three multilateral institutions—the World Bank Group's International Development Association (IDA), the International Monetary Fund (IMF), and the African Development Bank's African Development Fund (ADF)—agreed to provide full debt cancellation on eligible credits to countries that reached the HIPC completion point. In 2007, the Inter-American Development Bank announced the IADB-07 Initiative, which parallels the MDRI by providing 100 percent debt relief on eligible IADB credits to post–completion point HIPCs.

The debt-relief process consists of several stages (figure 6.1). Once a country satisfies the eligibility criteria, the executive boards of the IMF and IDA formally decide on its eligibility for debt relief. At this "decision point," the international community commits to providing debt relief in amounts established under the enhanced HIPC program. Immediately after the decision point, the country starts receiving interim relief on its

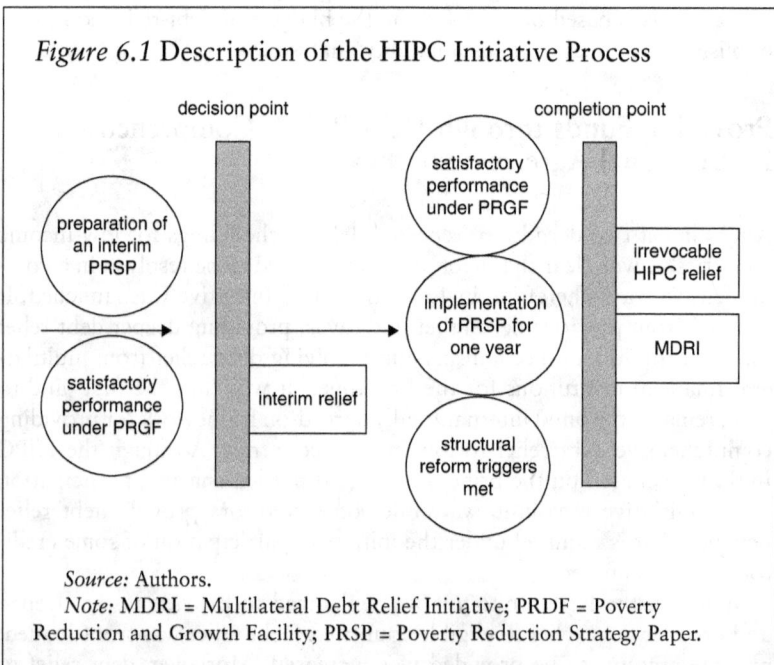

Figure 6.1 Description of the HIPC Initiative Process

Source: Authors.
Note: MDRI = Multilateral Debt Relief Initiative; PRDF = Poverty Reduction and Growth Facility; PRSP = Poverty Reduction Strategy Paper.

debt service from major creditors. It implements a program of reform to develop a satisfactory track record of development progress. A *satisfactory* track record is defined as (a) satisfactory performance under the IMF's Poverty Reduction and Growth Facility (PRGF), (b) implementation of the action plan in a Poverty Reduction Strategy Paper (PRSP) for one year, and (c) meeting specified structural reform triggers. After the executive boards of the IMF and IDA approve the country's track record, the country is deemed to have reached a "completion point." At that time, creditors' debt-relief commitments under the HIPC Initiative become irrevocable, and MDRI debt relief is approved and implemented shortly thereafter. Forty countries currently participate in the HIPC Initiative (table 6.1).

After a slow start, the past 12 years have witnessed significant progress in the implementation of the HIPC Initiative. As of April 2009, 35 countries have passed the decision point. Of the 35, 24 have reached the completion point and qualified for irrevocable debt relief under the HIPC Initiative and the MDRI. The overall assistance expected to be provided to the 35 post–decision point countries amounts to $85 billion in end-2008 net present value terms, including $28 billion in end-2008 net present value terms under the MDRI. This assistance represents, on average, about 50 percent of these countries' 2007 GDP. The debt burden of HIPCs is expected to fall by about 90 percent after completion point is reached.

Most HIPC debt relief has already been delivered. Total HIPC costs are estimated at $74 billion in end-2008 net present value terms, of which about half accrues to post–completion point countries. Debt relief to pre–decision point countries is estimated to cost $17 billion in end-2008 net present value terms. Most pre–decision point countries face tremendous

Table 6.1 Pre–Decision Point, Interim, and Post–Completion Point HIPCs
(as of April 2009)

Pre–decision point countries (5)	Interim countries (11)	Post–completion point countries (24)
Comoros, Eritrea, Kyrgyz Republic, Somalia, Sudan	Afghanistan, Central African Republic, Chad, Côte d'Ivoire, Democratic Republic of Congo, Guinea, Guinea-Bissau, Haiti, Liberia, Republic of Congo, Togo	Benin, Bolivia, Burkina Faso, Burundi, Cameroon, Ethiopia, The Gambia, Ghana, Guyana, Honduras, Madagascar, Malawi, Mali, Mauritania, Mozambique, Nicaragua, Niger, Rwanda, São Tomé and Principe, Senegal, Sierra Leone, Tanzania, Uganda, Zambia

Source: IDA and IMF, various HIPC documents.

challenges to satisfy the HIPC Initiative criteria. Almost half of pre–completion point countries have been affected by war in recent years, and many remain at high risk for conflict and/or political instability. With limited state capacity, these countries have particular difficulties in developing and implementing appropriate reform programs.

Reviewing Net ODA Flows to HIPCs

When the enhanced HIPC Initiative was introduced, in 1999, the IMF and the World Bank emphasized that "to be effective, the proposed enhanced (HIPC) Initiative needs to be reinforced by . . . increased aid flows—preferably in grant form—in support of such policies" (IDA and IMF 1999, p. 24). This aspect of additionality was reiterated in 2002, when stakeholders met in Monterrey, Mexico, to agree on common goals for financing development. The consensus reached there was that the "enhanced (HIPC) Initiative . . . should be fully financed through additional resources" (United Nations 2002).

The MDRI was intended to go further than the HIPC Initiative, by providing full debt relief in order to free up additional resources to help countries reach the MDGs. But unlike HIPC Initiative relief, MDRI debt relief does not change the net flows provided by some international financial institutions, because it reduces their annual allocation to a low-income country by an amount corresponding to the debt-service relief provided up front by the MDRI in that year.

Low-income countries experienced a sharp increase in external borrowing during the 1970s and 1980s. Having largely restricted access to private finance, they often contracted loans, either directly from the government or government export credit agencies or through private loans insured by an export credit agency. Unlike private creditors, who typically reduce their exposure when a country enters into payment difficulties, these official creditors responded in the form of "flow reschedulings" by the Paris Club as well as through new lending from multilateral agencies and some additional creditors from the export credit agencies. Moreover, some bilateral creditors (in particular, the then Soviet Union) continued to provide substantial financing to countries with which they had close ties.

Although payment difficulties of many low-income countries started in the 1980s, aid flows to HIPCs (net ODA) peaked in 1994, at about 17 percent of GDP (figure 6.2). Non–HIPCs also saw an increase in aid, with aid reaching about 10 percent of GDP at the mid-1990s. Thereafter, aid to HIPCs and non–HIPCs alike began a decline that was not reversed until after the Monterrey conference on financing development in 2002. Since then, aid (in particular, to HIPCs) has rebounded, but it has still not reached the levels of the early 1990s.

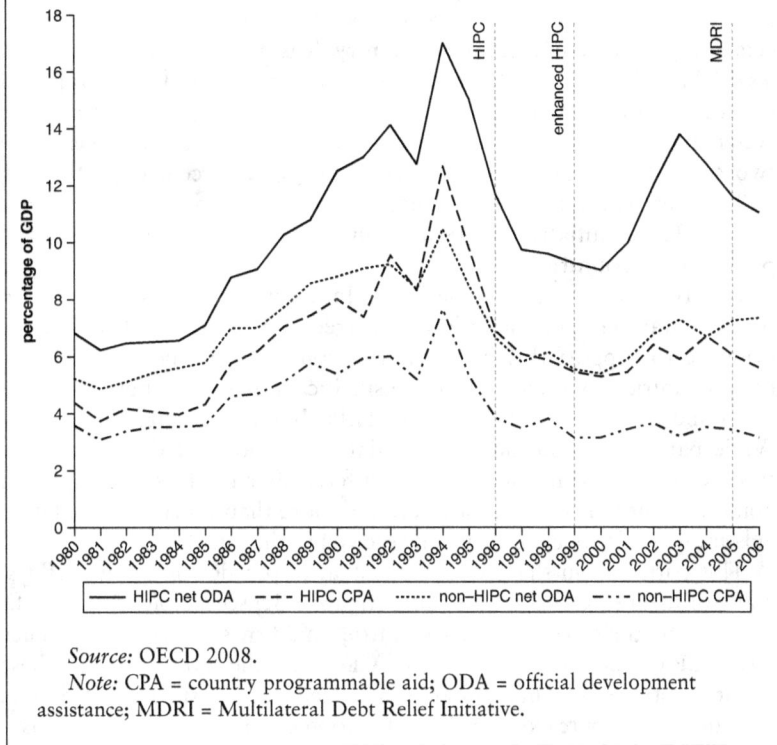

Figure 6.2 Net ODA to Low-Income Countries, 1980–2006

Source: OECD 2008.
  Note: CPA = country programmable aid; ODA = official development assistance; MDRI = Multilateral Debt Relief Initiative.

The pattern of net ODA in HIPCs and non–HIPCs is very similar (see figure 6.2). Countries that later became eligible for HIPC Initiative relief received more aid on average than did non–HIPCs during the 1980–2006 period.

The finding that before the launching of the HIPC Initiative, HIPCs were larger aid recipients than non–HIPCs is not surprising. After all, the reason they became eligible for the HIPC Initiative is that they were heavily indebted. Between 1996 and 2000, under the original HIPC Initiative, the gap in net aid received by countries receiving debt relief and those that did not remained virtually unchanged. HIPCs received more aid—on average, about 4 percentage points of GDP—than did non–HIPCs. This is about the same as the gap during the five years before HIPC Initiative relief but considerably more than the gap between these two groups in the early 1980s. Only after the enhancement of the HIPC Initiative did this gap widen somewhat.

Before trying to infer whether the HIPC Initiative has resulted in a greater aid transfer to eligible countries, it is useful to look at an alternative concept of aid. Country programmable aid (CPA) is a measure that is closer than net ODA to the cash flow available for development projects and programs in a recipient country. It is defined as total net ODA less debt relief, technical assistance, humanitarian and food aid, and interest payments made to creditors. Like net ODA, CPA for HIPCs has systematically exceeded CPA for non–HIPCs, but the gap between these two series has remained roughly constant, at 2 percent of GDP since 1990. There is little visual evidence in figure 6.2 to support the notion that the HIPC Initiative has resulted in a larger transfer of resources to participating countries.

It may be the case that the HIPC Initiative prevented a decline in resource transfers that might have occurred in its absence. There is some evidence to support this. Both interim countries and post–completion point countries continued to receive significant amounts of aid, both net ODA and CPA, since the start of the HIPC Initiative (figure 6.3a and b). While participating in the HIPC Initiative did not halt the aid decline, from which all low-income countries suffered after 1994, post–completion point and interim countries still received more than 6 percent of GDP in aid, comparable to levels they had received in the mid-1980s.

This pattern is in sharp contrast to that of pre–decision point HIPCs, many of them so-called fragile states (figure 6.3c; see chapter 4 for a definition of fragile states). In these countries, aid flows have collapsed since 1994. CPA is down to 2 percent of GDP, half the level of 1980. These countries still receive humanitarian and technical assistance, but donors no longer contribute extensively to development projects and programs.

In summary, participation in the HIPC Initiative has not caused a shift of donor resources toward HIPCs and away from non–HIPCs. But some HIPCs did face the prospect of a rapid decline in aid flows as a result of their debt-service obligations. Thanks to the HIPC Initiative, donors were able to flexibly respond to country needs through debt relief and maintain resource flows at historical levels.

At first sight, it may seem surprising that the billions of dollars allocated to debt relief have not resulted in greater cash flows to the countries on the receiving end. To understand this better, one must understand the details of aid accounting.

Aid is registered by OECD's Development Assistance Committee whenever a developing country receives a cash flow with a concessional element greater than 25 percent. Some aid is in the form of grants, but much aid has been in the form of low-interest credits. In aid accounting, no difference is made between receiving a grant of $100 and a credit for $100; in both cases, aid of $100 is recorded. In economic terms, the grant is clearly worth more to the recipient country, but this is not captured by the aid statistics until the repayment of the credit starts. At this point, the

Figure 6.3 Net ODA Flows to Post–Completion Point,
Interim, and Pre–Decision Point Countries, 1980–2006

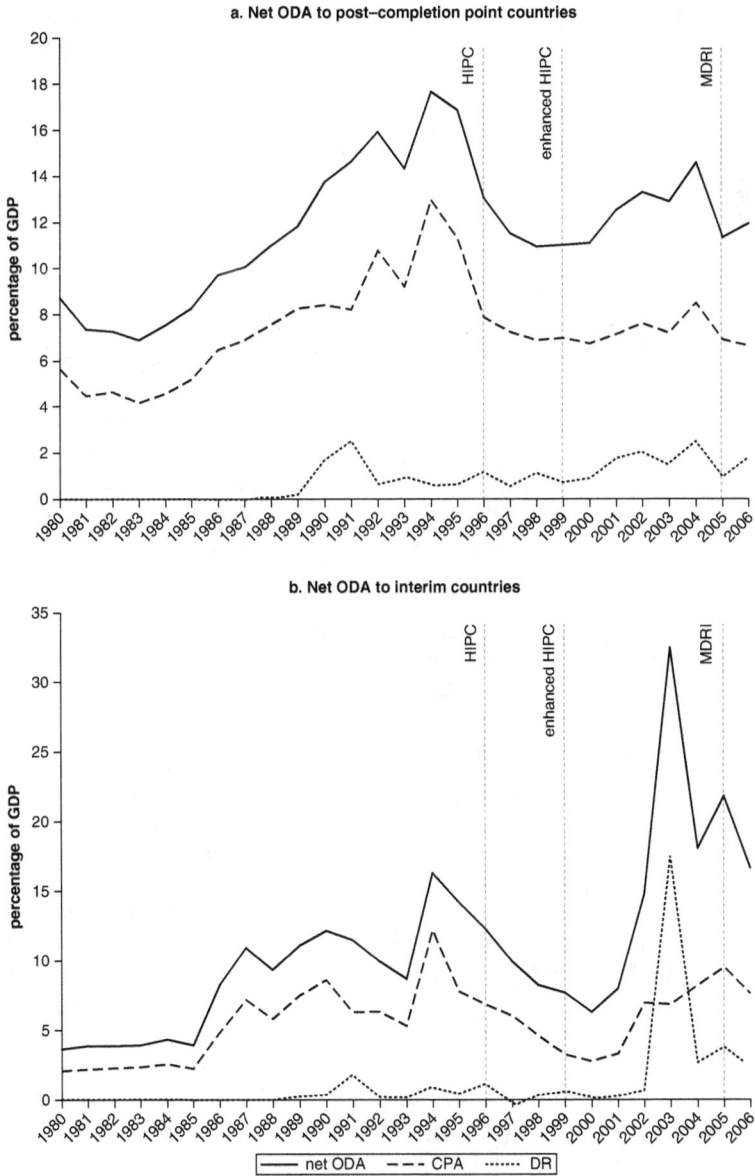

a. Net ODA to post–completion point countries

b. Net ODA to interim countries

net ODA   --- CPA   ...... DR

(continued)

Figure 6.3 (continued)

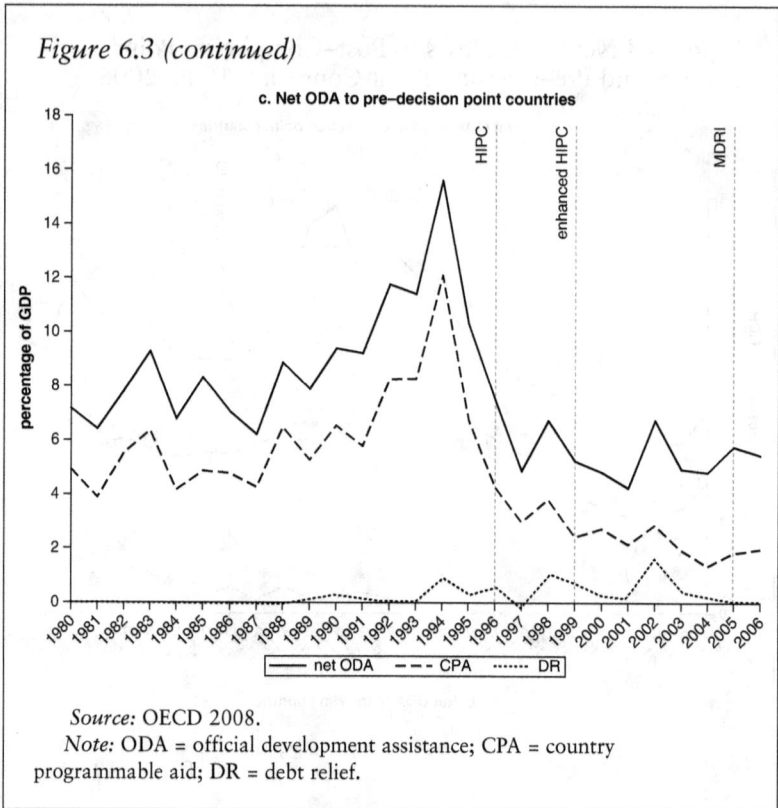

c. Net ODA to pre–decision point countries

Source: OECD 2008.
Note: ODA = official development assistance; CPA = country programmable aid; DR = debt relief.

repayment of the credit in a given year is subtracted from disbursements of new ODA grants and credits.

When debt relief is provided on a credit, it raises problems for accounting. If the debt payment forgiven is counted as more aid, then there is doubling counting: a country would be said to receive "aid" of $100 on receipt of the initial credit and again when the repayment was forgiven. To prevent double counting, therefore, an offset is recorded for concessional aid forgiveness.

The implication of this offset is that high levels of debt forgiveness may not translate into high levels of net ODA. In fact, MDRI does not affect ODA at the time of its implementation at all, because all the debt being forgiven was already counted as aid. However, everything else being equal, future net ODA flows will be higher, because debt-service payments from MDRI recipients will be lower. This explains the apparent discrepancy between the large numbers recorded as "debt relief" and the much smaller numbers recorded as net ODA.

The Impact of Debt Relief

Debt relief can affect development through several channels. It can (a) alter the debt dynamics and free up domestic resources; (b) eliminate debt overhang, thus enhancing investment and ultimately growth; (c) pave the way for additional borrowing; and (d) improve institutional quality as a result of the conditional policies associated with the HIPC Initiative process.

Growth

Did debt relief boost growth by eliminating the debt overhang? Answering this question is complicated by the fact that many factors affect growth. The period 2002–07 was a period of very rapid global growth and extraordinary movements in the terms of trade. Looking at growth over time by countries receiving debt relief does not give an accurate portrayal of the effect of debt relief on growth, because growth in all three groups of countries—post–completion point countries, interim countries, and non–HIPCs—rose during much of this period (figure 6.4).[9] Average

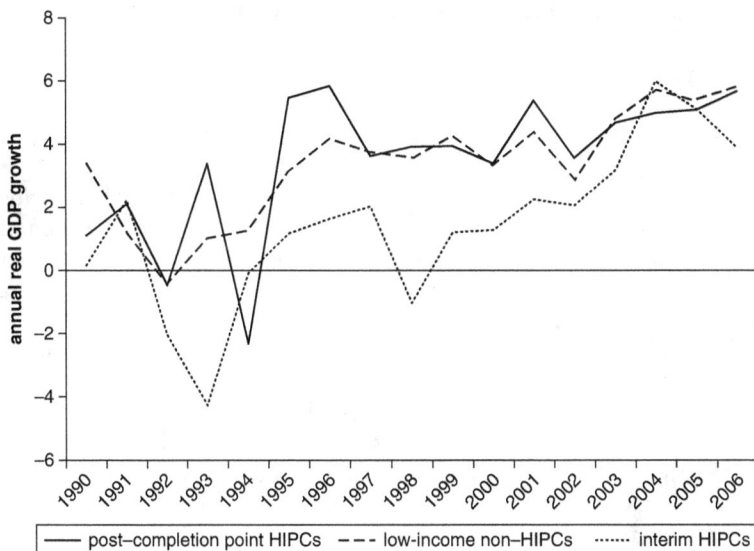

Figure 6.4 Annual Real GDP Growth in Post–Completion Point HIPCs, Interim HIPCs, and Non–HIPCs, 1990–2004

Source: World Bank 2008.

growth in non–HIPCs, however, accelerated most rapidly. There appears to have been little difference between the growth trends in interim and post–completion point countries in recent years.

Several studies look at the effect of debt relief on growth. Chauvin and Kraay (2005) find no significant effect on public spending, investment, or economic growth. Cordella, Ricci, and Ruiz-Aranz (2005) find a negative marginal relationship between debt and growth for countries with an intermediate level of indebtedness, but they do not find a significant effect for countries with a very high level of debt. They conclude that countries with good policies and institutions face a debt overhang when debt rises above 15–30 percent of GDP but that the marginal effect of debt on growth becomes irrelevant above 70–80 percent.

Debt Dynamics

The enhanced HIPC Initiative and particularly the MDRI led to a substantial debt-stock reduction in post–completion point countries. Debt dynamics, however, are driven by more than just the stock of debt. Critical variables include growth, the interest rate on new debt, changes in the real exchange rate over time, the level of the primary surplus, and a variety of contingent liabilities. If fundamentals driving debt are not fixed, then reduced debt levels will not be sustainable and debt will start to rise again.

To understand the contribution of debt relief to improving debt dynamics, we look at detailed budget data for each HIPC. If we assume that all borrowing is external, the fundamental drivers of debt D expressed in local currency can be expressed

$$\dot{D} = iD - PS + C - S + xD, \tag{6.1}$$

which states that the change in net debt is given by the new borrowings needed to fund interest payments on debt (iD, where i is the nominal interest rate on dollar debt) minus the primary surplus (PS) plus any contingent liabilities (C) the government may take on minus seigniorage (S) (interest-free high-powered money creation).[10] The term xD is the capital gain/loss on dollar-denominated debt, where x represents the percentage change in the nominal exchange rate expressed in local currency per dollar, so that smaller (larger) than x connotes a depreciation (appreciation). Contingent liabilities C are typically off-budget items. In some cases, they represent bailouts of the financial system, during which governments step in to protect bank deposits. In other instances, they are payments made by governments to bail out companies that are too big to fail or payments tied to a previously guaranteed level of activity. Private toll roads and utilities are examples of projects on which many developing country governments have had to pay unanticipated amounts to private companies. Corruption, unrecorded expenses, court-ordered judgments, payment of arrears, and other items enter into contingent liabilities. For developed countries, contingent liabilities tend to be very small, particularly when expressed as a percentage of GDP. But for developing countries, especially those with weak budget institutions, contingent liabilities can be very large.

It is convenient to express equation (6.1) in terms of the debt-to-GDP ratio, d, and to recognize the fact that debt for most low-income countries is denominated in foreign currency whereas GDP is in local currency. Thus, when the real exchange rate depreciates, the debt-to-GDP ratio tends to rise. In equation (6.2), r is the real dollar interest rate on debt (i – U.S. inflation); e is the depreciation of the real exchange rate (defined in local currency per dollar so that e larger than (smaller than) 0 means a real depreciation (appreciation); and g is the real growth rate of GDP:

$$\dot{d} = d(r + e - g) - ps + c - s. \tag{6.2}$$

The lower case letters ps, c, and s represent the variables PS, C, and S expressed as percentages of GDP.

Equation (6.2) shows that debt relief can fundamentally change debt dynamics when the sum of the interest rate and the rate of depreciation of the real exchange rate exceeds the growth rate of the economy. Thus, debt relief is particularly useful for slow-growing countries, for countries that face high interest rates, and for countries that face major pressures on their exchange rates because of difficulties in expanding exports and attracting private capital flows.

Equation (6.2) also highlights the role of the primary surplus and contingent liabilities. If significant borrowing is required to fund these items, then the debt ratio will rise even if debt stocks have been reduced to low levels.

There is also concern that countries that have received debt relief will start to borrow on commercial terms, increasing the effective interest rate they pay on debt. Any increase in interest rates would worsen debt dynamics. In order to understand the quantitative dimensions of the variables expressed in equation (6.2), we look at the change in the debt-to-GDP ratio for 41 low-income countries, using the same sample used in the previous section.

Debt relief has indeed had a sizable impact on the debt-to-GDP ratio of both post–completion point and interim countries. Among post–completion point countries, the debt-to-GDP ratio has fallen by very substantial amounts (figure 6.5). The overall decline in the debt ratio is much higher than the decline attributable to debt cancellation, suggesting that these countries would have shown a marked reduction in their debt ratios even in the absence of debt relief (assuming that debt relief does not affect growth).

Figure 6.5 Debt Decomposition in Post–Completion Point
HIPCs, Interim HIPCs, and Non–HIPCs, 1999–2007
(percentage of GDP)

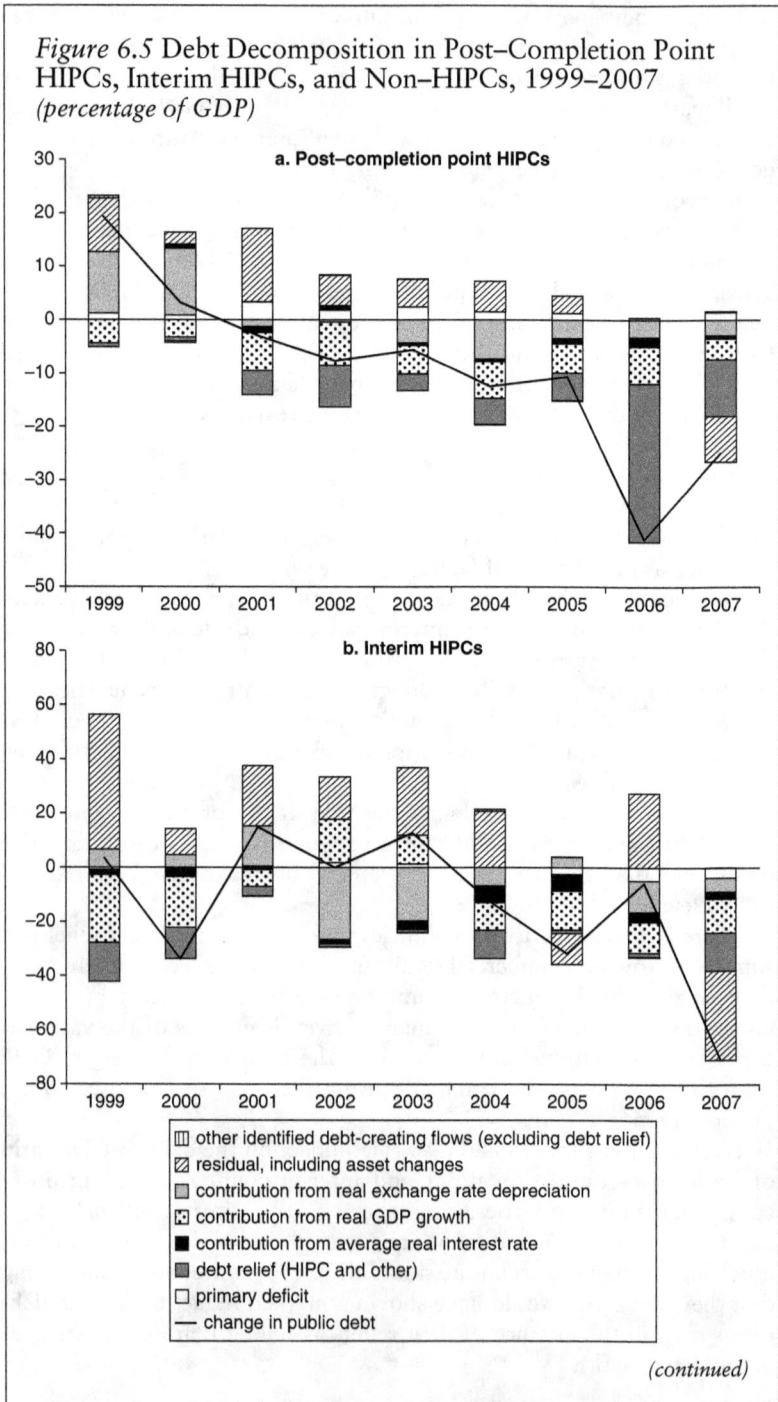

a. Post–completion point HIPCs

b. Interim HIPCs

⊞ other identified debt-creating flows (excluding debt relief)
▨ residual, including asset changes
▨ contribution from real exchange rate depreciation
⊡ contribution from real GDP growth
■ contribution from average real interest rate
▨ debt relief (HIPC and other)
☐ primary deficit
— change in public debt

(continued)

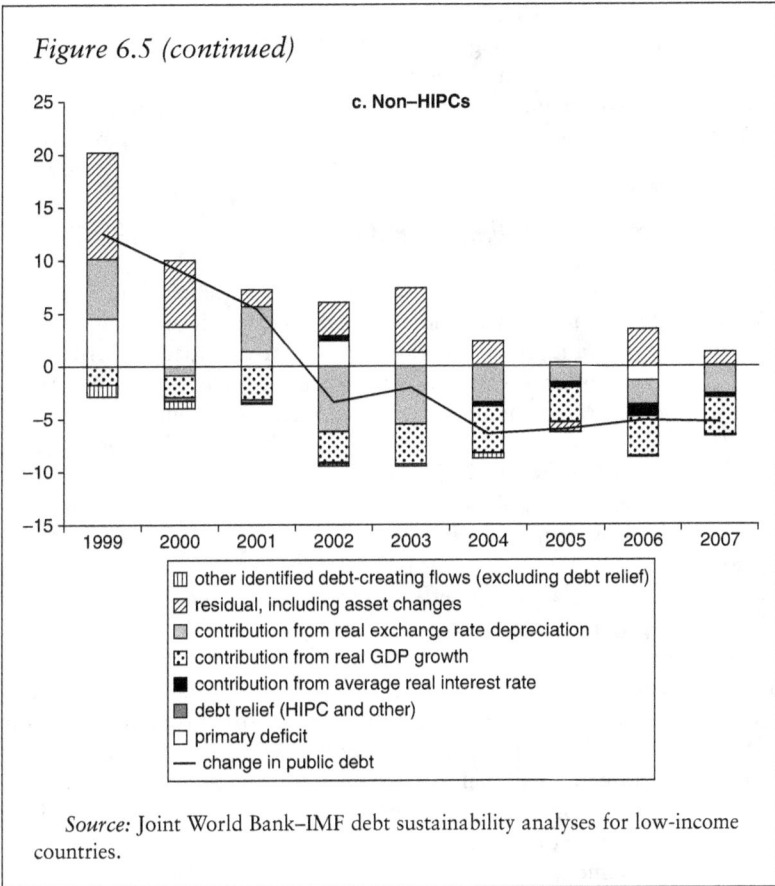

Figure 6.5 (continued)

c. Non–HIPCs

other identified debt-creating flows (excluding debt relief)
residual, including asset changes
contribution from real exchange rate depreciation
contribution from real GDP growth
contribution from average real interest rate
debt relief (HIPC and other)
primary deficit
— change in public debt

Source: Joint World Bank–IMF debt sustainability analyses for low-income countries.

The main additional factors behind the decline in debt in post–completion point countries are higher growth and the real appreciation of the currency, caused in part by strong commodity prices in recent years. These factors reduced the debt-to-GDP ratio by about 10 percentage points each year between 2001 and 2007.

Interim countries show the same pattern. There, too, debt ratios declined dramatically, but debt levels nevertheless remained high, with debt-to-GDP ratios in countries like Guinea and Haiti exceeding 350 percent.[11] The sharp reduction in debt in 2007 is attributable to the clearing of arrears for Liberia. In addition to debt relief, however, growth and the real exchange rate also contributed very significantly to the decline in the debt burden.

In interim countries, large contingent liabilities have been major drivers of debt buildup in the past. These countries often have weak public

management systems, so it is not surprising to see them faced with obligations that do not pass through the budget. Debt relief by itself cannot halt
such claims; improved institutional structures are needed. Non–HIPCs
also experienced declines in their debt ratios during this period: thanks to
growth and real exchange rate appreciation, their average debt-to-GDP
ratio fell to less than 50 percent.

Investment and New Financing Options

According to the debt overhang argument, debt relief should lead to
increased private investment. Some researchers, such as Arslanalp and
Henry (2005), argue, however, that debt relief provided to HIPCs had
little impact on either investment or growth, because the key constraint
to investment in these countries is not tax uncertainty but the absence of
functional economic institutions. As discussed above, there is evidence
that generous ODA helped HIPCs service their external debt. Still, markets may perceive debt relief positively. Raddatz (2009) concludes that the
MDRI had a positive impact on the financial assessment of firms operating
in countries benefiting from debt relief, but he argues that this may have
been caused by exchange rate effects and improved growth prospects for
the firms themselves rather than by debt relief.

Improved macroeconomic performance by some Sub-Saharan African
countries combined with debt relief led to increased interest by foreign
investors: private capital flows to Sub-Saharan Africa rose sharply, from
very low levels in 2002 to up $50 billion in 2007 (IMF 2009). These pri-
vate capital flows are still mainly equity foreign direct investment (FDI) in
the mineral sector, but there is an increase of inflows to other sectors, such
as banking and telecommunications, as well.

The improvement in policies and institutions in HIPCs reinforces the
improvement in creditworthiness brought about by debt relief. Some studies show a direct link between strong policies and a stronger capacity to
carry debt (Kraay and Nehru 2004). In the Debt Sustainability Framework
for Low-Income Countries of the World Bank and the IMF, countries with
better policies are permitted higher indicative debt thresholds.

These two channels of improved creditworthiness—the decrease in
absolute debt levels and the higher debt-carrying capacity associated
with reforms—have led some countries to explore new forms of borrowing, including on commercial terms. Four Sub-Saharan African countries, two of which are HIPCs, have successfully tapped international
capital markets: Ghana issued a $750 million bond in September 2007,
and the Republic of Congo (an interim HIPC) issued a $478 million
bond in December 2007 to replace defaulted London Club debt. Gabon,
which is not a HIPC, issued a $1 billion bond in December 2007 in the
context of debt relief provided by the Paris Club. Other countries plan
to follow.

A better policy environment and a boom in commodity prices have also made Sub-Saharan African countries more attractive to nontraditional creditors. While these creditors offer funds that allow countries to address large investment needs, the terms they offer are often nonconcessional, causing some concern that countries may return to situations of debt distress.

There is some hope that this time around new borrowing will be more beneficial to development than it was in the past. There is already talk that Africa represents a new frontier for financial markets (Nellor 2008). In a comparison between eight African "emerging markets" today and members of the Association of Southeast Asian Nations (ASEAN) in 1980,[12] just before an acceleration of their growth and mobilization of external resources, Nellor (2008) finds that the African economies compare favorably with the ASEAN economies on six of eight categories important to investors (inflation, financial depth, foreign exchange reserves, debt, FDI inflows, and portfolio inflows).[13] What is important for debt dynamics is the use to which the new flows are put.

In past years, several HIPCs have tried to develop local-currency bond markets. Local-currency bonds involve no currency risk for the borrower, improve the flexibility of financing, can be a means of developing local financial markets, and help sterilize aid flows. Domestic debt represented more than 30 percent of GDP in Ethiopia and Sierra Leone and about 20 percent of GDP in Cameroon.

Several African countries with solid growth performance and a benign debt sustainability outlook have succeeded in selling treasury bills in their own currency to foreign investors. Foreign investors have also been attracted by high-yield earning opportunities. For commodity-exporting countries, such as Nigeria and Zambia, rising commodities prices have raised expectation of future currency appreciation. Moreover, the relatively low correlation between African markets and other markets can provide opportunities for reducing portfolio risk and volatility.

Foreigners held about 11 percent of Ghana's domestic currency government debt, estimated at more than $400 million, at the end of June 2007. This share is reportedly even higher in Zambia, and foreigners seem to hold significant shares of domestic currency–denominated government debt in Tanzania and Uganda. All four countries have passed the HIPC completion point.

Overborrowing

Evidence from recent debt sustainability assessments confirms that debt sustainability is a concern in all pre–completion point HIPCs and in more than a third of low-income non–HIPCs (see chapter 5). Despite the significant decline of debt burdens thanks to debt relief, less than half of post–completion point HIPCs had low risk of debt distress in 2008. To prevent low-income countries from overborrowing, major creditors now provide a higher level of grants to countries with an elevated risk of debt distress under the Debt Sustainability Framework for Low-Income Countries. Still, several factors, including changes in the financial environment, have contributed to an increase in the risk of debt distress of completion point HIPCs. There is evidence of deterioration in the distribution of ratings, with the number of countries with high risk ratings increasing from two to four between 2007 and 2008.

Policy and Institutional Improvements

Countries receive debt relief only after developing a track record of a satisfactory reform program. If debt relief is the "sweetener" to encourage significant reform, the benefits from debt relief may be felt in longer-term institutional development and growth.

Among low-income countries, post–completion point countries have the best policies and have seen significant improvements in their policy performance over the past few years (figure 6.6).[14] That progress is consistent with the requirement that they implement satisfactory programs of reform.

Figure 6.6 CPIA Index for Low-Income Countries, 1999–2006

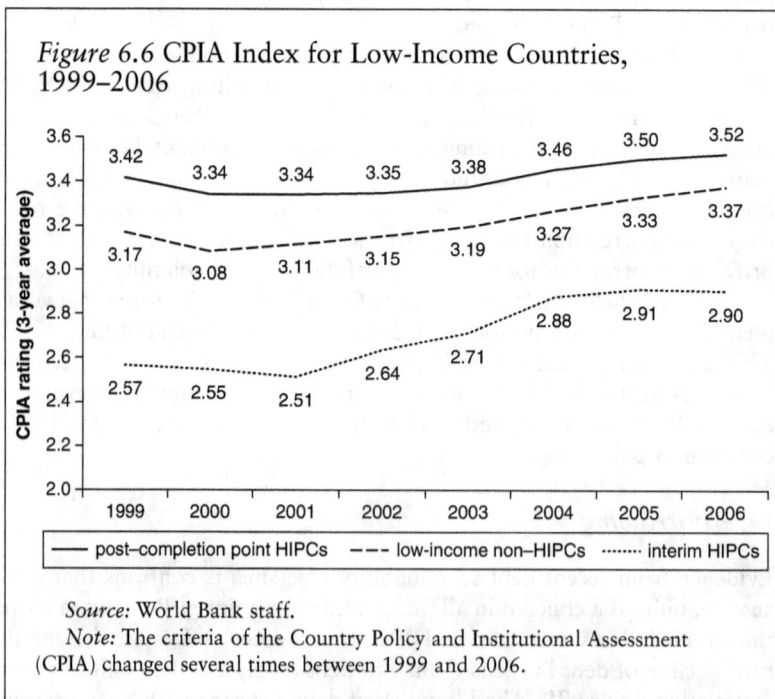

Source: World Bank staff.
Note: The criteria of the Country Policy and Institutional Assessment (CPIA) changed several times between 1999 and 2006.

Interim countries also seem to have improved their policies, albeit in a less smooth fashion. A period of poor policy performance until 2001 gave way to a spate of reforms, but the years between 2004 and 2006 appear to have seen stagnation in policies.

Non–HIPCs also show sustained policy improvement during this period. In fact, the gap between these countries and post–completion point HIPCs has narrowed in recent years.

The link between policy improvement and debt relief is more clearly seen when policies are compared before and after the completion and decision points (figure 6.7). Strong gains in policy performance are evident in the three years before completion point, and the momentum of these reforms seems to carry through to the years after the completion point has been reached.

A similar rate of improvement can be seen for countries after reaching the decision point. In fact, despite the fact that today's interim countries

Figure 6.7 CPIA Index without Debt-Policy Component in HIPCs before and after Completion and Decision Points

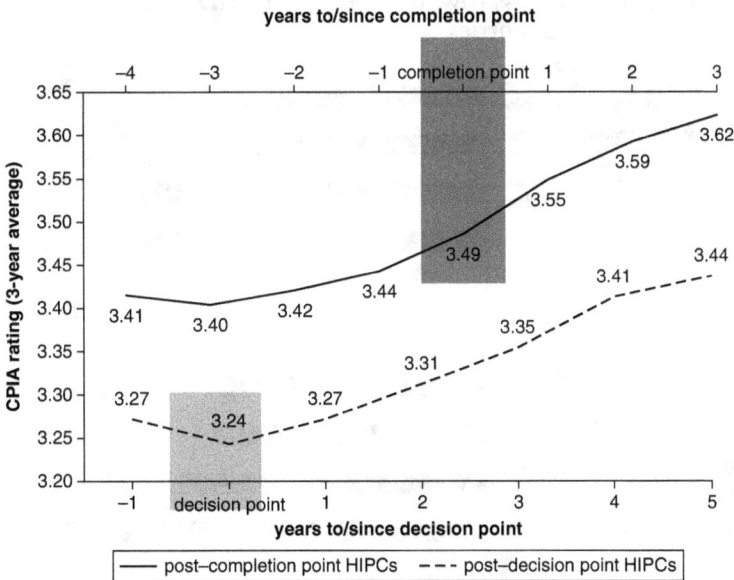

Source: World Bank staff.

Note: The criteria of the Country Policy and Institutional Assessment (CPIA) changed several times between 1999 and 2006.

are those that had some of the worst initial conditions of all HIPCs, they have already reached almost the same level of average policy performance as other HIPCs at their completion point.

Achieving the MDGs

Accelerated resource flows are required to help HIPCs meet the MDGs: both HIPCs and non–HIPCs have a significant distance to go to meet these goals (figure 6.8). Although post–completion point HIPCs have a demonstrated track record of better policy performance, this has yet to show up in better outcomes on MDG–related targets.

In education, health, and sanitation, HIPCs and non–HIPCs alike have achieved less than half the progress necessary to be on track to meeting their targets. It will take much more than finance to achieve these targets, but finance is probably a necessary condition for success. Using the new-found space created by debt relief offers the best hope for rapidly increasing expenditures on MDG–related programs.

Figure 6.8 Progress toward Meeting the MDGs in Low-Income Countries

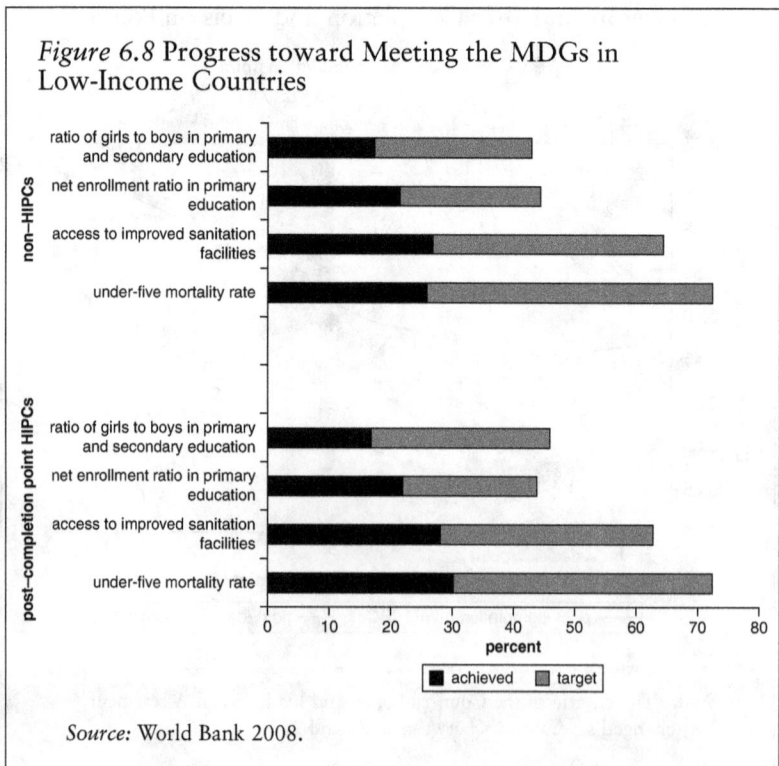

Source: World Bank 2008.

Concluding Remarks

Despite very significant debt relief provided to a set of developing countries through the HIPC Initiative and the MDRI, beneficiary countries have not been able to use the fiscal space afforded to increase their primary deficits. The evidence suggests that net resource transfers to HIPCs and non–HIPCs do not differ markedly. Moreover, as a share of GDP, the size of resource transfers today is at about the same level as in post–completion point HIPCs in the mid-1980s. The hope that debt relief would translate into significantly more resources appears not to have been realized.

Debt relief has had more success in avoiding a collapse of resource transfers to low-income countries. HIPCs that have completed or even initiated reform programs under the debt-relief initiatives have managed to reverse the declining trend in resource transfers.

Debt dynamics have been improved thanks to debt relief and the accompanying improvement in policies. HIPCs are in much stronger positions after passing the completion point, but they still have average debt levels of more than 40 percent of GDP. Moreover, debt dynamics have been improving as a result of other factors, including an environment of better growth, stronger exchange rates (as terms of trade improved), and reduced contingent liabilities in recent years. For interim countries, which still have large debt levels, the shocks to growth, exchange rates, and contingent liabilities could continue to drive debt dynamics even after full debt relief is afforded.

An improved debt sustainability outlook—accompanied by an enhanced security situation, better macroeconomic performance, and high commodity prices—has led to increased interest in Sub-Saharan Africa by foreign investors. Private capital flows have risen sharply since 2002. Although most of these private capital flows are equity FDI in the mineral sectors, several African countries have sold treasury bills in their own currency to foreign investors, and two HIPCs successfully placed international bonds. A better policy environment and the boom in commodity prices have also made Sub-Saharan African countries more attractive to nontraditional creditors. However, in the long run, the financing offered by these creditors might exacerbate debt sustainability, because funding terms are often nonconcessional. Private flows may also be volatile in today's tight credit markets.

Policies and institutions have become stronger in countries that have adopted reform programs—before the decision point, between the decision point and the completion point, and after the completion point. However, non–HIPCs have also improved policy performance, and there is no discernible difference in the rate of improvement in HIPCs and non–HIPCs, making it difficult to attribute the improvements to the HIPC Initiative.

Despite debt relief, the strengthening of institutions, and a relatively benign external environment during the past several years, post–completion point HIPCs are still far away from reaching the MDGs. Fiscal space seems not to have increased as a result of debt relief, although improvements in the debt sustainability outlook have contributed to increased interest by foreign investors, opening up new financing opportunities. Still, the debt sustainability outlook is highly sensitive to the terms of new financing, and the number of post–completion point countries with a high risk of debt distress is increasing. Improvement in the policy and institutional environment in these countries offers hope that resources will be used more effectively in the future than they have been in the past.

Notes

The authors are extremely grateful to Brian Pinto and Mona Prasad for invaluable comments. They would also like to thank Juan Pedro Schmid for providing useful data and relevant insights and Emeka Osakwe for conducting research assistance.

1. DAC counts only debt relief on nonconcessional debt as net ODA. Gross debt relief to Sub-Saharan Africa, including concessional aid, totaled $56 billion in 2006 (OECD 2008).

2. This does not necessarily apply to countries that are in arrears before debt relief, because their debt service may actually increase as arrears are rescheduled in the context of debt relief. Still, arrears clearance is generally an important step for accessing new finance that can lead to an increase in net transfers for a given country.

3. Several studies fail to find any tax reduction in HIPCs in Africa (see Cassimon and Van Compenhout 2006; Gupta, Powell, and Yang 2006; Kpodar and Unigovskaya 2008), although in at least one case, debt relief has been used to reduce domestic debt.

4. Because HIPC debt relief is linked to poverty-reducing expenditures, it would simply replace one form of expenditure (debt service) with another (poverty-reducing expenditures), leaving the overall budget deficit unchanged (see Burnside and Fanizza 2005).

5. *Overborrowing* is used here to mean borrowing more than the optimal level given the availability of high-return investment opportunities. The practical identification of overborrowing is fraught with difficulty.

6. See http://web.worldbank.org/WBSITE/EXTERNAL/TOPICS/EXTDEBT DEPT/0,,contentMDK:20701723~menuPK:64166739~pagePK:64166689~piPK: 64166646~theSitePK:469043,00.html.

7. Traditional debt relief generally allowed for a debt reduction of up to 67 percent in net present value terms.

8. To be eligible for debt relief under the HIPC Initiative, a country must satisfy the following criteria: (a) GDP per capita below $965 and to be IDA-only and PRGF eligible, (b) a net present value of debt-to-exports ratio after traditional debt relief beyond 150 percent, and (c) a track record of reform and sound policies through IMF- and IDA-supported programs.

9. The sample consists of 41 countries: 21 post–completion point countries, 9 interim countries, and 11 non–HIPCs. It covers countries for which there are adequate fiscal data on which to decompose debt.

10. In debt accounting, the primary surplus includes grants as revenues.

11. The implication of such numbers is that these countries have debt levels equal to the approximate total value of their capital stock.

12. The eight countries—Botswana, Ghana, Kenya, Mozambique, Nigeria, Tanzania, Uganda, and Zambia—account for 40 percent of the GDP of Sub-Saharan Africa excluding South Africa.

13. Of course, a comparison with ASEAN does not imply that debt distress will be avoided: several ASEAN countries suffered from major debt problems in 1997–98.

14. There is a minor bias in these figures, because debt sustainability is itself a component of the policy and institutional index, and debt sustainability automatically improves once debt relief has been granted. This effect is small, however, and does not materially affect the trends reported.

References

Arslanalp, S., and P. Blair Henry. 2005. "Is Debt Relief Efficient?" *Journal of Finance* 60 (2): 1017–51.

———. 2006. "Policy Watch: Debt Relief." *Journal of Economic Perspectives* 60 (1): 207–20.

Burnside, Craig, and Domenico Fanizza. 2005. "Hiccups for HIPCs? Implications of Debt Relief for Fiscal Sustainability and Monetary Policy." *Contributions to Macroeconomics* 5 (1): 1133.

Cassimon, D., and B. Van Campenhout. 2006. "Aid Effectiveness, Debt Relief and Public Finance Response: Evidence from a Panel of HIPC Countries." IOB–UA Working Paper 2006.02, Institute of Development Policy and Management, University of Antwerp, the Netherlands.

Chauvin, N. D., and A. Kraay. 2005. "What Has 100 Billion Dollars Worth of Debt Relief Done for Low-Income Countries?" *International Finance (Econ-WPA)* 0510001.

Cohen, D., and J. Sachs. 1986. "Growth and External Debt under Risk of Debt Repudiation." *European Economic Review* 30 (3): 529–60.

Cordella, Tito, L. Ricci, and M. Ruiz-Arranz. 2005. "Debt Overhang or Debt Irrelevance? Revisiting the Debt-Growth Link." IMF Working Paper 05/223, International Monetary Fund, Washington, DC.

Crespo Cuaresma, J., and G. Vincelette. 2008. "Debt Relief and Education in HIPCs." University of Innsbruck, Department of Economics, and World Bank, Economic Policy and Debt Department.

Dessy, Sylvain, and D. Vencatachellum. 2007. "Debt Relief and Social Services Expenditure: The African Experience 1989–2003." *African Development Review* 19 (1): 200–16.

Gupta, S., R. Powell, and Y. Yang. 2006. "Macroeconomic Challenges of Scaling Up Aid: A Checklist for Practitioners." IMF Working Paper 05/179, International Monetary Fund, Washington, DC.

IDA (International Development Association) and IMF (International Monetary Fund). 1999. "Modifications to the Heavily Indebted Poor Countries (HIPC) Initiative." IDA/SecM99-187/1, July 23, Washington, DC.

———. 2008. "Heavily Indebted Poor Countries (HIPC) Initiative and Multilateral Debt Relief Initiative (MDRI): Status of Implementation." IDA/Sec M2008-0561, August 25, Washington, DC.

International Conference on Financing for Development. 2002. "Resolutions of Heads of State and Government." Monterrey, Mexico, March 18–22.

IMF (International Monetary Fund). 2009. Regional Economic Outlook: Sub-Saharan Africa. April. Washington, DC.

Kpodar, E., and A. Unigovskaya. 2008. "Does Debt Relief under the HIPC Initiative Undermine Domestic Revenue Mobilization Effort?"

Kraay, A., and N. Vikram. 2004. "When Is External Debt Sustainable?" Policy Research Working Paper 3200, World Bank, Washington, DC.

Krugman, P. 1988. "Financing versus Forgiving a Debt Overhang." *Journal of Development Economics* 29 (3): 253–68.

MDG Africa Steering Group. 2008. *Achieving the Millennium Development Goals in Africa: Recommendations of the MDG Africa Steering Group.* June, http://www.mdgafrica.org/.

Nellor, D. 2008. "The Rise of Africa's 'Frontier' Markets." *Finance and Development* 45 (3).

OECD (Organisation for Economic Co-Operation and Development). 2008. *International Development Statistics.* Paris: OECD.

Raddatz, C. 2009. "Multilateral Debt Relief through the Eyes of Financial Markets." Policy Research Working Paper 4872, World Bank, Washington, DC.

United Nations. 2002. *Report of the International Conference on Financing for Development, Monterrey, Mexico.* New York: United Nations.

World Bank. 2008. *Global Monitoring Report 2008.* Washington, DC: World Bank.

———. *World Development Indicators.* 2008. Washington, DC: World Bank.

7

Sovereign Default Risk and Private Sector Access to Capital in Emerging Markets

Udaibir S. Das, Michael G. Papaioannou, and Christoph Trebesch

Corporations in emerging markets have gained unprecedented access to international capital markets in recent years (figure 7A.1 in the annex to this chapter). Many reasons have been cited for the strong rise in corporate external financing volumes in developing countries (see World Bank 2007 for a detailed discussion). One of the most prominent explanations is that sovereign risk has been very low over the past few years, as many emerging market countries made significant progress in reducing the vulnerability of their public sector balance sheets. It is widely believed that sovereign risk plays a crucial role in international capital flows and cross-border flows to individual firms (see, for example, Reinhart and Rogoff 2004). Despite this supposition, there is still little systematic evidence on the role of sovereign risk in capital flows to private corporations in developing countries.

This chapter analyzes how sovereign default risk affects private sector access to international capital markets, in the form of external credit (loans and bond issuances) and equity issuances.[1] As a first step, it extends the existing research on the effect of sovereign debt crises on corporate external credit for the period 1980–2004. As a second step, it broadens the analysis by investigating the role of additional measures of sovereign default risk (sovereign bond spreads and sovereign ratings) using a shorter sample for a more recent period (1993–2007). The results provide new insights into corporate access to capital in emerging markets during crisis periods, sovereign risk spillovers to the private sector, and the broad domestic costs of sovereign default.

Among the innovations of this chapter is its focus on emerging market corporate access to external capital markets. Only a few studies explicitly investigate emerging market countries' corporate access to foreign capital, and even fewer have focused on the link between sovereign risk and private sector external capital.[2] The growing importance of corporate external financing for emerging market and developing countries calls for more systematic analysis.

This chapter draws on extensive new data sets to analyze the link between sovereign risk and private sector access to capital markets. The dependent variables are constructed from firm-level data on corporate external loans, external bond issues, and equity issues from the Dealogic database. The advantage of this approach is that it avoids some potential biases of capital flow data on the aggregate country level and allows identification of capital flows to private corporations only (the data set distinguishes between private and publicly owned firms). In addition to unique firm-level data, the analysis also takes advantage of a new, comprehensive data set on sovereign debt crises and associated debt-renegotiation processes of the past three decades. This database was built by systematically evaluating more than 20,000 pages of case study material on crisis cases, as well as all standard reference books and other data sources (Enderlein, Müller, and Trebesch 2008; Trebesch 2009).

For the period 1980–2004, the results indicate that sovereign defaults to private creditors cause a drop in private sector external borrowing of more than 40 percent, an effect that lasts for one year after the crisis ends. This result offers a new insight, as existing studies find a strong adverse impact only for defaults to Paris Club creditors. This research also finds that delays in debt negotiations have adverse effects for private sector credit, whereas International Monetary Fund (IMF) programs have positive effects. Interestingly, delays caused by intercreditor disputes and litigation have no significant negative spillovers. Apparently, government behavior in distress situations has more important consequences for the domestic economy than does creditor behavior.

The results for the more recent period of 1993–2007 confirm the crucial role of sovereign risk for private sector access to capital.[3] This part of the study assesses the role of sovereign default risk in a broader sense, that is, beyond the effect of defaults and debt restructurings. The analysis also extends the coverage of corporate access to capital to include equity issues, given that equity capital has become an increasingly important alternative source of financing for emerging market firms since the early 1990s. Specifically, we find that higher sovereign bond spreads (taken from J.P. Morgan's Emerging Markets Bond Index [EMBI] Global) and lower sovereign ratings (taken from Standard & Poor's [S&P] and *Institutional Investor* magazine) have a strong negative effect on the volume of corporate credit or equity issued. At the same time, we find little evidence of the co-movement of public and private access to capital. In particular, the volume of government debt issued is only weakly related to the volume of private debt issued, both in normal times and during crisis episodes.

This chapter is organized as follows. The next section reviews the literature and provides a motivation for the need for more systematic research on the effects of sovereign risk and default on capital flows and private sector access to credit. The second section outlines the econometric methodology. The third section describes the analytical framework and presents the main results on the effects of sovereign defaults and crisis characteristics on private sector access to credit. The fourth section analyzes the effects of sovereign risk (spreads and ratings) on corporate capital access. The last section provides some concluding remarks.

Related Literature

This section reviews the related literature. First, it presents the general literature on capital flows of and access to financial markets by developing and emerging market countries. Then, it looks at studies analyzing the role of sovereign risk and ratings in capital flows in general and corporate access to credit in particular. Next, it summarizes the literature on the cost and consequences of sovereign default for the domestic economy, focusing on capital flows and financial market access.

Access to Capital in Emerging Markets

A large body of literature examines the determinants of capital flows to emerging markets (see Jeanneau and Micu 2002 and Bloningen 2005 for reviews). Studies such as Taylor and Sarno (1997), Montiel and Reinhart (1999), and Mody, Taylor, and Kim (2001) analyze capital flows in terms of "push and pull" factors. They find that both global trends in capital flows (push factors) and country-specific characteristics that reflect domestic fundamentals and investment opportunities (pull factors) are important determinants of portfolio, debt, and foreign direct investment (FDI) flows.

Increasing attention has been devoted to the role of political risk and institutions in recent years.[4] Alfaro, Kalemli-Ozcan, and Volosovych (2008) present evidence that low-quality institutions are the main impediment to cross-border capital flows in the form of FDI and portfolio investments. They underline the relevance of their findings in solving the "Lucas paradox" of limited capital flows to the developing world.[5] A number of related studies confirm the important role of politics and institutions for capital flows. Busse and Hefeker (2007) find that political risk and institutional quality, as measured by the *International Country Risk Guide* (*ICRG*) risk indicators, are crucial for FDI flows. Government stability as well as law and order seem to exert a particularly strong impact on the investment decisions of multinationals. Using the World Bank's Governance Indicators, Daude and Stein (2007) find that government instability and poor-quality laws, regulations, and policies, especially those imposing an excessive regulatory burden, are major deterrents to FDI. Papaioannou (2005) finds that the *ICRG* political risk index can explain much (more than half) of the variability in gross bilateral bank flows.

Most of these studies employ aggregate capital flow or stock data from the World Bank's Global Development Finance database, the IMF's *International Financial Statistics*, data from the Bank of International Settlement, or data from Lane and Milesi-Ferretti (2001). To date, however, few studies have differentiated between capital flows to private corporations and flows to governments or public companies.[6] Among the few studies that specifically analyze corporate capital market access in emerging markets are Eichengreen and Mody (2000) and World Bank (2007). Both studies estimate determinants of primary bond market credit spreads (issuance coupons) for corporate or sovereign borrowers using bond-by-bond and loan-by-loan data, respectively. They find that firm-level variables, as well as standard financial and macroeconomic variables, determine the level of corporate spreads.

Fostel and Kaminsky (2007) also use firm-level issuance data. They analyze access to capital in emerging markets in a manner similar to that used in this chapter, using aggregate firm-level data of debt and equity issuances from the Dealogic database. However, they aggregate total volumes (that is, sovereign, public, and corporate issues) and focus exclusively on six Latin American countries. Their results indicate that sound fundamentals do matter for capital market access in Latin America, but they attribute the rise in inflows since 2003 mainly to record increases in global liquidity.

Impact of Sovereign Risk and Ratings

Only a small body of literature examines the impact of sovereign risk on capital flows and corporate financial market access. Taking a broad historical perspective, Reinhart, Rogoff, and Savastano (2003) highlight the crucial role of sovereign risk for cross-border external capital. They show that countries usually lose all access to private capital markets when sovereign ratings fall below a critical threshold. In contrast, countries with very high ratings tend to have continuous access to capital, even during recessions and crisis periods. For the in-between group of countries—that is, middle-income emerging markets—access to capital is volatile and depends on various external and internal factors. In bad times, with ratings falling and fundamentals deteriorating, these countries face the risk of rapidly rising interest rates and a sudden loss of access to market financing.[7] The authors conclude that countries with weak political and institutional systems and a history of sovereign defaults are able to "tolerate" only very low levels of external indebtedness.

Reinhart and Rogoff (2004) expand the argument, emphasizing the link between historical defaults and today's sovereign risk levels. They list a number of stylized facts to argue that sovereign risk and capital market imperfections should be seen as the main reason for the Lucas paradox.

Kaminsky and Schmukler (2002) find that sovereign rating changes have a strong effect on both bond and stock markets in emerging markets. They show that a downgrade in ratings leads to an increase in bond market spreads of 2 percentage points and to a drop in stock market returns of 1 percentage point. Other studies find that sovereign risk has little impact. Alfaro, Kalemli-Ozcan, and Volosovych (2008), for example, find that sovereign risk, as measured by average ratings, is not a significant determinant of capital flows in a cross-sectional framework.[8]

In a similar vein, Kim and Wu (2008) analyze whether countries benefit when rating agencies assign credit ratings to the sovereign. They find that the provision of foreign currency long-term ratings by Standard & Poor's is associated with both financial development and cross-border capital flows. Ratha, De, and Mohapatra (2007, p. 3) confirm these findings, arguing that "having no rating . . . may have worse consequences than having a low rating." They conclude that sovereign risk ratings affect not only investment decisions in the international bond and loan markets but also the allocation of FDI and portfolio equity flows. Albuquerque (2003) tests the relationship between sovereign ratings and external capital flows more systematically. He finds ratings to matter substantially for the overall composition of country capital flows. Apparently, countries with lower ratings and higher political risk tend to have larger shares of FDI in total capital inflows. Albuquerque's findings are in line with those of Daude and Fratzscher (2008), who conclude that portfolio investments react more sensibly to changes in political risk than do FDI or debt flows.

The specific link between sovereign risk and corporate access to capital remains largely unexplored. Eichengreen and Mody (2000) and World Bank (2007) find that sovereign risk ratings do affect the size of corporate spreads and the likelihood of bond issuances. Hale (2007) concludes that sovereign risk can have an important impact on corporate financing choices between syndicated loans and bonds in emerging markets. Cruces (2007) finds sizable sovereign risk–related equity premia in stock markets of developing countries. According to him, corporations in countries with credit ratings in the default range have to pay much higher expected rates of return than companies based in nondefault countries. Borenzstein, Cowan, and Valenzuela (2007) indicate that sovereign risk can have a strong impact on corporate access to capital through the ratings channel. In particular, they find sovereign ratings to be the predominant explanatory factor for corporate ratings in a small set of emerging-market economies.

Implications of Sovereign Defaults

As sovereign risk reaches peak levels during episodes of sovereign default, it is reasonable to expect "top-down" risk spillovers to be particularly strong during and after default episodes. A relatively small body of empirical literature on the domestic cost of sovereign defaults indicates that this may be the case (see the comprehensive survey by Panizza, Sturzenegger, and Zettelmeyer forthcoming). For the recent crises in Argentina and Uruguay, Levy-Yeyati, Martinez Peria, and Schmukler (2004) find that sovereign distress affects the behavior of depositors and may thus contribute to bank runs. Along similar lines, Borenzstein and Panizza (2008) provide evidence that debt crises may trigger systemic banking crises.[9]

With regard to aggregate capital flows, Fuentes and Saravia (2006) find that FDI falls during and after sovereign defaults, especially from creditor countries that are "hurt" by the default. Levy-Yeyati (2006) and Panizza, Sturzenegger, and Zettelmeyer (forthcoming) provide evidence that private debt flows to developing countries tend to be procyclical, with strong outflows of loan and bond debt during and after debt-crisis episodes. Related to this, Richmond and Dias (2008) analyze the duration of capital market exclusion after sovereign defaults. They find that, on average, countries regain partial access to bond and bank transfers from private creditors after about five years. Both global liquidity and country characteristics, such as the sovereign risk rating and the budgetary balance, matter for the speed of renewed access.[10] They also find that, on average, larger economies regain market access twice as quickly as small countries.

To the best of our knowledge, only one study—Arteta and Hale (2008)—analyzes the specific effect of defaults on domestic corporations and their access to finance. (For related theoretical papers, see Sandleris 2008 and Mendoza and Yue 2008.) The authors use aggregate firm-level data on loan and bond issues from Dealogic as the dependent variable to assess the impact of default on corporate external borrowing. They find that sovereign debt crises and restructurings have a strong negative impact. After controlling for fundamentals and common shocks, they find the drop in foreign loans and bond issuance by domestic firms amounts to more than 20 percent during defaults. They find the decline in credit to be much more pronounced in defaults with official creditors; the effect of defaults to private creditors is small.

Analytical Framework

This study uses data from 31 major emerging-market economies to assess the effect of sovereign risk on the amount of capital issued by corporations (table 7A.1 in the annex to this chapter). The analysis consists of two main parts. In the first part, presented in the next section, we proxy sovereign risk by the occurrence of sovereign debt crises and analyze how sovereign defaults to private creditors affect private sector external credit. This part of the analysis builds on the econometric approach of Arteta and Hale (2008). It expands their data set, enabling us to test the robustness of some of their results and gain additional insights into the effects of debt-crisis resolutions.

In the second part, presented in the following section, we depart from a mere analysis of debt-crisis effects and focus on the more recent period of 1993–2007. In this part, sovereign risk is proxied by the level of sovereign bond spreads and by sovereign rating changes.

Formally, we estimate the effect of sovereign default risk on corporate access to capital based on the following reduced-form equation:

$$C_{it} = \alpha_i + \alpha_t + \beta_1 SOV\_RISK_{it} + X'_{it}\gamma + u_{it} \tag{7.1}$$

where C_{it} is a measure of capital to private corporations; α_i and α_t are country and year fixed effects, respectively; SOV_RISK is a measure of sovereign risk, which can be either ratings, spreads, or debt-crisis episodes; X'_{it} is a large set of control variables; and u_{it} are robust errors clustered by country.

The main dependent variable used is the volume of foreign bonds and syndicated loans issued by private domestic corporations by country and time period (month or quarter).[11] This variable is constructed by aggregating firm-level data on new debt issuances from the Dealogic database. Specifically, we retrieve all foreign corporate bond issues and foreign corporate syndicated loan contracts for 31 emerging-market economies for the period January 1980–December 2007. Later in the chapter, we employ an additional dependent variable that captures the volume of equity securities issued by domestic corporations by country and quarter, again aggregating firm-level data from Dealogic.[12] Because of our focus on access to capital of private domestic corporations, we exclude government firms and firms owned by foreign companies or multinationals from our sample.

For the selection of emerging-market countries, we follow Arteta and Hale (2008) and exclude countries that had only very limited access to foreign capital during the sample period.[13] The set of main explanatory variables, as well as the large set of economic control variables that might influence the supply and demand for credit and equity, is explained in detail in the next two sections.

Sovereign Debt Crises and Corporate Access to Credit

We first analyze the effect of emerging-market debt crises on the volume of corporate external credit during 1980–2004. We provide novel evidence on the issue using an updated data set on debt-crisis duration and crisis-related events from Trebesch (2008a, 2009).

Measuring Debt Crises and Crisis-Resolution Processes

The key explanatory variables in this type of analysis are time dummies on the occurrence of a debt crisis or a restructuring. For this reason, the definition of sovereign defaults and related events becomes crucial. In contrast to Arteta and Hale (2008), we focus on episodes of sovereign defaults to private creditors only; defaults and restructurings with official (bilateral or multilateral) creditors are controlled for only to check robustness. In line with other empirical studies (for example, Reinhart, Rogoff, and Savastano 2003; Tomz and Wright 2007; Panizza, Sturzenegger, and Zettelmeyer forthcoming) we also choose a narrower definition of debt crises than Arteta and Hale (2008). In particular, voluntary debt exchanges and swaps, which are part of routine liability management operations and do not involve a debt reduction (Medeiros, Polan, and Ramlogan 2007), are not regarded as relevant restructuring events.[14] We use revised data on the timing of restructuring agreements with private creditors.[15]

Another main difference between our work and that of Arteta and Hale (2008) is that they code the start of negotiations as the key event in capturing the start of debt-crisis episodes; periods of outright default without negotiations (for example, unilateral moratoria) are not measured explicitly. We code not only negotiation periods but also crisis periods that are not accompanied by negotiations, such as instances in which governments refuse to talk to creditors.[16] Accordingly, the start of debt distress is defined here as either the month of first missed payments beyond the grace period (the start of de facto default) or the beginning of debt talks and restructuring negotiations. The debt crisis ends with the successful closing of a debt-restructuring agreement. To assess the effect over the medium term, we include lags of up to three years of a debt-crisis dummy in the estimations. The three lag variables capture potential postcrisis effects for the period of 1–12 months, 13–24 months, and 25–36 months after the agreement.

In addition, we use new measures on debt-crisis characteristics as key explanatory variables, because we are particularly interested in the effects of delays and breakdowns in debt negotiations, as well as the occurrence of creditor coordination problems and litigation (for example, by vulture funds). Our focus on these issues stems from the extensive policy discussion on a standardized sovereign debt–restructuring mechanism and other mechanisms to improve debt crisis–resolution procedures (Krueger 2002; IMF 2003). One key claim in this debate was that delays in debt renegotiations, particularly delays induced by creditor coordination problems and creditor litigation, may lead to inefficient delays in debt restructurings and result in costly spillovers for the domestic economy. Very little evidence exists to analyze whether this is true. Here, we use three new variables to assess the relative role of government-induced crisis-resolution problems and creditor-induced delays, which could be caused by intercreditor disputes, holdout creditors, or litigation. These variables draw mainly on Trebesch (2008, 2009) and partly on Enderlein, Müller, and Trebesch (2008), who compile an archive on past debt-crisis cases and restructurings utilizing extensive case study material.

The three additional variables measure the following phenomena:

- The first additional variable measures negotiation delays stemming from political events. The used time dummy takes the value of 1 when unilateral government behavior leads to a delay or even breakdown in debt negotiations of more than three months in any given year. Instances in which governments explicitly refuse to initiate negotiations are also coded as delays.[17]
- The second variable captures cases of prerestructuring litigation toward debtor countries, which has been a frequent reason for delays in past crises. Episodes of litigation events take the value of 1 whenever we could identify that creditors had filed suit against a foreign sovereign and it was reported as an obstacle in the negotiations.
- The third variable captures episodes of creditor holdouts and intercreditor disputes. The dummy takes the value of 1 when disputes and coordination problems within the group of creditors led to negotiation delays of more than three months. Such creditor-induced delays are observed when holdout creditors reject a majority agreement. We also include an annual dummy for IMF programs that were in effect for more than five months in any given year. (The data on IMF standby agreements are from Dreher 2006).

Controlling for Fundamentals and Common Shocks

Some discussion of the control variables is necessary before turning to the results. To identify the true effect of debt crises on private sector credit and to avoid omitted-variable bias, it is necessary to control for a large set of economic and financial factors that might affect both the supply of and the demand for credit. We choose a set of control variables similar to that used by Arteta and Hale (2008).[18] The set of explanatory variables is constructed through principal component analysis, thus summarizing a large set of mutually correlated variables, with the additional benefit of bridging data gaps in some of the series. All original series are taken as monthly percentage deviations from their 25-year country-specific averages.[19] The resulting composite indexes can be grouped into five broad categories: an international competitiveness index, an investment climate and monetary stability index, a financial development index, a long-run macroeconomic prospects index, and an index on the global supply of capital. (A detailed overview of the variables and data sources is presented in the annex.) The indices of international competitiveness and long-run macroeconomic prospects may be viewed as proxies for a government's ability to pay. The index on investment climate and monetary stability and that on financial development proxy the corporate sector's financial and economic situation.

We explicitly control for currency and banking crises to account for common shocks. Currency crisis episodes are taken from Arteta and Hale (2007); data on systemic banking crises are from Laeven and Valencia (2008). In addition, to capture disruptions due to natural disasters, we use data on natural disasters from the International Emergency Disasters Database. In particular, we employ a dummy that takes the value of 1 whenever a government declared a state of emergency as the result of earthquakes, floods, storms, fires, or volcano outbreaks.[20] We also explicitly control for sudden stops in capital flows, as shown in the robustness analysis.

Finally, we include the real exchange rate, to account for possible currency mismatch effects on firms' balance sheets. A currency depreciation (that is, an increase in the real exchange rate) could lead to a drop in the demand for foreign credit, particularly when most of firms' revenues are denominated in domestic currency. With a weaker domestic currency, they would also need less "hard currency" credit to cover the same amounts of investments and expenses in domestic currency (see Arteta and Hale 2008 for a related, more detailed discussion).

Discussion of Results

This section presents the main results on the impact of debt crises on private sector external credit (table 7.1). Although the adjusted R^2 appears to be low, it tends to increase significantly (to 0.20–0.30) when the dependent variable is expressed in log form rather than as monthly percentage deviations from its 25-year average.[21] We therefore conclude that the low R^2 is not a major source of concern for the validity of our findings; for illustrative purposes, we prefer to show results as they are.[22] With this in mind, we find a strong negative effect of sovereign defaults on the volume of corporate borrowing. Even after controlling for a large set of fundamentals, we find that sovereign defaults to private external banks or bondholders lead to a drop in private sector credit by more than 40 percent, an effect that persists for one year after the crisis ends.

The strong adverse effect of defaults to commercial creditors is a novel insight on the domestic costs of default. It contrasts with the result of Arteta and Hale (2008), who find a strong adverse impact only for restructurings with Paris Club creditors. The impact coefficients for the variables capturing default episodes and restructuring agreements are also much larger than those in Arteta and Hale (2008), even though we employ a virtually identical set of explanatory variables.

Table 7.1 Sovereign Defaults and Private Sector External Borrowing (Entire Sample)

Variable	(1)	(2)	(3)	(4)
Default episode (private creditor)	−56.51** (21.12)	−46.69** (19.69)	−44.87* (22.53)	−38.72* (22.01)
Month of restructuring (private creditors)	−60.46*** (17.33)	−53.18** (20.60)	−52.04** (22.38)	−46.68** (22.01)
Default episode (official creditor)				−19.71 (13.79)
Month of restructuring (official creditors)				−21.76* (10.79)
Lag 1 (first year after agreement)	−64.31*** (23.03)	−68.93** (26.34)	−69.53** (28.70)	−69.39** (28.43)
Lag 2 (second year after agreement)	−31.13* (18.05)	−30.52 (27.97)	−32.95 (29.06)	−32.68 (28.77)
Index 1.1		−3.73 (3.47)	−2.20 (3.39)	−2.34 (3.44)
Index 1.2		−5.90** (2.20)	−5.05** (2.31)	−5.07** (2.28)
Index 2.1		−2.80 (8.72)	−3.07 (8.24)	−3.29 (8.20)
Index 2.2		7.77 (5.18)	3.16 (4.90)	2.29 (4.87)
Index 2.3		2.30 (5.84)	2.06 (6.36)	1.67 (6.46)
Index 3.1		15.81** (6.27)	16.32** (6.04)	15.99** (6.01)
Index 4.1		9.51*** (3.07)	8.04** (2.97)	8.14** (2.97)
Index 4.2		4.83 (4.91)	3.08 (4.55)	3.43 (4.58)
Index 6.1		−61.70*** (16.84)	−77.53*** (19.84)	−77.18*** (19.80)
Index 6.2		42.00*** (11.69)	54.59*** (14.15)	54.46*** (14.13)
Real exchange rate			−0.02*** (0.00)	−0.02*** (0.00)
Banking crisis			−24.08 (14.31)	−25.02* (14.17)

(continued)

Table 7.1 (continued)

Variable	(1)	(2)	(3)	(4)
Natural disasters			−14.41	−14.96
(dummy)			(15.22)	(14.65)
Currency crisis			−47.31***	−46.25***
			(13.49)	(13.48)
Constant	−59.57***	147.72**	199.69***	199.55***
	(20.12)	(58.43)	(69.01)	(68.75)
Number of observations	8,975	7,193	6,716	6,716
Adjusted R^2	0.042	0.051	0.054	0.054

Source: Authors' computations.

Note: The dependent variable is the total amount borrowed (corporate bonds and loans) as a percentage deviation from the mean. Robust standard errors clustered on country are in parentheses. The regressions include year and country fixed effects and dummies for issuances by mining and chemical industries.

*** Significant at the 1 percent level; ** significant at the 5 percent level; * significant at the 10 percent level.

To verify our results and assess the relative role of sovereign defaults to private versus official creditors, we also control for periods of Paris Club defaults and for agreements with official creditors. Hence, we add a dummy for debt renegotiation periods and a dummy for restructuring agreements with official creditors, relying on the original data by Arteta and Hale (2008). Defaults to private creditors appear to have a stronger effect than those to official creditors (column 4 of table 7.1). The commercial default and restructuring dummies have much higher negative coefficients than those of Paris Club defaults, yet another difference between our results and those of Arteta and Hale (2008).

Our results also provide new insights into crisis dynamics and the role of policy in crisis resolution. For the subsample of default episodes, we find that successful IMF programs (in particular, stand-by agreements) have a positive effect on private sector credit (table 7.2, column 2). This finding is in line with the literature on the catalytic role of IMF financing (see, for example, Bordo, Mody, and Nienke 2004; Mody and Saravia 2006) and provides some indication of the potential benefits of crisis-prone countries' cooperation with the IMF. Along similar lines, we find that breakdowns in debt renegotiations and outright refusals to negotiate with creditors have an additional negative effect on corporate borrowing, although the coefficient is only weakly significant (column 1). Overall, we find some evidence that defaults and the government's negotiation stance during default matter for private sector access to credit.

Table 7.2 Role of Debt-Crisis Characteristics (Subsample of Default Episodes)

Variable	(1)	(2)	(3)	(4)
Breakdown or refusal of negotiations	−22.24* (10.57)			
IMF program (stand-by agreements)		16.05** (7.06)		
Litigation by creditors (vulture funds)			13.33 (16.62)	
Intercreditor disputes (holdouts)				−6.10 (16.84)
Index 1.1	4.72 (5.99)	5.72 (5.97)	7.02 (6.29)	5.80 (5.60)
Index 1.2	5.12 (2.91)	3.81 (3.23)	3.82 (2.72)	4.37 (2.95)
Index 2.1	6.98* (3.37)	7.73* (3.68)	6.93* (3.27)	7.49* (3.64)
Index 2.2	0.17 (2.28)	0.73 (2.36)	0.51 (2.14)	0.72 (2.45)
Index 2.3	−2.40 (1.83)	−2.38 (1.86)	−2.56 (1.85)	−2.91 (2.24)
Index 3.1	19.84** (6.79)	19.51** (7.14)	19.06** (6.93)	19.28** (7.43)
Index 4.1	8.35** (3.32)	13.25** (5.02)	11.41** (4.06)	11.43** (4.72)
Index 4.2	8.87* (4.76)	8.22 (4.84)	8.18 (4.62)	8.57 (5.21)
Index 6.1	−40.51 (32.17)	−37.57 (31.85)	−38.68 (31.71)	−38.79 (31.94)
Index 6.2	25.94 (22.96)	23.59 (22.82)	24.03 (22.42)	24.25 (22.81)
Constant	215.72 (144.21)	192.99 (145.02)	198.73 (146.59)	201.36 (146.80)
Number of observations	1,041	1,041	1,041	1,041
Adjusted R^2	0.086	0.085	0.084	0.084

Source: Authors' computations.

Note: The dependent variable is the total amount borrowed (corporate bonds and loans) as a percentage deviation from the mean. Robust standard errors clustered on country are in parentheses. The regressions include year and country fixed effects and dummies for issuances by mining and chemical industries.

*** Significant at the 1 percent level; ** significant at the 5 percent level; * significant at the 10 percent level.

Creditor coordination problems have been the subject of much policy debate and a large body of literature.[23] Yet, as can be seen in table 7.2, the effect of prerestructuring litigation and intercreditor disputes or hold-outs is not significant. There is little indication that troublesome creditor actions during debt crises have negative spillovers on domestic firms and their borrowing abilities.

To validate the main findings of this section, we conducted a set of robustness checks (table 7B.1 in the annex). First, we reran all regressions using random instead of fixed-effect models. This proved not to have any major effect on the results. Second, we estimated the effect for various sub-periods. Interestingly, the effect of defaults and restructurings on private sector credit is much stronger in the 1990s than in the 1980s, a finding that is in line with Arteta and Hale (2008). One likely reason for this finding is the generally low supply of capital to emerging-market firms during the second half of the 1980s. Emerging-market external corporate borrowing reached precrisis (1981) levels only after the first Brady deals were concluded, in the early 1990s (see Sturzenegger and Zettelmeyer 2007 for a description of the Brady debt restructuring initiative).

Finally, we evaluate the extent to which the results depend on the specification and the number or type of variables included. In general, our results are very robust to specification changes, even when adding a variable on sudden stop episodes, taken from Frankel and Cavallo (2008) or Calvo, Izquierdo, and Mejia (2008).[24] However, our finding of the positive effect of IMF programs during crises turns out not to be overly robust. The variable for IMF programs turns insignificant in some specifications, in particular when adding a dummy variable for banking crises. Hence, the result on the possible catalytic role of IMF programs should be considered with some care.[25]

Impact of Sovereign Rating and Spread Changes on Corporate Capital Access

Having analyzed the effect of sovereign default in detail, we broaden our focus to additional measures and types of sovereign risk. This section first outlines the main effects of three other indicators of sovereign risk—sovereign bond spreads, sovereign credit ratings, and the volume of sovereign debt issuance—on corporate debt and equity issuances. It then presents our empirical findings, based on quarterly data from 26 major emerging-market economies for the period 1993–2007.

Measures of Sovereign Risk beyond Default Episodes

Following the exponential growth of emerging-market bond financing in recent years, sovereign default episodes have become a less representative measure of sovereign risk and thus a less reliable indicator of sovereign debt distress. Pescatori and Sy (2004) suggest the use of a broader indicator that takes into account turbulence in emerging bond markets, as measured, for example, by J.P. Morgan's EMBI. Along these lines, we analyze whether country-level sovereign bond spreads have an effect on quarterly corporate capital volumes. Typically, a government is regarded as distressed whenever the spread of its foreign bonds over U.S. Treasury securities of equivalent maturity exceeds 1,000 basis points.

We employ another continuous measure of sovereign default risk: sovereign ratings. As a baseline measure, we use the sovereign rating published in *Institutional Investor* magazine every March and September. Based on a large, standardized survey of leading banks and money management and security firms, the Institutional Investor Rating (IIR) is widely used in research. It has the advantage of having covered a large number of countries since the early 1980s (see Cruces 2006 for details). The IIR ranges from 0 to 100. A rating of 100 represents countries with the strongest debt-service capacity and the least possibility of defaulting; a rating of 0 represents countries with the weakest debt-service capacity and highest default risk.

Although nominal ratings are a good starting point, there is a possibility that the IIR measure is correlated with some of the fundamental variables that we aim to control for in the regressions. To address this issue, we regress our rating measure on a set of standard fundamentals, following Eichengreen and Mody (2000) and Garibaldi and others (2001).[26] The residuals of this first-stage regression are then used as the explanatory variable instead of the nominal IIR measure, with higher residual values indicating lower risk. In effect, this approach allows us to test whether country rating perceptions matter over and beyond changes in fundamentals. To further validate our findings, we use ratings data from Standard & Poor's. To this end, we transform the S&P rating scale into numerical values ranging from 0 (selective default) to 22 (AAA rating), with values averaged by quarter.

As a third indicator of the potential impact of sovereign risk on private sector capital access, we construct a "sovereign debt issuance" variable. This variable represents the volume of public debt raised on international capital markets for each of the countries in the sample. The rationale for employing this variable is that periods of no or low public debt issuance and higher sovereign risk spreads and lower ratings should also be associated with corporate "market closures" (Fostel and Geanakoplos 2008).[27] To construct this variable, we first retrieve all individual external bond issues and new syndicated loans by the government and publicly owned companies of each country, relying on the comprehensive Dealogic database. Then we aggregate the volumes of bond issues and loans by quarter and take their logarithms and construct a new dummy variable, "no sovereign issuance." This variable takes the value of 1 if no debt was raised by the public authorities or public corporations of a sample country in a given quarter.

Control Variables

Controlling for country fundamentals and global developments is important to properly identify the effects of sovereign risk on corporate capital access. In accordance with the previously cited literature on the determinants of capital flows, we include relevant variables that control for some of the main domestic and external factors. Annex table 7A.2 provides an overview of the explanatory variables employed, including summary statistics and data sources.

With regard to domestic factors, we include a quarterly measure of inflation based on the annual change in the consumer price index (CPI). Inflation is often taken as a first-best proxy for the stance of fiscal and monetary policies, with high rates of inflation indicating macroeconomic instability and weak economic policies.[28] As a second domestic factor, we use real (deflated by CPI) annual GDP growth. Strong economic activity may increase the domestic demand for external capital, and it may signal stronger ability to make future repayments to foreign investors. As an alternative measure, we also use growth based on quarterly industrial production indices (this indicator is available only for a much smaller number of observations). When equity issuances are considered, a more appropriate measure might be the growth in country stock market indices, measured on a quarterly basis. Given that this variable has reasonable coverage in the sample, we include it as a determinant of equity issuances in the baseline regressions. We expect a positive effect of stock market rallies on volumes issued.

To account for economic size effects, we include GDP per capita on a purchasing power parity basis in log form. In general, we expect more advanced emerging market countries to raise considerably more capital and to have more preferential access to external finance. We also include the real exchange rate to account for possible accounting effects (see above). In addition to these domestic economic factors, we include a measure of political stability, proxied by the composite score of political risk by the *International Country Risk Guide* (*ICRG*), which is available monthly. We expect higher values of political stability to foster capital access, as periods of stability are associated with a reduction of uncertainties, which serves as a positive investment signal.

Turning to external factors, we include a set of measures that are widely used in the literature. We include a proxy for the total capital flows to emerging markets. The variable used sums total bond, syndicated loan, and equity issuances of private sector firms in all of the 31 emerging markets listed in table 7.1 on a quarterly basis (figure 7A.1 shows the issuance of aggregate volumes over time). This measure (in log form) is intended to capture fluctuations in global liquidity. It is found not to be highly correlated with a country's capital issuance.[29] We expect total emerging-market issuance to have a strong positive effect on volumes issued by a country.

A second measure of investor perceptions about emerging-markets as a whole is the spread on the composite EMBI (quarterly average). This variable proxies risk aversion to debt investments in emerging-market economies and captures periods of emerging-market crises (such as the Asian and Russian crises in 1997 and 1998), which are usually accompanied by hikes in the composite EMBI spread. We expect higher overall EMBI spreads to reduce a country's corporate debt and equity issuance.

Finally, investor risk appetite can be proxied by VIX, the volatility index calculated by the Chicago Board Options Exchange. The VIX "fear index" measures market expectations of near-term volatility conveyed by S&P 500 stock index option prices. We also use the spread on high-yield corporate U.S. bonds, using the Lehman Brothers High Yield Bond Index.

Discussion of Results

Tables 7.3 and 7.4 highlight the main results on the effects of sovereign ratings. Table 7.5 shows a strong positive impact of the IIR and S&P rating on the volume of private sector borrowing, even after controlling for fundamentals and even when using the rating residual instead of nominal ratings. The better the country risk perceptions by investors and rating agencies, the larger the external borrowing volumes by domestic firms become.

To illustrate the quantitative importance of the individual factors, we multiply all estimated coefficients by the standard deviation of the respective variables. A one standard deviation increase in IIRs (16.4) results in a sizable increase in its coefficient (1.5). Only GDP per capita (column 3) has a larger quantitative effect. Another variable that is found to have a sizable economic effect is total issuance volumes in emerging markets. This finding indicates the crucial role of global liquidity for a country's level of access to international capital markets, confirming the results of Fostel and Kaminsky (2007).

The effects of sovereign ratings on equity issuances are weaker (table 7.4). Although the S&P rating has a positive and quantitatively important effect (column 2), its coefficient becomes insignificant when additional variables are controlled for, even when using the rating residual instead of nominal ratings. However, the crucial importance of total emerging-market issuance volumes and GDP per capita is confirmed. As expected, total capital flows to corporations in emerging markets and the size of the economy have a strong impact on the amount of equity issued by private firms in these countries.

Table 7.3 Effect of Sovereign Ratings on Corporate External Borrowing

Variable	(1)	(2)	(3)	(4)	(5)	(6)	(7)
Institutional Investor Rating (IIR)	0.09*** (0.01)						
Standard & Poor's rating		0.04** (0.02)					
Rating residual (based on IIR)			0.18*** (0.04)	0.18*** (0.04)	0.16*** (0.03)	0.18*** (0.04)	0.18*** (0.04)
Inflation		−0.00** (0.00)	−0.00 (0.00)	−0.00 (0.00)	−0.00 (0.00)	−0.00 (0.00)	−0.00 (0.00)
Growth		−0.01 (0.02)	−0.03 (0.02)	0.01 (0.02)	0.01 (0.02)	0.01 (0.02)	0.01 (0.02)
GDP per capita (purchasing power parity, log)		4.73*** (0.96)	4.39*** (0.88)				
Real exchange rate		−0.04*** (0.01)	−0.04*** (0.01)	−0.05*** (0.01)	−0.04*** (0.01)	−0.05*** (0.01)	−0.05*** (0.01)
Total capital flows to emerging-market economies		1.19*** (0.24)	1.06*** (0.25)	1.18*** (0.25)			
Political stability (International Country Risk Guide)					0.04* (0.02)		
Composite emerging-markets bond index						−0.00*** (0.00)	
VIX (volatility) Index							−0.01 (0.01)
Constant	0.42 (0.60)	−49.65*** (8.18)	−49.52*** (7.67)	−19.07*** (3.64)	−5.79*** (1.96)	−0.61 (1.78)	−4.24* (2.18)
Number of observations	1,828	1,356	1,311	1,382	1,367	1,382	1,382
Adjusted R^2	0.168	0.191	0.198	0.164	0.151	0.155	0.147

Source: Authors' computations.

Note: The dependent variable is the log of total amount borrowed (corporate bonds and loans). Robust standard errors clustered on country are in parentheses. Regressions include year and country fixed effects.

*** Significant at the 1 percent level; ** significant at the 5 percent level; * significant at the 10 percent level.

Table 7.4 Effect of Sovereign Ratings on Equity Issuances

Variable	(1)	(2)	(3)	(4)	(5)	(6)	(7)
Institutional Investor Rating	0.03		0.01				
	(0.02)		(0.03)				
Standard & Poor's rating		0.17**		0.13			
		(0.06)		(0.08)			
Inflation			-0.00	-0.00	-0.00**	-0.00	-0.00*
			(0.00)	(0.00)	(0.00)	(0.00)	(0.00)
Growth			-0.00	-0.01	-0.00	-0.00	-0.00
			(0.03)	(0.03)	(0.02)	(0.02)	(0.02)
GDP per capita (purchasing power parity, log)			4.33**	2.64	3.89*	4.46**	4.54**
			(2.06)	(1.83)	(1.92)	(2.04)	(2.05)
Real exchange rate			-0.02***	-0.02**	-0.01	-0.03***	-0.02***
			(0.01)	(0.01)	(0.01)	(0.01)	(0.01)
Stock index (annual growth)			0.01***	0.01***	0.01***	0.01**	0.01***
			(0.00)	(0.00)	(0.00)	(0.00)	(0.00)
Total capital flows to emerging-market economies			1.06***	1.11***			
			(0.28)	(0.29)			
Political stability (International Country Risk Guide)					0.06**		
					(0.02)		
Composite emerging-markets bond index						-0.00***	
						(0.00)	
VIX (volatility) Index							-0.02
							(0.02)
Constant	0.64	0.12	-44.19***	-31.47**	-33.60**	-32.67*	-34.44**
	(0.98)	(0.97)	(15.77)	(14.07)	(16.26)	(17.99)	(17.45)
Number of observations	1,828	1,600	1,145	1,138	1,218	1,219	1,219
Adjusted R^2	0.210	0.216	0.237	0.259	0.246	0.247	0.235

Source: Authors' computations.

Note: The dependent variable is the log of total corporate equity issued (in US$). Robust standard errors clustered on country are in parentheses. Regressions include year and country fixed effects.

*** Significant at the 1 percent level; ** significant at the 5 percent level; * significant at the 10 percent level.

Table 7.5 Sovereign Bond Spreads and Private Sector Capital

	Bonds and loans		Equity	
Variable	(1)	(2)	(3)	(4)
Emerging Markets Bond Index (EMBI) (country level)	−0.00*** (0.00)		−0.00*** (0.00)	
EMBI above 1,000 (dummy)		−0.83** (0.36)		−1.20** (0.51)
Inflation	−0.00*** (0.00)	−0.00*** (0.00)	0.00 (0.00)	0.00 (0.00)
Growth	−0.05** (0.02)	−0.05** (0.02)	−0.01 (0.03)	−0.02 (0.03)
GDP per capita (purchasing power parity, log)	5.10*** (1.24)	5.68*** (1.51)	3.48** (1.28)	4.11*** (1.36)
Real exchange rate	−0.00** (0.00)	−0.00** (0.00)	0.00 (0.00)	0.00 (0.00)
Total capital flows to emerging-market economies	1.18*** (0.32)	1.21*** (0.32)	1.13*** (0.32)	1.14*** (0.33)
Political stability (International Country Risk Guide)	0.04* (0.02)	0.05** (0.02)	0.04 (0.02)	0.04** (0.02)
VIX (volatility) Index	0.01 (0.01)	0.01 (0.01)	-0.02 (0.02)	-0.02 (0.02)
Constant	−51.89*** (10.75)	−57.97*** (13.06)	−39.01*** (10.06)	−45.12*** (10.73)
Number of observations	809	809	809	809
Adjusted R^2	0.207	0.198	0.308	0.305

Source: Authors' computations.
Note: The dependent variable in columns 1 and 2 is the log of total amount borrowed (corporate bonds and loans). The dependent variable in columns 3 and 4 is the log of total corporate equity issued. Robust standard errors clustered on country are in parentheses. The regressions include year and country fixed effects.
*** Significant at the 1 percent level; ** significant at the 5 percent level; * significant at the 10 percent level.

Our results also confirm the results of other studies on the role of political risk. We find the *ICRG* index to be a significant and quantitatively important determinant of both debt and equity volumes, with higher stability leading to higher cross-border capital flows. The coefficient of the composite EMBI spreads is significant and has a sizable quantitative effect. The higher overall sovereign risk of emerging-market countries leads to a drop in country-level access to foreign capital. In contrast, the effects of the VIX Index and the spread level on U.S. high-yield bonds, as measured by the Lehman Index, are insignificant.[30]

Other interesting findings relate to the role of sovereign bond spreads for private sector access to capital (table 7.5). EMBI spreads are a highly significant determinant, with regard to both external borrowing and equity issuances. This effect is quantitatively significant, as illustrated by the high negative coefficient of EMBI 1,000 (a dummy variable for periods in which spreads surpass the critical threshold of 1,000 basis points above the U.S. Treasury rate). This is further confirmation of our result that sovereign risk is a crucial factor for private sector access to capital in emerging markets.

We find only a weak link between public debt issuances and corporate access to capital (table 7.6). For the whole sample, the variable capturing the total amount of sovereign issuances is barely significant and has a low quantitative effect on corporate debt volumes and equity issuances; the dummy for the incidence of sovereign issuances by quarter is insignificant throughout. We obtain a similar result even when we examine a subsample of crisis periods. Although the "sovereign debt issuance" variable turns significant in a sample of debt-crisis periods (as defined above), the effect depends heavily on how crisis and distress episodes are defined. We find no effect of sovereign issuance on corporate issuance when a subsample of crisis episodes is identified by EMBI spreads above 1,000 basis points or by periods in which country credit ratings are in the default range (that is, when the IIR is below 25).[31] Thus, we find very weak evidence for a co-movement between public sector and private corporations' capital market access.

We check the validity of our results with additional analytical tests (table 7B.2 in the annex). First, we alter the specifications in various ways and include additional explanatory variables, in particular, variables capturing the development of domestic capital markets (domestic credit/GDP and stock market capitalization/GDP), taken from the updated data set of Beck, Demirgüç-Kunt, and Levine (2000). We include external and domestic factors (for example, U.S. interest rates, trade openness, G-7 growth, and a measure of sudden stop episodes, taken from Frankel and Cavallo (2008). Our main results are little affected, although the number of observations drops as a result of missing values in some of the additional variables.

Some results change when the regressions are run with random effects, with some variables showing higher coefficients at higher significance levels. In particular, we find a significant effect of rating levels on equity issuances. However, simple Hausman tests clearly indicate that it is necessary to include controls for fixed effects. Therefore, the baseline results that control for initial country conditions appear more reliable.

Table 7.6 Role of Sovereign Market Access

	Equity				Bonds and loans		
	Entire sample		Entire sample		Subsample of crisis periods		
Variable					Sovereign default and restructuring	Emerging-markets bond index spread > 1,000	Institutional Investor Rating < 25 (rating in default range)
	(1)	(2)	(3)	(4)	(5)	(6)	(7)
Volume of sovereign debt issuance (by country and quarter, log)	0.05* (0.03)		0.05* (0.03)		0.28*** (0.03)	0.00 (0.08)	0.04 (0.09)
No sovereign issuances (dummy)		0.23 (0.16)		0.23 (0.19)			
Institutional Investor Rating	0.01 (0.03)	0.01 (0.03)	0.04** (0.02)	0.04** (0.02)	0.05 (0.07)	0.13** (0.05)	-0.00 (0.00)
Inflation	-0.00 (0.00)	-0.00 (0.00)	-0.00** (0.00)	-0.00** (0.00)	-0.01** (0.00)	0.00 (0.00)	-0.00 (0.00)
Growth	-0.00 (0.03)	-0.00 (0.03)	-0.01 (0.02)	-0.01 (0.02)	0.26*** (0.03)	0.06 (0.04)	-0.26*** (0.06)

GDP per capita (purchasing power parity, log)	4.21* (2.04)	4.25** (2.04)	4.66*** (0.94)	4.68*** (0.95)	62.52*** (4.15)	-0.90 (3.93)	-2.52 (2.96)
Real exchange rate	-0.02*** (0.01)	-0.02*** (0.01)	-0.04*** (0.01)	-0.04*** (0.01)	-11.27*** (2.93)	-22.79* (11.23)	0.12*** (0.01)
Total capital flows to emerging-market economies	1.07*** (0.28)	1.08*** (0.28)	1.19*** (0.25)	1.20*** (0.25)	-1.16 (0.86)	-0.58 (1.10)	0.67 (1.61)
Stock index (annual growth)	0.01*** (0.00)	0.01*** (0.00)					
Constant	-43.35** (15.60)	-43.83*** (15.59)	-49.18*** (7.95)	-49.49*** (8.04)	-538.01*** (30.49)	19.25 (47.59)	12.39 (39.20)
Number of observations	1,145	1,145	1,356	1,356	44	68	72
Adjusted R^2	0.239	0.238	0.194	0.193	0.266	0.203	0.234

Source: Authors' computations.

Note: The dependent variable in columns 1 and 2 is the log of total amount borrowed (corporate loans and bonds). The dependent variable in columns 3–7 is the log of total corporate equity issued. Robust standard errors clustered on country are in parentheses. The regressions include year and country fixed effects. Columns 5, 6, and 7 are based on periods of sovereign debt distress only, defined as outright default or ongoing restructuring negotiations.

*** Significant at the 1 percent level; ** significant at the 5 percent level; * significant at the 10 percent level.

Finally, we estimate the model for different subperiods. In the more recent period (for example, the subsample 2001–07), the coefficients of domestic factors (such as ratings, inflation, and GDP per capita) tend to become smaller and less significant, whereas the coefficients for external factors (such as the composite EMBI spread or total emerging-market issuance volumes) tend to remain the same and are much more robust. This finding is in line with the findings of Fostel and Kaminsky (2007), who show that the role of global factors with respect to domestic factors has become more pronounced in the post–2000 period of high global liquidity.

Summary of Main Findings

The main findings of our analysis for the periods 1980–2004 and 1993–2007 can be summarized as follows:

- For the period 1980–2004, defaults to private creditors have a strong negative impact on corporate external borrowing, after controlling for fundamentals and shocks.
- Delays in debt renegotiations caused by government behavior have an additional negative spillover effect. Intercreditor disputes and creditor litigation against the sovereign appear to have no impact on domestic corporations in defaulting countries.
- For the period 1993–2007, a deterioration in risk perceptions (higher sovereign bond spreads and lower sovereign ratings) negatively affects corporate access to capital, in particular, the volume of corporate external borrowing.
- The volume of equity issuances is strongly influenced by the level of country bond spreads and little affected by sovereign rating changes.
- Economic development (per capita GDP) and external factors such as total capital flows to emerging markets are additional main determinants of corporate access to external credit and equity.
- The volume of sovereign loans and bond issuances has no statistically robust impact on the volume of corporate credit and equity in either the full sample or the subsample of crisis episodes. There is no evidence for close co-movement between public and corporate access to capital.

Concluding Remarks

Very few empirical studies have been conducted on "top-down" risk spillovers from sovereign to private entities in emerging-market countries, particularly with regard to corporate capital access conditions. Using data from 31 emerging economies from new data sets, this chapter provides new empirical evidence on the role of sovereign risk for private sector access to international capital markets. The results show that an increase in sovereign risk can have strong negative effects on the volume of corporate credit and equity issued.

The first part of the empirical analysis focuses on the role of sovereign debt crises. We provide novel evidence that defaults to private (not official) creditors have a strong impact on corporate external borrowing. Beyond the default effect per se, we find that debt-crisis characteristics matter. Delays in debt negotiations have adverse effects for private sector credit. Furthermore, we find (weak) indications that successful IMF programs have a positive effect on private sector access to credit during debt-crisis periods. Interestingly, however, there are no negative spillovers of delays caused by intercreditor disputes or litigation. It thus seems that in distress situations, government behavior has a greater impact than creditor behavior. Policy makers should take this finding into account when facing debt-restructuring negotiations.

The second part of the empirical analysis investigates the effect of sovereign risk in a broader framework and for a more recent period (1993–2007). It shows that both increasing sovereign spreads and deterioration in sovereign ratings have strong adverse effects on corporate external borrowing. Periods of higher sovereign risk are associated with a considerable drop in external debt issuances by major firms in the emerging-market countries under consideration. This result notwithstanding, we do not find persuasive evidence of co-movement of public and private market access. In fact, sovereign debt issuance is not an important predictor of the volume of external corporate capital raised in a given quarter.

Overall, emerging-market governments need to be aware of the potentially adverse effects for their domestic economies of negative country-risk perceptions by international investors and rating agencies. Government actions affecting sovereign risk (for example, threats to default on sovereign debt or delayed debt renegotiations) may have unintended consequences for the country's corporations. Put differently, emerging-market governments interested in fostering the development and growth prospects of domestic private firms should avoid policies or rhetoric that negatively influences the country's sovereign spreads and rating.

In view of the current financial crisis and global economic slowdown, it is likely that sovereign risk in emerging-market economies will be on the rise again in the short and medium terms. Our results indicate that this possible outcome could add to the potential constraints in the future external financing of firms in emerging-market and developing countries.

Annex 7A: Data and Descriptive Statistics

Figure 7A.1 Bond, Syndicated Loan, and Equity Issuance by Private Domestic Firms in Emerging Markets, 1993–2007

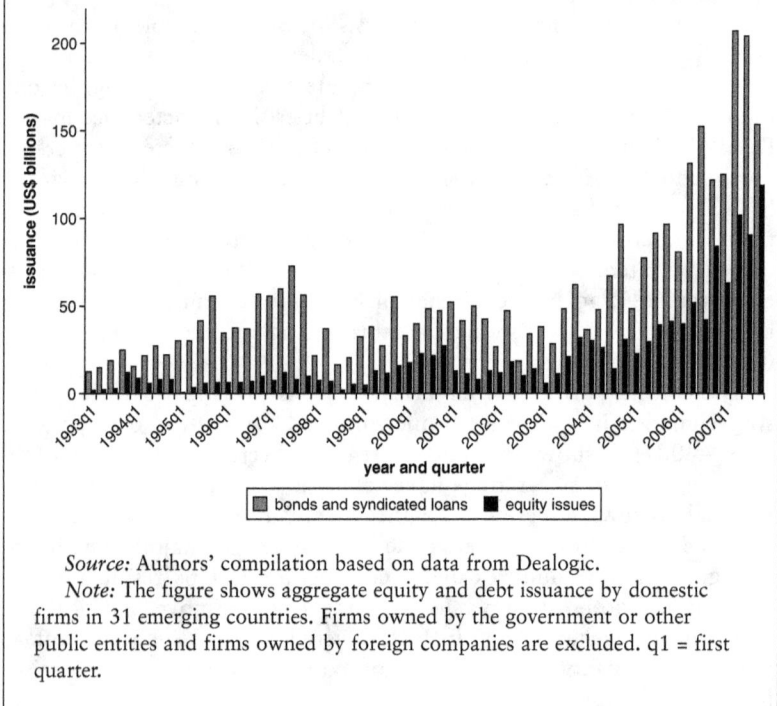

Source: Authors' compilation based on data from Dealogic.
Note: The figure shows aggregate equity and debt issuance by domestic firms in 31 emerging countries. Firms owned by the government or other public entities and firms owned by foreign companies are excluded. q1 = first quarter.

Construction of Index Variables (Sample 1980–2004)

The main control variables used in the analysis of debt-crisis effects are taken from Arteta and Hale (2008). They group their control variables in five broad categories and compose them in a set of indexes in the following way (data sources are shown in parentheses).

International Competitiveness. The degree of international competitiveness is likely to have an effect on firm performance and thus corporate demand for external credit. The index is constructed using data on changes in the terms of trade (United Nations Conference on Trade and Development), changes in the current account (IMF's *International Financial Statistics* [IFS]), changes in the real exchange rate (*IFS*), price indexes of each country's export commodities (Global Financial Data [GFD], *IFS*), and the volatility of export revenues (*IFS*). The index is scaled by trade

Table 7A.1 Economies Covered in the Analysis

Defaulters	Nondefaulters
Argentina	China
Brazil	Colombia
Chile	Croatia[a]
Mexico	Czech Republic[a]
Pakistan	Egypt, Arab Rep. of
Peru	Hong Kong, China
Philippines	Hungary
Poland	India
Romania	Indonesia
Russian Federation[a]	Korea, Rep. of
South Africa	Malaysia
Turkey	Qatar
Venezuela, R. B. de	Saudi Arabia
	Singapore
	Slovak Republic[a]
	Taiwan, China
	Thailand
	United Arab Emirates

Source: Authors' compilation based on Standard & Poor's 2007 and Enderlein, Müller, and Trebesch 2008.

Note: For the purposes of this study, defaulters are countries whose governments defaulted on debt obligations toward foreign private creditors between 1980 and 2004 or whose governments arranged a distressed debt restructuring at terms less favorable than the original terms.

a. Economies included from 1993 on only.

openness (imports + exports/GDP [*IFS*, GFD]). We use the same two principal components retained by Arteta and Hale (2007), naming them Index 1.1 and Index 1.2.

Investment Climate and Monetary Stability. This index accounts for foreign and domestic demand for investment and credit in the country, as well as short-run macroeconomic developments. It is composed of data on sovereign credit risk (IIR), the ratio of debt service to exports (Joint External Debt Hub), the ratio of investment to GDP (*IFS*), the real interest rate (*IFS*), the ratio of lending interest rate to deposit interest rate (*IFS*), the inflation rate (*IFS*), the ratio of domestic credit to GDP (*IFS*), and

Table 7A.2 Further Control Variables, 1993–2007

Variable	Number of observations	Mean	Standard deviation	Minimum	Maximum	Data source
Institutional Investor Rating	1,828	49.62	16.37	12.80	91.80	Institutional Investor magazine
Standard & Poor's rating (numerical)	1,600	13.21	4.09	0.00	22.00	Standard & Poor's
Emerging Markets Bond Index (EMBI) (country level)	861	492.67	781.72	20.41	6,626.88	J.P. Morgan/Datastream
EMBI above 1,000	861	0.08	0.28	0.00	1.00	J.P. Morgan/Datastream
Inflation (percent)	1,661	17.42	136.19	-5.87	4,448.81	Economist Intelligence Unit (EIU) data
Real annual growth (percent)	1,608	4.64	4.97	-23.08	47.88	EIU
GDP per capita (purchasing power parity, log)	1,604	8.85	0.96	6.57	12.29	EIU
Real exchange rate	1,760	4.53	17.24	0.01	183.67	EIU
Political stability	1,896	68.56	9.36	40.00	90.00	International Country Risk Guide
Stock market index (growth)	1,420	22.10	48.54	-68.89	873.24	EIU
VIX (volatility) Index	1,920	18.94	6.36	10.42	35.09	Bloomberg
High-yield spread	1,920	9.87	1.84	6.99	14.02	Lehman Brothers/Bloomberg
Total capital flows to emerging-market economies (log)	1,888	11.04	0.66	9.77	12.61	Dealogic

Source: Authors' compilation.

changes in the domestic stock market index (Ibbotson; GFD; Bloomberg). Three principal components used by Arteta and Hale (Indexes 2.1, 2.2, and 2.3.) are retained.

Financial Development. The development of the domestic financial system can be an important determinant of the demand for external credit in emerging markets. The index of financial sector development is constructed based on the ratio of stock market capitalization to GDP (GFD, *IFS*); the ratio of commercial bank assets to GDP (*IFS*); and the degree of financial account openness (IMF 2003; Glick and Hutchison 2005). The first principal component used by Arteta and Hale (Index 3.1.) is retained.

Long-Run Macroeconomic Prospects. Indicators of long-term macroeconomic prospects are likely to affect risk assessments of both domestic and foreign agents and thereby the demand and supply of corporate external credit. This index is constructed using the ratio of foreign debt to GDP (Joint External Debt Hub), the growth rate of real GDP (*IFS*), the growth rate of nominal GDP measured in U.S. dollars (*IFS*), and the unemployment rate (*IFS*). The first two principal components used by Arteta and Hale (Indexes 4.1 and 4.2) are retained.

Global Supply of Capital. The index capturing global "push" factors is based on the following variables: the Yale School of Management investor confidence index, the growth rate of the U.S. stock market index (GFD), the U.S. Treasury rate (Federal Reserve), the volume of gross international capital outflows from member countries of the Organisation for Economic Co-operation and Development (Lane and Milesi-Ferretti 2001), and the Merrill Lynch High Yield spread. Two principal components used by Arteta and Hale (Indexes 6.1. and 6.2.) are retained.

Finally, we include a small set of firm-level dummies. Some industries, such as firms in the chemical or mining sector, are particularly capital intensive; on average, these firms raise much larger bond or loan volumes than most other corporations. To capture some of the noise caused by financings of major investment projects in these sectors, we also include monthly dummies for debt issuances by chemical and mining corporations.

(Chapter continues on the following page.)

Annex 7B: Robustness Analysis

Table 7B.1 Robustness Analysis on the Effect of Sovereign Defaults

| | Entire sample | | | Subsample of default episodes | |
| | | | | Specification check (additional variables) | |
Variable	Random effects estimation (1)	With sudden stop (2)	1980s only (3)	(4)	(5)
Default episode (private creditor)	-21.90* (13.17)	-46.47** (21.96)	-9.53 (11.84)		
Month of restructuring (official creditors)	-39.57** (17.90)	-54.38** (21.54)	-18.56** (8.91)		
Lag 1 (first year after agreement)	-62.43** (25.78)	-72.45** (27.94)	-20.23* (11.74)		
Lag 2 (second year after agreement)	-24.96 (22.43)	-34.88 (27.53)	2.72 (19.62)		
Sudden stop		-42.99** (20.29)			
Breakdown in negotiations				-24.84** (11.09)	
IMF program (stand-by agreements)					14.27 (8.44)
Index 1.1	0.39 (2.83)	-2.07 (3.43)	1.82 (2.47)	1.57 (7.05)	2.81 (7.22)
Index 1.2	-5.20** (2.37)	-4.83** (2.35)	3.08 (4.05)	4.67 (2.70)	3.37 (3.14)
Index 2.1	-3.70 (7.80)	-3.04 (8.24)	-0.39 (1.14)	9.04* (4.28)	9.55* (4.86)
Index 2.2	7.00 (4.65)	3.02 (4.83)	2.52 (2.69)	0.90 (2.28)	1.47 (2.41)

Index 2.3	4.72	1.90	2.19	-4.18	-4.09
	(5.62)	(6.43)	(1.29)	(2.60)	(2.73)
Index 3.1	15.19**	16.91**	-4.22	23.06**	22.48**
	(5.91)	(6.23)	(3.37)	(7.65)	(8.30)
Index 4.1	8.21***	7.62**	-0.04	5.53	10.57**
	(2.91)	(3.10)	(4.67)	(3.87)	(4.04)
Index 4.2	4.21	2.77	6.05	7.98	7.21
	(4.28)	(4.66)	(5.64)	(5.72)	(5.94)
Index 6.1	-77.42***	-77.41***	-0.61	-44.21	-41.38
	(19.99)	(19.83)	(5.89)	(35.62)	(35.28)
Index 6.2	54.55***	54.51***	3.75	29.48	27.04
	(14.30)	(14.14)	(4.25)	(24.70)	(24.55)
Real exchange rate	-0.01**	-0.02***	0.01	0.01	0.02
	(0.00)	(0.01)	(0.01)	(0.05)	(0.07)
Banking crisis	-23.33*	-21.78	4.78	27.31*	25.16*
	(12.87)	(14.50)	(8.40)	(12.79)	(12.75)
Natural disasters (dummy)	-12.72	-14.57	-4.94	3.25	3.57
	(14.87)	(14.76)	(6.29)	(11.73)	(13.07)
Currency crisis	-41.32***	-42.74***	-15.03***	-8.75	-12.79
	(13.59)	(13.15)	(4.37)	(7.80)	(9.22)
Constant	197.02***	198.42***	-69.07***	255.72	232.18
	(67.85)	(68.73)	(21.33)	(156.79)	(158.01)
Number of observations	6,716	6,716	2,508	992	992
Adjusted R^2	0.055	0.055	0.020	0.086	0.083

Source: Authors' computations.

Note: The dependent variable is the total amount borrowed (corporate bonds and loans) as a percentage deviation from the mean. Robust standard errors clustered on country are in parentheses. The regressions include year and country fixed effects and dummies for issuances by mining and chemical industries.

*** Significant at the 1 percent level; ** significant at the 5 percent level; * significant at the 10 percent level.

Table 7B.2 Robustness Analysis on the Effect of Sovereign Ratings, 1993–2007

Variable	Random effects		Extended specification		Post–2000 period	
	Bonds and loans	Equity	Bonds and loans	Equity	Bonds and loans	Equity
	(1)	(2)	(3)	(4)	(5)	(6)
Institutional Investor Rating	0.06*** (0.01)	0.04* (0.02)	0.04** (0.02)	-0.02 (0.03)	0.04* (0.02)	0.04 (0.03)
Inflation	-0.00** (0.00)	0.00 (0.00)	-0.00 (0.00)	-0.00 (0.00)	-0.01 (0.01)	0.00 (0.01)
Growth	-0.00 (0.02)	0.04* (0.02)	-0.01 (0.02)	-0.01 (0.03)	-0.04 (0.03)	0.01 (0.03)
GDP per head (purchasing power parity, log)	1.02** (0.47)	0.34 (0.40)	4.80*** (1.67)	7.76*** (1.93)	6.01** (2.85)	-0.35 (1.93)
Real exchange rate	-0.03*** (0.00)	-0.01** (0.01)	-0.03*** (0.01)	-0.01 (0.01)	-0.08*** (0.01)	0.00 (0.01)
Total capital flows to emerging-market economies	1.14*** (0.24)	1.10*** (0.26)	1.04*** (0.31)	1.17*** (0.32)	0.99*** (0.29)	0.75** (0.30)

	(1)	(2)	(3)	(4)	(5)	(6)
Stock index (annual growth)					0.00	0.01***
					(0.00)	(0.00)
Sudden stop					-0.18	0.02
					(0.22)	(0.45)
Trade openness					-0.82	-1.69*
					(0.80)	(0.89)
Stock market capital to GDP					-0.45	0.46
					(0.34)	(0.73)
G7 growth					-0.61	1.29
					(1.90)	(2.98)
Constant	-18.29***	-13.67***	-49.25***	-78.71***	-62.87**	-3.39
	(4.61)	(4.18)	(14.34)	(16.92)	(25.40)	(17.72)
Number of observations	1,356	1,356	820	820	789	789
Adjusted R^2			0.137	0.140	0.178	0.278

Source: Authors' computations.
Note: The dependent variable in columns 1, 3, and 5 is the log of the total amount borrowed (corporate loans and bonds). The dependent variable in columns 2, 4, and 6 is the log of total corporate equity issued. Robust standard errors clustered on country are in parentheses. The regressions include year and country fixed effects.
*** Significant at the 1 percent level; ** significant at the 5 percent level; * significant at the 10 percent level.

Notes

Udaibir S. Das and Michael G. Papaioannou are staff members of the International Monetary Fund (IMF). The views expressed in this chapter are those of the authors and do not necessarily reflect the views of national authorities, the IMF, or IMF Executive Directors.

1. There is a growing body of literature on "bottom-up" risk transfers and private sector contingent claims (see, for example, Honohan and Laeven 2005; Gray, Merton, and Bodie 2007; Gapen and others 2008)

2. Among the few studies conducted are Eichengreen and Mody (2000), World Bank (2007), and Arteta and Hale (2008).

3. The analysis does not extend to the period of the current global financial crisis, because adequate 2008 data were not available for the set of countries included.

4. Portes, Rey, and Oh (2001), Gelos and Wie (2005), and Portes and Rey (2005) highlight informational frictions and lack of transparency as obstacles to equity and portfolio investments and financial asset transfers to emerging markets.

5. The Lucas paradox is the observation of low net capital flows from developed countries to developing countries despite high rate-of-return differentials.

6. A small body of literature examines the determinants of capital market access by sovereign borrowers (see, for example, Grigorian 2003; Gelos, Sandleris, and Sahay 2004; Erce 2008), and Fostel and Geanakoplos (2008) provide some stylized facts on sovereign bond issuances in emerging markets. However, the general link between sovereign and private sector access to external capital in emerging markets remains largely unexplored.

7. Kaminsky, Reinhart, and Vegh (2004) highlight the fact that ratings of middle-income countries tend to show much greater variability than ratings of high- or low-income countries.

8. Bevan and Estrin (2004) find that FDI flows to Eastern European countries are not affected by sovereign ratings. Their results are at odds with those of Garibaldi and others (2001), who do find an important role of sovereign risk for capital flows to transition economies.

9. Rose (2005) and Martinez and Sandleris (2008) find that sovereign defaults also affect trade flows. Levy-Yeyati and Panizza (2005) and Borenzstein and Panizza (2008) suggest that defaults tend to cause output losses.

10. A related study, by Zanforlin (2007), comes to roughly the same conclusion by applying probit and multivariate probit models.

11. The Dealogic data on bond and, particularly, syndicated loan spreads are very incomplete, making average spread levels per country and month/quarter too noisy to allow for a meaningful analysis. We therefore focus on issued volumes only.

12. It is not possible to disentangle the volumes of equity sold to domestic versus international investors. The results regarding equity thus represent corporate access to capital on both national and international markets.

13. Arteta and Hale (2008) exclude countries for which the total amount of bonds and loans is zero for more than 24 months out of the 264 months in the sample.

14. Given the focus on sovereign risk, we also exclude restructuring events of private-to-private debt, such as those in the Republic of Korea in 1997 and Indonesia in 1998.

15. Arteta and Hale (2008) rely on the list of restructuring events in the *Global Development Finance* report (World Bank 2002, 2003), a comprehensive and widely used source. Our coding process revealed that these lists contain a number of errors. Sometimes interim agreements are listed as final agreements. In other instances, agreements are listed as finalized although they were postponed or never implemented.

16. The definition of *crisis episodes* matters significantly. In some cases, such as Peru in the 1980s, governments were in default several years before engaging in restructuring negotiations with private creditors.

17. Note that delays caused by creditor coordination failure or outright inter-creditor disputes are explicitly excluded from the coding. Trebesch (2009) disentangles debtor- and creditor-induced delays explicitly.

18. We thank the authors for kindly sharing their extensive data set.

19. For coherence, we also measured the dependent variable of corporate credit as a monthly deviation from the 25-year average. Following Arteta and Hale (2008), we also deflate the amount of credit using the U.S. consumer price index in this part of the analysis.

20. To verify, we also use a dummy for cases in which the total number of affected people represented more than 5 percent of the population.

21. This transformation does not alter the main results. The effect of defaults on private sector credit is highly significant and robust when using the dependent variable in log form.

22. A main benefit of showing results as they are is that coefficient sizes are easy to interpret. In fact, the coefficients for the main dummy variable of default episodes simply represent the size of the percentage change in credit relative to what it would have been if no default had occurred that year. A further advantage is that results remain comparable to those in Arteta and Hale (2008).

23. Much of the debate focused on the effect of holdouts and "runs to the courthouse." Increasing attention has been devoted to the problem of vulture creditors in sovereign restructurings (Sturzenegger and Zettelmeyer 2007; Pitchford and Wright 2008).

24. Our main results on the effects of sovereign risk were robust even in an empirical setup with quarterly data for the post–1993 period.

25. Note, however, that the positive effect of IMF programs can be replicated in the quarterly data setup for the post–1993 period used below.

26. Based on the literature on the determinants of sovereign credit ratings (see Ratha, De, and Mohapatra 2007 for an overview), we include the following set of explanatory variables in the first stage: inflation, growth, log of GDP per head, total external debt to GDP, and total external debt to exports.

27. Of course, low volumes of government debt issuances may also be driven by demand effects (for example, periods during which the sovereign does not wish or need to borrow). See the discussion in Gelos, Sandleris, and Sahay 2004.

28. In the robustness analysis, we also use the ratio of budgetary balance to GDP to validate the findings relating to inflation. Fiscal account data are available only for a subset of countries and years, limiting the number of observations.

29. The simple correlation of total capital volumes (log) with logged country-level debt and equity issuances is 0.27 and 0.31, respectively.

30. Results are not reported but are available upon request.

31. Even an interaction term between sovereign ratings and sovereign debt issuance turned out to be insignificant with regard to corporate debt issuance.

References

Albuquerque, Rui. 2003. "The Composition of International Capital Flows: Risk Sharing through Foreign Direct Investment." *Journal of International Economics* 61 (2): 353–83.

Alfaro, Laura, Sebnem Kalemli-Ozcan, and Vadym Volosovych. 2008. "Why Doesn't Capital Flow from Rich to Poor Countries? An Empirical Investigation." *Review of Economics and Statistics* 90 (2): 347–68.

Arteta, Carlos, and Galina Hale. 2007. "Currency Crises and Foreign Credit in Emerging Markets: Credit Crunch or Demand Effect?" Working Paper 2007-02, Federal Reserve Bank of San Francisco.

———. 2008. "Sovereign Debt Crises and Credit to the Private Sector." *Journal of International Economics* 74 (1): 53–69.

Beck, Thorsten, Asli Demirgüç-Kunt, and Ross Levine. 2000. "A New Database on Financial Development and Structure." *World Bank Economic Review* 14 (3): 597–605.

Bevan, A., and S. Estrin. 2004. "The Determinants of Foreign Direct Investment into European Transition Economies." *Journal of Comparative Economics* 32 (4): 775–87.

Blonigen, Bruce A. 2005. "A Review of the Empirical Literature on FDI Determinants." NBER Working Paper 11299, National Bureau of Economic Research, Cambridge, MA.

Bordo, Michael, Ashoka Mody, and Oomes Nienke. 2004. "Keeping Capital Flowing: The Role of the IMF." *International Finance* 7 (3): 421–50.

Borensztein, Eduardo, Kevin Cowan, and Patricio Valenzuela. 2007. "Sovereign Ceilings 'Lite'? The Impact of Sovereign Ratings on Corporate Ratings in Emerging Market Economies." IMF Working Paper 07/75, International Monetary Fund, Washington, DC.

Borensztein, Eduardo, and Ugo Panizza. 2008. "The Costs of Sovereign Default." IMF Working Paper 08/238, International Monetary Fund, Washington, DC.

Busse, Matthias, and Carsten Hefeker. 2007. "Political Risk, Institutions and Foreign Direct Investment." *European Journal of Political Economy* 23 (2): 397–415.

Calvo, Guillermo A., Alejandro Izquierdo, and Luis-Fernando Meja. 2008. "Systemic Sudden Stops: The Relevance of Balance-Sheet Effects and Financial Integration." NBER Working Paper 14026, National Bureau of Economic Research, Cambridge, MA.

Cruces, Juan. 2006. "Statistical Properties of Sovereign Credit Ratings." *Emerging Markets Review* 7 (1): 27–51.

———. 2007. "The Value of Pleasing International Creditors." Universidad Torcuato di Tella Department of Economics, Buenos Aires.

Daude, Christian, and Marcel Fratzscher. 2008. "The Pecking Order of Cross-Border Investment." *Journal of International Economics* 74 (1): 94–119.

Daude, Christian, and Ernesto Stein. 2007. "The Quality of Institutions and Foreign Direct Investment." *Economics and Politics* 19 (3): 317–44.

Dreher, Axel. 2006. "IMF and Economic Growth: The Effects of Programs, Loans, and Compliance with Conditionality." *World Development* 34 (5): 769–78.

Eichengreen, Barry, and Ashoka Mody. 2000. "Lending Booms, Reserves and the Sustainability of Short-Term Debt: Inferences from the Pricing of Syndicated Bank Loans." *Journal of Development Economics* 63 (1): 5–44.

Enderlein, Henrik, Laura Müller, and Christoph Trebesch. 2008. "Debt Disputes: Measuring Government Coerciveness in Sovereign Debt Crises." Hertie School of Governance, Berlin.

Erce, Aitor. 2008. "A Structural Model of Sovereign Debt Issuance: Assessing the Role of Financial Factors." Working Paper 0809, Bank of Spain, Madrid.

Fostel, Ana, and John Geanakoplos. 2008. "Leverage Cycles and the Anxious Economy." *American Economic Review* 98 (4): 1211–44.

Fostel, Ana, and Graciela L. Kaminsky. 2007. "Latin America's Access to International Capital Markets: Good Behavior or Global Liquidity?" NBER Working Paper 13194, National Bureau of Economic Research, Cambridge, MA.

Frankel, Jeffrey A., and Eduardo A. Cavallo. 2008. "Does Openness to Trade Make Countries More Vulnerable to Sudden Stops, or Less? Using Gravity to Establish Causality." *Journal of International Money and Finance* 27 (8): 1430–52.

Fuentes, Miguel, and Diego Saravia. 2006. "Sovereign Defaulters: Do International Capital Markets Punish Them?" Documentos de Trabajo 314, Instituto de Economía, Pontificia Universidad Católica de Chile, Santiago de Chile.

Gapen, Michael, Dale Gray, Cheng Hoon Lim, and Yingbin Xiao. 2008. "Measuring and Analyzing Sovereign Risk with Contingent Claims." *IMF Staff Papers* 55 (1): 109–48.

Garibaldi, Pietro, Nada Mora, Sahay Ratna, and Jeromin Zettelmeyer. 2001. "What Moves Capital to Transition Economies?" *IMF Staff Papers* 48 (4): 6.

Gelos, Gaston R., and Shang-Jin Wei. 2005. "Transparency and International Portfolio Holdings." *Journal of Finance* 60 (6): 2987–3020.

Gelos, Gaston R., Guido Sandleris, and Ratna Sahay. 2004. "Sovereign Borrowing by Developing Countries: What Determines Market Access?" IMF Working Paper 04/221, International Monetary Fund, Washington, DC.

Glick, Reuven, and Michael Hutchison. 2005. "Capital Controls and Exchange Rate Instability in Developing Countries." *Journal of International Money and Finance* 24 (3): 387–412.

Gray, Dale F., Robert C. Merton, and Zvi Bodie. 2007. "New Framework for Measuring and Managing Macrofinancial Risk and Financial Stability." NBER Working Paper 13607, National Bureau of Economic Research, Cambridge, MA.

Grigorian, David A. 2003. "On the Determinants of First-Time Sovereign Bond Issues." IMF Working Paper 03/184, International Monetary Fund, Washington, DC.

Hale, Galina. 2007. "Bonds or Loans? The Effect of Macroeconomic Fundamentals." *Economic Journal* 117 (516): 196–215.

Honohan, Patrick, and Luc Laeven. 2005. *Systemic Financial Crises.* Cambridge, U.K.: Cambridge University Press.

IMF (International Monetary Fund). 2003. "Fact Sheet: Proposals for a Sovereign Debt Restructuring Mechanism." Washington, DC. http://www.imf.org/external/np/exr/facts/sdrm.htm.

Jeanneau, Serge, and Marian Micu. 2002. "Determinants of International Bank Lending to Emerging Market Countries." BIS Working Paper 112, Bank for International Settlements, Basel, Switzerland.

Kaminsky, Graciela L., Carmen M. Reinhart, and Carlos A. Vegh. 2004. "When It Rains, It Pours: Procyclical Capital Flows and Macroeconomic Policies." NBER Working Paper 10780, National Bureau of Economic Research, Cambridge, MA.

Kaminsky, Graciela L., and Sergio L. Schmukler. 2002. "Emerging Market Instability: Do Sovereign Ratings Affect Country Risk and Stock Returns?" *World Bank Economic Review* 16 (2): 171–95.

Kim, Suk-Joong, and Eliza Wu. 2008. "Sovereign Credit Ratings, Capital Flows and Financial Sector Development in Emerging Markets." *Emerging Markets Review* 9 (1): 17–39.

Krueger, A. 2002. "A New Approach to Sovereign Debt Restructuring." International Monetary Fund, Washington, DC.

Laeven, Luc, and Fabian Valencia. 2008. "Systemic Banking Crises: A New Database." IMF Working Paper 08/224, International Monetary Fund, Washington, DC.

Lane, Philip R., and Gian Maria Milesi-Ferretti. 2001 "The External Wealth of Nations: Measures of Foreign Assets and Liabilities for Industrial and Developing Countries." *Journal of International Economics* 55 (2): 263–94.

Levy-Yeyati, Eduardo. 2006. "Optimal Debt: On the Insurance Value of International Debt Flows to Developing Economies." IDB Working Paper 575, Inter-American Development Bank, Washington, DC.

Levy-Yeyati, Eduardo, and Ugo Panizza. 2005. "The Elusive Costs of Sovereign Defaults." RES Working Paper 4485, Inter-American Development Bank, Research Department, Washington, DC.

Levy-Yeyati, Eduardo, Maria S. Martinez Peria, and Sergio L. Schmukler. 2004. "Market Discipline under Systemic Risk: Evidence from Bank Runs in Emerging Economies." Policy Research Working Paper 3440, World Bank, Washington, DC.

Martinez, Jose Vicente, and Guido Sandleris. 2008. "Is It Punishment? Sovereign Defaults and the Decline in Trade." Business School Working Paper 2008-01, Universidad Torcuato di Tella, Buenos Aires.

Medeiros, Carlos I., Magdalena Polan, and Parmeshwar Ramlogan. 2007. "A Primer on Sovereign Debt Buybacks and Swaps." IMF Working Paper 07/58, International Monetary Fund, Washington, DC.

Mendoza, Enrique G., and Vivian Z. Yue. 2008. "A Solution to the Default Risk–Business Cycle Disconnect." NBER Working Paper 13861, National Bureau of Economic Research, Cambridge, MA.

Mody, Ashoka, and Diego Saravia. 2006. "Catalysing Private Capital Flows: Do IMF Programmes Work as Commitment Devices?" *Economic Journal* 116 (513): 843–67.

Mody, Ashoka, Mark P. Taylor, and Jung Yeon Kim. 2001. "Modelling Fundamentals for Forecasting Capital Flows to Emerging Markets." *International Journal of Finance & Economics* 6 (3): 201–16.

Montiel, Peter, and Carmen M. Reinhart. 1999. "Do Capital Controls and Macroeconomic Policies Influence the Volume and Composition of Capital Flows? Evidence from the 1990s." *Journal of International Money and Finance* 18 (4): 619–65.

Panizza, Ugo, Federico Sturzenegger, and Jeromin Zettelmeyer. Forthcoming. "The Law and Economics of Sovereign Debt and Default." *Journal of Economic Literature.*

Papaioannou, Elias. 2005. "What Drives International Bank Flows? Politics, Institutions and Other Determinants." ECB Working Paper 437, European Central Bank, Frankfurt.

Pescatori, Andrea, and Amadou N. R. Sy. 2004. "Debt Crises and the Development of International Capital Markets." IMF Working Paper 04/44, International Monetary Fund, Washington, DC.

Pitchford, Rohan, and Mark L. J. Wright. 2008. "Holdouts in Sovereign Debt Restructuring: A Theory of Negotiation in a Weak Contractual Environment." Department of Economics, University of California, Los Angeles.

Portes, Richard, and Helene Rey. 2005. "The Determinants of Cross-Border Equity Flows." *Journal of International Economics* 65 (2): 269–96.

Portes, Richard, Helene Rey, and Yonghyup Oh. 2001. "Information and Capital Flows: The Determinants of Transactions in Financial Assets." *European Economic Review* 45 (4): 783–96.

The PRS (Political Risk Services) Group. Various years. *International Country Risk Guide Annual.* Syracuse, NY: The PRS Group.

Ratha, Dilip, Prabal De, and Sanket Mohapatra. 2007. "Shadow Sovereign Ratings for Unrated Developing Countries." Policy Research Working Paper 4269, World Bank, Washington, DC.

Reinhart, Carmen M., and Kenneth S. Rogoff. 2004. "Serial Default and the 'Paradox' of Rich-to-Poor Capital Flows." *American Economic Review* 94 (2): 53–58.

Reinhart, Carmen M., Kenneth S. Rogoff, and Miguel A. Savastano. 2003. "Debt Intolerance." *Brookings Papers on Economic Activity* 34 (1): 1–70.

Richmond, Christine, and Daniel Dias. 2008. "Duration of Capital Market Exclusion: Stylized Facts and Determining Factors." Department of Economics, University of California, Los Angeles.

Rose, Andrew K. 2005. "One Reason Countries Pay Their Debts: Renegotiation and International Trade." *Journal of Development Economics* 77 (1): 189–206.

Sandleris, Guido. 2008. "Sovereign Defaults: Information, Investment and Credit." *Journal of International Economics* 76 (2): 267–75.

Standard & Poor's. 2007. "Sovereign Defaults and Rating Transition Data: 2006 Update." February.

Sturzenegger, Federico, and Jeromin Zettelmeyer. 2007. *Debt Defaults and Lessons form a Decade of Crises.* Cambridge, MA: MIT Press

Taylor, Mark P., and Lucio Sarno. 1997. "Capital Flows to Developing Countries: Long- and Short-Term Determinants." *World Bank Economic Review* 11 (3): 451–70.

Tomz, Mike, and Mark L. J. Wright. 2007. "Do Countries Default in 'Bad Times'?" *Journal of the European Economic Association* 5 (2–3): 352–60.

Trebesch, Christoph. 2008. "Delays in Sovereign Debt Restructurings: Should We Really Blame the Creditors?" Department of Economics, Free University of Berlin.

———. 2009. "The Cost of Aggressive Sovereign Debt Policies: How Much Is the Private Sector Affected?" IMF Working Paper 09/29, International Monetary Fund, Washington, DC.

World Bank. 2002. *Global Development Finance 2002: Financing the Poorest Countries.* Washington, DC: World Bank.

———. 2003. *Global Development Finance 2003: Striving for Stability in Development Finance.* Washington, DC: World Bank.

———. 2007. *Global Development Finance 2007: The Globalization of Corporate Finance in Developing Countries.* Washington, DC: World Bank.

Zanforlin, Luisa. 2007. "Reaccessing International Capital Markets after Financial Crises: Some Empirical Evidence." IMF Working Paper 07/136, International Monetary Fund, Washington, DC.

8

Lessons from Market-Access Countries on Public Debt Sustainability and Growth

Brian Pinto and Mona Prasad

his chapter focuses on sovereign debt in developing countries with access to international capital markets.[1] Included in this set are middle-income countries as well as some low-income countries, such as India. We refer to these countries as *market-access countries*. Low-income countries that have benefited from debt relief in connection with the Heavily Indebted Poor Countries (HIPC) Initiative and the Multilateral Debt Relief Initiative (MDRI) are likely to join the ranks of these market-access countries in the coming years.

There is a sharp distinction between developing countries whose governments rely predominantly on market borrowings (that is, access to international capital markets) and those that do not. The second group relies mostly on official creditors (multilateral and bilateral) and but for rare exceptions, is not subject to sudden stops in capital flows.[2] Net transfers to countries in this group usually remain positive irrespective of the level of indebtedness, especially when they suffer negative external shocks. In addition, the "market versus official creditors" distinction carries over to fundamental topics such as debt restructuring and the incentives and objectives of both creditors and debtors.

The landscape now prevailing in a number of post–completion point HIPCs, many in Africa, is characterized by sharply reduced debt-to-GDP ratios, low per capita incomes, underdeveloped domestic debt markets, limited access to international capital markets, and heavy dependence on official development assistance (ODA). But as a sign of changing times, private capital flows into Africa reportedly exceeded official aid flows for the first time in 2006 (IMF 2008, p. 45). Debt relief coupled with the search for yield that characterized Western investor behavior until the subprime crisis hit in fall 2007 was a major factor, according to the International Monetary Fund (IMF 2008). The investment climate in these countries also strengthened as a result of major reforms and rapid growth between 2000 and 2007, a trend that has been interrupted by the U.S. subprime crisis and recession.

This chapter draws on the experience of market-access countries over the past two decades to gain insights into the links between sovereign debt and development that could serve as a basis for advising low-income countries as they eye market-access status. Given their massive developmental needs and limited taxation capacity, governments in low-income countries need to borrow domestically and externally. The experience of market-access countries suggests that the journey from low-income to market-access status should be undertaken cautiously and that ODA should be used in the interim as domestic fiscal and financial institutions are strengthened.

The chapter is organized as follows. The next section discusses debt dynamics and the importance of the government's intertemporal budget constraint. The following section looks at the crises of the 1980s and 1990s and the resultant debt overhang. The third section examines the responses to unsustainable debt dynamics/levels by market-access countries over the past decade. The fourth section explores the links between public debt and growth. The last section summarizes the lessons learned from market-access countries.

Debt Dynamics

The standard flow version of the government's budget constraint in discrete time is given by the equation

$$d_t - d_{t-1} = pd_t - ndfs_t + \frac{r_t - g_t}{1 + g_t} d_{t-1}, \tag{8.1}$$

where d is the end-of-period debt-to-GDP ratio, pd is the primary-deficit-to-GDP ratio, $ndfs$ is the nondebt-financing-sources-to-GDP ratio, r is the real interest rate, g is the real growth rate, and t is time period. (For a derivation, see the technical annex in Aizenman and Pinto 2005.) Changes in the debt-to-GDP ratio are explained by the primary deficit, the real interest rate, and the real growth rate; other factors, including privatization receipts (which form a part of nondebt financing sources), could also play a role.

Until the crises of 1997–98, the effect of the real exchange rate on debt burdens was largely overlooked.[3] The Russian Federation's poor growth and public finance performance over the period 1995–97, which preceded its August 1998 meltdown, illustrates the extent to which an appreciating real exchange rate can mask unsustainable debt dynamics (table 8.1).

During 1995–97, the primary deficit was high; real interest rates on ruble treasury bills easily exceeded 25 percent, with interest payments rising as a share of both GDP and revenues; and real GDP growth was either negative or close to zero. Based on equation 8.1, one would have expected a dramatically rising debt-to-GDP ratio. In fact, it barely budged, remaining at about 50 percent, fueling a sense of complacency. The ratio was stagnant because starting in mid-1995, the sharp real appreciation of the ruble— itself a consequence of the exchange rate–based disinflation program— yielded capital gains on the large percentage of dollar-denominated debt in total government debt. In 1996 alone, the real appreciation of the ruble reduced the debt-to-GDP ratio by 8 percent of GDP. But the real exchange rate was overvalued and on an unsustainable trajectory, as became apparent after the public debt crisis of 1998 (Kharas, Pinto, and Ulatov 2001). The Russian experience of 1998 underscores the importance of assessing real overvaluation, particularly if a large share of public debt is denominated in foreign currency.

Two other factors—private sector balance sheet mismatches and contingent liabilities of the government—also matter. The East Asian crisis of 1997–98 showed that currency and maturity mismatches on the balance sheets of banks and corporations (which borrowed short term in dollars and invested long term in local currency assets) could precipitate mass bankruptcy if the exchange rate collapsed. This in turn could force a fiscally costly bailout (table 8.2).

Table 8.1 Public Finances and Economic Growth in the Russian Federation, 1995–98

Year	Primary deficit (percentage of GDP)	Interest payments (percentage of GDP)	Interest payments (percentage of cash plus noncash revenue)	Government debt (US$ billions)	Government debt (percentage of GDP)	Real annual GDP growth (percent)
1995	2.2	3.6	28	170	50	–4.0
1996	2.5	5.9	47	201	48	–3.4
1997	2.4	4.6	38	218	50	0.9
1998	1.3	4.6	43	242	75	–4.9

Source: Kharas, Pinto, and Ulatov 2001.

Table 8.2 Estimated Bank Bailout Costs during the East Asian Crisis, by Country, 1997–2001

Country	Gross fiscal cost (percentage of average nominal GDP)
Indonesia	56.8
Korea, Rep. of	31.2
Malaysia	16.4
Philippines	13.2
Thailand	43.8
Vietnam	10.0

Source: Laeven and Valencia 2008.

Debt dynamics are influenced mainly by primary deficits, real interest rates, and growth rates. Real exchange rates and contingent liabilities also play important roles, as the crises of 1997–98 showed (box 8.1).

Because debt needs to be serviced through future taxation, which if insufficient could result in undesirably high inflation or costly default, debt sustainability and solvency become critical. A market-access country has a debt sustainability problem when its existing mix of fiscal policies needs to be changed in order to avoid an explosion in its debt-to-GDP ratio. This could happen if, for example, the government is running a structural primary deficit (that is, noninterest spending exceeds total revenues) and the real interest rate is greater than the real growth rate. In this case, the debt-to-GDP ratio will grow without bound in the absence of corrective policies until a crisis results (recall equation 8.1). The crisis could take the shape of a burst in inflation (which serves as a capital tax on domestic currency debt) or a debt default, the anticipation of which could have knock-on effects that could lead to a collapse in the exchange rate, a spike in interest rates, a run on banks (which tend to invest in government securities), and a plunge in growth.[4]

If, however, corrective policies are implemented in good time or there is a dramatic increase in the growth rate, a crisis can be avoided. In this sense, a debt sustainability problem need not translate into a solvency problem (that is, a situation in which the debt-to-GDP ratio reaches a level that is no longer serviceable). Such a situation would occur if the present value of future primary surpluses expressed as a percentage of GDP (at a discount rate equal to the real interest rate minus the growth rate) were less than the current debt-to-GDP ratio.[5] The policy implications are that a country running primary fiscal deficits today will need to run offsetting surpluses in the future and that procrastination is costly, because postponing adjustment to a burdensome debt situation will require an even greater fiscal effort down the road.

Box 8.1 What Factors Affect a Country's Level of Debt?

- Fiscal deficit = primary deficit + interest payments.
- Change in nominal debt = primary deficit + interest payments − (seigniorage + privatization proceeds).
- Interest payment = nominal interest rate × nominal debt.
- The faster the economy grows, the lower the debt-to-GDP ratio is.
- If some of the debt is in dollars, a nominal depreciation (appreciation) will raise (lower) the level of debt in domestic currency.
- Debt can also rise if the government bails out banks or guarantees are called (contingent liabilities).

Source: Authors.

This brings to the fore the centrality of the government's intertemporal budget constraint, which essentially says that debt dynamics are influenced by the potential for future revenues and growth prospects. These factors are crucial, as is the market's assessment of solvency. Hence, debt sustainability is a forward-looking exercise, and the factors affecting it are captured in the government's intertemporal budget constraint. The history of macroeconomic management also plays an important role in the market's assessment of debt sustainability, as Reinhart, Rogoff, and Savastano (2003) note.

From External Debt Overhang to Public Debt Sustainability

Until the macroeconomic crises of 1997–98, the focus of the developing-country debt literature tended to be on a country's total external debt, public plus private. This was motivated by the debt crisis of the 1980s and Latin America's "lost decade," even though much of this debt eventually ended up on the government's balance sheet as a result of private sector bailouts, debt-for-equity swaps, debt buybacks, and the Baker and Brady Plan resolutions of the crisis. The focus on external debt also fit well with the two-gap theory of development, which posited that developing-country growth was constrained by either a shortage of national savings or the foreign exchange needed for critical imported inputs. However, external indebtedness has been strongly associated with crisis and an increase in macroeconomic vulnerability rather than with rapid growth (World Bank 2005). Caution is therefore called for to avoid accessing the international capital markets prematurely.

One of the most useful policy concepts to emerge from the 1980s debt crisis was that of the external debt overhang, developed by Krugman (1988) and Sachs (1989).[6] This theory has three parts:

- *Definition.* An overhang exists whenever the market does not expect the debt to be fully repaid (that is, it expects a partial or total default). Debt then trades at a discount in the market relative to its face value, with a higher discount connoting a higher probability of default.
- *Impact.* When a country has a debt overhang, it is unlikely to be able to attract new sovereign inflows, even for projects with high economic rates of return (this is the essence of a debt overhang), and it would be vulnerable to a sudden stop. Existing creditors want to exit, and potentially new creditors are deterred by the prospect of an immediate capital loss. Firms would be reluctant to invest even in profitable projects for fear that their returns would be taxed away to service the debt; politicians would balk at implementing difficult reforms because the growth and taxation benefits would be captured by external creditors (Corden 1989).
- *Resolution.* A debt write-down would potentially benefit the country and creditors alike, but a collective-action problem makes such action difficult because individual creditors would prefer to free ride on debt reduction by other creditors and gain on their entire holding of the country's debt, as the secondary market price would tend to rise after the reduction. This free-rider problem formed the rationale for the Brady Plan announced in March 1989, whereby the U.S. government threw its weight behind a coordinated debt reduction to break the deadlock on the Latin American debt crisis.

If the Brady Plan gave respite, it did not last long. Financial liberalization of the external sector in the early 1990s appears to have enhanced vulnerability rather than growth (Gourinchas and Jeanne 2006; Prasad, Rajan, and Subramanian 2006; Aizenman, Pinto, and Radziwill 2007). The combination of fixed exchange rates, unsustainable debt dynamics, and open capital accounts proved hazardous to economic health. Another series of crises developed starting in 1997, this time involving public debt either as a fundamental cause (as in Argentina, Russia, and Turkey, where unsustainable debt dynamics propelled a crisis) or as an absorber of the costs of the crisis (as in Indonesia, the Republic of Korea, and other countries, where bank bailouts increased public debt [recall table 8.2]). Two large debt defaults occurred, in Russia (1998) and in Argentina (2001). Whereas Russia was able to restructure its debt within two years of its crisis, Argentina has still not reached full agreement with its private or official (Paris Club) creditors.

Substantial rescue packages orchestrated by the IMF and the World Bank played a role, especially in the East Asian countries. Neither the degree of coordinated official intervention nor the scale of debt reduction was as great as during the 1980s debt crisis, however. Nevertheless, the debt crises of the 1990s became a watershed in debates about development policy, with attacks unleashed on capital account convertibility, on the policy recommendations included in the Washington Consensus (Williamson 1990), and on the very utility of external borrowing and access to international capital flows as a way of promoting investment and growth.

Since the string of public debt crises that began in 1997, there has been a sea change in the way governments in market-access countries manage their public finances and macroeconomic policy more generally. Policy makers are apt to look at the links between public finances and growth differently, refocusing their attention away from short-run concerns about fiscal deficits and inflation toward longer-run concerns centered on the government's intertemporal budget constraint. There has also been a marked shift in focus from external to public debt.

In the policy literature, the concerns surrounding the external debt overhang have morphed into concerns about public debt sustainability and solvency. Investment and growth are likely to suffer in countries experiencing debt sustainability problems because of high real interest rates, macroeconomic uncertainty, and uncertainty about future taxation. In this sense, the negative effects are similar to those described earlier for an external debt overhang (although to the extent that part of the public debt is held by external creditors, the incentives for the government may differ).

Public Debt Sustainability in Market-Access Countries: Insights from the Past Decade

This section examines ways in which market-access countries can address their debt sustainability problems. It also assesses the effectiveness of debt guidelines and proposed instruments in preventing crises and provides empirical highlights from the past decade.

How Can Market-Access Countries Address Debt Sustainability Problems?

What should a government faced with unsustainable debt levels do? The answer depends on a country-specific diagnostic. Some options countries have tried over the past decade are described below.

Increase the Primary Surplus. Increasing the primary surplus amounts to reducing debt the old-fashioned way—by paying it off. Countries that increase their primary surpluses often do so by cutting public capital expenditure instead of raising taxes or cutting noninterest current expenditure. Such an approach is shortsighted to the extent that long-run growth and taxes (and hence the solvency of the government) could be adversely affected by the resulting infrastructure gaps. If this is the case, interest rates might not fall, because the fundamental fiscal problem will not have been addressed. In contrast, generating a higher primary surplus by increasing revenue mobilization through improvements in tax policy and administration or eliminating inefficient subsidies would help. Many countries may lack the scope for such measures, face political constraints, or both, however.

The observation that many market-access countries, especially in Latin America, were cutting public investments in infrastructure fueled the so-called "fiscal space" controversy, succinctly expressed by Calderon, Easterly, and Servén (2003, p. 133), who note that "fiscal adjustment through public infrastructure compression can be largely self-defeating in the long run, because of its adverse effect on growth and hence on the debt-servicing capacity of the public sector." The authors blame the international financial institutions for focusing on short-run stabilization, fiscal deficits, and gross public debt instead of long-run solvency, defined by net debt and the government's intertemporal budget constraint. As an alternative to raising primary surpluses at the expense of infrastructure, the fiscal space argument would suggest that a better strategy might be to borrow even more and invest in infrastructure. The debt-to-GDP ratio might rise in the short run, but solvency would actually be strengthened. The key condition is that the marginal financial return to the government (namely, user charges plus the tax collected on the marginal product of the extra spending on infrastructure) exceed the marginal cost of borrowing plus the rate of capital depreciation (see Servén 2007 for a derivation).

Even if we assume the Servén marginal condition is met, governments may not be able to borrow the money needed at what might be regarded as reasonable interest rates because of myopic capital markets (infrastructure projects involve long gestation periods) or past credibility or default problems that make new creditors reluctant to come in. In addition, high initial public indebtedness enhances vulnerability to exogenous shocks, as the subprime crisis eloquently attests.[7] Public debt sustainability problems thus have similar effects as the corporate debt overhang in that even profitable public investment infrastructure projects may have to be forgone until indebtedness is lowered.

Restructure Debt. The evidence on successfully restructuring debt (defined as changing the debt currency composition or terms before the scheduled maturity) in an attempt to address debt sustainability concerns is not encouraging. In particular, voluntary market-based exchanges do not seem to work. The reason is simple: a voluntary market-based exchange is unlikely to result in a reduction in the present value of debt obligations, because this would run counter to the interests of the creditors, and is therefore incapable of improving debt sustainability. Worse yet, an attempt to voluntarily restructure debt may not simply be neutral in the Modigliani-Miller sense; it may backfire and actually hasten a crisis. In both Russia (1998) and Argentina (2001), attempts to restructure debt in order to stave off a macroeconomic crisis actually precipitated one. In the context of the 1998 Russian crisis, Kharas, Pinto, and Ulatov (2001) argue that not only was the rescue package costly, but it also actually triggered the crisis.[8]

To see how this happened, suppose a country has a debt sustainability problem and the market is pricing the government's debt at default levels. This means there are basic concerns about the government's ability to service the debt, which can be verified by looking at revenue mobilization and growth, prospects for both of which were dim at that time in Russia. By bringing in senior debt, a rescue package by an international financial institution reduces the chances that the bonds held by the private sector will be serviced. In these circumstances, especially if the exchange rate is fixed, a boost to official reserves as a result of a rescue package by the international financial institutions provides the perfect opportunity for private sector holders of local-currency debt to exit, precipitating a speculative attack and subsequent crisis. In such a case, the rescue package has the twin effects of "demoting" private creditors while providing them with a means of escape at the precrisis exchange rate. Because restructuring debt does not address the core problems underlying unsustainable debt dynamics, it is unlikely to work in isolation. (For a formal analytical argument, see Aizenman, Kletzer, and Pinto 2005.)

Default. Another option is a forced, one-sided restructuring, resulting in a significant haircut for private creditors, domestic and external. Typically, such restructurings follow a suspension of debt service if not an outright default. After their crises had occurred, both Russia and Argentina were able to reduce their debt burdens through negotiated deals, but Argentina's renegotiation was much more tortuous and is still not fully complete. Although defaults accompanied by forced restructurings reduce indebtedness, they are costly in terms of disruption and reputation.[9] Not surprisingly, the nature of the outcome and the speed with which it is reached depend upon the relative bargaining power of the government and its creditors.

Russia was able to restructure its debt within two years of its August 1998 meltdown and at attractive terms. Its agreement with the London Club, concluded in August 2000, involved an estimated debt reduction of 50 percent in present value terms. The inducement was that the securities involved, which were legally the liability of the Soviet-era Vneshekonombank, would be replaced by Russian Eurobonds; the threat was that Vneshekonombank could be allowed to go bankrupt, creating a legal nightmare for creditors.[10]

It is difficult to know who ultimately lost and gained, because the market value of the securities involved rose from a paltry $1.8 billion in October 1998 to $14 billion just before the exchange (see Pinto, Gurvich, and Ulatov 2005). In addition, Russia was able to obtain the support of the IMF, which made a distinction between Russian and Soviet-era debt in which the debt that was restructured was treated as Soviet-era debt. Thus, the law under which the debt is issued, political support, and bargaining power all make a difference.

Do Nothing and Hope That the Country Grows Out of Its Indebtedness. Sitting back and hoping that a country will grow out of its debt is unlikely to work. Malaysia was able to reduce its debt-to-GDP ratio significantly after it had exceeded 120 percent in the mid-1980s, but this achievement rested on a fundamental redefinition of the role of the state, from being a sponsor of affirmative action based on setting up nonfinancial public sector enterprises to playing a more supportive role, with a focus on encouraging private sector–led growth.

Likewise, the pickup in Indian growth rates after 2003 has helped with its high public indebtedness. The cumulative impact of gradual reform in taxes, trade, and the domestic financial sector and careful macroeconomic management after 1991 (building up foreign exchange reserves, adopting a flexible exchange rate, and shifting toward long-term rupee debt) has been substantial. Initially, these reforms affected public finances negatively, reducing revenues and weakening debt dynamics, as became evident during the late 1990s. The beneficial impact on growth was seen only after 2003, suggesting that macroeconomic reforms may bear fruit only after a lag and that some deterioration in debt dynamics may be unavoidable in the interim (as the fiscal costs are borne up front).[11]

It is very likely that countries transitioning from lower-income to market-access status will experience this sort of deterioration in debt dynamics before growth dividends kick in. The process of strengthening fiscal and financial institutions in low-income countries could require rationalizing tax rates, cutting import tariffs, eliminating financial repression, delicensing businesses, strengthening supervision and monitoring agencies, and designing and implementing reporting systems for debt and capital inflows, to cite just a few possible reforms.[12] A number of these reforms could reduce government revenues in the short run, although they would go a long way toward strengthening the microfoundations of growth and hence increasing long-run solvency. However, there could be a lag of several years before growth picks up; managing the interim could be daunting. Two factors that have been found to cushion the process are a cautious approach to capital account liberalization and a country's inflation and credit history (remaining "debt tolerant," in the parlance of Reinhart, Rogoff, and Savastano 2003).

Reputation and the Role of the Market

Markets tend to be more tolerant toward countries that have a history of sound macroeconomic management: both Malaysia and India were able to accumulate significantly higher levels of debt than are conventionally considered safe without ending up in crisis. In this sense, debt intolerance or vulnerability to crisis even at low levels of external debt is a consequence of adverse past debt outcomes in emerging economies, which are in turn directly affected by the way public finances are managed. On the basis of institutional investor ratings between 1979 and 2002 and the ratio of total external debt (public plus private) to GNP between 1970 and 2000, Reinhart, Rogoff, and Savastano (2003) classify market-access economies by their level of debt intolerance based on the incidence of adverse credit events. They find that for highly debt-intolerant countries, safe external debt thresholds could be as low as 15–20 percent of GNP.[13]

A fundamental assumption in the theoretical debt literature is that Ponzi schemes are ruled out—that is, debt cannot grow faster than GDP forever. This condition is in danger of being violated when the government runs a primary deficit, the real interest rate exceeds the growth rate, and debt obligations are rolled over.[14] One can think of distinct instances in the past decade or so in which countries have done this (Russia after mid-1995 and in the lead-up to its 1998 meltdown; India during 1997–2002, when its chronic primary deficits began to be accompanied by real interest rates exceeding the growth rate). This does not necessarily mean that the country is insolvent: corrective action can always be taken. Yet unlike India, Russia was unable to avoid its disruptive crisis of 1998. The key point is the market's assessment of whether credible corrective action will be taken on time, which is bound to be influenced by the country's inflation and default history—one way of looking at the debt-intolerance hypothesis of Reinhart, Rogoff, and Savastano (2003). Alternatively, the market may be myopic and not give the country a chance. Market perceptions thus play a key role in determining safe threshold debt levels for market-access countries (although this does not imply that the market is always right; it is prone to myopia and herd behavior).

How Effective Are Debt Guidelines and Proposed Instruments in Preventing Crises?

The focus on crisis avoidance is manifested in attempts to pin down guidelines for what constitutes a sustainable debt level. There have also been attempts to develop and foster debt instruments with equity-type features (such as GDP–indexed bonds). Empirical evidence, however, suggests that debt guidelines or rules-of-thumb do not work well in practice and that there has been limited appetite for new instruments.

Rules-of-Thumb for Sustainable Debt Levels. The Maastricht Treaty for participation in the European Monetary Union required a reduction of the government's debt-to-GDP ratio to at least 60 percent. Comparing this benchmark with the debt levels of Argentina, India, and Russia during the 1996–2007 period is instructive (figure 8.1).

Both Russia in 1998 and Argentina in the lead-up to the 2001 crisis had debt levels below the 60 percent threshold. Conversely, large countries like India escaped a crisis during the turbulence of the late 1990s despite government debt levels far in excess of 60 percent of GDP. These findings suggest that other factors also weigh in, such as the possible overvaluation of the real exchange rate, the currency and maturity composition of government debt, balance sheet mismatches in the private sector and contingent liabilities, and the dynamics of the debt as influenced by the prospects for growth and tax collections. All these factors are eventually captured in the government's intertemporal budget constraint.

Financial Engineering. Proponents of the "original sin" hypothesis (Eichengreen, Hausmann, and Panizza 2002) argue that developing-country debt crises reflect the failure of the market to develop suitable instruments that would enable market-access countries to borrow long term in their own currencies. The 2007 report by the Inter-American Development Bank, *Living with Debt,* reinforces the original sin hypothesis. It reviews and analyzes the evolution of sovereign debt in Latin America and the Caribbean over the past two centuries, identifying debt structure and composition as

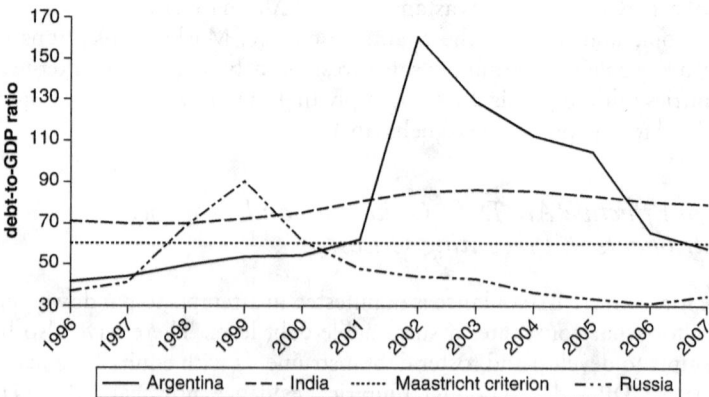

Figure 8.1 Maastricht Debt-to-GDP Ratio Criterion and Ratios in Argentina, India, and Russia, 1996–2007

Source: IMF 2008.

the critical determinants of vulnerabilities. Given this finding, the study advocates the use of instruments such as contingent debt contracts with equity-type features, inflation-indexed debt instruments, and a shift toward domestic currency–denominated debt. Such a move would ensure a debt structure that would limit the risk of sovereign finance and enable the use of sovereign debt as an instrument for growth.

Notwithstanding their theoretical appeal, contingent debt instruments have not been warmly embraced by the markets or developing countries. Instruments such as GDP–indexed bonds, for example, in which the interest rate is positively correlated with growth, have not taken off. Their lack of popularity could reflect technical or incentive-related problems in measuring GDP accurately and punctually or network externalities that make it costly for an individual country to take the initiative. The idea behind these market innovations and prescriptions was to use financial engineering as a means to reduce vulnerabilities and improve debt sustainability. Their limited use reinforces the argument that strengthening fiscal fundamentals is far more important and that financial engineering cannot replace weak fundamentals.

The experience of Brazil buttresses this argument. Although the Brazilian government made a concerted effort to stay away from hard-currency debt after 1999, the local-currency debt it issued tended to be indexed to short-run interest rates, the exchange rate, or the price level. The proportion of nominal (unindexed) bonds fell from 60 percent in 1996 (when credibility was high following the successful stabilization of 1994) to less than 3 percent in 2002, as a result of economic and political uncertainty associated with the presidential election and its aftermath (Gill and Pinto 2005). The basic point is that debt maturity and currency composition are not one-sided policy choices made by a country but endogenous to more fundamental variables such as credibility, reputation, and government solvency as perceived by the market.

Empirical Highlights from the Past Decade

All the major market-access countries sought to reduce their indebtedness following the crises that began in 1997 (including by default and forced restructuring). The degree of success varied. In general, countries were successful in running higher primary surpluses, building up foreign exchange reserves, and shifting toward flexible exchange rates and domestic-currency debt. Despite similar policy responses, success in reducing indebtedness (as measured by the public-debt-to-GDP ratio) and in reigniting growth has varied considerably. East Asian countries have fared much better than other countries, for two reasons. First, except in the Philippines, East Asian governments traditionally carried little debt and therefore had greater capacity to absorb the shock associated with the 1997–98 crisis. Second, these governments boasted stronger credit histories.[15]

The situation has been more challenging in Argentina, Brazil, Russia, and Turkey, where unsustainable public debt dynamics were a fundamental cause of macroeconomic crisis. In these countries, growth was low and interest rates and fiscal deficits high in the lead-up to their crises. Turkey saw more immediate results in terms of reducing indebtedness and restoring long-run growth than did Argentina or Brazil. Argentina resumed growing in 2003 and has been growing rapidly since, but concerns remain about debt dynamics and subnational fiscal policies. Brazil has been growing since 2000, albeit at a relatively slow rate. After its wrenching 1998 crisis, growth resumed rapidly in Russia following a large real depreciation of its currency and the hardening of budgets for the government, firms, and banks, although the challenge of diversifying the economy away from oil, gas, and minerals remains.

Public Debt and Growth

An important—and unsurprising—finding from the past decade is that a combination of debt intolerance (high inflation and a bad credit history) and unsustainable debt dynamics is not good for growth. The reasons for this are familiar: real interest rates are likely to be high, crowding out private investment; the government might be forced to cut capital expenditure, further hurting growth because of complementary cutbacks in private investment, which might be deterred by infrastructure gaps; and macroeconomic uncertainty is likely to be high regarding inflation and relative prices as well as future tax rates. These factors conspire to weaken the investment climate.

A key new insight is that the combination of unsustainable debt dynamics and debt intolerance acts in a fashion similar to the external debt overhang. The government may not be able to borrow for and invest in projects even with high rates of return (those meeting the marginal condition derived in Servén 2007) as a shortcut to increasing net worth and restoring creditworthiness without first reducing its indebtedness. This is so because without the restoration of a government's credibility, interest rates could rise in response to the additional borrowing, reflecting the reluctance of creditors to lend new sums of money, eventually violating the Servén marginal condition. For this reason, we remain skeptical about the "fiscal space" argument articulated earlier.

Suppose a policy maker in a low-income country starting out afresh after HIPC–MDRI relief would like to use debt in support of growth. What advice could one give? The optimal debt literature (summarized elegantly in Barro 1999) has three main prescriptions:

- Tax rates should be smoothed or kept constant to the extent possible.
- Optimal fiscal policy should be either pro- or countercyclical over the business cycle, depending on the assumptions made about the

demand versus the wealth effects of fiscal policy; the nature of the
credit constraints faced by individuals, firms, and the government;
and the interaction between domestic and international credit constraints (Perotti 2007).
- Under uncertainty, indexed debt instruments should be issued where
available.

These policy prescriptions are meant for high-income countries concerned about smoothing fluctuations in the business cycle; they are likely
to be of limited value to low-income countries trying to raise long-run
growth while minimizing crisis-induced volatility. Thus, although the optimal debt literature is the natural first port of call, it is not particularly
helpful in offering immediate guidance to low-income countries seeking
to graduate to market-access status, a transition that will require major
transformations in their tax systems and fiscal and financial institutions.

We now turn to the empirical policy-based literature to see what
it has to offer. As Easterly (2005, p. 1033) notes in the context of the
effects of economic policies on growth, "The list of national economic
policies that have received most extensive attention are fiscal policy,
inflation, black market premiums on foreign exchange, financial repression vs. financial development, real overvaluation of the exchange rate,
and openness to trade." This focus, combined with the observation that
Latin America performed poorly on many of these variables, led Williamson (2000, p. 251) to set down the Washington Consensus in 1990
as the "lowest common denominator of policy advice being addressed
by the Washington-based institutions to Latin American countries as
of 1989." The Washington Consensus covered expenditure (redirection
toward fields offering both high economic returns and the potential to
improve income distribution), tax reform (to reduce marginal tax rates),
liberalization of foreign direct investment, privatization, deregulation
(to abolish entry and exit barriers), and tightening of secure property
rights. It pointedly excluded capital account liberalization.

In an apparent reference to the Washington Consensus, the Commission on Growth and Development notes that "in recent decades governments were advised to 'stabilize, privatize, and liberalize'" (Commission
on Growth 2008, p. 5).[16] It observes that there is merit in this prescription but that it is not enough. Based on its examination of 13 episodes
of sustained high growth (defined as an average annual growth rate
of 7 percent or more for 25 years or longer), it identifies five common
ingredients: openness (importation of knowledge and exploitation of
global demand); macroeconomic stability (modest inflation and sustainable public finances); leadership and governance (credible commitment to
inclusive growth and capable administration); market allocation (prices
guide resources and resources follow prices); and future orientation (high
investment and high saving).

These ingredients and the "stabilize, privatize, and liberalize" dictum of the Washington Consensus have one thing in common: a direct bearing on public finances. Trade openness is likely to involve cutting tariffs, with an adverse impact on revenues; sustainable public finances would call for balance in the government's intertemporal budget constraint; market allocation might require liberalization of interest rates (reduction in implicit financial repression taxes) and cuts in subsidies (hardening budgets for firms); and future orientation would call for reducing macroeconomic uncertainty, without which horizons are likely to be short. Even good leadership and governance would translate into how public finances are managed, including the transparent selection of public investment projects and tax reform.

The experience of market-access countries over the past decade suggests that "stabilize, privatize, and liberalize" is in dire need of reinterpretation. Stabilization is more than the low inflation and small fiscal deficits Fischer (1993) emphasized; it also means sustainable debt dynamics and a balanced intertemporal budget for the government, which are more complicated to assess and measure. Privatization refers ultimately to a set of incentives to use and allocate resources well: the varied experiences of the transition economies during the 1990s (the Czech Republic, Poland, and Russia all had different strategies) showed that privatization had to be accompanied by hard budgets, competition, and transparent corporate governance if it was to deliver the intended benefits. With regard to liberalization, in his classic 1985 article, Diaz-Alejandro cautioned that countries that liberalized their capital accounts in the presence of weak domestic financial systems or trade-tax distortions risked inefficient resource allocation and a possible financial crash.

Conflating the Commission on Growth (2008) recommendations with the "growth diagnostics" of Hausmann, Rodrik, and Velasco (2005) once again suggests that public finances have a key role to play. It is hard to think of any binding constraint that needs relaxing that does not have implications for the public finances. No wonder former U.S. Treasury Secretary Larry Summers quipped that IMF stood for "It's Mostly Fiscal."

Conclusions

The key empirical insights that emerge from the public debt crises in market-access countries during the 1990s can be summarized as follows:

- *The way in which stabilization is viewed has changed.* A new mindset has emerged that focuses on the government's intertemporal budget constraint instead of short-run fiscal deficits and inflation. The focus of debt has shifted from external to public debt, although the most recent turmoil highlights the importance of both public (domestic plus external) and total external (public plus private) debt. The reason for the new focus is that the clean-up of the government's balance sheet has in many cases been accompanied by a large increase in private external debt.

- *The market is the ultimate arbiter of what level of debt is sustainable.* Rules-of-thumb on what constitutes a safe debt-to-GDP threshold (such as the Maastricht criteria or even criteria generated by cross-country regressions) are of limited use and could lead to unjustified complacency.

- *Fiscal fundamentals dominate financial engineering.* Debt intolerance ("it's the country's fault," because of its inflation and credit history) finds more empirical support than does original sin ("it's the market's fault," appropriately engineered instruments will solve the problem). A good debt structure (in the sense of IDB 2007) will help reduce vulnerability to a crisis but is not a one-sided policy choice. Moreover, the set of debt structure–related choices available will be severely constrained for debt-intolerant countries.

- *Market-access countries have been reforming and self-insuring.* As a rule, market-access countries have been seeking to reduce indebtedness (measured by the debt-to-GDP ratio) in order to spur growth. They have adopted common policies after the crises that began in 1997–98, including shifting toward domestic debt and flexible exchange rates; running higher primary surpluses; building up reserves; and in many cases, strengthening financial and fiscal systems.

- *A natural hierarchy has emerged in postcrisis responses.* This consists of first reducing indebtedness (measured by the debt-to-GDP ratio) and only then thinking about better aligning fiscal policy with growth. This two-step route appears more feasible than the "fiscal space" prescription of immediately borrowing more for infrastructure in order to raise long-run growth.

- *Market-access countries have been relying on themselves.* What countries themselves have been doing in response to the public debt crises after 1997 is much more significant than what the international financial institutions or market innovation have been able to do to help. Self-insurance (understood as a comprehensive fiscal and financial package) is the name of the game.

Low-income countries should not expect a smooth ride to market-access status, and they should make every effort to avoid crises—prevention is better than cure. Doing so requires extensive groundwork in strengthening fiscal and financial institutions and maximizing the use of available ODA in the transition to predominantly market-based financing.

The experience of market-access countries with public debt and development highlights the importance of good management of public finances and the government's intertemporal budget constraint. Keeping debt on a sustainable trajectory is likely to have reinforcing spin-off benefits through greater market access to less risky debt structures in terms of currency and maturity. It also has important linkages to growth: it provides macroeconomic stability, reduces uncertainty about future inflation and tax rates, and creates a facilitating environment for private investment by undertaking complementary public investments. Such synergies fit well with the Washington Consensus, the common ingredients in sustained fast-growth episodes identified by the Commission on Growth, and the "growth diagnostics" framework of Hausmann, Rodrik, and Velasco (2005).

It is hard to imagine low-income countries financing their development strategies without accumulating public debt, which in the future will come increasingly from the domestic and international capital markets rather than official creditors. Such borrowing is essential because low-income countries have huge infrastructure and social needs, limited taxation capacity, and low savings rates. Moreover, future generations are likely to be richer than the current generation, justifying borrowing, especially for long-gestation projects.

Low-income countries exiting the HIPC Initiative and MDRI processes and eyeing market-access status can learn from the experience of market-access countries over the past decade in order to avoid making the mistakes they did. Will they have the political will and foresight to do so? Only time will tell.

Notes

1. Unless explicitly noted otherwise, *debt* refers to public debt, both domestic and external. The terms *public debt* and *sovereign debt* are used interchangeably.

2. In Kenya, official creditors suddenly cut aid flows in the early 1990s on governance grounds. The move led to severe macroeconomic problems and a major scandal as the central bank launched special incentive schemes to boost foreign exchange reserves (Bandiera, Kumar, and Pinto 2008).

3. Glick and Kharas (1986) discuss real exchange rate movements in the context of optimal external borrowing.

4. The reader will readily recognize the burst of inflation outcome as the famous result of Sargent and Wallace (1981).

5. The intuition is that the growth rate of debt is equal to the rate of interest, whereas the growth rate of the debt-to-GDP ratio is the difference between the interest rate and the growth rate. Primary surpluses are available to pay off debt and thereby slow its rate of growth. For a simple derivation, see Aizenman and Pinto (2005).

6. This concept owes its origins to Myers (1977) in the corporate finance context. The idea is that if a firm's income is not sufficient for it to service its existing debt, it will find difficulty in attracting new financing, even for investment projects with a positive net present value, because much or possibly all the net present value could be appropriated by existing debt holders. Firms thus end up forgoing profitable new investment opportunities, reducing growth.

7. One of the reasons why market-access countries have been resilient so far is precisely because their governments cleaned up their balance sheets and built up reserves as part of a self-insurance strategy following the last round of crises, a point returned to later in this chapter.

8. Together with dollar Eurobond issues and a debt swap out of ruble treasury bills into long-term dollar bonds, the first tranche of the rescue package raised Russian public debt in dollars by 8 percent of postcrisis GDP in the 10 weeks leading up to the crisis (Kharas, Pinto, and Ulatov 2001).

9. For a comprehensive and authoritative account of the sovereign debt defaults of the past decade, see Sturzenegger and Zettelmeyer (2006), who find that countries rarely engage in "strategic" default, usually doing so only after all other options fail.

10. Vneshekonombank was the Soviet-era bank responsible for managing external debt.

11. See Pang, Pinto, and Wes (2007) for an analysis of India's macro-fiscal-growth developments after 1991.

12. For example, among seven African countries examined in an IMF (2008) study, Zambia was the only one in which private capital flow data, including portfolio flows, are compiled by the central bank and stock exchange on a monthly basis. Notwithstanding its impressive fiscal reforms since 2004, Nigeria is described as having "only limited capacity to monitor portfolio inflows" (p. 59).

13. Reinhart, Rogoff, and Savastano (2003) focus on a country's total external debt (public plus private). This chapter looks at total public debt (domestic plus external).

14. This does not mean that the government is insolvent or that debt will grow faster than GDP forever, unless there is simply no hope of future primary surpluses.

15. Between 1824 and 2001, the Republic of Korea, Malaysia, Singapore, and Thailand had not a single episode of external debt default (Reinhart, Rogoff, and Savastano 2003).

16. Williamson (2000) notes that this policy slogan does not do justice to the Washington Consensus. The comparison in Rodrik (2008) of the list of reforms in the Washington Consensus and the ingredients for rapid growth from the Growth Commission brings out their similarity. The main differences are the Growth Commission's emphasis on country context (diagnostic rather than presumptive) and the key role of governance.

References

Aizenman, Joshua, Kenneth M. Kletzer, and Brian Pinto. 2005. "Sargent-Wallace Meets Krugman-Flood-Garber, or Why Sovereign Debt Swaps Do Not Avert Macroeconomic Crises." *Economic Journal* 115 (503): 343–67.

Aizenman, Joshua, and Brian Pinto. 2005. *Managing Economic Volatility and Crises: A Practitioner's Guide*. Cambridge, U.K.: Cambridge University Press.

Aizenman, Joshua, Brian Pinto, and Artur Radziwill. 2007. "Sources for Financing Domestic Capital: Is Foreign Saving a Viable Option for Developing Countries?" *Journal of International Money and Finance* 26 (5): 682–702.

Bandiera, Luca, Praveen Kumar, and Brian Pinto. 2008. "Kenya's Quest for Growth: Stabilization and Reforms—But Political Stability?" Policy Research Working Paper 4685, World Bank, Washington, DC.

Barro, Robert J. 1999. "Notes on Optimal Debt Management." Department of Economics, Harvard University, Cambridge, MA.

Calderon, Cesar, William Easterly, and Luis Servén. 2003. "Infrastructure Compression and Public Sector Solvency in Latin America." In *The Limits of Stabilization: Infrastructure, Public Deficits, and Growth in Latin America*, ed. William Easterly and Luis Servén, 119–38. Washington, DC: World Bank.

Commission on Growth and Development. 2008. *The Growth Report: Strategies for Sustained Growth and Inclusive Development*. Washington, DC: World Bank.

Corden, W. Max. 1989. "Debt Relief and Adjustment Incentives." In *Analytical Issues in Debt*, ed. J. A. Frenkel, M. P. Dooley, and P. Wickham, 242–57. Washington, DC: International Monetary Fund.

Diaz-Alejandro, Carlos. 1985. "Goodbye Financial Repression, Hello Financial Crash." *Journal of Development Economics* 19 (1–2): 1–24.

Easterly, William. 2005. "National Policies and Economic Growth: An Appraisal." In *Handbook of Economic Growth* 1A, ed. Philippe Aghion and Steven Durlauf, 1016–56. Amsterdam: North-Holland.

Eichengreen, Barry, Ricardo Hausmann, and Ugo Panizza. 2002. "Original Sin: The Pain, the Mystery, and the Road to Redemption." Paper prepared for the conference "Currency and Maturity Matchmaking: Redeeming Debt from Original Sin," Inter-American Development Bank, Washington, DC, November 21–22.

Fischer, Stanley. 1993. "The Role of Macroeconomic Factors in Growth." *Journal of Monetary Economics* 32 (3): 485–512.

Gill, Indermit, and Brian Pinto. 2005. "Sovereign Debt in Developing Countries with Market Access: Help or Hindrance?" In *Financial Crises Lessons from the Past, Preparation for the Future*, ed. Gerard Caprio, James A. Hanson, and Robert E. Litan, 87–120. Washington, DC: Brookings Institution Press.

Glick, Reuven, and Homi Kharas. 1986. "The Costs and Benefits of Foreign Borrowing: A Survey of Multi-Period Models." *Journal of Development Studies* 22 (2): 279–99.

Gourinchas, Pierre-Olivier, and Olivier Jeanne. 2006. "The Elusive Gains from International Financial Integration." *Review of Economic Studies* 73 (3): 715–41.

Hausmann, Ricardo, Dani Rodrik, and Andres Velasco. 2005. "Growth Diagnostics." http://ksghome.harvard.edu/~drodrik/barcelonafinalmarch2005.pdf.

IDB (Inter-American Development Bank). 2007. *Living with Debt: How to Limit the Risks of Sovereign Finance*. Economic and Social Progress in Latin America 2007 Report. Washington, DC: IDB.

IMF (International Monetary Fund). 2008. *World Economic and Financial Surveys. Regional Economic Outlook: Sub-Saharan Africa. APR08*. Washington, DC: IMF.

Kharas, Homi, Brian Pinto, and Sergei Ulatov. 2001. "An Analysis of Russia's 1998 Meltdown: Fundamentals and Market Signals." *Brooking Papers on Economic Activity* 1: 1–50.

Krugman, Paul. 1988. "Financing vs. Forgiving a Debt Overhang." *Journal of Development Economics* 29 (3): 253–68.

Laeven, Luc, and Fabian Valencia. 2008. "Systemic Banking Crises: A New Database." IMF Working Paper WP/08/224, International Monetary Fund, Washington, DC.

Myers, Stewart C. 1977. "Determinants of Corporate Borrowing." *Journal of Financial Economics* 5: 147–75.

Pang, Gaobo, Brian Pinto, and Marina Wes. 2007. "India Rising: Faster Growth, Lower Indebtedness." Policy Research Working Paper 4241, World Bank, Washington DC.

Perotti, Roberto. 2007. "Fiscal Policy in Developing Countries: A Framework and Some Questions." Policy Research Working Paper 4365, World Bank, Washington, DC.

Pinto, Brian, Evsey Gurvich, and Sergei Ulatov. 2005. "Lessons from the Russian Crisis of 1998 and Recovery." In Managing Economic Volatility and Crises: A Practitioner's Guide, ed. Joshua Aizenman and Brian Pinto, 406–38. Cambridge, U.K.: Cambridge University Press.

Prasad, Eswar, Raghuram G. Rajan, and Arvind Subramanian. 2006. "Patterns of International Capital Flows and Their Implications for Economic Development." Federal Reserve Bank of Kansas City Journal Proceedings, 119–58.

Reinhart, Carmen, Kenneth Rogoff, and Miguel Savastano. 2003. "Debt Intolerance." Brookings Papers on Economic Activity 1: 1–74.

Rodrik, Dani. 2008. "Spence Christens a New Washington Consensus." Economists' Voice, July.

Sachs, Jeffrey. 1989. "The Debt Overhang of Developing Countries." Debt Stabilization and Development, ed. G. A. Calvo, R. Findlay, P. Kouri, and J. B. de Macedo, 80–102. Cambridge, MA: Blackwell.

Sargent, Thomas J., and Neil Wallace. 1981. "Some Unpleasant Monetaristic Arithmetic." Federal Reserve Bank of Minneapolis Quarterly Review 5 (3): 1–17.

Servén, Luis. 2007. "Fiscal Rules, Public Investment and Growth." Policy Research Working Paper 4382, World Bank, Washington, DC.

Sturzenegger, Federico, and Jeromin Zettelmeyer. 2006. Debt Defaults and Lessons from a Decade of Crises. Cambridge, MA: MIT Press.

Williamson, John. 1990. "What Washington Means by Policy Reform." In Latin American Adjustment: How Much Has Happened? ed. J. Williamson, 7–20. Washington, DC: Institute for International Economics.

———. 2000. "What Should the World Bank Think about the Washington Consensus?" World Bank Research Observer 15 (2): 251–64.

World Bank. 2005. Economic Growth in the 1990s: Lessons from a Decade of Reform. Washington, DC: World Bank.

Part III

Odious Debt

9

The Concept of Odious Debt: Some Considerations

Vikram Nehru and Mark Thomas

The debate on "odious" debt has grown in intensity in recent years. Some advocacy groups and civil society organizations have invoked the concept in their manifestos for unilateral debt repudiation by developing countries. The concept was used as a possible justification for canceling the debt of post-Saddam Iraq.

The expression *odious debt* may mean different things to different people, largely because they use it to achieve different objectives. It is hardly surprising then that the participants in this debate tend to speak past one another.

This chapter summarizes the terms of the debate on a controversial subject and examines how the underlying motivating forces driving the debate can be addressed in a constructive way. The first section identifies the main features of the traditional concept and categories of odious debt and briefly examines whether a rule allowing its repudiation may be said to have emerged in international law. The second section considers recent attempts to expand the traditional concept and categories of odious debt and asks whether they are sufficiently precise to contribute to the solution of the problems they are meant to address. The last section identifies ways in which lenders and borrowers can address, or have indeed addressed, the concerns underlying the concept of odious debt.

Traditional Concept and Categories of Odious Debt

Initially, the term *odious debt* identified debt that a state or a government had contracted with a view to attaining objectives that were prejudicial to the major interests of the successor state or government or of the local population. It covered debt contracted with an international legal subject (a state) under legal agreements governed by international law.[1] The issue of the existence of an international legal doctrine on odious debt can arise within the context of litigation before international courts and arbitral tribunals and before national courts.[2] With respect to financial agreements governed by a national legal system, the question (not addressed here) is whether a national, as opposed to an international, doctrine on odious debt exists.[3]

As a rule, international law requires a successor government to honor the public debt of a predecessor regime (Jennings and Watts 1992). However, if the question is not one of succession of governments but one of succession of states, the law becomes uncertain. The extent to which a successor state is bound to honor the public debt of the replaced state is a matter of controversy. The solution reflected in the 1983 Vienna Convention on succession of states in respect of state property, archives, and debt is not immune from difficulties (Brownlie 2003).[4] This may partly explain why it has not been widely accepted or entered into force.[5]

War, Subjugation, and Regime Debt

Historically, the theory of odious debt has been developed mainly in the writings of Anglo-American jurists (Bedjaoui 1977). The English lawyer John Westlake (1910) discussed odious debt (without using this term) in his treatise on international law at the beginning of the past century, but the name most often linked to the emergence of a doctrine of odious debt is that of Alexander Nahum Sack, who wrote on the subject in the 1920s, when he lived in Paris as a Russian expatriate. Sack identified three categories of odious debt, namely, "war debt" (debt incurred when the government of a state contracts debt "with a view to waging war against another state" [Sack 1927, p. 165]); "subjugation debt" (debt incurred when the government "contracts debts to subjugate the population of part of its territory or to colonize it by members of the dominant nationality") [p. 158]), and "regime debt" (debt incurred when a despotic regime "contracts a debt, not for the needs and in the interest of the state, but to strengthen its own despotic regime" [p. 157]). This division has proved helpful in the treatment of the topic by later writers and is therefore adopted in this chapter.

War Debt. Successor states have sometimes rejected war debt contracted by a predecessor state to sustain its war effort against their supporters. A case in point is the treatment of South Africa's war debt when Great Britain annexed the Transvaal, in 1900, after the Boer War. In its opinion to the Colonial Office, the Crown Counsel denied the existence of any international legal principle that would compel the British government to recognize obligations incurred during or in contemplation of the war.

There have also been cases in which, out of political expedience, successor states have assumed the war debt of predecessor states. An example is the assumption of a percentage of Austria's war debt by the former Czechoslovakia after World War I.[6] This uneven practice induced such an attentive observer as Feilchenfeld (1931) to doubt whether a specific international customary rule had emerged exempting war debt from assumption in the case of annexation or dismemberment.

Subjugation Debt. The classic case of rejection of a subjugation debt is the repudiation by the United States of the Cuban debt contracted by Spain, allegedly on the ground that the debt had been imposed on Cuba against its will and contracted for not to benefit Cuba but rather to keep it under Spanish domination and to suppress the war of independence. In opposition to this claim, Spain argued that this debt had been contracted on behalf and for the benefit of Cuba and had contributed to the island's economic development. The 1898 Treaty of Peace, which ended the dispute, seemed to uphold the United States's argument, in that neither the United States nor Cuba assumed the subjugation debt contracted by Spain. However, in this case (as in the case of war debt), the view that a successor state should be relieved of responsibility for any debt contracted by a predecessor state to subjugate a territory did not go unchallenged. In 1905, Frantz Despagnet argued that this view "opens the way to all manner of disputes as to the utility of expenditure incurred by the dismembered country for the portion that is separated from it; it encourages the most arbitrary and most iniquitous solutions" (Despagnet 1905, p. 11, quoted in Bejaoui 1977). Nor has the practice of states been consistent in its application. For instance, although it declared its readiness to assume certain debt before the Dutch capitulation to Japan on Java on March 8, 1942, and on Sumatra on April 7, 1942, Indonesia refused to assume various debt after those dates, especially those resulting from Dutch military operations against the Indonesian national liberation movement. At a roundtable conference in 1949, Indonesia and the Netherlands agreed on a formula of debt apportionment that departed from the principle of repudiation of subjugation debt. Although Indonesia later denounced the agreement, it remains questionable whether a customary international rule allowing the repudiation of subjugation debt really exists.[7]

Regime Debt. As a rule, arguments based on the nonenforceability of war and subjugation debt have been used within the context of state succession. The case of regime debt is different. Following a change in government, successor governments sometimes refuse to honor the debt contracted by the previous regime, because it was contracted in the exclusive interest of the predecessor regime, not to the benefit of the state or its population. The traditional example is that of the loans extended by the Royal Bank of Canada to Frederico Tinoco, a former secretary of war of Costa Rica, who, at the time of the loans in question, was the head of the Costa

Rican government, having overthrown the previous government in 1917. Tinoco's government lasted two years; the loans were contracted in the months before he left the country. Great Britain started arbitral proceedings against Costa Rica to force the new government to honor Tinoco's debt. The sole arbitrator (William Howard Taft, a former U.S. President and, at the time of the arbitration, the U.S. Chief Justice) held that the transactions involving Tinoco were "full of irregularities" and that the Royal Bank of Canada knew that the money would benefit only Tinoco, not the state or the people of Costa Rica. The new Costa Rican government was therefore right in declining its responsibility for the repayment of the loans (United Nations 1923). In this arbitral award, there was no recognition of any international customary norm allowing a successor government to repudiate the debt contracted for personal gain by the predecessor government. Rather, there was a factual analysis of the irregular transactions and the consideration that the lender knew how the funds were being used.

Lack of an International Legal Norm on Odious Debt

Treaties of peace and other international agreements may have indirectly recognized the claims of successor states to repudiate war and subjugation debt, but they have not led to any codification treaty embodying a general rule on odious debt. The International Law Commission (a subsidiary organ of the United Nations (UN) General Assembly entrusted with the task of codifying and progressively developing international law) was faced with a proposal to include an article on odious debt in its draft articles on the succession of states in respect of state property, archives, and debt. These articles were the basis for the international conference that adopted the 1983 Vienna Convention. Having discussed the proposed articles presented by its special rapporteur (Mohammed Bedjaoui, who later became president of the International Court of Justice), the Commission concluded that "the rules formulated for each type of succession of States might well settle the issues raised by the question and might dispose of the need to draft general provisions on it" (International Law Commission 1979, para 43). In declining a request to adopt a draft article on odious debt, the International Law Commission remarked that the practical issues that the concept is intended to address could be settled in other ways.

A similar conclusion can be reached regarding the question of whether a rule on odious debt has developed in the other main source of international law, international custom.[8] International law distinguishes mere usages from customs. A *usage* is a practice that does not reflect a legal obligation, such as the ceremonial tradition of saluting at sea. In contrast, a *custom* is a consistent and general practice (the objective element of custom) accompanied by a sense of legal obligation (the subjective element of custom, called *opinio juris*). A distinctive feature of custom is its general sphere of validity, whereby a customary norm (other than a local custom) is binding on all states, except those that have objected to it since its inception (the principle of the "persistent objector").[9]

War, subjugation, and regime debt have been repudiated and found not transferable to a successor state or government. However, it is highly doubtful that these instances amount to a general practice or that the states and governments concerned have acted with the conviction of following a legally binding rule. It is questionable that the two constitutive elements of international custom—general practice and *opinio juris*—have materialized in the case of an alleged international customary rule on odious debt or, better, an exception based on customary international law to the operation of the principle *pacta sunt servanda* on treaty compliance.[10] Yianni and Tinkler (2007, p. 771) reach the same conclusion, noting that "neither the threshold for state practice nor *opinio juris* have been met."

A fortiori, the attempts that have been made to link odious debt to the invalidity of treaties for the violation of norms of *jus cogens* remain controversial. Pursuant to Article 53 of the Vienna Convention on the law of treaties (an article many regard as reflecting customary international law and as therefore binding on all states), a treaty is void if it is in conflict with a peremptory norm of general international law (*jus cogens*)—that is, a norm "accepted and recognized by the international community of States as a whole as a norm from which no derogation is permitted and which can be modified only by a subsequent norm of general international law having the same character."[11]

What would be the norm from which the derogation would determine the nullity of a financial agreement extending an odious debt? Obviously, it would be an international norm on odious debt, which, as noted earlier, is hardly an international customary norm let alone a norm "accepted and recognized by the international community of States as a whole" (an expression implying a higher burden of proof). If the norm in question were meant to be one of the classic examples of *jus cogens* (such as the prohibition of genocide or acts of aggression), the difficult task, to be assessed on the specific circumstances of each case, would remain of establishing a link between such a norm and the financial agreement in question. This leads to the conclusion that the class of debt that could be classified as odious because of the derogation of a norm of *jus cogens* would be narrow, if existing at all.

Ex Ante Declarations of Odiousness

A recent proposal suggests having some internationally accepted entity or individual(s) declare ex ante that certain regimes are odious (Jayachandran and Kremer 2006). This idea constitutes a bridge between the traditional and expanded concepts of odious debt. It would put lenders on notice that loans to such regimes could be repudiated by successor regimes with the support of the international community unless the lender could demonstrate that due diligence had been used to ensure that the loan proceeds were used for legitimate purposes. But even such a seemingly appealing approach has many weaknesses. First, who would declare ex ante that regimes are odious? Second, on which decisive factors would this arbiter distinguish odious from nonodious regimes—unrepresentative government, ethnic cleansing, racial discrimination, denial of fundamental human rights? Third, how would such declarations be treated in national courts with jurisdiction to resolve debt disputes? Although, as King (2007) recently put it, the problems with the ex ante model may outweigh its advantages,[12] there is nothing preventing governments (as has indeed happened) from imposing sanctions on, and prohibiting lending to, regimes that they consider odious, either unilaterally or through their participation in international organizations.[13]

Conclusions

Three conclusions can be drawn from the analysis in this section. First, the traditional concept of odious debt is not open ended but restricted to easily identifiable categories (war, subjugation, and regime debt) in the context of the succession of states or governments. Second, even within these strict limits, no customary international rule (let alone a norm of *jus cogens*) allowing the repudiation of odious debt seems to have emerged from the scattered instances of state practice and arbitral decisions, nor has any codification treaty embodied an exception based on the odiousness of the debt. Third, proposals to declare ex ante that certain regimes are odious have their own weaknesses, some practical, some conceptual, and have consequently gained little traction. It is therefore not surprising that Iraq and South Africa, to take just two recent examples of countries with new governments that inherited substantial sovereign debt, chose not to repudiate it unilaterally on the grounds that they were odious but instead chose to negotiate debt restructuring with their creditors.[14]

Expanded Concept and Categories of Odious Debt

The debate on the traditional concept of odious debt focused on whether debt obligations may be repudiated by successor states or governments under exceptional circumstances. Recent decades have seen a rising chorus of demands by nongovernmental and civil society organizations to apply the concept of odious debt to new and different subcategories. The objectives behind these demands are as different as the groups advancing them. Some seek a legal basis for the cancellation of debt owed by developing countries. Others want to punish international lenders for what they see as irresponsible and reckless lending. Yet others are keen to suppress odious regimes by starving them of the flow of capital.[15]

The revived concept of odious debt and its newly articulated sub-categories differ from the traditional concept and categories in several ways. First, the limited setting of the succession of a state or government has been abandoned; the new concept is advocated in the case of state or governmental continuity as well. Second, instead of a case-by-case analysis of individual loans with a view to determining whether they have given rise to odious debt, there is a tendency to conduct an overall assessment of the odious nature of the borrower (that is, odious debtors rather than odious debt are identified). Such an extension rests in part on the concept of fungibility—namely, that loans ostensibly provided for one purpose can release monies already allocated for that purpose for an entirely different purpose, with or without the knowledge of the lender. Third, greater emphasis is placed on the lender's actual or presumed knowledge (and ensuing accountability) of how the borrower will use the borrowed funds. Fourth, unlike the traditional concept and categories of odious debt considered above, there is no appeal to any international customary rule that would justify the new concept and categories. Instead, the stress is on the moral or political unacceptability of repayment.

This expanded concept of odious debt and its various subcategories can be found in some of the international literature and in advocacy materials produced by various nongovernmental organizations. But these documents often lack the precision necessary to allow for meaningful debate. For example, sometimes within the same article, the epithet *odious* is ascribed to lenders, regimes, countries, and debt. Moreover, many articles identify different categories of odiousness.

For reasons of convenience, this chapter focuses on three types of odious debt: "criminal," "unfair," and "ineffective" debt.[16] Although it is not easy to find a common thread that connects them, the term *illegitimate* is sometimes used to encompass all these categories. (At other times, the term is used to describe a category of its own.) Illegitimate debt is debt "that the borrower cannot be required to repay because the original loan or conditions attached to that loan infringed the law or public policy, or because they were unfair, improper, or otherwise objectionable" (Hanlon 2006, p. 125). It refers to "loans which are so bad that by making them a bank has failed in its fiduciary responsibilities, and has no right to collect on those loans" (Hanlon 2007, p. 41). This argument imposes a greater measure of legal responsibility on creditors, even when creditors do not have the power or authority to control the borrowers' actions once the loan is disbursed. Such considerations have led to the concept of "know your client" in retail and commercial banking, which requires lenders to guard against reckless behavior.[17]

"Criminal" Debt

The category of "criminal" debt encompasses loans that involve corruption and kickbacks. Proponents of this category argue that debt repayments by a country are unjust if the original loans to the governments were stolen by officials or businesspeople or the debt was incurred to rescue an economy ravaged by corruption. (Domestic financial transactions or loans that are misused as a result of corruption are considered to be completely different and do not fall within this category. They are categorized as purely domestic affairs, which are consequently the subject of national law and domestic legal procedures.) An essential ingredient of this line of reasoning is that international lenders should be made wholly or partly responsible for the fiscal burden of the misuse of the loan if they were aware in advance that a part of the loan would be illegally siphoned off or they had the leverage to prevent (or at least greatly diminish) the illegal misuse of such loans.

Attractive as the above line of argument may seem, various considerations weaken it. First, once a loan is committed and disbursed by a lender to a sovereign borrower, any subsequent transaction between the sovereign and any other national unit, entity, or individual is, as a rule, a domestic financial transaction subject to national laws and legal procedures and therefore usually outside the reach of international law. It therefore follows that the fiscal burden of any loss should be borne by the country, with the accompanying incentive on the country's law enforcement institutions to recover such losses from the corrupt perpetrators causing the loss.[18]

Second, proponents of the concept of criminal debt are often unclear whether the required prior knowledge of lenders (as a necessary condition) should be with respect to an individual loan or more broadly to the financial climate within a country. Although lenders may know that corruption exists in a country, they may not have any concrete knowledge of plans to siphon proceeds from any individual loan (indeed such ignorance would appear highly likely, given that corrupt officials are not in the habit of advertising their intention to conduct an illegal activity). This raises the question of the burden imposed on creditors of the information they need to have in order to be held responsible for any wrongful act. Within the context of state-to-state relations, the International Law Commission has written that a state "providing material or financial assistance or aid to another State does not normally assume the risk that its assistance or aid may be used to carry out an internationally wrongful act"(Para. 4 of the 2001 Commentary on Draft Article 16, Draft Articles on Responsibility of States for Internationally Wrongful Acts with Commentaries [http://untreaty.un.org/ilc/texts/instruments/english/commentaries/9_6_2001.pdf]). The relevant point here is that actual, not presumed, knowledge may trigger responsibility.

Third, proponents of the concept of criminal debt do not clarify how one assesses the lender's ability to influence the borrower's actions. This leaves open the extent to which an international lender can be held responsible for the alleged corruption of the nationals of the borrowing country.[19]

"Unfair" Debt

The category of "unfair" debt includes a wide variety of debt that either has been incurred for activities considered inappropriate or contains unacceptable conditions, such as usurious interest rates or policy demands that are inconsistent with the borrower's national laws.[20] (The international law equivalent would be lending that violates the purposes and principles of Articles 1 and 2 of the UN Charter, including such all-encompassing principles as the prohibition on aggression, the protection of fundamental human rights, and the right to self-determination.) In the context of national law, courts have determined that repayment demands can be considered illegal on the grounds that the terms of the original loan were usurious, that the lenders perpetrated fraud on the borrowers, or that the lenders broke other national laws in order to extend the loan.

"Ineffective" Debt

The category of "ineffective" includes loans that do not reach their developmental purpose and loans directly linked to capital flight. This line of argument differs from the previous two in that it recognizes that projects can fail and the development purposes of loans not be reached even when there is no corruption and all applicable national and international laws are followed.

Such a line of argument needs scrutiny, for its equivalent would be that domestic lenders to private borrowers should not be repaid when commercial projects fail. This, of course, is not the usual practice in most financial systems. On the contrary, when commercial projects fail because of commercial risk, bankruptcy laws almost without exception require that lenders be among the first to be repaid (after all production costs and arrears to suppliers have been met). Indeed, this is the defining characteristic of debt contracts, as opposed to other financial contracts, such as equity participation. In international lending, especially to poor countries for developmental purposes, the risks of failure are at least as high as those faced in private transactions: development finance is a risky enterprise in which a certain degree of project failure is inevitable given the multiplicity of the challenges poor countries face. It is faulty logic to suppose that one can secure only those development successes that all agree are crucial without taking the risks that entail failure from time to time.

But there is more to the question of lender responsibility than realism about outcomes. National financial laws do not require lenders to pay the costs for project failure for two reasons. First, the act of lending cannot usually be considered the proximate cause of the failure of a project or activity, under any scenario. Second, and more important, allowing loans to be repudiated because they were ineffective could create incentives for irresponsible behavior by borrowers (moral hazard), because the costs would be borne by the lenders. In economic terms, debt contracts are incentive compatible with maximizing the chances of project success because at the margin, they make those responsible for project execution (the borrowers) the sole beneficiaries of that success.

Another line of argument for declaring ineffective debt as odious derives from a more sophisticated line of reasoning. The essence of this argument rests on the principle that advisers to governments should be held legally accountable for their advice and that failed projects are sometimes the result of poor advice provided by the lender. Where loans and advice are bundled together, the liability of the adviser for a failed project should be the nonpayment of the loan itself.

Even this more sophisticated line of reasoning is subject to many of the same shortcomings as above, for several reasons. First, finding advisers responsible for the failure would require isolating their advice from the more general context of the country's circumstances and identifying it as the sole or main cause of the failure. Second, even if it could be established that the advisers had given poor advice, there is little logic to suggest that this frees borrowers from the need to repay their loans. There are no contracts that underwrite advisory services with loan nonpayment. Third, a legal system making advisers culpable for failure would prevent any delivery of technical advice, especially if that technical advice were provided for free or as part of a broader aid package (much as making nonpayment an outcome of financing a failed project would lead to a drying up of development finance). Fourth, the incentive structure of such a possibility would exacerbate the dangers of moral hazard, because it would encourage the reckless use of loans if there were a sense that the cost of failure would be borne by others.

Conclusions

The wide body of literature on the topic does not yet provide a clear concept of odious debt in the expanded versions in which the term is used today. The categories proposed often overlap and lack clarity, and they tend to apply the concept with equal facility and often at the same time to loans, regimes, countries, and debt. This lack of precision and the array of practical objections it creates make it difficult to accept an expanded concept of odious debt based on current proposals, although such conceptual expansion has been advanced in recent discourse (if not reflected in the practice of states).

It is important to establish what such a rejection does and does not imply. There is no doubt that on occasion, lenders, through a lack of diligence or a misunderstanding of the needs of the borrower, contribute to poor outcomes in the sovereign states they finance. Independent evaluation of impact, quality-at-entry assessments, and operational safeguards all exist to minimize this risk; they also indicate the risk is real. The key element of the approach suggested by proponents of an expanded odious debt doctrine is that in some subset of these cases, borrowers should be allowed to repudiate their debt, either on the basis of new legal principles or at the determination of some newly created international arbiter.

That such a system could be set up is not at issue; its likely consequences are the crux of the debate. There are good reasons why much finance—including development finance to sovereign states—is provided in the form of debt. The reflows from successful repayments allow a leveraging of the scarce overseas development assistance provided by donors, which is vital if the Millennium Development Goals (MDGs) are to be met in many countries. Lenders' systems need to provide maximum due diligence to make sure that funds lent contribute to success in the borrowing country. But just as fundamentally, debt contracts keep the bulk of the incentives for success where they should be—at the level at which the funds are used. There may be scope for other forms of financial contracts within the architecture of development finance (for example, greater equity stakes by international institutions in certain projects) to better align the incentives for success when borrowers may not be the main parties involved in project execution. But such an assertion is a long way from encouraging the repudiation of contracts, something that as a general policy prescription is not the way to build an investment climate propitious for economic growth and social development.

Of equal concern are the likely effects of a legalistic approach to odious debt on development finance. Lenders' ability to keep providing finance to poor countries, whether in the official sector or in the private sector, depends on their balance sheets, present and future. Lenders would be obliged to "price in" the future possibility that their loans would at some undetermined point in the future and possibly, despite their best efforts, be declared odious. The likely effects on the flows of finance to developing countries are not hard to discern (see, for example, Rajan 2004 for a compelling account on this topic). This would be doubly counterproductive at a time when donor countries are aiming to increase, not decrease, financial flows to the poorest nations in pursuit of the MDGs. A different approach is therefore required to address the concerns that motivate many of the proposals grouped under the banner of odious debt.

Improvement of Lending and Borrowing Practices

Proponents of the expanded concept of odious debt argue that lenders must be held accountable for illegitimate debt. The underlying objectives for such a proposition are in principle laudable, as they aim to ensure that international lending to developing countries reduces corruption (or, at the very least, does not encourage it). Proponents of the expanded concept also argue that holding lenders accountable is in accordance with national and international laws and would ensure that loans are used to achieve developmental outcomes. Expanding the concept of odious debt to cover illegitimate debt may also provide some legal support for the unilateral repudiation of debt by sovereign borrowers.

Taking lenders to court to force them to meet these objectives runs into various problems, however, most serious among which is the risk of disrupting international financial flows to developing countries. The same objectives can be met in other ways. The best approach does not seem to be to convert uncertain concepts and categories into law but rather to rigorously identify the problem; assess whether even partial answers to the problem already exist (and search for reasonable solutions in the interest of borrowers and lenders alike if they do not); and maintain the continued healthy functioning of the international financial system.

Fighting Corruption in International Lending

Perhaps the most important factor motivating the call for the cancellation of odious debt is the conviction that loan proceeds are often embezzled by corrupt officials and leaders in borrowing countries, leaving it to future administrations and generations to pay back debt for which they receive none of the benefits. Corrupt practices deserve not only moral outrage but also a thoughtful plan for dealing with them most effectively. National governments, elected bodies, and civil society organizations can all help thwart corrupt practices. In addition, external lenders can commit to follow good lending practices that may help remedy the problem over time. Not least among such practices is assessment of the pecuniary and nonpecuniary risks of lending, the full disclosure of these to shareholders and the borrower, and the development of ways to mitigate these risks so that the probability of the loan being misused is reduced. Some steps lenders could take include the following:

- Examine the overall governance standards in the borrowing country, including anticorruption programs and measures.
- Require that projects considered at high risk of corruption include anticorruption action plans that build on knowledge gained from the experience of implementing previous projects and draw on tried and tested requirements for transparency and oversight, possibly including enhanced disclosure provisions, civil society oversight, complaint-handling mechanisms, policies to reduce opportunities for collusion, mitigation of fraud and forgery risks, and specified sanctions and remedies.

- Put in place well-publicized mechanisms that allow the public and internal whistleblowers to come forward with allegations of corruption, with adequate safeguards to protect them against possible reprisals. Such allegations need to be investigated thoroughly by the lender as well as the borrowing authorities, in full conformity with national laws and regulations. Any evidence emerging from investigations of wrongdoing should be made public and handed over to the authorities for appropriate action consistent with the laws and regulations of the country concerned.
- Reserve the right to cancel part of the loan and seek reimbursement of any funds that have been misused if covenants in loan agreements are breached or loan proceeds are not used for their intended purposes. Those found guilty should be prosecuted by borrower governments to the full extent possible under national law.
- Put in place mechanisms for the debarment of firms and individuals found to participate in fraud or corruption. Governments and the international community should make every effort to recover stolen government assets, including money stolen from sovereign loans. Lenders and borrowers could publicize instances of fraud and corruption and the remedial measures taken, and they could join forces to develop systems that make such crimes harder to commit.

These examples of good lending practices can be complemented by new initiatives, such as the Stolen Assets Recovery (StAR) Initiative (box 9.1), to strengthen the array of anticorruption measures countries can implement. In recent years, countries as diverse as Nigeria, Peru, and the Philippines have enjoyed some success in securing the repatriation of assets stolen by their corrupt former leaders. Success, however, has been neither easy nor quick.

Ensuring the "Fairness" of Loans

Just as lenders can play an important proactive role in protecting their loans from fraud and corruption, they can exercise appropriate due diligence to ensure that the loans themselves are the results of processes and procedures consistent with the laws of the borrowing country and expected good practice according to international standards. Steps they can take include the following:

- Provide ample opportunities within the country to comment on, criticize, and shape the proposed loan, and stress a country representative's freedom to decline the loan throughout the loan preparation, appraisal, and approval process.
- Subject loans to intensive preparation, evaluation, appraisal, and negotiation—with full participation by the authorities of the country

Box 9.1 The Stolen Assets Recovery (StAR) Initiative

To help developing countries seeking to recover stolen assets, in 2007 the UN Office on Drugs and Crime and the World Bank jointly developed the Stolen Assets Recovery (StAR) Initiative. The initiative aims to deter asset theft and facilitate the recovery of assets stolen through acts of corruption.

Stolen assets are frequently hidden in developed-country financial centers and often include bribes paid by multinational corporations. The StAR Initiative helps countries that are parties to it implement the UN Convention against Corruption (http://www.unodc.org/unodc/crime_convention_corruption.html), which entered into force in 2005 as the first global anticorruption agreement.

StAR has developed pilot programs to help specific countries recover stolen assets by providing technical assistance and support to improvements in public financial management, investigative capacity, and fiscal transparency to prevent future looting. Through monitoring programs with the voluntary agreement of the countries concerned, StAR aims to help countries ensure that recovered assets are used effectively in support of development.

concerned and when appropriate, by civil society and other relevant groups—and publicly disclose the final appraisal documents. Depending on the applicable laws, regulations, and procedures, this process could include scrutiny by elected representative bodies.

- Require legal opinions regularly, from acceptable counsel, confirming that the loan agreement in question is legally binding in accordance with its terms and has been approved in conformity with the internal laws and procedures of the borrowing country.

Of course, such steps could raise the cost of loan preparation, which might be a disincentive for lenders (and borrowers, if it raises the cost of borrowing). The increased costs of loan preparation may be seen as an investment in obtaining potential benefits, however (for the borrower, better use of the loan proceeds; for the lender, a lower risk of default on the loan).

Improving the Effectiveness of Loans

To meet the concerns that underlie proposals to declare ineffective debt as odious, lending institutions could adopt a variety of measures. Before considering these measures, it is worth reiterating that as a rule, loan agreements do not create a link between the final success of the loan proceeds and the borrower's repayment obligation. The reason why they do not is simple. One of the key aspects of international lending to sovereigns is the borrower's "ownership" and complete control of the use of the proceeds and the acknowledgment that the lender's role is limited to assisting the borrower in achieving the aims it has itself set and for which it has requested financial assistance. Moreover, as argued above, loan agreements usually do not include a link between the repayment obligation and the final success of the financial assistance because it is recognized that (a) the success of a project entails risks that are usually outside the control of lenders, who also face greater risks because they have less information than borrowers (information asymmetry); (b) such a link would reduce incentives for borrowers to make the project a success (because part of the cost of failure would be borne by the lender); and (c) such a feature would give these loans an equity, rather than a debt, characteristic.

International lenders could nevertheless engage in efforts to ensure that the risks of inappropriate use are managed to the extent possible. These could include the following:

- Include covenants in loans that require the loan proceeds be used for their intended purposes, and conduct subsequent supervision (in which the borrower and the lender cooperate) designed to ensure that proceeds are being used for and achieving their intended purposes.
- Together with the sovereign borrower's authorities, regularly conduct evaluations of the use of the loan proceeds and whether such loans have achieved their intended purposes. These evaluations may be conducted independently of the management of these institutions. Results could be made public.
- Apply higher standards of probity and more stringent safeguards than normal in lending to countries in which economic management institutions are weak and controls over the use of public resources are inadequate. (Implementing such a policy is difficult in practice, because there are few objective indicators on which such judgments can be based.)

Differentiating between Official and Commercial Creditors

Good lending practices of the sort described in this section could apply to official as well as commercial creditors. Because the shareholders of official creditors are sovereigns, the policies of bilateral and multilateral financial institutions tend to be driven by public policy considerations. Shareholders in these institutions tend to apply constant pressure to improve lending practices, in part because they are concerned about the development impact of the finance provided by these agencies and in part because they are sensitive to concerns raised by nongovernmental and civil society organizations in their own countries and in developing countries. This pressure has led to improved lending practices in some official lending institutions, although room for improvement no doubt remains considerable.

One might think that commercial creditors would have less incentive to improve lending practices, especially if implementing such practices imposes additional costs. But the existence of the Equator Principles suggests otherwise. The Equator Principles are a set of 10 benchmarks against which 52 of the world's most prominent commercial financial institutions have agreed to determine, measure, and manage the social and environmental risks associated with project financing (http://www.equator-principles .com/index.html). One of the key motivations for this initiative was the perceived importance of mitigating credit and reputational risk—a good example of how commercial considerations can potentially lead to socially desirable results. Supported by the International Finance Corporation (one of the institutions of the World Bank Group), the Equator Principles also facilitate collaboration and learning among member financial institutions on the interpretation and application of broader good-practice lending policies.

Of course, as important as they are, good lending practices by official or commercial lending institutions cannot by themselves guarantee the appropriate use of loan proceeds for development purposes. The responsibility of achieving this result ultimately rests with the borrower.

Dealing with Unsustainable Debt Stocks

If loans become the subject of fraud, embezzlement, or corruption, they can quickly accumulate to the point that they become unsustainable. Proponents of the expanded concept of odious debt would like to see a legal basis for the unilateral repudiation of debt stocks if such unsustainable debt is found to be odious. But there are other ways to deal with the problem of unsustainable debt stocks.

Although misused loans can quickly accumulate into unsustainable debt, not all unsustainable debt is the result of misused loans. Loans can be used well and nevertheless fail to achieve their desired results, for a variety of reasons. Circumstances can change, the economic environment affecting investments can suddenly deteriorate for reasons outside governmental control, natural disasters can strike, or the design of the investment can prove to have been faulty from the start. When such unforeseeable situations (shocks) occur, debt can accumulate (Kraay and Nehru 2006).

That countries must either pay their unsustainable debt or repudiate it is a false dichotomy. In practice, countries usually choose the middle path of restructuring their debt when it becomes unsustainable. Such restructurings usually involve losses to creditors and therefore tend to be the result of prolonged and complex negotiations. But they do provide a useful alternative to repudiation that allows borrowing countries to maintain good relations with their creditors. As noted earlier, Iraq and South Africa chose not to repudiate the large sovereign debt they inherited from the previous region, instead negotiating their restructuring with their creditors.

In the case of commercial creditors, debt restructuring negotiations have been between the sovereign and creditor committees such as the London Club or, as in more recent cases, representatives of bondholders. With official creditors, debt restructurings have usually taken place in the context of the Paris Club, an informal group of official creditors whose role is to find coordinated and sustainable solutions to payment difficulties experienced by sovereign debtors. The most prominent recent examples of large Paris Club debt-reduction deals are those for Nigeria and Iraq.

Multilateral creditors are governed by international frameworks on the treatment of debt problems in developing countries.[21] Most notable among these are the Heavily Indebted Poor Countries (HIPC) Initiative and the Multilateral Debt Relief Initiative (MDRI), which together have provided—and are expected to provide further—significant debt reduction to the poorest, most heavily indebted countries of the world. These initiatives implicitly recognize that the debt accumulated by recipient countries has reached a point at which it cannot be repaid without imposing unacceptable hardship on the population.

In addition to participating in international debt-reduction initiatives, some international lenders have independently and voluntarily forgiven debt owed to them by developing countries. The most recent example is that of the Norwegian government, which, in the 2007 national budget, cancelled, *ex gratia* and not out of any legal obligation, 520 million Norwegian kroner (about $78 million) of official debt owed by Ecuador, the Arab Republic of Egypt, Jamaica, Peru, and Sierra Leone stemming from the Norwegian Ship Export Campaign (1976–80). The Norwegian government considered this campaign a development policy failure and consequently assumed "shared responsibility" for the debt that followed. This debt cancellation was additional to Norway's ordinary overseas development assistance.

Resolving Disputes

Disputes inevitably arise between lenders and borrowers. Usually, loan agreements include clauses on the settlement of disputes. For loans from commercial creditors to sovereign borrowers, the jurisdiction for the settlement of disputes belongs to local courts, such as those of New York or London, which may apply laws that protect debtors against litigants who may be seeking repayment despite evidence of bribery or "unclean hands" on the part of the lender or the embezzlement of state funds by corrupt agents or public officials under cover of government bureaucracy. In the case of loan agreements to which international institutions are parties, the settlement of disputes is usually devolved to arbitrators. However, in practice, such disputes are usually resolved through direct negotiations between the parties, without any need to resort to arbitration.

Conclusions

Many of the concerns raised by proponents of the expanded concept of odious debt have been fueled by moral outrage and the need for a just system of international lending to sovereigns. Such concerns can be addressed by improving the practices of international lenders and sovereign borrowers. Despite some promising steps in this direction, much remains to be done. Rather than relying on an elusive expanded concept of odious debt, with the many costs to developing countries that this would entail, it seems more practical to assess what can be done to improve lending and borrowing practices at a more quotidian level. This approach has the advantage of channeling the valid concerns that underpin the debate on odious debt into constructive and widely shared efforts.

Notes

1. A debt contracted by a state with a nonsovereign may give rise to an international claim through diplomatic protection, a possibility that is not examined here.

2. See, for example, the reference to the fact that "the [People's Republic of China] asserted as a long-established principle of international law that 'odious' debts are not to be succeeded to . . . a view they continue to advance, but do not explicitly rely on, in making this motion to dismiss" in *Marvin L. Morris, Jr., Plaintiff, against the People's Republic of China, and others, Defendants. Gloria Bolanos Pons, and others, Plaintiffs, against The People's Republic of China, and others, Defendants,* U.S. District Court for the Southern District of New York, 478 F. Supp. 2d 561; 2007 U.S. Dist. LEXIS 20784, decided March 21, 2007.

3. According to Khalfan (2003, p. 71), "It is unclear whether the laws of England and of New York, properly interpreted, provide support for the 'odious' debt doctrine. Given the interest of these jurisdictions in maintaining their positions as key financial centers, their courts are likely to reject the 'odious' debt doctrine." While an argument based on the doctrine of odious debt may not succeed in municipal courts, other arguments (which are as varied as the existing legal systems) may succeed in reaching the same result.

4. The convention (available at http://untreaty.un.org/ilc/texts/instruments/english/conventions/3_3_1983.pdf) provides for the passing of the public debt to the successor (unless it is a newly independent state), with a reduction according to an equitable proportion.

5. By the end of June 2009, only seven states had acceded to the Convention.

6. On the cases of the South African and Austrian war debts and other instances of state practice, see Bedjaoui (1977).

7. On the Cuban and Indonesian subjugation debts, see Bedjaoui (1977).

8. For the limited purposes of this chapter, there is no need to examine the third source of international law, namely, the "general principles of law recognized by civilized nations." In the committee of jurists that prepared Article 38(1) of the Statute of the International Court of Justice (for what, at the time, was the Permanent Court of International Justice), there was no consensus on the meaning of this phrase. Moreover, despite occasional references to general principles (sometimes co-mingled with equitable considerations [see, for example, Howse 2007]) in the legal literature on odious debt, there has been almost no sustained effort to investigate a plurality of national legal systems (assuming such principles

have their origin in national law) with a view to showing that the exception to the repayment of odious debt is indeed a "general principle of law recognized by civilized nations."

9. On the principle of the "persistent objector" and whether it applies to norms of *jus cogens*, see Ragazzi (1997).

10. Article 26 of the 1969 Vienna Convention on the law of treaties (*pacta sunt servanda*) reads as follows: "Every treaty in force is binding upon the parties to it and must be performed by them in good faith." The Vienna Convention entered into force in 1980. Its text is available at http://untreaty.un.org/ilc/texts/instruments/english/conventions/1_1_1969.pdf.

11. Article 64 of the Vienna Convention embodies the principle of *jus cogens superveniens* in stating, "If a new peremptory norm of general international law emerges, any existing treaty which is in conflict with that norm becomes void and terminates."

12. King (2007, pp. 659–60) identifies three main problems with this approach: "The first problem is that such an institution [entrusted with the task of designating certain regimes ex ante as odious] will likely designate very few regimes as odious. . . . A second problem is that declaring a regime, rather than a set of actions, to be odious is a rather 'nuclear' type of option and is unlikely to be deployed until the regime reaches pariah status. . . . Both the first and second problems lead inexorably to the third, and indeed perhaps the most significant, problem: if a given regime is not so designated, a creditor can rely on this fact in lending to it. In other words, and quite ironically, the idea of calling this model the 'due diligence' model is highly misleading. It would eliminate the need for any diligence at all."

13. Under the UN Charter, pursuant to its powers in the area of peace and security, the Security Council can make decisions that are binding on states. On this ground, the Security Council has imposed economic sanctions and prohibited members from undertaking certain financial transactions with targeted states. However, even in such rare instances, all the Security Council can do is create a legal obligation for states not to enter into financial transactions. The authority of the Security Council does not extend to rendering invalid such transactions. In other words, noncompliance by a state with a Security Council's prohibition to enter into a financial transaction would trigger the international responsibility of such a state but would not invalidate the financial transaction in question.

14. The reference to these two cases is limited to the fact of the final decision to negotiate a debt restructuring rather than repudiate odious debt unilaterally. These decisions were obviously the result of the specific circumstances prevailing in these two countries (as is always the case for such decisions), which need not be analyzed here.

15. These three examples do not exhaust the universe of motivations. Other examples include parties looking for a legal defense to protect themselves against creditors seeking repayment or those attempting to carve out a role for themselves as international arbiters of disputes between international creditors and sovereign borrowers.

16. The literature has spawned several other categories of odious debt, including "unpayable," "onerous," "unsustainable," "dubious," "honorific," and other kinds of debt.

17. Adams (2005) writes, "Already, private sector financiers are careful to establish their due diligence and evidentiary basis to defend today's loans in future." Much sovereign lending takes the form of more generalized financial support, however, through general budget support from official lenders or bond financing on international capital markets. In these cases, the issue of the use of funds is rendered rather vague.

18. The point of the importance of incentives can be made the other way round: if any obligation to repay is rendered null by the misuse of funds, could this not create incentives for said misuse?

19. Overstating the policy reach of lenders to sovereigns is not limited to the debate over the legitimacy of debts. In the debate on conditionality, for example, opponents of the notion often assume that the lender exerts an extremely high degree of control over the borrower's actions. Ironically, when such control is not exerted and bad outcomes follow—in the case of criminal debt, for example—greater control by lenders is deemed not only feasible but also desirable.

20. On its Web site (http://www.jubileedebtcampaign.org.uk), Jubilee refers to "debts that a country can't afford to repay without meeting its people's basic needs . . . debt on unfair terms, such as very high interest rates; and debts contracted illegally, where proper processes weren't gone through." The term *unfair* is used here to cover a variety of categories from the literature, not all of which use this term.

21. Some commercial entities have canceled their claims on similar grounds, but these cases have usually been the result of pressure generated by negative publicity in the media.

References and Other Resources

Abrahams, Charles Peter. 2002. "The Doctrine of 'Odious Debts.'" LL.M. thesis, Rijks Universiteit, Leiden, the Netherlands. http://www.odiousdebts.org/odiousdebts/publications/ApartheidDebtThesis.pdf.

Adams, Patricia. 1991. *Odious Debts: Loose Lending, Corruption and the Third World's Environmental Legacy*. Toronto: Earthscan. Excerpts at http://www.odiousdebts.org/odiousdebts/index.cfm?DSP=content&ContentID=53.

———. 2004. *Iraq's Odious Debts*. Policy Analysis 526, Cato Institute, Washington, DC. http://www.cato.org/pubs/pas/pa526.pdf.

———. 2005. Letter to the Editor. *Finance and Development* 42 (2). http://www.imf.org/external/pubs/ft/fandd/2005/06/letterto.htm.

Anderson, Kevin H. 2005. "International Law and State Succession: A Solution to the Iraqi Debt Crisis?" *Utah Law Review* 401 (2): 401–42.

Bedjaoui, Mohammed. 1977. "Succession of States in Respect of Matters Other Than Treaties." In *Yearbook of the International Law Commission*, vol. II, part 1. http://untreaty.un.org/ilc/publications/yearbooks/Ybkvolumes(e)/ILC_1977_v2_p1_e.pdf.

Bonilla, Stephania. 2006. "A Law-and-Economics Analysis of Odious Debts: History, Trends and Debates." http://ssrn.com/abstract=946111.

———. 2007. "Towards a Solution to Odious Debts and Looking at Creditors' Incentives." http://ssrn.com/abstract=1007698.

Brownlie, Ian. 2003. *Principles of Public International Law*, 6th ed. Oxford, U.K.: Oxford University Press.

Buchheit, Lee C., G. Mitu Gulati, and Robert B. Thompson. 2007. "The Dilemma of Odious Debts." *Duke Law Journal* 56 (1201): 1205–8.

Despagnet, Franz. 1905. *Cours de droit international public*, 3rd ed. Paris: Elibron Classics.

Feilchenfeld, Ernst. 1931. *Public Debts and State Succession*. New York: Kraus Reprint Co.

Foorman, James L., and Michael E. Jehle. 1982. "Effects of State and Government Succession on Commercial Bank Loans to Foreign Sovereign Borrowers." *University of Illinois Law Review* 1: 9–38.

Frankenberg, Günter, and Rolf Knieper. 1984. "Legal Problems of the Over-Indebtedness of Developing Countries: The Current Relevance of the Doctrine of Odious Debts." *International Journal of the Sociology of Law* 12: 415–28.

Garner, James Wilford. 1938. "Germany's Responsibility for Austria's Debts." *American Journal of International Law* 32: 766–75.

Gelpern, Anna. 2005. "What Iraq and Argentina Might Learn from Each Other." *Chicago Journal of International Law* 6 (391): 391–414.

Gruber, Annie. 1986. *Le droit international de la succession d'états.* Brussels: Bruylant.

Hanlon, Joseph. 2006. "Defining 'Illegitimate Debt': When Creditors Should Be Liable for Improper Loans." In *Sovereign Debt at the Crossroads: Challenges and Proposals for Resolving the Third World Debt Crisis*, ed. Chris Jochnick and Fraser A. Preston, 109–32. New York: Oxford University Press.

———. 2007. "Wolfowitz, the World Bank, and Illegitimate Lending." *Brown Journal of World Affairs* 13 (41): 41–54.

Hoeflich, M. H. 1982. "Through a Glass Darkly: Reflections upon the History of the International Law of Public Debt in Connection with State Succession." *University of Illinois Law Review* 1: 39–70.

Howse, Robert. 2007. "The Concept of Odious Debt in Public International Law." UNCTAD Discussion Paper, July, United Nations Conference on Trade and Development, Geneva. http://www.unctad.org/Templates/Download.asp?docid =8960&lang=1&intItemID=2101.

International Law Commission. 1979. "Report of the International Law Commission on the Work of Its Thirty-First Session." *Yearbook of the International Law Commission*, vol. II, Part 2. New York: United Nations.

Jayachandran, Seema, and Michael Kremer. 2006. "Odious Debt." *American Economic Review* 96 (1): 82–92.

Jennings, Robert, and Arthur Watts, eds. 1992. *Oppenheim's International Law*, vol. 1, *Peace*, 9th ed. London: Longman.

Jochnick, Chris. 2006. "The Legal Case for Debt Repudiation." In *Sovereign Debt at the Crossroads: Challenges and Proposals for Resolving the Third World Debt Crisis*, ed. Chris Jochnick and Fraser A. Preston, 132–57. New York: Oxford University Press.

Kaiser, Jürgen, and Antje Queck. 2004. "Odious Debts—Odious Creditors? International Claims in Iraq." Dialogue on Globalisation Occasional Paper 12, March 24. Friedrich-Ebert-Stiftung, Berlin. http://www.odiousdebts.org/odiousdebts/ publications/iraqpaper.pdf.

Khalfan, Ashfaq. 2003. "Sites and Strategic Legal Options for Addressing Illegitimate Debt." CISDL Working Paper, Centre for International Sustainable Development Law, Montreal.

Khalfan, Ashfaq, Jeff King, and Bryan Thomas. 2003. "Advancing the Odious Debt Doctrine." CISDL Working Paper, Centre for International Sustainable Development Law, Montreal.

King, Jeff A. 2007. "Odious Debt: The Terms of the Debate." *North Carolina Journal of International Law and Commercial Regulation* 32: 605–68.

Kraay, Aart, and Vikram Nehru. 2006. "When Is External Debt Sustainable?" *World Bank Economic Review* 20 (3): 341–65.

Kremer, Michael, and Seema Jayachandran. 2002. "Odious Debt." NBER Working Paper 8953, National Bureau of Economic Research, Cambridge, MA. http://www.nber.org/papers/w8953.pdf

Lothian, Tamara. 1994–95. "The Criticism of the Third-World Debt and the Revision of Legal Doctrine." *Wisconsin International Law Journal* 13: 421–70.

Ludington, Sarah, and Mitu Gulati. 2008. "A Convenient Untruth: Fact and Fantasy in the Doctrine of Odious Debts." *Virginia Journal of International Law* 48: 595–639.

Mahmud, Mohammad. 2000. "Illegitimacy of Odious and Dubious Debt." *Pakistan and Gulf Economist*, May 29–June 4.

Mancina, Emily F. 2004. "Sinners in the Hands of an Angry God: Resurrecting the Odious Debt Doctrine in International Law." *George Washington International Law Review* 36: 1239–62.

Mandel, Stephen. 2006. "Odious Lending: Debt Relief as If Morals Mattered." New Economics Foundation, London. http://www.jubileeresearch.org/news/Odiouslendingfinal.pdf.

Marcelli, Fabio. 2004. *Il debito estero dei paesi in via di sviluppo nel diritto internazionale.* Rome: Giuffré.

Menon, P. K. 1991. *The Succession of States in Respect to Treaties, State Property, Archives, and Debts.* Lewiston, NY: Edwin Mellen Press.

Michalowski, Sabine. 2007. *Unconstitutional Regimes and the Validity of Sovereign Debt: A Legal Perspective.* Aldershot, U.K.: Ashgate Publishing.

Ochoa, Christiana. 2008. "From Odious Debt to Odious Finance: Avoiding the Externalities of a Functional Odious Debt Doctrine." *Harvard International Law Journal* 49: 109–59.

O'Connell, Daniel Patrick. 1967. *State Succession in Municipal Law and International Law,* vols. I and II. Cambridge, U.K.: Cambridge University Press.

Paulus, Christoph G. 2005. "Odious Debts vs. Debt Trap: A Realistic Help?" *Brooklyn Journal of International Law* 31 (83): 83–102.

———. 2007. "The Concept of Odious Debts: A Historical Survey." Duke Law School Legal Studies Paper 179, Durham, NC.

Ragazzi, Maurizio. 1997. *The Concept of International Obligations Erga Omnes.* Oxford, U.K.: Oxford University Press.

Rajan, Raghuram. 2004. "Odious or Just Malodorous? Why the Odious Debt Proposal Is Likely to Stay in Cold Storage." *Finance and Development* (December), International Monetary Fund, Washington, DC. http://www.imf.org/external/pubs/ft/fandd/2004/12/pdf/straight.pdf.

Reinisch, August. 1995. *State Responsibility for Debts: International Law Aspects of External Debt and Debt Restructuring.* Vienna: Bohlaud.

Sack, Alexander Nahum. 1927. *Les effets des transformations des états sur leurs dettes publique et autres obligations financières.* Paris: Recueil Sirey.

———. 1932–33. "The Juridical Nature of the Public Debts of States." *New York University Law Quarterly Review* 10: 341–58.

Stiglitz, Joseph E. 2003. "Odious Rulers, Odious Debts." *Atlantic Monthly,* November. http://www.odiousdebts.org/odiousdebts/index.cfm?DSP=content&ContentID=8577.

————. 2006. "Ethics, Markets and Government Failures, and Globalization: Perspectives on Debt and Finance." In *Sovereign Debt at the Crossroads: Challenges and Proposals for Resolving the Third World Debt Crisis*, ed. Chris Jochnick and Fraser A. Preston, 158–73. Oxford, U.K.: Oxford University Press.

Tamen, Anaïs. 2003. "La doctrine de la dette 'odieuse' ou l'utilisation du droit international dans les rapports de puissance." Dissertation presented during the Third Meeting of the Droit International du Comité pour l'Annulation de la Dette du Tiers-Monde, Amsterdam, December 11. http://www.dette2000.org/data/File/detteillegitime/ladoctrine/ladoctrinedelado_anaistamen_janv04.pdf.

United Nations. 1923. *United Nations Reports of International Arbitral Awards.* New York: United Nations.

Weisburd, A. Mark. 2008. "Reflections on 'A Convenient Untruth.'" *Virginia Journal of International Law* 48: 641–45.

Westlake, John. 1910. *International Law.* Part I: *Peace.* Cambridge, U.K.: Cambridge University Press.

Yianni, Andrew, and David Tinkler. 2007. "Is There a Recognized Legal Doctrine of Odious Debts?" *North Carolina Journal of International Law and Commercial Regulation* 32 (4): 749–72.

10

Odious Debt as a Principal-Agent Problem

Frederico Gil Sander

I n principle, debt is contracted by a country's government on behalf of its population for the purpose of providing public goods, such as public investments or consumption smoothing. However, because of asymmetric information between governments and the population, public debt is sometimes used instead for the private benefit of government officials, including for ensuring their hold on power by repressing the population through violent means. The concept of "odious" debt—traditionally defined as debt incurred without the consent of the population and not for their benefit (Sack 1927)—is therefore closely related to a principal-agent problem in which, because of limited observability of the actions of governments, the agents contracting debt (the government) do not use it for the benefit of the principals (the population), who are ultimately responsible for repaying it.

A number of civil society organizations have called for the cancellation of such odious debt, arguing that creditors should bear responsibility for aligning the interests of governments and their populations. These advocates suggest that this can be accomplished by restricting loans to certain types of governments or spending resources to ensure that loan proceeds are used for the benefit of the population. Lenders who fail to do so would lose the right to enforce their claim through the courts. This chapter analyzes the implications of this policy proposal for the welfare of the populations using a game-theoretical framework that models the principal-agent problem between governments and populations.

Borrowing—whether by governments or private entities—is characterized by at least two agency relationships: one between borrowers (the agents) and creditors (the principals), another between the actors responsible for contracting debt (the agents) and those who ultimately bear the burden of servicing it (the principals). Both problems must be solved by providing agents with appropriate incentives so that their interests are aligned with those of the principals. Although the nature of the problems of sovereign and private borrowing is similar, their solutions are fundamentally different.

The agency problem between borrowers and creditors is straightforward: having contracted debt, absent any constraints, the borrower would prefer not to repay it. The solution to the problem depends on the availability of appropriate incentives for debt repayment. Creditors of firms can rely on the legal system to credibly reassign the property rights of assets from the borrower to the creditor in case of default.

The transfer of property rights from a sovereign borrower to its creditors through the courts poses substantial challenges, as noted by several authors at least since Eaton and Gersovitz (1981). Creditors would not be expected to be able to attach assets located in the borrowing country (although there have been exceptions in the past),[1] and any judgments obtained in foreign courts would (generally) be enforceable only in those jurisdictions and therefore limited to assets located therein. Although cross-border enforcement is possible in principle (through gunboats, for example), there is widespread agreement that such enforcement is politically untenable today.[2] Some authors argue that, in the absence of direct enforcement, sovereign borrowing needs to be self-enforcing through market reactions, such as higher interest rates, credit rationing for defaulting countries, or both. The precise nature of the enforcement mechanisms available to creditors of sovereign nations, as well as the empirical evidence for the effectiveness of different mechanisms, has been the subject of an extensive body of literature, discussed in detail in Dömeland, Gil Sander, and Primo Braga (2009).

This chapter focuses instead on the principal-agent problem between those responsible for negotiating and contracting loans and those who ultimately bear the costs of repayment. In the case of a company, management makes borrowing decisions, but shareholders ultimately bear the costs of debt service. In the case of sovereign borrowing, governments are responsible for negotiating and contracting loans, but the country's population bears the burden of debt service through future taxation. In both cases, the parties responsible for entering into the loan contract may not be in the same position at the time the loan must be repaid, and in both cases, the agents may attempt to invest in overly risky projects or to misappropriate the proceeds of the loans for their own benefit.[3]

In the case of private borrowing, the solution to the problem lies in collapsing the agency relationship to ensure that the borrower and payer are the same (as is the case of consumer borrowing or borrowing by a sole proprietorship or partnership) or enforcing shareholder protection laws, such as those that require the disclosure of information and create civil and criminal liability for executives that provide false or misleading information. Managers in private firms may have incentive contracts that condition their compensation on performance.

In the case of sovereign borrowing, the solution to the agency problem must rely on more limited mechanisms. With the possible exception of a very small number of countries in which the national wealth is indistinguishable from that of its rulers, collapsing the agency relationship is not possible. The enforcement of anticorruption and transparency laws (analogous to the laws that protect shareholders from management fraud) is ultimately conducted by the government itself; new agency problems emerge that make the enforcement of such fiscal probity laws less effective than that of private contracts. Perhaps most important, contingent compensation contracts for government leaders do not seem to exist in practice (for example, in no country does the president or prime minister earn a bonus for exceptional economic growth).[4] The only form of incentives provided to government executives is the possibility that they can be replaced.

This agency problem between governments and the population they serve is ultimately at the heart of the debate over the cancellation of odious or otherwise "illegitimate" debt. This category of debt—which in this chapter also includes "war," "ineffective," "regime," and "subjugation" debt—is characterized by the fact that the proceeds from the borrowing were not used for the benefit of the population of the country. The cancellation of odious debt, it is argued, would help correct for the incentives for governments to use loan proceeds in the interests of their populations by pressuring lenders to ensure that loans are made only to governments—or purposes—that are aligned with the interests of the population.

There are essentially three types of proposals in this regard. The first, advocated by many civil society organizations, is to audit existing debt portfolios and repudiate debt deemed illegitimate. This would correct the moral hazard problem ex post (from the point of view of the population) and create incentives for lenders to be more careful in future lending, because they would always face the risk of a debt audit.

The second proposal, put forward by Bolton and Skeel (2007) and Jayachandran and Kremer (2006), would be for an international body (such as the United Nations [UN] Security Council) to declare regimes odious ex ante, in which case all loans contracted by the odious regime would in principle be repudiated by the successor government. In a related version of this proposal, once a regime is deemed odious, only loans that could be justified as benefiting the population would not be repudiated later.

A third proposal, aimed at ensuring that loan proceeds are used judiciously but without affecting the enforceability of loans, is that of "responsible lending." This proposal calls for greater oversight of all sovereign lending by creditors (for example, by suspending loan disbursements if serious corruption problems are encountered in the project the loan is financing) (see, for example, Nehru and Thomas 2009).

This chapter considers the impact of the three types of proposals in an agency model of politics in the vein of Ferejohn (1986) and Persson, Roland, and Tabellini (1997), in which the primary incentives provided to government executives are the possibility that they can be replaced— through elections in a democratic environment or through the overthrow of the government in a nondemocratic one. The model is modified to include two features relevant to the odious debt debate, namely, that governments finance their activities partly by borrowing from foreign creditors and that governments may seek to remain in power by using government resources to provide public goods to the population or to repress the population through violence.

The chapter is organized as follows. The first section discusses the relation between this chapter and the literature on odious debt. The second section presents a simple political agency model with international borrowing, in which governments may engage in borrowing for investments or repression. The third section describes the equilibrium of the model under the baseline of no changes to the current international debt market and then compares the welfare properties under the benchmark with those arising from the three proposed odious debt frameworks. It also extends the model in order to analyze the implications of an odious debt framework for the likelihood of collusion between creditors and odious regimes. The last section summarizes the chapter's conclusions and discusses possible extensions of the model.

Relation to the Literature

An extensive body of literature debates the existence of an odious debt doctrine in international law, proposes alternative formulations for a new or expanded framework for the cancellation of odious debt, and discusses alternatives for its implementation (see Nehru and Thomas 2009 for a summary of the literature). In contrast, few studies consider the problem from the point of view of economic theory. Those that have (Kremer and Jayachandran 2002; Jayachandran and Kremer 2006; Choi and Posner 2007) do not explicitly analyze the impact of an odious debt framework on the political agency problem ultimately at the heart of the debate, and none explicitly models the politics involved.

Jayachandran and Kremer (2006) and the working paper version (Kremer and Jayachandran 2002) consider a model in which an odious regime borrows to smooth consumption. The authors develop an equilibrium model of sovereign credit markets, which are supported by the possibility that creditors may seize overseas assets of borrowers. Under a legal framework of loan sanctions, this transfer of assets in case of nonpayment is precluded when a loan is made to an odious regime, which eliminates equilibria with lending to that regime. This result depends, however, on successor regimes always being nonodious. In the model, the imposition of loan sanctions increases the welfare of the population, which would no longer be saddled with debt that had not been used for their benefit.

Choi and Posner (2007) note that the argument in Jayachandran and Kremer (2006) also depends on odious governments always wasting loan proceeds. They point out that loan sanctions would not necessarily dry out funding to odious states but only increase the costs of finance, because default would occur if the dictator were overthrown but debt would likely be repaid as long as the odious regime were still in power and seeking new loans. If dictators remain in power when their loans come due, they would repay them in order to access new loans, implying a positive probability of repayment even for an odious regime under loan sanctions. Choi and Posner consider the impact of an increase in loan costs on the consumption-investment choice of odious governments. Their model—which assumes that the probability of overthrowing the dictator is the same regardless of whether the dictator consumes or invests the loan proceeds—actually suggests that loan sanctions do not change the incentives of odious governments. In order to have an effect, implementation of the odious debt doctrine must also increase the probability of overthrowing the dictator (they argue that this would be the case because the benefits to the population of overthrowing the regime are greater if the new regime can then repudiate its debt). In this case, under certain parameter values, populations are worse off under loan sanctions.

Allowing successor governments to repudiate debt incurred by previous regimes does not necessarily increase the likelihood of overthrowing a dictator. The evidence from trade sanctions is mixed (regimes subject to trade sanctions are not more likely to be overthrown), and in any case, new representative governments already have the possibility of repudiating their predecessors' debt. Successor regimes usually honor debt because of fear of legal penalties if they repudiate but also (perhaps mainly) because of possible market penalties that cannot be legislated away. The assumption that introducing an odious debt doctrine increases the likelihood of the regime being overthrown also appears to be at odds with the idea that the probability of replacing the regime is unaffected by the government's choice between investment and consumption, which has a direct impact on the utility of the population in the model.

This chapter departs from Jayachandran and Kremer (2006) in several respects. First, as in Choi and Posner (2007), the motive for borrowing may be investment rather than consumption smoothing. Empirical evidence for a consumption-smoothing motive for sovereign borrowing is weak at best: Levy-Yeyati (2008) shows that sovereign borrowing by developing countries is procyclical rather than countercyclical. The motive for repayment is not central to the model presented here, which simply assumes the existence of an exogenous punishment against default.

The main difference between this chapter and the existing economics literature on odious debt is the explicit modeling of the principal-agent relationship between the government and its population. Modeling the relationship in this way allows for the analysis of the effects of different policy prescriptions on both the incentives for a government to use repression and its incentives to invest in public goods.

The Model

In this section, I motivate and set up a simple model with which to analyze the implications of different odious debt frameworks on the welfare of the populations under both odious and nonodious regimes. Although the model is highly simplified, it captures the trade-off governments must make between trying to remain in power by providing public goods or using violence, and it allows analysis of the implications of different proposals for the cancellation of odious debts on this trade-off.

Motivation and Setup

I model the relationship between the government and the population as a principal-agent problem: the population "hires" the government to deliver certain public goods on its behalf, but the incentives of the government are not naturally aligned with those of the population, because the politicians in the government may prefer to divert resources for their private consumption rather than investing those resources in the delivery of public goods. As in Ferejohn (1986) and Persson, Roland, and Tabellini (1997), voters may control the government by threatening to replace politicians unless they deliver a minimum level of public goods. In the model, the government can remain in power by delivering public goods or by using repression and violence. I denominate governments that choose repression as a means to remain in power as odious, but it is important to note that even nonodious governments may act against the interests of the population by exploiting information asymmetries.

The motivation for borrowing in the model comes from a nonlinear (bulky) technology for public investments, for which the government is assumed to have insufficient resources in the first period. Because the investments have positive expected net returns, it would therefore be optimal to borrow. Borrowing (or at least some borrowing) may also take place to finance repression, government consumption, or redistribution.

This chapter does not consider the reasons why governments repay their debt in the first place (this is a fundamental question of international finance, because creditors' ability to enforce their claims through the legal system is far more limited against countries than against firms). The literature identifies a number of possible channels that compel countries to repay their debt, including reputational costs; penalties, such as litigation costs or trade sanctions; limitations on access to finance in the short term; and long-term increases in the cost of finance. There is no consensus as to the relative importance of these channels from an empirical perspective, and even the theoretical literature is divided: the classic article by Bulow and Rogoff (1989) argues that reputational costs alone are not sufficient to prevent strategic defaults, whereas other authors (for example, Wright 2003) suggest that reputation among creditors allows for borrower reputation to have value. In this chapter, I simply assume that some enforcement mechanism exists and that loan sizes are limited by a hypothetical penalty cost.

Because I rule out inability to pay (by assuming that revenues in the repayment period are always greater than the loan size), default can occur only when default penalties are removed. Although it is not at all clear that implementing an odious debt framework removes the costs of default discussed above, I take this as a best-case scenario assumption. Therefore, if the odious debt framework is in place, countries default when the framework allows them to do so.

Production

Consider an economy with just two goods, guns and butter. Guns are consumed only by the government for the purpose of repressing the population and remaining in power. Butter may be consumed by both the population and the government. Guns are not produced domestically; they must be imported (or smuggled) into the country. Butter is perishable and cannot be imported, but it may be produced domestically if the government builds a milk-processing plant. Building the butter factory requires a risky lump-sum investment: a fixed amount I is required, with a positive probability that it will be diverted (because of corruption, civil strife, or other factors) or otherwise considered unsuccessful, in which case nothing is built. If the investment is successful, it has both private (internal) and public (external) returns (through the creation of employment, the building of roads needed to transport the butter to town, and so forth).

The production function for butter is given by

$$y_t = (1 + x)I_t\theta_t, \tag{10.1}$$

where I_t is investment, x is the public (external) returns, and θ_t is the stochastic returns that are identically and independently distributed such that with probability p, the return is $\theta_t = \theta > 1$ and with probability $1 - p$, $\theta_t = 0$ (that is, the project fails). Investment is lumpy, such that $y_t = 0$ for

$I_t < I$ and $y_t = n(1 + x)I\theta_t$ if $(n + 1)I < I_t < nI$ (therefore, it is optimal to invest only in multiples of I). I later make an assumption on the available financing to ensure that $I_t \in \{0, I\}$.

Governments have an endowment $b_1 < I$ in the first subperiod and therefore must borrow to build the butter factory. In the second period, the government collects domestic revenues of b_2. There are no domestic or external savings available to the government.

Credit Markets

I consider competitive, risk-neutral commercial lenders who are assumed to behave according to the nonarbitrage condition

$$(1 - p_D)(1 + i)d + p_D R = (1 + j)d, \tag{10.2}$$

where p_D is the probability of default, i is the interest rate charged to the borrower, R is the recovery value in case of default, and j is the risk-free world interest rate. For simplicity, I assume that $j = 0$ and $R = 0$, so that the no-arbitrage condition reduces to $1 + i = \left(\dfrac{1}{1 - p_D}\right)$.

As noted above, I do not explicitly model the question of why sovereign borrowers repay their debt at all. Instead, I assume that a punishment P is available to lenders such that they can make loans as large as D (where D is such that $2I > D + b_1 \geq I$) and be ensured of payment as long as the country has the resources to pay, which I also assume. I do not separate the portion of P attributable to reputational or legal costs (that is, the portion of the punishment that may be removed by an odious debt framework). In addition, by precluding loans that would allow investments of $2I$, I simplify output by restricting the analysis to $y_t = \{0, (1 + x)\theta I\}$.

Because D is fixed, I assume, as a convention, that $d = \dfrac{D}{1 + i} = D(1 - p_D)$ are the loan proceeds, which vary with p_D, and that D is the fixed repayment amount consistent with P.[5] I assume $b_2 \geq D$, so that without an odious debt framework, $p_D = 0$ and $D = d$. Therefore, under the base case, there are no defaults in equilibrium regardless of regime type or use of the loan. This reflects evidence that potentially odious regimes are no more likely to default than nonodious ones, including in the case of transition from odious to nonodious regimes (as was the case in postapartheid South Africa).

Creditors cannot costlessly observe whether loan proceeds are used for consumption, repression, or investment, but a monitoring technology is available at a fixed cost k. Because creditors are competitive, the verification technology will not be used in equilibrium unless the choice between repression and consumption affects the probability of default (and therefore their profits).

Politics

Governments maximize their own utility subject to the constraint that they may be replaced by the population. There are two possible political systems: one in which governments spend resources on repression, another in which incumbent governments forgo repression and rely instead on the provision of public goods to garner electoral support to remain in power. Broadly speaking, the political systems can be characterized as dictatorship and democracy, where democracy refers to a political system in which voters may hold politicians accountable on the basis of delivery of public services.

Let g denote expenditures on guns. To keep the model simple, I assume that if the government spends an amount $g_t = G$, it remains in power with exogenous probability q and that there is no benefit to spending any more. Therefore, $g_t \in \{0, G\}$. (Later, I provide a possible motivation for the probability q as the probability of the realization of the actual costs of keeping power.) In the model, I term *odious* those governments that choose $g_t = G$. Because even odious regimes that invest capture the entire private output of the investment, the population is always better off with a nonrepressive regime. I assume that $b_1 > G$, so that the government may engage in repression even without external borrowing. This seems to be a reasonable assumption, given that many countries that are currently cut out of the international financial system nonetheless find resources to spend on repression.

When governments choose $g_t = 0$, voters use a retrospective voting rule based on minimum utility cutoff. That is, they reelect governments that provide at least a minimum utility level and otherwise elect a new government.

A key assumption needed for the tractability of the model is that the external effects of investments are not observable to voters at the time of the election and that voters therefore must base their decision only on the private output of the factory. I motivate this assumption by noting that external effects sometimes benefit only the next generation of voters, as may be the case, for example, if previously credit-constrained workers in the factory can now afford to educate their children. Voters observe only $(1 - \gamma)I_t\theta_t = \{0, (1 - \gamma)I\theta\}$, where γ is the fraction of the investment's output captured by the government as rents. Because I and θ are exogenous, the rule is equivalent to setting a threshold on γ.

To ensure that the game is stationary and to focus on the moral hazard problem, I assume that each country has only one type of politicians, with the type given by the level of "ego rents" w they receive from being in power (politicians with higher w are more attached to power than those with lower w). In practice, different countries may have different types of politicians; I assume that a given country only has one type.

Finally, I assume that the present value of costs from allowing a government always to expropriate the private output of investment for a current voter is greater than the external benefits for future generations. Therefore, each generation of voters is indifferent between a kleptocrat (who appropriates all private output but invests) and an autocrat who does not invest.

Preferences and Government Budget Constraint

I assume that both the population and the government are risk neutral and have linear utility functions. For simplicity, there is no discounting. The instantaneous utility function of the population of generation g at time t is given by

$$u_{g,t} = (1 - \gamma)I_t \theta_t + (x\, I_{g-1}\theta_{g-1}) + b_2 - D. \tag{10.3}$$

As noted above, the benefits of private investment affect the utility of the next generation only. The government's instantaneous utility function is given by

$$v_t = w + d + b_1 - g_t + (\gamma\theta_t - 1)I_t. \tag{10.4}$$

Governments maximize the expected utility function

$$E[v_t] = w + d + b_1 - g_t + (\gamma\theta p - 1)I_t + \Pr[\text{reelection}]V^{B,G}, \tag{10.5}$$

where $V^{B,G}$ are continuation values for governments that choose, respectively, to build butter factories or buy guns. Utility is maximized subject to the government's budget constraint

$$d + b_1 \leq g_t + I_t \tag{10.6}$$

as well as by constraints on reelection.

Timing

I consider an infinitely repeated game with three subperiods (figure 10.1). In subperiod 1, the government contracts a loan and decides whether to remain in power through repression (that is, buy guns) or through the provision of public goods. In subperiod 2, the returns to investing are revealed and the government decides whether to divert the investment for consumption or undertake the investment. In subperiod 3, the population observes the output, the loan is repaid, and elections take place.

Note that once the government chooses to consume the proceeds of the loan, elections are trivial because the government either accepts that it will

Figure 10.1 Sequence of Actions in an Infinitely Repeated
Game with Three Subperiods

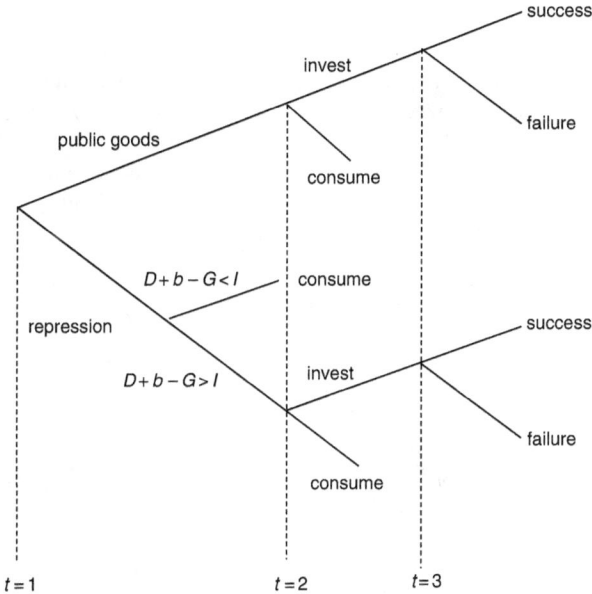

Source: Author.
Note: D = debt; b = budget; G = guns spending; I = investment amount;
t = time.

not be reelected or knows that it will remain in power through the use of
repression. In addition, the assumptions on timing ensure that the government will never undertake a failed investment, choosing instead to consume
the loan proceeds, because voters would observe the same outcome.

Equilibrium

I begin by analyzing a benchmark model of international debt markets
without an odious debt framework in place; this is the baseline against
which I compare the models modified with the different frameworks.

Two cases must be considered depending on the budget constraint
faced by the government. The first corresponds to governments that cannot afford to engage simultaneously in repression and investment (that is,
$d + b_1 - G < I$). The second corresponds to governments that are able to

undertake both activities (that is, $d + b_1 - G \geq I$). Following the analysis of the baseline case, I analyze the three proposed odious debt frameworks and compare them with this baseline.

Baseline Case 1: Odious Regimes Cannot Invest

Consider the case in which the government's budget constraint (equation 10.6) is characterized by $d + b_1 - G < I$, with $d = D$. In this case, the government's choice to use repression precludes it from also investing. The government then has three choices: use repression, forgo repression and invest, or forgo repression and consume. The incentive-compatibility constraint for the government to choose to enter electoral politics rather than to engage in repression is given by

$$w < \left(\frac{(1-p)G + (1-q)p(\gamma\theta - 1)I}{q - p} \right) - D - b_1. \tag{10.7}$$

The right-hand side of equation (10.7) is increasing in G, because the higher the cost of repression, the smaller the number of types of politicians that will avail themselves of repression. It is also increasing on I as long as $\gamma\theta > 1$ (that is, if the investment yields positive returns to the government), and it is monotonically increasing on γ and θ only if $q > p$, which I assume to be true. This implies that the probability of staying in office is greater for the repressive government than for the "democratic" government, which makes sense because otherwise, investment strictly dominates repression. The assumption that the government observes θ before investing guarantees positive returns; if investment also ensured a higher probability of reelection (that is, if $p > q$), there would clearly be no use for repression.

As $(q - p)$ decreases, more types of politicians choose to provide public goods rather than engage in repression. Therefore, $q - p$ can be viewed as an institutional variable. In fact, in many developing countries, the probability of the success of public investments does appear to be lower (even if the returns may be high) because of capacity and other institutional constraints; in contrast, the probability of staying in power that can be "bought" for a fixed amount is likely decreasing on the level of income, as the population has more at stake and would be more compelled to overthrow a dictator.

Another consequence of the magnitude of $q - p$ is that decreasing resources make investment more likely (as long as it is affordable), because the benefits of staying in power are a function of the residual (that is, net of spending on guns and investment resources). Therefore, fewer residual resources reduce the benefit of staying in office (which is biased toward repression by $q > p$).

The equilibrium entails manipulating equation (10.7) to identify $w = w_1^*$, the level of the ego rent parameter above which politicians choose repression regardless of the level of γ_1 and γ^*, the optimal fraction of the output that voters must allow politicians to appropriate when $w < w_1^*$ to ensure that investment is incentive compatible. Naturally, the higher w_1^* is, the larger is the number of types of politicians who will choose to abstain from repression, and the lower γ is, the greater is the utility of voters. Proposition 1 summarizes the equilibrium (all proofs appear in the annex):

Proposition 1. *For the case in which* $d + b_1 - G < I$, *governments always choose to engage in repression when*

$$w > \left(\frac{(1-p)G + (1-q)p(\theta - 1)I}{q - p} \right) - D - b_1 \equiv w_1^*.$$

When $w \le w_1^*$, *governments choose to engage in electoral competition and are reelected if they deliver utility* $u \ge (1 - \gamma_1^*)I\theta + b_2 - D$, *where* $\gamma_1^* \in \{0, \gamma_1\}$ *is the optimal fraction of investment returns that is transferred to the government in the form of rents. For*

$$w \le \left(\frac{(1-p)G - (2p-1)(1-q)I}{q - p} \right) - D - b_1 \equiv w_1^{\gamma=0},$$

$\gamma_1^* = 0$; *and for* $w_1^{\gamma=0} < w \le w_1^*$,

$$\gamma_1^* = \gamma_1 = \left(\frac{(w + D + b_1)(q - p) - (1-p)G}{\theta I(1-q)p} \right) + \left(\frac{2p-1}{\theta p} \right).$$

Proposition 1 shows that there are two cutoffs for w that in turn give rise to three regions for w: (a) $w > w_1^*$ (repression is always chosen); (b) $w_1^* \ge w > w_1^{\gamma=0}$ ($\gamma^* = \gamma_1 > 0$); and (c) $w \le w_1^{\gamma=0}$ ($\gamma^* = 0$) (figure 10.2). Note that in case (b) the population must accept a higher level of γ than required simply to provide incentives for a politician to invest rather than consume. Therefore, the threat of repression forces higher transfers to the government.

Note that whether a government is odious depends on its type. However, where a government falls in the spectrum (that is, how close to w_1^* it is) will affect the consequences for any odious debt framework.

The model has two potentially interesting features that are applicable to developing countries. The first is the role that the threat of repression plays in increasing the rents that accrue to the government. For the intermediate w types, governments may be able to extract more rents under a democratic setting by threatening (though not actually using) repression. In this simple model, where the incentive compatibility for investing rather than consuming the loan investment amount is always met (see the proof

Figure 10.2 Relationship between Level of "Ego Rents" and Required Transfer to Government

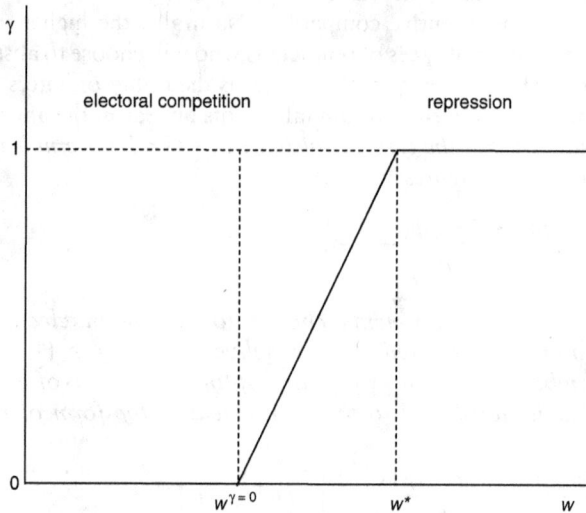

Source: Author.

in the annex), $\gamma^* > 0$ provides a measure of the threat of repression and is decreasing on the returns to investment (θ) and the cost of repression (G) but increasing on w, D, and b_1.

The second feature is the "natural resource curse." As discussed earlier, as long as engaging in repression provides better chances of remaining in power than does delivering public goods (that is, $q > p$), a higher endowment b_1 makes investment less likely up to the point at which both investment and repression become affordable. But, as shown below, even as a higher endowment makes investment affordable, repression will still be used to ensure the government's hold on power.

Baseline Case 2: Odious Regimes Can Invest

The analysis of the case in which odious regimes may invest is similar to the first case, except that the benefits of engaging in repression are greater, because the government can accrue the full output of the investment project and incur only a probability ($1 - q < 1 - p$) of being replaced. The government must still trade off these benefits with the cost of repression. The government has four choices: use repression and invest, use repression and consume, forgo repression and invest, and forgo repression and consume.

The incentive-compatibility constraint for the government to choose to enter electoral politics rather than to engage in repression is given by

$$w + D + b_1 < \left(\frac{1-p}{q-p}\right)G + \left(\frac{1-q}{q-p}\right)(\gamma\theta - 1)pI - \left(\frac{1-p}{q-p}\right)(\theta - 1)pI. \quad (10.8)$$

As in the previous case, I derive the cutoff values of w that indicate when the government will always choose repression and when the governments will not require transfers in order to provide the public good.

Proposition 2. *In the case in which $d + b_1 - G > I$, governments always choose to engage in repression when*

$$w > w_2^* = \left(\frac{1-p}{q-p}\right)G - (\theta - 1)pI - D - b_1.$$

When $w \le w_2^*$, governments choose to engage in electoral competition and are reelected if they deliver utility $u \ge (1 - \gamma_2^*)I\theta + b_2 - D$, where $\gamma_2^* \in \{0, \gamma_2\}$ is the optimal share of investment returns that must be transferred to the government in the form of rents. For

$$w \le \left(\frac{(1-p)G - (2p-1)I(1-q)}{q-p}\right) - D - b_1 \equiv w_2^{\gamma=0},$$

$\gamma_2^* = 0$; *for $w_2^{\gamma=0} < w \le w_2^*$,*

$$\gamma_2^* = \left(\frac{(w + D + b^1)(q-p)}{(1-q)pI\theta}\right) + \left(\frac{(1-p)(\theta - 1) + 1 - q}{(1-q)pI\theta}\right)pI - \left(\frac{(1-p)}{(1-q)\theta}\right)\left(\frac{G}{pI}\right).$$

As in baseline Case 1, there are two cutoff levels of w that give rise to three regions: (a) $w > w_2^*$ (repression is always chosen); (b) $w_2^* \ge w > w_2^{\gamma=0}$ and $\gamma_2^* > 0$; and (c) $w \le w_2^{\gamma=0}$ ($\gamma_2^* = 0$), where $w_2^{\gamma=0}$ is the cutoff above which $\gamma_2^* > 0$, given by

$$\left(\frac{1-p}{q-p}\right)(G - \theta pI) - D - b_1.$$

Note that $w_1^* > w_2^*$, which is consistent with the fact that more types of government will engage in repression given the added ability to undertake investments. In general, a higher w^* implies higher welfare, because it is associated with fewer types above w^* that engage in repression.

Other comparative statics are similar to those in the previous case. Notably, a small difference between q and p leads to higher values of w_2^*, making repression less attractive. As noted above, although a higher b_1

may eventually increase welfare by allowing the country to invest, as long as $q > p$, the government will continue to engage in repression.

Ex Ante Framework (Loan Sanctions)

I consider an ex ante odious regime framework in the vein of that suggested by Jayachandran and Kremer (2006), whereby an appropriate institution (for example, the UN Security Council or the International Monetary Fund) would declare a regime odious, in which case all loans made to it from that point on would be unenforceable by the relevant courts and the usual default provisions in commercial or official debt contracts would not be triggered. The key feature of the ex ante framework is that the debt of the odious regime must be considered legitimate until the appropriate institution declares it odious. As Jayachandran and Kremer argue, this would preserve legitimate lending by ensuring creditors that they would be punished only if they knowingly lent to a regime that acted against the interests of its population, where "knowingly" would be precisely defined by the pronouncement of the international body.

I model the loan-sanctions regime as removing all penalties for default (by successor governments) on debt contracted by regimes declared to be odious by a suitable international body. This is the most optimistic assumption about the impact of the policy, because in reality it is questionable whether an odious debt framework would entirely remove the reputational and legal penalties of defaulting (see Dömeland, Gil Sander, and Primo Braga 2009).

As Choi and Posner (2007) note, the probability of default under the loan-sanctions framework depends on whether the odious regime is replaced. As long as the regime remains in power, it will not be eligible for debt forgiveness (in terms of the model, punishment P would still be imposed) and will therefore have to continue to repay its debt. I assume that odious regimes are replaced by nonodious ones with probability $1 - q$. Recall that $(1 - p_D)(1 + i)d + p_D R = (1 + j)d$. For $R = j = 0$ and $p_D = 1 - q$, yielding $i = \left(\dfrac{1-q}{q}\right)$. Under this policy, governments choosing repression can borrow only $d = qD < D$, where D is the repayment amount compatible with the enforcement mechanism. This applies only to governments declared odious, which I assume are limited to those using repression.

Rewriting the incentive-compatibility constraint for this case results in

$$\left(\frac{1-p}{q-p}\right)G + \left(\frac{1-q}{q-p}\right)p(\theta-1)I + \left(\frac{1-2q+qp}{q-p}\right)D - b_1 = w^*_{1,LS}. \qquad (10.9)$$

Proposition 3 summarizes the comparison between the cutoff levels of w given by the loan-sanctions framework relative to the baseline scenarios discussed earlier.

Proposition 3. *Under the loan-sanctions framework, the welfare of the population increases relative to the baseline scenario in countries in which the government has $w < w^*_{1,LS}$, where*

$$w^*_{1,LS} = \left(\frac{1-p}{q-p}\right)G + \left(\frac{1-q}{q-p}\right)p(\theta-1)\ I + \left(\frac{1}{q-p}\right)(D-d-(Dq-dp))$$
$$-b_1 > w^*_1;$$

welfare is unchanged in countries in which $w > w^*_{1,LS}$ and $d + b_1 - G > I$ or $D + b_1 - G < I$; and welfare is reduced when $w > w^*_{1,LS}$ and $d + b_1 - G < I$, but $D + b_1 - G > I$.

Under the loan-sanctions policy, countries with governments of type $w < w^*_{1,LS}$ benefit because the government chooses to switch from using repression to investing, or if it was already investing, the threat of using repression is reduced, allowing voters to demand lower rents for the government; this is true whether or not the government can afford to engage in both repression and investment. Governments of type $w > w^*_{1,LS}$ use repression. If $d + b_1 - G > I$, the government also continues to invest; the impact of the loan sanctions on the population is therefore neutral. In cases in which $D + b_1 - G > I$ but $d + b_1 - G < I$ and $w > w^*_{1,LS}$, the population is worse off, because the government continues to use repression but now chooses not to invest.

Ex Post Framework (Debt Audits)

Under an ex post framework, international laws would be changed to allow governments succeeding odious regimes to challenge (through litigation) debt contracted by odious regimes. Unlike the ex ante framework, lenders would not be sure which governments would later be found odious, even if they were aware that there was a high probability that a regime would later be considered as such. Even regimes that lenders may strongly believe are nonodious may later be regarded as odious. For example, Jayachandran and Kremer (2006) suggest that Trudjman's Croatia could be considered an odious regime, although many Croatians consider Trudjman a national hero.

The ex post framework is modeled by assuming that creditors cannot observe whether governments engage in repression but rather observe a signal $\omega = \{0,G\}$ such that $\Pr[g = 0|\omega = 0] = s$. For simplicity, assume that $\Pr[g = G|\omega = G] = s$. In this case, default occurs if both (a) the regime is eventually found to be odious through the litigation process, which occurs with probability s if the signal was G and $(1 - s)$ if the signal was 0 and (b) the dictator is out of power in the repayment period, which occurs with probability $1 - q$. To keep things simple, I assume that governments that choose to engage in repression know they will be sending a signal $\omega = G$ with probability s, so that $\Pr[\omega = G|g = G] = \Pr[\omega = 0|g = 0] = s$.

Given that the lender observes $\omega = G$, the probability of default is $s(1-q)$ and $d^o = D(1-(1-q)s)$. If the lender observes $\omega = 0$, the probability of default is such that $d'' = D(q + s(1-q))$. Therefore, if s is close to 1 (that is, there is a high correlation between the use of repression and its signal), $d'' \approx D$, whereas if s is close to $\frac{1}{2}$, $d^o \approx d''$.

Proposition 4 summarizes the equilibrium under a debt-audit framework in international debt markets and compares the welfare implications with those of the baseline case.

Proposition 4. *Under the debt-audit framework, the welfare of the population increases relative to the baseline scenario in countries in which the government is of type $w < w^*_{1,DA}$, where*

$$w^*_{1,DA} = \left(\frac{1-p}{q-p}\right)G + \left(\frac{(1-q)p(\theta-1)I}{q-p}\right)$$

$$+ \left(\frac{(1-p)(1-q)}{q-p}\right)(2s-1)D - d'' - b_1 > w^*_1;$$

is unchanged in countries in which $w > w^*_{1,DA}$ and $d^o + b_1 - G > I$ or $D + b_1 - G < I$; and is reduced in countries in which $w > w^*_{1,DA}$ and $d^o + b_1 - G < I$, but $D + b_1 - G > I$. These results require that the signal of whether a regime is odious be informative—namely, $s > \left(\frac{1-q}{2-q-p}\right)$, which is satisfied for $s > \frac{1}{2}$. Increases in s increase welfare, and as $s \to 1$, the debt-audit framework converges to the loan-sanctions framework. Therefore, the debt-audit framework is dominated by the loan-sanctions framework for all $s < 1$.

The loan-sanctions framework dominates the ex post debt-audit framework in at least two ways. First, for $s < 1$, $w^*_{LS} > w^*_{DA}$, implying that any given type w that does not choose repression under the loan-sanctions framework will also not choose repression under the debt-audit framework; the converse is not true. Second, for countries in which $D + b_1 > I$ but $d'' + b_1 < I$, the debt-audit framework, but not the loan-sanctions framework, leads to a decrease in welfare, because the (likely nonodious) government is no longer able to invest. Finally, although not always captured in the welfare of the population, unlike loan sanctions, the debt-audit framework implies higher borrowing costs to all nonodious regimes.

This discussion assumes that regimes rather than individual loans may be found to be odious ex post. In this model, because loan proceeds are fungible and $b_1 > G$, a loan-by-loan audit would not identify gun purchases, although such audits may identify episodes during which the government used loan proceeds for its own consumption. To be consistent with the starker definition of an odious regime as one that uses violence to repress the population, I focus on an audit of the regime.

Ex Ante Loan Certification (Responsible Lending)

The responsible lending framework requires lenders to abide by certain standards (for example, the Equator Principles) in order to ensure that loans are enforceable. Once a loan is judged to have met those standards, it cannot be repudiated on the grounds that it is illegitimate, even if the project fails or it is later discovered that the money was used illegally. Moreover, the loan cannot be repudiated if the successor government claims its predecessor regime was odious.

The implications of the responsible lending framework depend on the ex post status of loans that do not meet the standard. If such loans are regarded as legitimate and enforceable, governments and creditors would be able to effectively opt out of the framework, in which case commercial creditors would be unlikely to adopt the regime. The second possibility would be for a loan that does not meet the standard to be unenforceable (that is, it is by default assumed by the courts to be illegitimate). A third possibility—that the legitimacy of loans not covered could be litigated—is similar but not equivalent to the ex post (debt-audit) approach. The key difference lies in the parties' advance knowledge of the legal implications of a repudiation under an ex ante but not an ex post framework.[6]

In modeling the responsible lending framework, I assume that loans that do not meet the standards of responsible lending are unenforceable and can be repudiated by any government without incurring punishment. If lenders were only required to verify that loan proceeds are not used to purchase guns in order to secure enforceability of their claims, the ultimate impact of the policy would be to raise financing costs, as governments would simply use domestic resources to buy guns (since $b_1 > G$ by assumption). This results in financing terms implicitly given by $d_{RL} = D - k$, where k is the verification cost. I therefore assume that lenders must verify that the funds are spent on the investment project (rather than used for buying guns or for the consumption of the government). I assume that lenders cannot observe the realization of θ before the investment is started. This implies that lenders will engage in some projects that are ex post inefficient.

Proposition 5. *Under the responsible lending framework, the welfare of the population increases relative to the baseline scenario in countries in which the government is of type* $w < w^*_{1,RL}$, *where*

$$w^*_{1,RL} = \left(\frac{(D - k + (p\theta - 1)I)(1 - q) + G(1 - p)}{q - p} \right) - b_1 > w^*_1 \quad if$$

$$k < \left(\frac{D(1 - p) - (1 - q)(\theta - 1)pI}{1 - q} \right).$$

If $w_1^* < w < w_{2,RL}^*$, welfare increases if

$$k > \left(\frac{(1-q)(1-p)}{(q-p)} \right) I.$$

Welfare also increases in countries in which $D - k + b_1 - G < I$ but $D + b_1 - G > I$ and $w_{2,RL}^* > w > w_2^*$. Welfare decreases if monitoring costs are too high (when both investment and repression are precluded) or too low (when both investment and repression are possible).

If the government was previously able to afford both repression and investment, the higher financing costs could make investment unaffordable, reverting to results of the case in which $D + b_1 - G < I$ applies. Assuming the government can still afford both repression and investment at the higher borrowing cost $D - k$, I calculate

$$w_{2,RL}^* = \left(\frac{(1-p)G}{q-p} \right) - D + k - b_1 - (p\theta - 1)I.$$

Interestingly, because now both types of governments can obtain loans, it is again the case that more budgetary resources (such as loans) lead to greater incentives to use repression to hold on to power. Therefore, higher monitoring costs, which reduce the budget, actually prevent the use of repression. Therefore, $w_{2,RL}^* > w_2^*$ for $k > 0$.

Although the threat of repression is lower, because the government is forced to invest even when it knows a project will fail, rent transfers to the government are generally higher:

$$\gamma_{2,RL}^* = \left(\frac{(w + D - k + b_1)(q - p) - (1-p)G + p(\theta - 1)(1-p)I + (1-q)I}{(1-q)Ip\theta} \right)$$
$$< \gamma_1^* \text{ if}$$

$$k > \left(\frac{(1-q)(1-p)}{(q-p)} \right) I > 0.$$

Therefore, if

$$k > \left(\frac{(1-q)(1-p)}{(q-p)} \right) I,$$

welfare is unambiguously increased; $k > 0$ ensures that fewer governments choose repression but requires higher rents. The different effects of monitoring costs on countries able to afford both repression and investment implies that k must be within a certain range to ensure that welfare is raised relative to the baseline, namely,

$$\left(\frac{(1-q)(1-p)}{q-p}\right)I < k < \left(\frac{D(1-p)-(1-q)(\theta-1)pI}{1-q}\right).$$

Comparing $\gamma^*_{1,RL}$ and γ^*_1, I note that $\gamma^*_{1,RL} < \gamma^*_1$ if

$$k < \left(\frac{D(1-p)-(1-q)(\theta-1)pI}{1-q}\right).$$

This is a different condition from the one above ensuring that more countries choose to engage in investment rather than repression because of the need to compensate for the fact that governments must invest even when they know a project will be unsuccessful. In cases in which countries cannot afford to both invest and engage in repression, the responsible lending framework increases the number of governments that choose to invest. It may, however, also increase the required transfers to the government, because the government can no longer divert loan proceeds in cases in which it is known in advance that the investment financed by the loan will fail.

The incentive compatibility for investing or consuming the loan does not apply here, because I assume that once the government accepts the loan, it accepts that it will be monitored and unable to divert the proceeds to consumption. Although in principle the government would have incentives to truthfully reveal information to lenders about the prospects of the project, I preclude bargaining between the government and the lenders in this case.

The responsible lending regime is especially effective for governments that are not investing, because such governments would be unable to borrow at all if they wanted to continue to rule through repression. For governments that can afford to invest and use repression, the impact on welfare of the population is mixed. On the one hand, at any level of monitoring costs k, there is a clear effect of lowering the incentives for repression. On the other hand, by forcing governments to invest when a project may turn out to be unsuccessful, this framework requires transferring higher rents to the government.

Comparing the responsible lending with the loan-sanctions frameworks, I note that $w^*_{1,RL} > w^*_{1,LS}$ if k is sufficiently low, specifically $k < (qD - (1 - q)I)(1 - p)$. This is feasible (that is, $k > 0$) if $q > \dfrac{I}{D+1}$.

Creditor Collusion

In this model, creditors are indifferent between lending to different regimes. This characterization of debt markets is shared—and criticized—by some civil society organizations, which have called for creditor coresponsibility, suggesting that creditors should discriminate against regimes deemed odious. The argument for an odious debt framework is often made in this context, suggesting that it would create such discrimination.

The discussion above suggests that different odious debt frameworks may have this result, albeit often at a cost to nonodious regimes as well. In this section, I modify the model to analyze how the introduction of an odious debt framework could change the incentives for collusion between creditors and odious regimes and result in a bias toward lending to odious regimes.

Suppose the exogenous probability of reelection q corresponds to the probability of $G' = G^L < b_1$ (that is, repression is "affordable"). If the government cannot afford sufficient repression (if $G' = G^H > D + b_1$), it is overthrown, which yields $\Pr[G = G^H] = 1 - q$. Assume that the revelation of G' takes place after the revelation of θ. Given that G^H is unaffordable by definition, a government that engages in repression chooses G^L and accepts the probability of being overthrown, exactly as before.

Given that politicians are risk neutral and creditors are always repaid, the equilibrium under the scenario without an odious debt framework is the same as in the previous discussion with loans in the amount of D, the maximum enforceable amount. In particular, creditors have no incentive to help troubled repressive regimes. Because they are already lending at the highest level given the available enforcement mechanisms, any attempt to save the odious regime by making repression affordable inevitably leads to default and losses. Alternatively, the creditor knows it will be repaid by the next regime and therefore has no incentives to help the one being overthrown.

This modification does have implications when an odious debt framework is in place. Consider the case of an ex ante odious regime framework, and recall that creditors lend $d = qD$ to odious regimes when q cannot be affected by loan size. If creditors can make additional loans following the revelation of the cost of repression, they now have an incentive to support the odious regime and agree to obtain a partial repayment in the next period.

The zero-profit condition becomes $D - (1 - q)d^{sup} = d'$ (here $d^{sup} = G^H - D$), the supplemental, nonenforceable loan made once the cost G' is revealed. Solving for d', I obtain $d' = (2 - q)D - G^H(1 - q)$, which is greater than d (the amount lent to odious regimes under the ex ante approach) if $G^H < 2D$ and equal to d otherwise. Therefore, it is possible that by reducing the likelihood that creditors are paid if an odious regime is overthrown, the introduction of an odious debt framework could increase the incentives for creditors to lend to odious regimes that would otherwise be replaced.

Directions for Future Research and Conclusions

This chapter makes a first attempt at analyzing different proposals to address the odious debt problem. A number of extensions could be pursued. On a technical level, the model contains a number of nonlinear assumptions. Extensions to more continuous models (in the probability of project success or the required amount of investment, for example) would be useful to verify whether the conclusions are robust.

Another extension would be to separate reputational and direct punishments for default. With a more refined definition of punishment for default, the loan-sanctions framework—which seems to create the fewest distortions, because of the assumption that it would not change the cost of borrowing of nonodious regimes—may turn out to be more similar to the debt-audit regime than to the model presented in this chapter. Because odious regimes face market exclusion, higher financing costs, or both under the loan-sanctions regime, these methods for enforcing existing nonodious loans become ineffective. If reputational (or market) punishments are indeed an important reason why countries repay their debt, a regime that is declared odious has no incentive to honor debt it acquired before the declaration of odiousness (and which therefore is not eligible for "no-punishment" repudiation), because the borrower has already been excluded from credit markets. Lenders would price their loans in the expectation that a regime could be declared odious, and the analysis would be closer to that of the debt-audit framework. The extent to which this would create welfare losses or gains will be closely related to how well lenders can predict which regimes will be declared odious. Like the debt-audit framework, it would entail an increase in borrowing costs for all regime types.

It would also be useful to consider an extension to official creditors. Official creditors do not make lending decisions through nonarbitrage conditions; rather, most lending is done at concessional (that is, below-market) rates. For official creditors, $(1 - p_D)(1 + i)D + p_D R \ll (1 + j)D$, with the difference financed by the budget of the official creditors, partly mitigated by their preferred creditor status. In the limited context of the model presented here, one would expect that official creditors may respond more severely than commercial creditors. For example, in the loan-sanctions model, official creditors would be expected to stop lending to odious regimes entirely (one could argue that this is already the case with some countries). In addition, official creditors already have relatively strict policies in place requiring verification of the use of proceeds.

Although it focuses on relatively simple trade-offs, the analysis in this chapter suggests that among the different odious debt frameworks, the least promising is the ex post debt-audit framework, which is welfare dominated by the loan-sanctions framework. The relative merits of the responsible lending and loan-sanctions frameworks are ambiguous and depend on the cost of verifying that loans are used appropriately.

None of the proposed frameworks provides an unambiguous improvement in the welfare of the population, which cautions against drawing easy policy conclusions. Ambiguity on the effects of the different policy proposals emerges from the possibility of diversion of domestic resources from investment to repression and from the offsetting effects of different policy proposals on the threat of repression and the required transfer to the government. Moreover, the assumption that successor governments would not face any market punishment under an odious debt framework is a strong one, as is the assumption that a loan-sanctions framework would entirely remove the punishment imposed on a defaulting country even if it were allowed to do so.

Framing the problem as one of political agency does, however, highlight the importance of promoting effective expenditure-tracking mechanisms and budget transparency as a means of ensuring that not only the proceeds of loans but also all public resources are used in the interests of the population rather than for the private gain of politicians in government. Indeed, in Gil Sander (2009), I show that reducing the cost of information acquisition by voters improves their control over the government, promotes the alignment of interests between governments and their population, and reduces the incurrence of odious debt.

Annex Proofs

Proposition 1

I first write the incentive-compatibility constraint that ensures the politician refrains from using repression, assuming that investing (rather than consuming the investment funds) is also incentive compatible. The constraint is given by

$$w + D + b_1 - G + qV^G < w + D + b_1 + p(\gamma\theta - 1)I + pV^B \text{ or}$$

$$qV^G - pV^B < G + p(\gamma\theta - 1)I. \tag{10A.1}$$

In this expression, V^G is the continuation value for a government that chooses to purchase guns, and V^B is the continuation value for a government that chooses to invest in a butter factory. Attention is restricted to stationary equilibria, in which politicians choose the same strategies each period. Solving for $V^{G,B}$ and replacing the result in equation (10A.1) yields equation (10.7) in the text:

$$w < \left(\frac{(1-p)G + (1-q)p(\gamma\theta - 1)I}{q - p} \right) - D - b_1.$$

By setting $\gamma = 1$, I define

$$w_1^* \equiv \left(\frac{(1-p)G + (1-q)p(\theta - 1)I}{q - p} \right) - D - b_1$$

as the critical level of w such that by the linearity of the inequality on γ, any government with $w > w_1^*$ will choose repression independent of γ. For $w \leq w_1^*$, voters set the optimal γ_1^* that maximizes their utility, subject to incentive compatibility for the government. Given the simple linear forms in the model, utility maximization implies minimizing the value of γ to just ensure that incentive compatibility is met.

There are two potential incentive-compatibility conditions on γ. The first incentive-compatibility constraint on γ states that the government that forgoes repression should choose to invest rather than consume when it observes that $\theta_t = \theta$. This constraint is given by $(\gamma\theta - 1)I + V^B \geq 0$, or $\gamma \geq \left(\dfrac{I - (w + D + b_1)}{\theta I} \right) \equiv \gamma_0$. Because $I \leq D + b_1$ (that is, the budget constraint for investment must be met), the right-hand side of this inequality is negative even if $w = 0$. Therefore, this incentive compatibility is not binding, and voters can set γ_0 to zero.

The second incentive-compatibility constraint on γ is given by equation (10.7) in the text. Modifying it as a function of γ yields $\gamma \geq \left(\dfrac{(w + D + b_1)(q - p) - (1 - p)G + (1 - q)pI}{\theta(1 - q)pI} \right) \equiv \gamma_1$. Because $\gamma \in (0, 1)$ and voters will provide the smallest possible value of gamma such that the appropriate incentive-compatibility condition is met, $\gamma^* \in \{0, \gamma_1^*\}$, where $\gamma_1^* = \min\{\gamma_1, 1\}$ is the lowest transfer the population must make to ensure that the politician does not choose repression.

Equation (10.7) is binding (and $\gamma_1 > 0$) when $w \geq \left(\dfrac{(1 - p)G - (1 - q)pI}{q - p} \right) - D - b_1 \equiv w_1^{\gamma = 0}$. Moreover, $w_1^{\gamma = 0} < w < w_1^*$, because w_1^* is monotonically increasing on γ.

Finally, I must prove the optimality of the cutoff rule by showing that neither the government nor the voters can gain by deviating from this strategy. Given that the voting rule must rely on the observable output, that the external benefits of the investment are not observable during voters' lifetimes, and that each country has a single (known) type of politician, voters cannot improve their welfare by reelecting a government that delivers zero output (except for the knife-edge case of $w = w_1^*$). For $w < w_1^*$, if voters were to reelect a government that delivers no private output from the investment (that is, for $\gamma^* = 1$), the government would have an incentive to set $\gamma = 1$ at all times, although it would still be willing to invest and not use repression at a lower level of γ. From the point of view of the government, deviation is not profitable because it is not possible to extract higher rents from the population. Because voters cannot transfer the external benefits of the investment to the government, they cannot offer rents greater than $\gamma = 1$, a level that voters are already willing to offer as long as it ensures that the government does not resort to repression. Voter welfare is also not increased if governments that deliver public services are not reelected, as that would change the incentives of politicians toward using repression or demanding higher rents. Therefore, voters are at least indifferent toward using the cutoff rule or another rule, implying that the cutoff rule is consistent with optimizing behavior.

Proposition 2

The analysis of the second case is similar to the first, except that the benefits of engaging in repression are greater, because the government can capture the full output of the investment project and incur only a probability $q < p$ of being replaced. The government must still trade off these benefits with the cost of repression.

As in the previous case, I begin by identifying the incentive-compatibility constraint for avoiding repression, assuming the government has the right incentives to invest:

$$w + D + b_1 - G + p(\theta - 1)I + qV^G < w + D + b_1 + p(\gamma\theta - 1)I + pV^B \text{ or}$$

$$qV^G - pV^B < G. \tag{10A.2}$$

As above, I solve for the continuation values,

$$V^B = \left(\frac{w + D + b_1 + p(\gamma\theta - 1)I}{1 - p}\right) \text{ and } V^G = \left(\frac{w + D + b_1 - G + p(\theta - 1)I}{1 - q}\right).$$

Replacing the continuation values above in equation (10A.2) yields

$$w < \left(\frac{1-p}{q-p}\right)G + \left(\frac{1-q}{q-p}\right)(\gamma\theta - 1)pI - \left(\frac{1-p}{q-p}\right)(\theta - 1)pI - D - b_1. \tag{10A.3}$$

I define w_2^*, the cutoff ego-rent above which a government will always choose to use repression regardless of the amount of rents voters allow the government to keep, in a manner similar to that used in the previous case, as

$$\left(\frac{1-p}{q-p}\right)G - (\theta - 1)pI - D - b_1 \equiv w_2^*.$$

Regardless of whether the government uses repression, the incentive-compatibility condition for investing (given $\theta_t = \theta$) is the same as before

$$\gamma \geq \left(\frac{I - (w + D + b_1)}{\theta I}\right) \tag{10A.4}$$

and still implies $\gamma^* = 0$ because now $d' + b_1 > I + G \gg I$.

Rewriting equation (10A.3) in terms of γ yields

$$\gamma \geq \left(\frac{(w+D+b_1)(q-p)}{(1-q)pI\theta}\right) + \left(\frac{(1-p)(\theta-1)+1-q}{(1-q)pI\theta}\right)pI$$

$$- \left(\frac{(1-p)}{(1-q)\theta}\right)\left(\frac{G}{pI}\right) \equiv \gamma_2.$$

Therefore, as in baseline Case 1, there are two cutoffs for w that give rise to three regions of w: (a) $w > w_2^*$ (repression is always chosen); (b) $w^* \geq w > w_2^{\gamma=0}$ (10A.3 is binding and $\gamma^* > 0$); and (c) $w \leq w_2^{\gamma=0}$ ($\gamma^*= 0$), where $w_2^{\gamma=0}$ is the cutoff at which $\gamma^* > 0$ and is given by

$$\left(\frac{1-p}{q-p}\right)(G-\theta pI) - D - b_1.$$

The argument for the optimality of the retrospective voting rule is similar to that used in the previous case, as the government would have an incentive to deviate from any voting rule if it could be reelected despite delivering no output.

Proposition 3

I begin by analyzing the effects of $d < D$ on w_1^*. In this case, because $d' + b_1 - G < I$, reducing $d' = d < D$ for regimes choosing repression implies that baseline Case 1 applies (the government cannot afford to both invest and use repression). Rewriting the incentive-compatibility constraint for this case results in

$$\left(\frac{1-p}{q-p}\right)G + \left(\frac{1-q}{q-p}\right)p(\theta-1)I + \left(\frac{1-2q+qp}{q-p}\right)D - b_1 = w_{1,LS}^*.$$

Comparing $w_{1,LS}^*$ with w_1^*, $q < 1$ implies that $w_{1,LS}^* > w_1^*$. Therefore, some government types that previously would have chosen repression now choose to invest.

As before, $\gamma_0 = 0$ and

$$\gamma_{1,LS} = \left(\frac{(b_1+w)(q-p)-(1-p)G}{(1-q)\theta pI}\right) - \left(\frac{(D-d-(Dq-dp))}{(1-q)\theta pI}\right) + \left(\frac{1}{\theta}\right) < \gamma_1.$$

Therefore, with the threat of repression reduced, the equilibrium level of rents also decreases.

For governments that could previously afford both investment and repression ($D + b_1 - G > I$), two outcomes are possible. If $d + b_1 - G < I$, the analysis is as in baseline Case 1. Because $w_{1,LS}^* > w_1^* > w_2^*$, government types between $w^*_{1,LS}$ and w^*_2, which would previously have chosen repression (and investment), now choose to invest only. However, governments with type $w > w^*_{1,LS}$ now cease to invest and continue to undertake repression, reducing overall welfare.

For countries in which $b_1 + d - G > I$, the incentive-compatibility constraint for not using repression and the critical value $w^*_{2,LS}$ are given by

$$w < \left(\frac{1-p}{q-p}\right)G + \left(\frac{(\gamma\theta-1)(1-q)-(\theta-1)(1-p)}{q-p}\right)pI$$
$$+ \left(\frac{(1-p)(D-d)}{q-p}\right) - D - b_1 \text{ and}$$
$$w^*_{2,LS} = \left(\frac{1-p}{q-p}\right)G - (\theta-1)pI - D - b_1 + \left(\frac{(1-p)(D-d)}{q-p}\right).$$

Because $w^*_{2,LS} > w^*_2$ by the last term, the impact of the loan-sanctions regime is to reduce the incentives for using repression as a tool.

Finally, I derive

$$\gamma_{2,LS} = \left(\frac{\begin{array}{c}(q-p)(w+D+b_1)-(1-p)G-(1-p)(D-d)\\ +(\theta-1)(1-p)pI+(1-q)pI\end{array}}{(1-q)pI\theta}\right) < \gamma_2.$$

In order to see why this inequality holds, notice that

$$\gamma_2 - \gamma_{2,LS} = \left(\frac{(1-p)(D-d)}{(1-q)pI\theta}\right).$$

This demonstrates that, as expected, rents are reduced along with the threat of repression.

Proposition 4

I begin by analyzing the effects of $d^{o,n} < D$ on w^*_1. In this case, because $d' + b_1 - G < I$, reducing $d' = d^{o,n} < D$ for regimes choosing repression implies that baseline Case 1 applies (the government cannot afford to both invest and use repression). Rewriting the incentive-compatibility constraint for this case results in

$$w < \left(\frac{1-p}{q-p}\right)G + \left(\frac{(1-q)p(\gamma\theta-1)I}{q-p}\right) + \left(\frac{1-p}{q-p}\right)(d^n-d^o)-d^n-b_1.$$

This inequality corresponds to

$$w^*_{1,DA} = \left(\frac{1-p}{q-p}\right)G + \left(\frac{(1-q)p(\theta-1)I}{q-p}\right) + \left(\frac{1-p}{q-p}\right)(d^n - d^o) - d^n - b_1.$$

Replacing $(d^n - d^o)$ with the definition of the two debt levels, I obtain

$$w^*_{1,DA} = \left(\frac{1-p}{q-p}\right)G + \left(\frac{(1-q)p(\theta-1)I}{q-p}\right)$$
$$+ \left(\frac{(1-p)(1-q)}{q-p}\right)(2s-1)D - d^n - b_1,$$

which is monotonically increasing in s.

When $s = 1$,

$$w^*_{1,DA} = \left(\frac{1-p}{q-p}\right)G + \left(\frac{(1-q)p(\theta-1)I}{q-p}\right) + \left(\frac{pq-2q+1}{q-p}\right) D - b_1 = w^*_{1,LS}.$$

Comparing $w^*_{1,DA}$ with w^*_1, $w^*_{1,DA} > w^*_1$. This requires $(D - d^n)q + (d^n - d^o) > (D - d^o)p$, or, expressed as a condition on the quality of

the signal, $s > \left(\dfrac{1-q}{2-q-p}\right)$, which is true as long as the signal is informative

$\left(s > \dfrac{1}{2}\right)$.

Because in baseline Case 1 investment precludes repression, $\gamma_0 = 0$ and

$$\gamma_{1,DA} = \left(\frac{(w+d^n+b_1)(q-p)-(1-p)G-(1-p)(d^n-d^o)+(1-q)pI}{(1-q)pI\theta}\right) < \gamma_1$$

if $s > \left(\dfrac{1-q}{2-q-p}\right)$. Thus, as above, as long as the signal is informative, the threat of repression is decreased. The debt-audit policy also creates the possibility that $d^n + b_1 < I$, which decreases voter welfare under the model as the government must resort to repression.

For governments that previously could afford both investment and repression $(D + b_1 - G > I)$, two outcomes are possible. If $d^o + b_1 - G < I$, the analysis is as in baseline Case 1. Depending on the quality of the signal, some types of governments that had engaged in repression start investing and others stop investing and continue to use repression. If the signal is not informative, more government types choose repression.

For countries in which $b_1 + d^o - G > I$, I derive the incentive compatibility for not using repression and the critical value $w^*_{2,DA}$:

$$w < \left(\frac{1-p}{q-p}\right)G + \left(\frac{(\gamma\theta-1)(1-q)-(\theta-1)(1-p)}{q-p}\right)pI$$

$$+ \left(\frac{(1-p)(d^n-d^o)}{q-p}\right) - d^n - b_1 \text{ and}$$

$$w^*_{2,DA} = \left(\frac{1-p}{q-p}\right)G - (\theta-1)pI - d^n - b_1 + \left(\frac{(1-p)(d^n-d^o)}{q-p}\right).$$

I can show that $w^*_{2,DA} > w^*_2$, because $(D - d^n)(q - p) + (1 - p)$ $(d^n - d^o) > 0$. Therefore, the debt-audit regime also reduces the incentives for using repression for governments that invest.

Finally, I derive

$$\gamma_{2,DA} = \left(\frac{\begin{array}{c}(w + d^n + b_1)(q-p) - (1-p)G - (1-p)(d^n - d^o)\\ + pI(\theta-1)(1-p) + pI(1-q)\end{array}}{pI(1-q)\theta}\right) < \gamma_2.$$

In order to see why this inequality holds, notice that

$$\gamma_2 - \gamma_{2,DA} = \left(\frac{(d^n - d^o) - (D - d^o)p + (D - d^n)q}{p\theta I(1-q)}\right),$$

which was shown to be greater than zero as long as the signal is informative.

Proposition 5

For the case in which $d' + b_1 - G < I$, no loans are available to regimes that choose to use repression (because investment is not affordable), and the incentive-compatibility condition becomes

$$w + b_1 - G + qV^G < w + D - k + b_1 + (p\gamma\theta - 1)I + pV^B.$$

In addition, the government that invests must pay the monitoring cost k and cannot consume I if $\theta_t = 0$. Therefore, the cost I must be paid with probability 1.

Replacing V^B and V^G yields

$$w < \left(\frac{(D - k + (p\gamma\theta-1)I)(1-q) + G(1-p)}{q-p}\right) - b_1.$$

I derive $w^*_{1,RL}$ as before:

$$w^*_{1,RL} \equiv \left(\frac{(D - k + (p\theta-1)I)(1-q) + G(1-p)}{q-p}\right) - b_1.$$

Note that $w^*_{1,RL} > w^*_1$ if k is sufficiently low, namely, if

$$k < (1-p)\left(\left(\frac{D}{1-q}\right)-I\right).$$

For $w \le w^*_{1,RL}$, the optimal $\gamma^*_{1,RL}$ that maximizes voter utility subject to incentive compatibility for the government is given by

$$\gamma^*_{1,RL} = \left(\frac{(w+b_1)(q-p)-G(1-p)-(D-k)(1-q)+(1-q)Ip\theta}{(1-q)Ip\theta}\right).$$

The critical value of w above which $\gamma^*_{1,RL} > 0$ is given by

$$w^{\gamma=0}_{1,LR} = \left(\frac{(1-p)G-(1-q)Ip\theta+(D-k)(1-q)}{q-p}\right)-b_1 > w^{\gamma=0}_1 \quad \text{if}$$

$$k < \left(\frac{D(1-p)-(1-q)(\theta-1)pI}{1-q}\right).$$

If $\theta > \left(\frac{1}{p}\right)$, then $(1-p)\left(\left(\frac{D}{1-q}\right)-I\right) > \left(\frac{D(1-p)-(1-q)(\theta-1)pI}{1-q}\right)$.
Therefore, if $k < \left(\frac{D(1-p)-(1-q)(\theta-1)pI}{1-q}\right)$, welfare is unambiguously
increased; if $\left(\frac{D(1-p)-(1-q)(\theta-1)pI}{1-q}\right) < k < (1-p)\left(\left(\frac{D}{1-q}\right)-I\right)$, then
governments are more likely to invest, but required rents increase.

Notes

The author wishes to thank John Londregan and Thomas Romer for helpful comments and discussions. Financial support from the Debt Department of the Poverty Reduction and Economic Management network at the World Bank is gratefully acknowledged.
    1. Creditors seized railroads in Chile and Costa Rica in the late 19th century.
    2. Tomz (2007) argues that even prominent historical examples of this type of enforcement may overstate its role.
    3. In both cases, there is a possibility that all cash flows can be misappropriated, including those coming from loans.
    4. See Besley (2004) for a discussion of the impact of wages of politicians in a political agency model.
    5. I assume that loans do not pay interest but instead are sold at a discount (that is, the proceeds are less than the repayment obligation) that provides the appropriate returns.

6. Although it is left for further research to analyze this third case, the fact that only loans outside the framework can be litigated provides certainty to creditors who do abide by it and is not exactly equivalent to the debt-audit case, in which a lender observing a signal $\omega = 0$ may still be challenged in court.

References

Besley, Timothy. 2004. "Paying Politicians: Theory and Evidence." *Journal of the European Economic Association* 2 (2–3):193–215.

Bolton, Patrick, and D. Skeel. 2007. "Odious Debts or Odious Regimes?" *Law & Contemporary Problems* 70 (4): 83–108.

Bulow, Jeremy, and Kenneth Rogoff. 1989. "Sovereign Debt: Is to Forgive to Forget?" *American Economic Review* 79 (1): 43–50.

Choi, Albert, and Eric A. Posner. 2007. "A Critique of the Odious Debt Doctrine." *Law & Contemporary Problems* 70 (3): 33–52.

Dömeland, Dörte, Frederico Gil Sander, and Carlos A. Primo Braga. 2009. "The Economics of Odious Debt." In *Debt Relief and Beyond: Lessons Learned and Challenges Ahead,* ed. Carlos A. Primo Braga and Dörte Dömeland, 261–92. Washington, DC: World Bank.

Eaton, Jonathan, and Mark Gersovitz. 1981. "Debt with Potential Repudiation: Theoretical and Empirical Analysis." *Review of Economic Studies* 48 (2): 289–309.

Ferejohn, John. 1986. "Incumbent Performance and Electoral Control." *Public Choice* 50 (1–3): 5–25.

Gil Sander, Frederico. 2009. "Electoral Control with Costly Information Acquisition." Woodrow Wilson School of Public and International Affairs, Princeton University, Princeton, NJ.

Jayachandran, Seema, and Michael Kremer. 2006. "Odious Debt." *American Economic Review* 96 (1): 82–92.

Kremer, Michael, and Seema Jayachandran. 2002. "Odious Debt." NBER Working Paper 8953, National Bureau of Economic Research, Cambridge, MA.

Levy-Yeyati, Eduardo. 2008. "Optimal Debt? On the Insurance Value of International Debt Flows to Developing Countries." *Open Economies Review.* http://www.springerlink.com/content/341625364273142t/.

Nehru, Vikram, and Mark Thomas. 2009. "The Concept of Odious Debt: Some Considerations." In *Debt Relief and Beyond: Lessons Learned and Challenges Ahead,* ed. Carlos A. Primo Braga and Dörte Dömeland, 205–27. Washington, DC: World Bank.

Persson, Torsten, Gerard Roland, and Guido Tabellini. 1997. "Separation of Powers and Political Accountability." *Quarterly Journal of Economics* 112 (4): 1163–202.

Sack, Alexander N. 1927. *Les effets des transformations des états sur leurs dettes publiques et autres obligations financières.* Paris: Recueil Sirey.

Tomz, Michael. 2007. *Reputation and International Cooperation: Sovereign Debt across Three Centuries.* Princeton, NJ: Princeton University Press.

Wright, Mark L. J. 2003. "Reputations and Sovereign Debt." Working paper, Department of Economics, Stanford University, Stanford, CA.

11

The Economics of Odious Debt

Dörte Dömeland, Frederico Gil Sander, and
Carlos A. Primo Braga

In recent years, some civil society organizations have stepped up their advocacy for the cancellation of *odious debts,* broadly defined, for the purposes of this chapter, as loans to sovereign borrowers that are not used in the interest of the population. They argue that odious debts should be cancelled on moral grounds and advocate the implementation of a framework that would exempt governments that repudiate odious debts from any legal consequences. The aim of this chapter is to increase the understanding of the economic implications of instituting such a framework.[1]

All borrowing—whether by governments (sovereign borrowing) or private entities—is characterized by at least two potential conflicts of interest: the one between creditors and borrowers and the one between those responsible for contracting debt and those who ultimately bear the burden of servicing it.[2] Ensuring the alignment of interests within each pair is a fundamental problem in contract theory. The nature of the problems is similar for sovereign and private borrowing, but their solutions are fundamentally different (figure 11.1).

The incentive problem between creditors and borrowers is straightforward: having contracted debt, the borrower would prefer not to repay it. The creditor lends, however, only if it has a reasonable expectation of being repaid. To solve this problem, creditors of private entities can rely on the judicial system to reassign the property rights of assets from the borrower to the creditor should the borrower default. This not only ensures that borrowers have the correct incentives to repay but also provides incentives for creditors to enforce their claims, because the prejudicial consequences for a defaulting debtor provide creditors with a direct benefit. Both creditors

Figure 11.1 Conflicts of Interest in Sovereign Debt

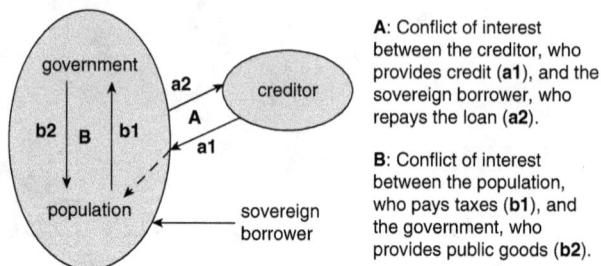

A: Conflict of interest between the creditor, who provides credit (**a1**), and the sovereign borrower, who repays the loan (**a2**).

B: Conflict of interest between the population, who pays taxes (**b1**), and the government, who provides public goods (**b2**).

Source: Authors.

and borrowers gain from the enforcement mechanism, which allows the trade of resources to take place.

The solution is less simple for sovereign borrowing, and there is great controversy as to the practical reasons why countries comply with their contractual obligations and repay their debts. As noted by several authors at least since Eaton and Gersovitz (1981), the transfer of property rights from a sovereign borrower to its creditors through the courts poses substantial challenges. Creditors would not be expected to obtain favorable judgments in courts of the borrowing country, and judgments obtained in foreign courts are generally enforceable only in a subset of jurisdictions and limited to assets located therein. Although cross-border enforcement is possible in principle (through gunboats, for example), this is politically untenable today, and there is evidence that even well-known historical examples of "gunboat enforcement" may overstate its role (see Tomz 2007). Some authors have therefore argued that sovereign borrowing needs to be self-enforcing (or enforced by the market) through optimal reactions by creditors that would lead, for example, to the exclusion of defaulting countries from future borrowing. A lack of coordination among creditors can, however, easily undermine self-enforcement, making it more difficult for creditors to be repaid once a sovereign creditor declares default.[3]

Solving the second incentive problem—between those responsible for negotiating and contracting the loans and those that bear the burden of repayment—is even more complex in the context of sovereign borrowing. The design and enforcement of anticorruption and transparency laws (analogous to the laws that protect shareholders from management fraud) are ultimately conducted by the public authorities of the sovereign borrower, not by an independent party. Most important, outcome-contingent compensation (that is, contracts for government leaders, such as those that exist for managers of private firms) does not exist (in no country, for example, does the president earn a bonus for exceptional economic growth or for implementing good governance).[4] The main form of incentives provided to government executives is the desire to remain in power.

This agency problem between government executives and their population is ultimately at the heart of the debate over the cancellation of odious debts. After all, the definitions of the term proposed in the literature all tend to argue that the proceeds from the borrowing were not used for the benefit of the population of the country.[5] Proponents of the different policy approaches on odious debt argue that placing responsibility for ensuring that loans to sovereign borrowers are aligned with the interests of the population on lenders would solve this incentive problem.

This chapter identifies four policy approaches to odious debt. The odious regimes framework argues that no debts incurred by a regime deemed odious should be enforceable. Under an ex post version of this framework, successor regimes can argue (through litigation) that the predecessor regime was odious and, therefore, that debt contracted by the predecessor need not be honored. In practical terms, this would imply that successful litigation would prevent courts from attaching assets to enforce the repayment of a debt contracted by the odious regime. Under an ex ante version of the odious regimes framework, put forward by Jayachandran and Kremer (2006) and Bolton and Skeel (2007), an international body (such as the United Nations [UN] Security Council) would declare certain regimes odious and agree that courts in member countries would not enforce debt contracts entered with such regimes.

The odious loan framework argues that loans that were used against the interest of the population should be cancelled or declared unenforceable. Such a framework would provide incentives for creditors to enter the second agency relationship, in order to reduce the risk of not being repaid. Under the ex post version of this framework, old loans are audited and those deemed illegitimate (regardless of the regime that contracted them) are repudiated. Under the ex ante version of this framework, creditors must undertake sufficient due diligence to certify that a loan is being used for legitimate purposes. If it does so, the loan could not later be deemed odious.

All proposals implicitly assume that the enforcement of sovereign borrowing takes place through the legal system—and therefore, that borrowers would indeed repudiate odious debts if they were legally allowed to do so.[6] Put differently, proposals assume that borrowers would face no costs for a debt default that is legally sanctioned by an odious debt framework. Although this seems plausible at first sight, the extent to which legal enforcement is effective in the context of sovereign debt is unclear. Moreover, some authors argue that the costs of market enforcement dominate those of legal enforcement. Even without an odious debt framework, a country could repudiate its debts for any reason. To be beneficial to a debtor country, and ultimately a country's population, a proposed policy approach must reduce the existing costs of repudiation.

In this chapter, we draw from the literature on sovereign debt to address two questions that are relevant for the odious debt debate: what are the costs that countries would experience if they were to repudiate debts deemed in any way odious, and how would the implementation of the odious debt policies mentioned above change these costs? Throughout the chapter, we recognize that there is an important distinction between commercial creditors (including bondholders) and official creditors (both bilateral and multilateral). Commercial lenders are assumed to maximize profits, whereas official creditors are motivated by noncommercial interests, such as political incentives and poverty reduction. One would expect these differences to lead to distinct behaviors.

The chapter is organized as follows. The next section reviews the enforcement mechanisms identified in the literature and the estimates of their relative importance. The second section discusses how the different proposals for an odious debt doctrine in international law could affect these costs. The last section draws conclusions.

The Costs of Debt Repudiation

Three broad categories of sanctions have been discussed as mechanisms to enforce sovereign debt contracts: political, legal, and market mechanisms (table 11.1). Although political enforcement (for example, gunboat diplomacy) could, in principle, enforce sovereign debts, there seems to be consensus that this type of enforcement is untenable politically in the 21st century.

The relevance of legal and market-related enforcement mechanisms is controversial, in both the theoretical and the empirical literature. In general, researchers recognize that legal enforcement can be pursued, although its role is generally much less important than in the context of private borrowing. Most of the theoretical literature that argues in favor of a prominent role for legal enforcement does so as a residual, a consequence of ruling out the importance of market enforcement mechanisms.

Types of Enforcement

Political enforcement refers to actions imposed by governments from creditor countries in response to a default. It includes military action, trade or other diplomatic sanctions, and external control of the country's finances (for example, customs revenues).[7] Political enforcement does not require a court ruling on the default. Its main characteristic is that it involves the act of a sovereign government (or governments) against another.

Table 11.1 Cost to Borrowers of Repudiating Debts Contracted with Official and Commercial Creditors

Type of enforcement	Cost of defaulting to official creditors	Cost of defaulting to commercial creditors
Political	"Gunboats" (military intervention or pressure) Trade sanctions External control of a country's finances	
Legal	Restrictions on access to new financing Comparability of treatment clauses	Asset seizures Cross-default Legal barriers to access to finance (for example, trade credits)
Market (self-enforcing mechanisms)	Reduced ability to lend in the long term (resource constraints)	Higher costs of financing Limited access to new financing (for example, trade credits) Capital flight Impact on domestic economy

Source: Authors.

Legal enforcement refers to the costs that emerge as the result of legal proceedings or from the activation of contractual clauses. This category includes asset seizures, the activation of cross-default clauses, and expenses incurred in the process of litigation (lawyers' fees, the time government officials must spend assisting in the process, and so forth). It also includes consequences (such as difficulty in obtaining new financing) that arguably would not have been experienced absent litigation.[8] Delays to restructuring defaulted debt caused by legal action or contractual obligations (for example, unanimity clauses) may also be included as legal costs if such delay is costly to the country (for example, if it cannot borrow while it remains formally in default). Unlike political enforcement, legal enforcement does not necessarily take place in the sovereign borrower's jurisdiction.[9] Rather, legal proceedings usually take place in the courts of the creditor countries, implying that only assets that are outside the borrowing country are available for seizure and attachment by the courts (unless procedures for recognizing foreign judgments in the borrowing country are in place).

Market enforcement refers to the impact of a default (or risk of default) on the borrower's access to new financing. As a consequence of default, the cost of new loans may be higher or the amount of available financing lower. This mechanism is also frequently referred to as *reputation*. For our purposes, it is useful to think of reputation as the contract's self-enforcement feature that would emerge without any legal or political enforcement. The proposed odious debt policies may affect legal costs; they are unlikely to affect the self-enforcing nature of sovereign debt contracts.

Two main types of theoretical models explain why a default leads to restrictions in a country's access to finance. First, in adverse selection models, there are two types of governments: "good payers" and "bad payers."[10] A default provides a signal that the government is of the bad payer type, which implies higher financing costs. Second, in certain moral hazard models, if countries are motivated to borrow to smooth consumption during bad times, a possible equilibrium of the repeated-borrowing game would be for creditors to exclude defaulting countries from borrowing in the future to enforce payment (Eaton and Gersovitz 1981).[11] A related model (Grossman and Van Huyck 1989) differentiates between "excusable" defaults (debts a country is unable to pay because of a negative shock) and "nonexcusable" defaults (debts a country is able but unwilling to pay), with only nonexcusable defaults leading to exclusion from the credit markets.

Higher interest rates and limitation on new financing are expected to have economywide impacts. A country's reputation in repaying its sovereign debt could affect other economic areas, such as trade or foreign direct investment, with economywide repercussions (see, for example, Kletzer and Wright 2000). Moreover, some reputational models suggest that a default signals a "bad type" not only with regard to sovereign debt but also with regard to property rights in general, which may lead to capital flight. The government's inability to borrow externally combined with capital flight would exert pressure on the domestic economy through effects on the exchange rate and the domestic public debt. Finally, domestic financial institutions may hold the government debt, which could create a link between a domestic banking crisis and a default on sovereign obligations.

Enforcement by Type of Creditor

Although market enforcement applies primarily to commercial creditors, official creditors mimic some enforcement mechanisms associated with the market by reducing (or suspending) lending to borrowers who default to them. Although a political decision could be made to remove these sanctions, we consider them legal enforcement mechanisms, because they are generally anchored in the creditors' statutes. For example, default to multilateral creditors generally triggers a contractual suspension of new disbursements.

Official creditors have also used litigation in the past, albeit largely indirectly through the sale of claims to private creditors that then attempt to enforce them through the legal system.[12] Another example of contractual enforcement used by official creditors is the comparability of treatment clause found in all Paris Club debt-restructuring agreements, which requires borrowers to seek comparable debt reduction from other bilateral creditors as well as from commercial creditors. It thus serves a similar purpose as a cross-default clause in some debt contracts by preventing countries from seeking debt reduction on their official debt without defaulting to commercial creditors as well.

Finally, although the overall amount of resources available to official creditors is ultimately a political decision, it is affected by default or the risk thereof. Lost flows from nonpayment directly reduce official creditors' resources for new lending. Moreover, a high risk of default requires greater provisions by some creditors, which reduces the amounts available for new lending.

Empirical Evidence

This section presents empirical evidence on the use of political and legal enforcement by creditors. It also provides anecdotal evidence on the costs associated with these enforcement mechanisms.

Political Enforcement. Much empirical evidence exists regarding the use of political enforcement, such as military intervention or foreign control of a country's economy.[13] Alfaro, Maurer, and Ahmed (2008) argue that the imposition of the "Roosevelt Corollary"—whereby, during the first quarter of the past century, the United States intervened in Latin American countries that had difficulties servicing their debts—reduced the financing costs of the countries in which it intervened. Mitchener and Weidenmier (2005), for example, estimate the probability of political enforcement in case of default between 1870 and 1913 (the gold standard era) at 25 percent. They find that yield spreads declined by about 800 basis points and that the defaulting country experienced an almost 100 percent reduction in the amount of time it remained in default when sovereign default was punished with political sanctions.

The relationship between default and political sanctions may, however, have been spurious, as Tomz (2007) points out. Before World War I, he notes, countries that defaulted were indeed more often targets of military intervention than countries that serviced their debts. But, he argues, political sanctions were more likely for defaulters because they were often already involved in other disputes. As an example, he argues that the military intervention in República Bolivariana de Venezuela in 1902—one of the most prominent examples of "gunboat" enforcement—was not caused by that country's default on its foreign bonds but rather by other acts against British and German interests. Specifically, although the Venezuelan government defaulted on bonds held by British and German investors in 1901, it had been in default four times between 1847 and 1901, without any intervention by the British military. On the basis of an analysis of historical documents, Tomz argues that the real motivation for the 1902 intervention was several previous confrontations between the Venezuelan navy and British vessels in the Caribbean.

With respect to trade sanctions, notwithstanding strong evidence that trade volumes are lower following default (see discussion below), there is little evidence that government-imposed overt trade sanctions have been used to enforce sovereign debt contracts, at least in the past 30 years. Martinez and Sandleris (2008) report that they could not find a single instance of substantial and overt trade sanctions in 116 sovereign defaults with private creditors and 269 with official creditors over the past 30 years.

Regardless of whether political enforcement was ever effective, it is incompatible with existing international law. Moreover, there seems to be a consensus against such intervention.

Legal Enforcement. An extensive body of literature analyzes the legal mechanisms available to creditors and debtors in the context of sovereign debt (see, for example, Waibel 2003; Sturzenegger and Zettelmeyer 2007). Although such laws as the U.S. Foreign Sovereign Immunities Act of 1976 and the U.K. State Immunity Act of 1978 have stripped sovereign immunity related to commercial transactions, a key principle discussed in this literature is sovereign immunity. Following a bellwether U.S. Supreme Court decision in *Republic of Argentina v. Weltover* (1992), which upheld that sovereign debt constituted a nonprotected activity under the U.S. Sovereign Immunities Act, a number of other lawsuits were brought forward against defaulting sovereign borrowers, with a mixed record of success. As Sturzenegger and Zettelmeyer (2007) note, both creditors and borrowers have honed their legal tactics—creditors to expand their abilities to seize assets, borrowers to avoid seizures.

A related body of literature on sovereign bankruptcy analyzes the optimality of existing contractual characteristics of sovereign debt and the need for a sovereign debt–restructuring mechanism (see, for example, Rogoff and Zettelmeyer 2002; Bolton and Jeanne 2007). This literature focuses on the tension between the ex post and ex ante efficiency of certain aspects of sovereign bond contracts. Clauses that make debt restructuring difficult (for example, those that require unanimity among holders to modify the repayment terms of the contract) make default more costly; ex ante they therefore reduce the risk premium borrowers must pay. However, once a default occurs, such clauses are inefficient. Ex post both the defaulting borrower and a majority of creditors would prefer that restructuring were easier, because of the deadweight losses associated with a protracted restructuring. Most of this literature is theoretical, however, and simply acknowledges that delays in reaching an agreement are costly in a broad sense.

Empirical evidence on the average or aggregate importance of legal costs in enforcing sovereign debt contracts and estimates of their magnitude are generally not available. Case study evidence suggests that the ability of creditors to ultimately obtain payments or asset transfers from sovereign borrowers—what may be called "direct legal sanctions"—appears to have been limited. Creditors have been able to obtain judgments in a number of cases, but they have found it difficult to collect on them. This difficulty is reflected in the fact that only a small number of creditors (so-called "distressed asset" funds) is usually involved in lawsuits. Despite unusually harsh terms for creditors following Argentina's default in 2001—for example, a reduction in the present value of the obligations on the order of 70 percent—more than 75 percent of creditors accepted the restructuring offered by the government in 2005 instead of engaging in lawsuits. This willingness to accept a substantial "haircut" reflected the expectation by most investors that the potential for recovery through legal means was limited.

Estimates of actual litigation costs (the expenses governments must incur on lawyer and court fees) as well as the opportunity cost of government officials who work on the litigation are rarely addressed in the literature. Although those costs may be trivial in most cases (especially relative to the costs of asset seizure), they can be significant for small economies and large relative to the original claim amount (box 11.1).

Recognizing that recent cases of sovereign default were very costly for both debtor countries and creditors, in 2001 the International Monetary Fund (IMF) proposed creating a sovereign debt–restructuring mechanism to deal with unsustainable debt burdens of emerging-market countries. The proposal involved establishing a universal legal framework to facilitate negotiations and to empower creditors to approve a debt-restructuring agreement with a debtor country that would bind minority dissenting creditors. The agreement could precede or follow an event or default. At the same time, the IMF also considered a complementary approach, in which debt restructurings could be facilitated by enhanced use of certain contractual provisions in sovereign debt contracts.[14]

Even if the expected direct legal costs of defaulting may be limited, there is evidence that the threat of litigation alone acts to restrict the access of countries to certain types of financing, at least in the short term. This applies particularly to trade financing, which relies on short-term credits and letters of credit. Alexander (1987) notes that countries find it difficult to obtain letters of credit during default, because creditors may fear that repayments on these new credit lines could be seized, even if temporarily, by litigating creditors. This fear forces countries to conduct roundabout transactions, which Alexander claims reached 10–15 percent of the value of trade in one case. Indeed, it is possible that all types of borrowing are restricted by the risk of seizures. Consistent with this hypothesis, very few countries issue new debt before reaching a restructuring agreement with their creditors. Tomz (2007) reports that between 1820 and 1870, a single loan was issued by a country that was in default and had not yet restructured its obligations.

The line between these (indirect) legal costs and market enforcement (discussed below) is blurry: it is possible that creditors would reestablish

Box 11.1 Noga vs. the Russian Federation

Noga, a Swiss company, entered into a contract with the Russian Federation to exchange oil for certain products it agreed to export. Russia explicitly waived its right to sovereign immunity under the contract.

In 1993, Russia repudiated the contract and offered to settle it under London Club terms (that is, with a discount on the amount of claims outstanding). Noga sued and obtained judgments in Luxembourg and Switzerland to freeze Russian government bank accounts worth $700 million. The judgments led Russia to establish a shell company to hold its offshore assets. In 1996, the Luxembourg accounts were unfrozen, without payment being made to Noga. In 1997, a Swedish arbitration court awarded Noga $63 million, a fraction of the $800 million Noga had sought. Russia refused to pay, and the lawsuits continued.

In 2000, several lawsuits were filed in various jurisdictions. A French court ordered the seizure of bank accounts of some 70 Russian entities connected with the state, including the Russian embassy in Paris and its delegation to the United Nations Educational, Scientific and Cultural Organization (UNESCO). Within a few months of the award, a judge dismissed the case and ordered Noga to pay damages to Russia. A French presidential decree was required to prevent the seizure of Russian President Vladimir Putin's personal aircraft at Orly airport, and Noga obtained a judgment to impound a Russian ship in the French port of Brest. Once again, the suit was later dismissed and Noga ordered to pay damages. Noga also lost a suit filed in the United States requesting the seizure of uranium allegedly owned by Russia.

In June 2001, Noga attempted to seize Russian fighter jets at the Le Bourget air show, outside Paris. The planes were scrambled ahead of the bailiffs, after the Russian contingent was warned by the show organizers, who also helped drag the planes to the end of the runaway, gave permission for an emergency takeoff, and opened an air corridor.

The case continued in Swiss courts, which ruled in favor of Noga in 2002. In 2005, 54 paintings from the Pushkin Museum of Fine Arts, insured for $1 billion, were seized on their way back from Switzerland to Russia. The Swiss government intervened, and the paintings were returned to Russia. In 2006, there were reports that a Russian-born U.S. investor had purchased the debt from Noga for an undisclosed amount. It is not clear whether Noga still has claims against the Russian government.

By March 2006, Noga reported that it had spent $40 million in legal expenses over the years, and it estimated that Russia had spent twice as much. As of May 2008, the Russian government had plans to sue Noga for damages under previous seizure orders.

Source: Wright 2002.

credit more quickly absent legal threats and find alternative coordination devices to punish defaulting countries absent the threat of litigation. We are not aware of a study that attempts to separate these two channels. Alfaro, Maurer, and Ahmed (2008) provide some insight by testing empirically the comparative effectiveness of political and legal enforcement. They compare the evolution of borrowing costs following two important events: the announcement of the Roosevelt Corollary, considered by most authors to mark a period in which political sanctions were widely used to enforce sovereign debt, and the landmark 1996 decision in *Pravin v. Peru*, which signaled to investors that courts could be used to force payments from creditors. The authors find evidence that political enforcement reduced borrowing costs, whereas the impact of legal sanctions was "weak at best" (Alfaro, Maurer, and Ahmed 2008, p. 26). Nevertheless, because the data used to test the legal enforcement hypothesis begin after what is probably an even more influential legal decision from the point of view of investor expectations—the 1992 U.S. Supreme Court decision in *Republic of Argentina v. Weltover*—their conclusions must be accepted with caution.

The literature is silent on actual estimates of the costs arising from legal enforcement by official creditors. The recent case of Argentina's default is illustrative. Argentina defaulted on its Paris Club debt in 2002. Since then, many of the government-controlled insurance agencies, export-import banks, and other institutions linked to Paris Club members have been prevented from extending insurance or loan guarantees for projects in Argentina because of the default to the Paris Club. In the absence of such guarantees or insurance, many investors shy away from riskier projects. In 2007, for example, the first $1.1 billion phase of a $3.3 billion infrastructure project to extend passenger rail service in greater Buenos Aires met with little interest from investors. The cost of these sanctions has become more relevant over time. In September 2008, Argentina indicated that it planned to use $6.7 billion of its international reserves to clear its arrears to the Paris Club, thus reopening short-term trade credits and insurance and guarantees for investment projects financed by companies from Paris Club member countries. However, as the 2008 global financial crisis brought liquidity constraints to the fore, the plan was postponed.

This case study is suggestive of the mechanism that may lie behind the results of Rose (2005), who examines defaults to official creditors. He finds that bilateral trade (between creditor and borrower) declines by 8 percent a year following a default, an effect that lasts 15 years. Using instrumental variables techniques, Rose and Spiegel (2002) find a significant positive effect of bilateral trade on bilateral lending patterns: an increase of 1.0 percent in bilateral trade increases bilateral lending by 0.4 percent. These results must be accepted with some caution, because defaults to official and commercial creditors are correlated. Moreover, as discussed below, some authors question whether there is a fall in bilateral trade or just a fall in overall trade, which may be correlated with the cause of the default (a negative shock) and simply persist beyond the default.

The paucity of empirical evidence on the costs of legal enforcement notwithstanding, it is likely that they are not trivial, especially indirect costs related to the effect of legal threats on a country's ability to enter into short-term credit agreements and the statutory suspension of credit from official credit agencies that provide trade credit, insurance, and guarantees. Direct legal costs have been important in specific cases, such as *Elliot Associates v. Banco de la Nación,* in which Peru was forced to settle with Elliot to avoid defaulting on all creditors of its Brady bonds for purely legal reasons. The evidence on the overall impact of this (and similar) cases appears weak, however, as reported by Alfaro, Maurer, and Ahmed (2008) and illustrated by the small fraction of creditors that rejected Argentina's restructuring offer.

Market (Self-) Enforcement. The empirical relevance of market enforcement of sovereign debt contracts has been investigated extensively. Many researchers have studied the types of self-enforcing sanctions most commonly predicted by the theoretical literature: higher borrowing costs, difficulty in accessing credit, or both. They find some evidence that in the short term, defaulting countries face higher financing costs and difficulty in accessing credit. However, the effects are muted, at best, beyond a relatively short period following the resolution of the default.

Another strand of the literature looks at the effects of sovereign defaults on the aggregate economy, which is likely to be influenced (if not caused) by the market reaction to the default. These aggregate effects include impacts on GDP and trade. Although defaults are clearly correlated with drops in GDP and trade, the causation mechanisms are open to debate.

Most analysts find a positive but small impact of default on the long-term cost of borrowing. Lindert and Morton (1991) find that defaults in the 19th century and the 1930s did not imply higher borrowing costs in the 1970s; long-term effects appear negligible. De Paoli, Hoggarth, and Saporta (2006) find that for a given debt-to-GDP ratio, past defaulters generally pay higher interest rates. For example, during the period 2003–05, the 3 nondefaulters in their sample faced lower spreads than did 10 out of the 12 defaulters, even though in most cases the defaulters had lower debt burdens. Flandreau and Zumer (2004) find that in the period 1880–1914, interest rates jumped by 500 basis points immediately following a default, by 90 basis points in the year following the end of the default episode, and by 45 basis points 10 years after the default. Özler (1993) considers the impact of defaults between 1820 and 1930 and the post–World War II period on loans extended over the period 1968–81. He finds that defaults before the 1930s did not have any impact on credit terms. The impact of a default is estimated at 20 basis points in the 1930s and 30 basis points following postwar IMF stand-by arrangements.

Borensztein and Panizza (2006a) also find that the effect of default on spreads is short lived.

The evidence on access to new financing is similar: defaulting countries eventually recover market access, but, not surprisingly, they have problems accessing the markets before the default is resolved and immediately after the default. As mentioned earlier, Tomz (2007) finds that only one country issued debt between 1820 and 1870 while it was still in default. Eichengreen (1987) finds no relationship between default in the 1930s and borrowing after 1945. Gelos, Sahay, and Sandleris (2004) find that the median number of years countries are excluded from the markets following a default fell from four in the 1980s to zero in the 1990s. The Inter-American Development Bank (IDB 2006) notes that from the 1930s to the 1960s, all Latin American countries were largely excluded from world capital markets, regardless of whether they had defaulted in the 1930s. Conversely, the lending boom of the 1990s did not exclude countries that had defaulted in the 1980s.

English's (1996) study on the external borrowings of U.S. states in the early 1840s corroborates the evidence that market enforcement plays a role. Before the Civil War, the federal government did not guarantee the foreign debt of U.S. states; given the status of the U.S. states, neither political nor legal enforcement was possible at that time. Until the early 1840s, most U.S. states never defaulted, some were temporarily in default or partially repudiated their debts, and two states (Florida and Mississippi) repudiated their debts entirely. All states that did not default were able to borrow again in the 1840s and 1850s, and all but three states had more debt in 1860 than in 1841. The states that repudiated all their debt did not issue new bonds. The situation of states that partially defaulted fell somewhere in between, with yields on their bonds remaining elevated for several years.

Of course, the costs of market enforcement may be different for different types of government. According to Tomz (2007), creditors assess a country's "type" based on whether the same type of government is still in power and whether that government has defaulted or repaid at a time when the opposite could have been expected (for example, a repayment during a recession or a default during a boom). In a separate paper (Tomz 1998), he notes that most defaults during the trough of the Great Depression were fully expected and therefore could not have affected the reputation of the borrowers. This would explain why the effects on later borrowing costs were muted.

In contrast, the markets rewarded countries that were expected to default but did not: in the 1930s, prices on Argentine bonds reflected a 50–70 percent probability of default. As a consequence of not defaulting in difficult times, Argentina was one of the only countries that issued debt in New York and London during the Depression. Özler (1993) notes that countries that had recently acquired sovereignty in the 1960s and 1970s faced borrowing costs that were as high as countries that had defaulted in earlier decades since they had not yet formed a reputation. Similarly, English (1996) finds that the U.S. states that had repudiated their debt in the early 1840s were able to borrow again only after new Northern-backed governments were installed (see also Tomz 2007).

A default is often associated with a decline in trade. One possible channel through which this occurs, discussed in the previous section, is the shortage of short-term trade credits. The decline in trade would thus be the consequence of default. Another possibility is that trade falls in line with the overall economy and is thus related to the cause rather than the consequence of a default. Rose (2005) and Rose and Spiegel (2002) support the hypothesis that, regardless of the cause, trade declines follow rather than cause defaults. Similarly, Borensztein and Panizza (2006b) find that, for each year in which the sovereign is in default, an industry in the 75th percentile of the nonexporter/exporter continuum would see its growth drop 1.7 percentage points relative to the 25th percentile. This effect lasts only as long as the country is in default, and it holds for defaults on bank loans, not bonds. Alexander (1987) and Cline (1987) provide anecdotal evidence that Peru and Bolivia suffered severe reductions in their access to short-term trade credits as a consequence of their "confrontational" approach. Martinez and Sandleris (2008) argue that the declines observed by Rose (2005) are actually declines in overall trade: once this trend is taken into account, no significant effect on bilateral trade is found. Similarly, Tomz (2007) argues that between the two world wars, governments did not service their debts in proportion to their trade with creditors, which would be expected if the reduction in trade were a result of default.

Many researchers have attempted to measure the overall correlation between GDP growth and sovereign default. A commonly cited estimate puts default costs at 2 percent of GDP growth (Sturzenegger 2002).[15] De Paoli, Hoggarth, and Saporta (2006) report much higher output losses, on the order of 7 percent a year for their median country. These measures are not very informative, however, because the mechanisms through which GDP growth falls are even less well specified than those in the case of trade. Moreover, there is substantial evidence that countries default in bad times, when their GDP growth is trending downward, thus making it difficult to distinguish between a sanction in anticipation of default and the cause of the default itself. Tomz and Wright (2007) find that output is 1.4 percent below trend during periods of default and 0.2 percent above trend when the borrower is in good standing. Levy-Yeyati and Panizza (2006) find that when the frequency of the data is changed from yearly to quarterly, growth rates in the postdefault period are never significantly lower than in normal times. In contrast, recessions are a significant 3 percent deeper during default episodes.

De Paoli, Hoggarth, and Saporta (2006) and others relate the growth costs to the fact that sovereign defaults are connected to currency and banking crises.[16] Often the domestic financial sector holds government debt (including external debt, as was the case in Argentina) or its own financing is affected through the sovereign "ceiling," namely, the risk that governments may impose restrictions on the exit of foreign exchange during an episode of default. However, it is very difficult to determine whether a banking crisis, a currency crisis, or both occur at the same time or after a debt default. Given the evidence that countries generally default in bad times, one should consider the output costs of default with appropriate caution.

Most of the discussion on market enforcement focuses exclusively on commercial creditors. Debt write-offs affect the resource constraints of official creditors as well. For example, as of 2008, the expected debt relief to be provided under the Highly Indebted Poor Countries (HIPC) Initiative and the Multilateral Debt Relief Initiative (MDRI) by bilateral and multilateral creditors was estimated at $95 billion in net present value terms (IDA and IMF 2008).

In short, there is evidence that defaults affect a country's ability to obtain credit, especially in the short term, which affects trade patterns of the defaulting country. The impact of these costs appears to be short lived, but given the severity of the recessions that lead to default (or, alternatively, the effort that some countries appear to exert to avoid default), they must be large. The degree of pain of the default serves as a signal that the default was a matter of inability rather than unwillingness to pay. Thus, if one accepts Tomz's reputational theory, it should not affect the ability of the country to regain access to markets.

Summary of Costs of Repudiation

The legal and market costs of default, especially through their effect on trade, may be large. Although there is limited evidence for the relevance of direct legal costs or permanent increases in the cost of financing, credit constraints seem to emerge in the short term as a consequence of market enforcement, the threat of litigation, and statutory constraints by official agencies.

It is difficult to separate the short-term impact on access to finance that emerges from legal or market enforcement—indeed, it is very plausible that the legal system acts as a coordination device for creditors. Although legal costs cannot be ignored, the balance of the evidence does not favor the view that they dominate. Several studies (Özler 1993; Rose 2005) find effects that last well beyond the immediate aftermath of the default, thus well beyond the length of legal proceedings or suspensions caused by default. English (1996) plausibly argues that lenders to U.S. states in the 1840s imposed market-access restriction without any apparent ability to obtain legal enforcement. The small number of creditors pursuing legal remedies in a given default and the many commercial banks that chose to delay declaring a default (and instead used the legal system) in the 1980s also points to an important, if not dominant, role for market rather than legal enforcement.

Notwithstanding the empirical difficulty in separating legal and economic sanctions, in the next part of the analysis, we continue to impose the abstract separation between legal and market costs. Only legal costs can be expected to be reduced by the proposed odious debt policies, as Kremer and Jayachandran (2002) recognize.

The literature does not provide estimates of the magnitude of the legal and market costs imposed by official creditors, but the practical implications of default to such creditors are more clear-cut. Countries in default to the Paris Club are unable to access official export credits and related agencies from other Paris Club creditors, unless a restructuring agreement is reached. Default to multilateral creditors also triggers a contractual suspension of new disbursements from those creditors. The impact of defaults on the ability of official creditors to provide development finance has not been studied in detail, but in the absence of compensating transfers from donors, a higher number of defaults would limit the long-term ability of official creditors to maintain their lending levels.

Potential Impact of Implementing Odious Debt Policy Proposals

In the previous section, we argue that the costs to a country that decides to repudiate its debt are only partly determined by the legal actions available to creditors. In the case of debts to commercial creditors, some (probably most) of the costs that emerge in case of repudiation arise from market enforcement. In the case of debts to official creditors, most of the costs are indeed likely to be linked to legal action—although not in the sense of international commercial law, where odious debt policy proposals have been explored, but rather as a result of the application of the statutes of these official creditors.

In this section, we consider the impact of the implementation of different odious debt policy proposals on the costs identified in the previous section. We divide these proposals into those concerned with all borrowing done by specific regimes, which we term *odious regime frameworks* (Bolton and Skeel 2007), and those that are concerned with the legitimacy of specific loans, which we term *odious loan frameworks*. For each of the two types, we consider separately the impact of an ex ante and an ex post version of the proposal on the costs of defaulting to official and commercial creditors. In all cases, we ask how the proposed policy would alter the costs of repudiating odious loans compared with the existing costs of repudiation.

Under an odious regime framework (table 11.2), all debts contracted by a regime deemed odious are declared unenforceable. Under an ex post

Table 11.2 Ex Ante and Ex Post Odious Debt Frameworks

Framework	Ex ante	Ex post
Odious regime	An international body is charged with declaring regimes odious. All loans to regimes declared odious are not enforceable.	Successor regimes argue, through litigation, that the predecessor regime was odious and that its debts should therefore not be honored.
Odious loan	Loans certified to comply with the framework's standards are enforceable; those that do not may not be.	Disbursed loans are audited, and borrowers sue for cancellation of loans found to be odious.

Source: Authors.

version of this framework, successor regimes can argue (through litigation) that the predecessor regime was odious and that debt contracted by them therefore need not be honored. In practical terms, this would imply that successful litigation would prevent creditors from attaching assets to enforce the repudiation of a debt contracted by the odious regime. Under an ex ante version of the odious regime framework, an international body would declare certain regimes odious and invite national courts not to enforce debt contracts entered into with such regimes. (As a variant, acting under its peace and security powers, the UN Security Council could adopt legally binding decisions to that effect.)

Under an odious loan framework, loans used against the interest of the population are cancelled or declared unenforceable. Under the ex post version of this framework, previously contracted loans are audited and those deemed odious are challenged in the courts, which may not enforce obligations they find illegitimate. Under the ex ante version of this framework (which is closely related to the responsible lending approach; see, for example, Nehru and Thomas 2009), creditors must undertake sufficient due diligence to certify that a loan is being used for legitimate purposes, with the expectation that such a loan would not later be deemed odious.

Before we proceed with a systematic analysis of the impact of these different policies on the costs identified earlier, we must consider whether odious debt policies may create new costs. If regimes are barred from borrowing—or the costs of financing increase—as a result of the implementation of an odious debt framework, at least three new costs could plausibly emerge:

- Odious regimes may default on debt previously contracted by nonodious regimes, leaving successor governments with a large stock of arrears on debt that is, according to the policy proposal, legitimate and should therefore be repaid.

- The consumption/investment choice of an odious regime may be distorted in a way that is not in the interests of the population (Choi and Posner 2007; Gil Sander 2009).
- Odious regimes may substitute borrowing with more intensive exploitation of nonrenewable natural resources (Choi and Posner 2007), a topic discussed in greater detail by Ochoa (2008, p. 159), who concludes that "alternative sources [of financing for odious regimes] may often result in more long-term damage to the people and the territory of a country than debt."

Odious Regimes

This section analyzes the ex post and ex ante odious regime frameworks. It assesses the legal and market costs of each framework.

Ex Post Framework. We assume that an ex post odious regime framework would allow a government to argue in front of an appropriate forum (for example, the International Court of Justice or another relevant court or arbitral tribunal entrusted with the settlement of disputes between the parties to the loan agreement in question) that its predecessor regime was odious and that therefore no loan made to the regime can be enforced or trigger the usual default provision in commercial contracts or official debt agreements. Under this version of the framework, the change in legal costs related to commercial debt is ambiguous, albeit likely similar to what it would be without the framework. Successor governments would have to argue that their predecessors had been odious. Given the time required to establish the odious nature of the previous regime through litigation, the ex post framework would probably not improve access to financing (that is, there may still be a shortage of short-term credits as a result of fear of attachment, which may lead to a reduction in trade). The costs of engaging in litigation would still have to be incurred. Successful litigation would allow workout at favorable terms, although it is difficult to estimate the magnitude of such improvement in terms. Argentina received a reduction of more than 70 percent of the nominal amount of its debt from commercial creditors without an odious debt framework in place. Nevertheless, the legal costs are likely to be lower than under a loan-by-loan approach, because a decision to declare a regime odious would presumably cover all the debts contracted by it.

If the ex post odious regime framework does reduce the costs of repudiating odious debts, the costs of borrowing for all countries are likely to increase, because creditors would price in an expected probability of the regime being declared odious (and thus a higher probability of defaulting). This increase in borrowing costs would be higher for regimes that are most likely to be odious. Indeed, there are likely to be cases in which new lending dries up altogether as a result of the high risk of repudiation. In many cases, however, uncertainty about the regime type will remain, causing legitimate regimes (that is, regimes that are never declared odious) to incur higher borrowing costs.

Because the willingness of creditors to offer new loans is an important incentive for debt repayment, if the ex post odious regime framework succeeds in restricting access of odious regimes to new loans, those regimes may be more likely to default on earlier (and therefore legitimate) debt. Moreover, there may be an adverse selection effect: those creditors that are most committed to the spirit of the framework (and do not extend loans to potentially odious regimes) will be punished with defaults on loans contracted by predecessor regimes, whereas "rogue" creditors that lend to regimes after they are declared odious are likely to be repaid (at least as long as the odious regime is in power). Thus, even if the framework punishes the rogue creditors once the odious regime is overthrown, the successor regime may have to deal with large amounts of arrears on legitimate debt, often incurring substantial penalties in addition to interest on overdue principal and being cut off from lending until arrears are cleared.

The impact on legal costs related to official debt under the ex post odious regime framework are also ambiguous (table 11.3). Lending by many official creditors is related to a country's quality of polices and institutions. It tends to dry up in countries with severe policy failures. To the extent that the framework institutionalizes the restriction of lending to odious regimes, there will be less "odious debt" to be worked out. But incentives for odious regimes to default on legitimate debt would increase. Official creditors generally do not lend into arrears, and it is unlikely that the framework,

Table 11.3 Cost Implications of Ex Post Odious Regime Framework

Creditor	Legal cost	Market cost
Commercial	Litigation costs must still be incurred and are likely to be similar to those incurred under the status quo.	Difference between pre- and postrepudiation borrowing costs declines, largely because of higher predefault costs for all borrowers.
Official	Litigation costs and costs associated with arrears clearance must still be incurred and are likely to be similar to those incurred under the status quo.	Volume of official lending resources could decrease.

Source: Authors.

with its requirement of a litigation process to determine whether a regime is odious, would speed up debt workouts relative to the existing restructuring mechanisms. The effects of restrictions on short-term credits would likely remain unchanged. Because official creditors would also be unable to predict perfectly which regimes will be deemed ex post odious, in the long run the availability of resources could be decreased overall given a fixed lending envelope and fixed borrowing costs.

The ex post odious regime framework is likely to reduce the welfare of countries that have legitimate regimes by raising their borrowing costs (to reflect the risk of being declared odious ex post). The welfare impact on countries under odious regimes is ambiguous but likely to be negative: legal costs are unlikely to be reduced, and for the non-odious successor regime, it could imply that any benefits from reduced lending to odious regimes are likely to be offset by the cost of dealing with costly legitimate arrears left by the preceding odious regime.

Ex Ante Framework. We consider an ex ante odious regime framework in the vein of that suggested by Jayachandran and Kremer (2006), whereby an appropriate institution (for example, the UN Security Council) would declare a regime odious on the basis of human rights violations or financial mismanagement. As a consequence, all loans made to it from that point on would be unenforceable, and the usual default provision in commercial or official debt contracts would not be triggered. The key feature of the ex ante version of the odious regime framework is that the debt contracted by the odious regime would be legitimate until the appropriate institution declares it odious; otherwise, the same analysis of the ex post version applies. As Jayachandran and Kremer argue, this would preserve legitimate lending by ensuring creditors that they would be "punished" only if they knowingly lent to a regime that acts against the interest of its population, where *knowingly* would be precisely defined by the declaration.

Under the ex ante version of the odious regime framework, the legal costs related to repudiating commercial debt contracted by the odious regime are likely to decline. Indirect legal costs—such as the potential difficulty in obtaining letters of credit and other short-term trade financing—are also likely to decline, because there would be no delay in establishing the illegitimacy of odious loans. However, legal costs would be associated with the workout of arrears on legitimate debt, which the new regime would be expected to inherit from the predecessor odious regime, which, as argued earlier, would have no incentive to repay creditors unwilling to lend to them. Because by definition these would be arrears on legitimate debt, the terms of the workout are unlikely to be at more favorable terms than would be available without the policy in place.

The market costs related to repudiating commercial debt contracted by the odious regime are likely to decline, in part because of an increase in borrowing costs predefault. The increase in borrowing costs will depend on the probability that existing regimes will be declared odious as well as the probability that odious regimes will be replaced by nonodious regimes. An open question is whether markets would consider repudiation in those circumstances justifiable and would coordinate not to punish the country. This is one possible equilibrium, as Kremer and Jayachandran (2002) show, but there are others in which restrictions to finance could emerge.[17]

Because odious regimes are likely to accumulate arrears on legitimate debt (at least to some creditors), restrictions in the availability and cost of financing for nonodious regimes is likely to be proportional to the probability that regimes would be declared odious. Thus, some of the same concerns raised with respect to an ex post regime still arise.

Under the ex ante version of the odious regime framework, the legal costs related to repudiating official debt contracted by the odious regime are ambiguous (table 11.4). Although lending to odious regimes—and hence the amount of debt odious regimes could default on—would decrease, the incentive to default on legitimate debt would increase for these regimes, leading to costs associated with the clearance of arrears

Table 11.4 Cost Implications of Ex Ante Odious Regime Framework

Creditor	Legal cost	Market cost
Commercial	Legal costs associated with default on odious debt would decline, but the expected costs associated with the default by the odious regime on legitimate debt would likely increase.	If the market coordinates around the declaration of odiousness as a justifiable default, borrowing costs would not increase as a result of default; the costs of default would thus fall. Borrowing costs are likely to increase to all borrowers, however, if there is a greater probability of default overall.
Official	Legal costs associated with default on odious debt would decline, but the expected costs associated with the default by the odious regime on legitimate debt are likely to increase.	Possible effects on the lending volume of official creditors are unclear.

Source: Authors.

on debt contracted by a nonodious government, which are unlikely to be lower than existing costs for restructuring official debt.

The ex ante odious regime policy proposal has some advantages over the ex post proposal in that it clearly identifies which loans are enforceable. In both cases, however, benefits may be limited by the higher borrowing costs for all regimes that would result if borrowing restrictions made odious regimes more likely to default on nonodious debt. Moreover, identifying odious regimes would lead to nontrivial practical difficulties of achieving international consensus. The behavior of official creditors would be unlikely to change drastically, because many already refuse to lend to certain regimes.

Odious Loans

This section analyzes the ex post and ex ante odious loan frameworks. It assesses the legal and market costs of each framework.

Ex Post Framework. The ex post odious loan proposal suggests that sovereign debt portfolios be audited and loans deemed odious be repudiated, regardless of the type of regime that contracted the debt.[18] Governments would argue in front of an appropriate forum (for example, a court or arbitral tribunal entrusted with settling disputes between the parties) that, based on the results of its audit, the loan is odious and the court or arbitral tribunal should therefore not pronounce on its repayment.

Legal costs related to repudiating odious commercial debt under the ex post odious loan framework are likely to be higher than those associated with current default mechanisms. Direct legal costs would increase, because costly and time-consuming debt audits and costly litigation would be required to argue that the loans are odious. Moreover, indirect legal costs are unlikely to be changed. Given the lag to establish the odious nature of the debt in legal proceedings, this version of the framework would probably not improve access to financing restricted by legal means.

Market costs related to repudiating commercial debt under the ex post odious loan framework depend on whether the probability of default would increase and the recovery value decrease. As noted earlier, it is possible that legal costs under this framework increase, leaving unchanged the probability of default.[19] However, because the expected recovery in case of a default could be reduced, creditors may compensate by increasing borrowing costs. This would also be the case if creditors incur more due-diligence expenses. Therefore, market costs would either be similar to or higher than they would be without the framework, and borrowing costs could increase for all countries. Although odious regimes are likely to find it more costly to obtain loans, it is likely that the incentives for the odious regimes to default on legitimate debt—especially from commercial creditors—will be smaller under the loan-by-loan approach than under the regime-by-regime one. Thus, although it is still possible that odious regimes may have higher incentives to default on legitimate debt, this effect would likely be less severe than under an odious regime framework.

Legal costs related to repudiating official debt under the ex post odious loan framework would most likely increase. Direct legal costs, such as the costs of litigation, would be higher than under the odious regime case, given the need for a costly and time-consuming debt audit. Because official creditors may also be expected to undertake additional efforts of due diligence of new loans (as many already do), the repudiation of any loan found ex post to be odious would involve short-term indirect legal costs.[20]

Another source of the increase in costs is the high degree of subjectivity of certain definitions of *odious debt*. As Nehru and Thomas (2009) note, categories such as "ineffective" debt are often difficult to define and to identify in practical terms. It would be very difficult to differentiate between a project that was good ex ante (that is, one with high expected returns that was well aligned with the interests of the population and therefore desirable) that happened to fail and a project that failed because it was bad ex ante. In particular, broad definitions of odious debt would either drive up existing due-diligence costs or, more likely, lead to a possible market effect in official lending away from risky projects. Such an effect would be welfare reducing, because it would imply that many projects that could realize high returns would not be financed or would be financed at higher costs by other creditors.

The ex post odious loan framework creates an unambiguous increase in legal costs (table 11.5). It is thus likely to be pursued primarily in cases

Table 11.5 Cost Implications of Ex Post Odious Loan Framework

Creditor	Legal cost	Market cost
Commercial	Legal costs are very likely to increase, because debt audits are likely to be costly and time consuming to conduct.	Predefault costs are likely to increase, because the costs associated with establishing that loans are not odious will rise and the expected recovery of loans in case of default could decrease.
Official	Legal costs are likely to increase, especially if the definition of *odious* is ambiguous.	Lending volumes and willingness to extend loans for higher-risk projects may decline.

Source: Authors.

in which the prospect of full cancellation, compared with a partial cancellation possible under the current legal framework, compensates for the higher legal costs. Borrowing costs (or the increase in costs postrepudiation) would rise as a result of stricter due diligence or lower expected returns. Moreover, depending on how broad the definition of *odious loan* is, there could be a tendency for both commercial and official creditors to shy away from riskier projects that nonetheless have high ex ante returns and would therefore be in the interests of the country's population.

Ex Ante Framework. The ex ante odious loan framework is similar to the concept of responsible lending, because it would require lenders to abide by certain lending standards (for example, the Equator Principles). However, it could go beyond a responsible lending framework, because loans that do not comply with predefined standards could be questioned on legitimacy grounds. Once a loan is judged to have met those standards, it cannot be repudiated on the basis that it is illegitimate, including, for example, in the case in which a project fails or it is later discovered that the money was used for purposes other than those originally intended.

The costs of an ex ante odious loan framework, especially for commercial creditors, depends on the ex post status of loans that do not meet the responsible lending standard. If loans that do not meet the standard are regarded as legitimate and enforceable, governments and creditors would be able to effectively opt out of the framework to avoid the additional costs of complying with standards. A second possibility would be for a loan that does not meet the standard to be unenforceable (that is, it is presumed illegitimate). A third possibility—that the legitimacy of loans that are not covered could be litigated—is equivalent to the ex post approach, because the key difference between ex ante and ex post frameworks lies in the parties' knowledge of the legal implications of repudiation in the ex ante but not in the ex post framework.

In the first scenario (in which all loans are presumed to be enforceable), one might expect that most countries and creditors would wish to avoid the high costs of due diligence beyond what is legally required to guarantee enforcement (that is, comparable to what currently exists) and would opt out of the framework, in which case costs would not be affected. Nevertheless, commercial creditors may welcome such a framework, because it enhances their reputation for corporate social responsibility, and governments may wish to incur the costs as a signal to their voters that they are engaging in a worthwhile project. Moreover, if the loans could be questioned ex post, participating in the framework would likely improve the likelihood of enforcement. We consider below the implications of a stronger version of the current system—namely, declaring all noncompliant loans to be illegitimate in principle.

The effect of this framework on litigation costs related to commercial debt is unclear. Certifying that loans meet the framework's criteria would increase costs. But ex ante frameworks generally reduce the need for legal proceedings, because they preclude arguments of illegitimacy if the government tries to repudiate a loan that was certified to meet the standards of the framework or if creditors try to recover on a loan that was not certified as meeting the appropriate standards.

Market costs of repudiating loans not meeting the standards of the framework are likely to fall, as creditors that adopt the framework are unlikely to coordinate punishment with a nonparticipant lest they provide incentives for free-riding. Costs of predefault financing would increase for all countries, however, proportionally to the increased cost associated with adopting the policy. These additional costs would not be seen in interest rates charged. Instead, they would appear as an increase in the "all-in" cost of the loan, which includes preparation costs.

Compared with the other policies, the ex ante odious loan framework probably creates the smallest incentive for regimes to default on legitimate debt, because even odious regimes retain access to finance for certain projects. Nevertheless, the incentives to default could still increase relative to the current situation (without any odious debt policy), if the costs of verifying the legitimacy of loans are prohibitively high.

By avoiding all ex post legal proceedings and building on existing due-diligence practices, the ex ante odious loan framework would likely reduce overall legal costs of restructuring debt to official creditors. However, lending costs from these creditors could increase if additional due-diligence costs are added. Moreover, as in the ex post loan approach, official creditors may shy away from projects in which the costs of meeting the proposed standards would be very high, even if these projects might be in the interest of the population.

An ex ante odious loan framework in which loans that do not meet the framework's standards are not enforceable has some attractive features relative to the other proposals. Most notably, it appears to actually reduce ex post legal costs without substantially raising market costs for commercial or official lenders (table 11.6). However, these benefits are not without their costs: increased due-diligence requirements would increase overall borrowing costs, which would be borne largely by all borrowers, including those with adequate control systems. Moreover, costs would increase for high-risk projects, which could make them nonviable.

Finally, designing such a framework would be challenging, especially because most of the benefits from such a framework depend on being able to define criteria that prevent the ex post repudiation of the debt. Current governments, especially of market-access countries, and their creditors are unlikely to favor a system that would force all loans to require costly due-diligence expenses, especially if the requirements are broad.

Table 11.6 Cost Implications of Ex Ante Odious Loan
Framework

Creditor	Legal cost	Market cost
Commercial	Predefault costs rise, because verifying the legitimacy of loans can be costly. Postdefault costs are lower, because the legal status of loans is established ex ante.	Predefault costs rise, because verifying the legitimacy of loans can be costly. Postdefault costs fall, because creditors participating in the framework would not help a nonparticipant in "punishing" the borrower.
Official	As above.	Predefault costs rise, lending volume falls, or both, because verifying the legitimacy of loans can be costly.

Source: Authors.

Conclusion

The objective of ensuring that governments use the proceeds from external loans for the benefit of their population is a laudable one. Odious debt frameworks, however, are unlikely to offer a costless solution. The policies proposed by civil society organizations (with the possible exception of the ex ante loan policy) do little to unambiguously reduce the costs of defaulting on loans deemed to be illegitimate—and therefore to dissuade lending for illegitimate purposes. Frameworks based on regime-type definitions pose tremendous challenges for the body or bodies charged with adjudicating on the type of regime; they also create incentives for despots to default, especially to those creditors most committed to the goals of the framework. Frameworks based on individual loans entail high direct legal costs of auditing loan portfolios and litigating or certifying that each loan complies with the framework's standards. Ex ante frameworks appear superior to ex post ones because they minimize the impact on nonodious governments, but they do not remove all uncertainty: under such frameworks, many countries will be penalized for the probability of being declared odious even if they are never so declared, and worthwhile but risky projects may not be undertaken.

The ex ante odious loan policy seems to be the least distortionary. Although it may entail higher costs ex ante, a well-designed policy could improve the use of loan proceeds and reduce other effects. However, it would still lead to an increase in borrowing costs. Moreover, even a well-designed ex ante odious loan policy does not avoid the problem of the fungibility of resources: if odious regimes cannot borrow to buy weapons or line their private bank accounts, they may use domestic revenues or exploit natural resources more intensively. A loan-by-loan approach is effective only in ensuring that loan proceeds are used in the interest of populations living in countries in which a large volume of financial flows is associated with external loans, as is the case in most low-income countries. As a consequence, the proposed odious debt policies are likely to increase the borrowing costs in countries that require access to relatively cheap external loans in order to finance their development needs.

A loan-by-loan approach—or indeed any framework that focuses exclusively on debt—would not address the important issues of improving public financial management and building and using domestic budget monitoring systems (that is, the building of capacity for the country's own population and civil society to monitor the expenditure of all resources administered by the state, not only those that arise from external borrowing). In sum, our analysis suggests that the economic costs of odious debt policies are nontrivial and should be carefully considered by governments and organizations involved in this debate.

Notes

1. For a detailed discussion of the different definitions of *odious debt* and their reflection in law, see chapter 9.

2. The creditor in the first relationship is the country, represented by the government. The creditor is therefore not one actor acting independently but rather the outcome of the first agency relationship: the government acting on behalf of the population.

3. Bulow and Rogoff (1989) argue that noncreditor banks would profit from selling an insurance contract to the defaulting country (using the defaulted amount as a premium) that would remove the consumption-smoothing motive for borrowing, thus rendering market exclusion an ineffective punishment. They conclude that only the existence of direct enforcement (such as legal threats) can ensure sovereign debt repayments.

4. The recently instituted $5 million prize to "well-behaved" African presidents, funded by Sudanese telecoms entrepreneur Mo Ibrahim, could be considered a proxy for such a concept (see Reuters Foundation 2006).

5. The emergence of a doctrine of odious debts is generally linked to Alexander Nahum Sack (1927), who identified three categories of odious debts: (a) "regime debts" (created when a despotic regime "contracts a debt, not for the needs and in the interest of the state, but to strengthen its own despotic regime"); (b) "subjugation debts" (created when the government "contracts debts to subjugate the population of part of its territory or to colonize it by members of the dominant nationality"); and (c) "war debts" (created when the government of a state contracts debts "with a view to waging war against another state"). However, the concept of odious debt as currently used by civil society organizations has been expanded to include "criminal," "ineffective," and "unfair" debts and debts "used against the interest of

the population." There are practical difficulties in determining whether debts were contracted against the interest of the population, an issue that is not addressed in this chapter.

6. The current debate hinges largely on the assumption that borrowers would indeed repudiate odious debts if they were legally allowed to do so (see chapter 9 of this volume by Vikram Nehru and Mark Thomas). In their working paper, Kremer and Jayachandran (2002) examine the effect of an odious debt regime on both market and direct enforcement. Curiously, in the published version of the paper (Jayachandran and Kremer 2006), they consider legal costs as the sole enforcement mechanism.

7. Mitchener and Weidenmier (2005) refer to political sanctions as "supersanctions."

8. For example, creditors tried to stop Argentina from proceeding with its debt-restructuring transaction by asking the courts to seize the bonds tendered in the exchange as an Argentine asset. The exchange stalled in March 2005, when an offshore fund moved to seize the default bonds that Argentina had accepted for the exchange (see Gelpern 2005).

9. Exceptions exist: some Latin American railroads were seized by creditors in the late 19th century (Mitchener and Weidenmier 2005).

10. Adverse selection models were introduced by Akerlof (1970), who noted that relevant characteristics of actors (in this example, the willingness of governments to repay) are often observed only imperfectly, forcing creditors to rely on estimates. When types are indistinguishable, the average willingness to pay is below that of "good payers" but above that of "bad payers." Because borrowing costs can rely only on the average, costs are too high for good payers, who may choose not to borrow, and too low for bad payers. Therefore, there will be an (adverse) self-selection of bad payers in the market. This situation can be partly remedied by credible signals of creditworthiness, such as credit ratings, guarantees, or licensing practices.

11. Moral hazard models imply that actions are imperfectly observed. Instances of moral hazard emerge, for example, when it is not possible to distinguish whether a default is a result of inability or unwillingness to repay. Moral hazard may tempt borrowers to claim inability to pay when they are actually simply unwilling to do so.

12. One example is the case *Donegal vs. Zambia*. In 1979, Romania provided a $15.4 million credit facility to Zambia (to support the acquisition of agricultural machinery, vehicles, spare parts, and technical assistance). Zambia defaulted in 1981. In 1999, Donegal International (a distressed debt fund) offered to buy the debt, and Romania sold the debt to Donegal for $3.2 million (on a claim with a face value of $30 million). In 2007, Britain's High Court ruled that Donegal could claim $15.4 million. (For more information, see IDA and IMF 2008.)

13. An example is the case of the Egyptian default at the end of the 19th century. A costly war with Ethiopia and lavish government spending led Egypt's debt to increase by a factor of 14 over a 13-year period; by 1876, the country was essentially bankrupt. Ismail, the khedive of Egypt, declared a unilateral partial default on the outstanding bonds. In response, the British and French governments demanded to intervene in the country's finances and pressured the Ottoman sultan to depose Ismail and replace him with his son. British and French officials took control of government revenue, managing it in the interests of the private creditors. For details, see Chowdhry (1991).

14. For more information on the sovereign debt–restructuring mechanism, visit http://www.imf.org/external/np/exr/facts/sdrm.htm. Setzer (2008) provides an in-depth discussion of why the IMF proposal failed, illustrating the difficulties of building international consensus behind any major change in global financial regulation.

15. The cost is measured as the difference between observed and trend GDP growth.

16. See Laeven and Valencia (2008) for an updated survey of episodes of banking, currency, and sovereign debt crises.

17. Whether markets would perceive the successor to an odious regime that defaults on odious debt as a "bad" payer and whether markets would punish successor governments because they cannot coordinate around the declaration of odiousness remains unclear (see Kremer and Jayachandran 2002).

18. The audit of the Ecuadorian Comisión para la Auditoria Integral de la Deuda Pública (CAIC), established in 2007 to investigate Ecuadorian loans contracted in the period 1976–2006, is an example of this ex post loan framework.

19. If legal costs under an odious debt framework are higher than those related to default because of inability to pay, countries will opt out of the framework and claim inability to pay.

20. Of course, these legal costs would not apply if a creditor unilaterally announced the cancellation of certain loans, because in this case the borrowing country would not repudiate its loan. For example, Norway announced in 2006 that it would unilaterally and without conditions cancel $80 million in ship export debt owed by five countries. The government stated: "The [Ship Export] campaign represented a development policy failure. As a creditor country Norway has a shared responsibility for the debts that followed. In cancelling these claims Norway takes the responsibility for allowing these five countries to terminate their remaining repayments on these debts." Norway also indicated that the unilateral cancellation of the ship export debt would be implemented outside the cooperative framework of the Paris Club of creditor countries but that this unilateral forgiveness would be a one-off debt relief policy measure and that all future debt forgiveness would be affected through multilaterally coordinated debt relief operations (http://www.regjeringen .no/nb/dep/ud/Pressesenter/pressemeldinger/2006/Cancellation-of-debts-resulting -from-the-Norwegian-Ship-Export-Campaign-1976-80.html?id=272158).

References

Akerlof, George. 1970. "The Market for Lemons: Quality Uncertainty and the Market Mechanism." *Quarterly Journal of Economics* 84 (3): 488–500.

Alexander, Lewis S. 1987. *The Legal Consequences of Sovereign Default*. Washington, DC: Federal Reserve Board.

Alfaro, Laura, Noel Maurer, and Faisal Ahmed. 2008. "Gunboats and Vultures: Market Reaction to the 'Enforcement' of Sovereign Debt." Harvard Business School, Boston, MA.

Bolton, Patrick, and Olivier Jeanne. 2007. "Structuring and Restructuring Sovereign Debt: The Role of a Bankruptcy Regime." IMF Working Paper 07/192, International Monetary Fund, Washington, DC.

Bolton, Patrick, and David Skeel. 2007. "Odious Debts or Odious Regimes?" Research Paper 07–30, University of Pennsylvania, Institute for Law and Economics, Philadelphia.

Borensztein, Eduardo, and Ugo Panizza. 2006a. *The Cost of Default*. Washington, DC: Inter-American Development Bank.

———. 2006b. "Do Sovereign Defaults Hurt Exporters?" RES Working Paper 1018, Research Department, Inter-American Development Bank, Washington, DC.

Bulow, Jeremy, and Kenneth Rogoff. 1989. "A Constant Recontracting Model of Sovereign Debt." *Journal of Political Economy* 96 (February): 155–78

Choi, Albert, and Eric Posner. 2007. "A Critique of the Odious Debt Doctrine." *Law and Contemporary Problems* 70 (Summer). http://www.law.duke.edu/shell/cite.pl?70+Law+&+Contemp.+Probs.+33+(summer+2007).

Chowdhry, Bhagwan. 1991. "What Is Different about International Lending?" *Review of Financial Studies* 4 (1): 121–48.

Cline, William R. 1987. *Mobilizing Bank Lending to Debtor Countries.* Washington, DC: Institute for International Economics.

De Paoli, Bianca, Glenn Hoggarth, and Victoria Saporta. 2006. "Output Costs of Sovereign Defaults: Some Empirical Estimates." Financial Stability Paper 1, Bank of England, London.

Eaton, Jonathan, and Mark Gersovitz. 1981. "Debt with Potential Repudiation: Theoretical and Empirical Analysis." *Review of Economic Studies* 48 (2): 289–309.

Eichengreen, Barry. 1987. "Till Debt Do Us Part: The U.S. Capital Market and Foreign Lending 1920–1955." CEPR Discussion Paper 212, Centre for Economic Policy Research, London.

English, William 1996. "Understanding the Costs of Sovereign Default: American State Debts in the 1840s." *American Economic Review* 86 (1): 289–309.

Flandreau Marc, and Frederic Zumer. 2004. *The Making of Global Finance, 1880–1913.* Paris: Organisation of Economic Co-operation and Development.

Gelos, R. Gaston, Ratna Sahay, and Guido Sandleris. 2004. "Sovereign Borrowing by Developing Countries: What Determines Market Access?" IMF Working Paper 04/221, International Monetary Fund, Washington, DC.

Gelpern, Anna, 2005. "After Argentina." Newark Research Paper 011, Rutgers School of Law, New Brunswick, NJ.

Gil Sander, Frederico. 2009. "Odious Debt as a Principal-Agent Problem." In *Debt Relief and Beyond: Lessons Learned and Challenges Ahead,* ed. Carlos A. Primo Brago and Dörte Dömeland, 229–60. Washington, DC: World Bank.

Grossman, Herschel I., and John Van Huyck. 1989. "Sovereign Debt as a Contingent Claim: Excusable Default, Repudiation, and Reputation." NBER Working Paper 1673, National Bureau of Economic Research, Cambridge, MA.

IDA (International Development Association) and IMF (International Monetary Fund). 2008. "The Heavily Indebted Poor Countries (HIPC) Initiative and Multilateral Debt Relief Initiative (MDRI): Status of Implementation Report." Washington, DC. http://siteresources.worldbank.org/INTDEBTDEPT/ProgressReports/21899739/HIPCProgressReport20080912.pdf.

IDB (Inter-American Development Bank). 2006. *Living with Debt: How to Limit the Risks of Sovereign Finance.* Washington, DC: IDB and Harvard University Press.

Jayachandran, Seema, and Michael Kremer. 2006. "Odious Debt." *American Economic Review* 96 (1): 82–92.

Kletzer, Kenneth, and Brian Wright. 2000. "Sovereign Debt as Intertemporal Barter." *American Economic Review* 90 (3): 621–39.

Kremer, Michael, and Seema Jayachandran. 2002. "Odious Debt." NBER Working Paper 8953, National Bureau of Economic Research, Cambridge, MA.

————. 2006. "Odious Debt." *American Economic Review* 96 (1): 82–92.

Laeven, Luc, and Fabian Valencia. 2008. "Systemic Banking Crises: A New Database." IMF Working Paper 08/224, International Monetary Fund, Washington, DC.

Levy-Yeyati, Eduardo, and Ugo Panizza. 2006. "The Elusive Costs of Sovereign Defaults." CIF Working Paper 11/2006, Centro de Investigación en Finanzas, Universidad Torcuato di Tella, Buenos Aires.

Lindert, Peter, and Peter Morton. 1991. "How Sovereign Debt Has Worked." In *Developing Country Debt and the World Econ*omy, ed. Jeffrey D. Sachs, 225–35. Chicago: University of Chicago Press for the National Bureau of Economic Research.

Martinez, Jose Vicente, and Guido Sandleris. 2008. "Is It Punishment? Sovereign Defaults and the Decline in Trade." Business School Working Paper 2008-01, Universidad Torcuato di Tella, Buenos Aires.

Mitchener, Kris, and Marc Weidenmier. 2005. "Supersanctions and Sovereign Debt Repayment." NBER Working Paper W11472, National Bureau of Economic Research, Cambridge, MA.

Nehru, Vikram, and Mark Thomas. 2009. "The Concept of Odious Debt: Some Considerations." In *Debt Relief and Beyond: Lessons Learned and Challenges Ahead*, ed. Carlos A. Primo Brago and Dörte Dömeland, 205–28. Washington, DC: World Bank.

Ochoa, Christiana. 2008. "From Odious Debt to Odious Finance: Avoiding the Externalities of a Functional Odious Debt Doctrine." *Harvard Journal of International Law* 49: 109–59.

Özler, Sule. 1993. "Have Commercial Banks Ignored History?" *American Economic Review* 83 (3): 608–20.

Reuters Foundation. 2006. "Thumbs Up or Down for African Prize?" October 27. http://www.alertnet.org/db/blogs/22870/2006/09/27-133957-1.htm.

Rogoff, Kenneth, and Jeromin Zettelmeyer. 2002. "Bankruptcy Procedures for Sovereigns: A History of Ideas 1976–2001." IMF Working Paper, International Monetary Fund, Washington, DC.

Rose, Andrew 2005. "One Reason Countries Pay Their Debts: Renegotiation and International Trade." *Journal of Development Economics* 77 (1): 189–206.

Rose, Andrew, and Mark Spiegel. 2002. "A Gravity Model of Sovereign Lending: Trade, Default and Credit." *Working Papers in Applied Economic Theory* 2002–09. San Francisco: Federal Reserve Bank of San Francisco.

Sack, Alexander 1927. *Les effets des transformations des états sur leurs dettes publique et autres obligations financières*. Paris: Recueil Sirey.

Setzer, Brad. 2008. "The Political Economy of the SDRM." Project on Debt Restructuring and Sovereign Bankruptcy, Initiative for Policy Dialogue, Columbia University, New York.

Sturzenegger, Federico. 2002. "Default Episodes in the 90s: Factbook and Preliminary Lessons." Universidad Torcuato di Tella, Buenos Aires.

Sturzenegger, Federico, and Jeromin Zettelmeyer. 2007. *Debt Defaults and Lessons from a Decade of Crisis*. Cambridge, MA: MIT Press.

Tomz, Michael. 1998. "Do Creditors Ignore History? Reputation in International Capital Markets." Paper presented at the International Congress of the Latin American Studies Association in Chicago, IL, September 24–26.

————. 2007. *Reputation and International Cooperation: Sovereign Debt across Three Centuries.* Princeton, NJ: Princeton University Press.

Tomz, Michael, and Mark L. J. Wright. 2007. "Do Countries Default in 'Bad Times'?" *Journal of the European Economic Association* 5 (2–3): 352–60.

Waibel, Michael. 2003. "Sovereign Debt Restructuring." Diss., Seminar für Internationales Voelkerrecht, Universität Wien, Vienna.

Part IV

Debt Management

12

Government Debt Management in Low-Income Countries

Phillip Anderson and Eriko Togo

The financial landscape facing beneficiaries changed dramatically following debt relief from the Heavily Indebted Poor Countries (HIPC) Initiative and the Multilateral Debt Relief Initiative (MDRI). With the decline in debt levels, there has been a significant reduction in the budgetary burden from servicing the debt. The new fiscal space has created renewed optimism and allowed countries to reallocate public expenditure to achieve the Millennium Development Goals and long-term growth objectives, including the goal of reaching middle-income status. These ambitious programs require substantial investments in human and physical capital, which will require additional financing above the projected official sector financing, including multilateral and bilateral donors.

In many low-income countries, the completion of HIPC Initiative and MDRI debt relief occurred at a time when global financial markets were characterized by high levels of liquidity and international investors seeking opportunities with higher yields and risks. Given the historically low yields that could be earned in advanced countries, this led to large capital inflows to developing countries, including low-income countries.

The confluence of debt relief and capital availability created new borrowing opportunities in low-income countries. Some countries gained access to nonconcessional sources of financing from new creditors, through new instruments, and increased financial choices. In 2007, for example, Gabon, Georgia, and Ghana entered the international capital markets by issuing Eurobonds. Kenya, Malawi, Uganda, and Zambia, which planned to issue Eurobonds, were quoted spreads of 350–500 basis points over U.S. Treasury securities. Foreign investors also entered the domestic debt markets, holding as much as 20 percent of domestic debt outstanding in certain markets.

The recent financial crisis and the resultant credit crunch have highlighted the risks of nonconcessional borrowing. As market conditions deteriorated dramatically and quickly over the course of 2008, market-access opportunities suddenly closed for debut issuers, as indicated by the prohibitive trading spreads of bonds issued by comparable credits of about 1,500 basis points over the U.S. Treasury rate. Foreign investors in the domestic debt market also pulled out, as funds faced redemptions and required liquidity to pay back investors. The experience revealed the new challenges market debt presents to managing the government debt portfolio and heightened awareness of the importance of prudent government debt management to avoid the risk of reaccumulating unsustainable debt.

This chapter illustrates the historical context in which government debt-management practices evolved in more advanced countries and draws lessons for low-income countries. A hypothesis developed in earlier studies is that the challenges faced by middle- and low-income countries are similar in type but that the degree and severity are greater in low-income countries. This chapter presents some evidence to this effect, drawing on early results from the World Bank's Debt Management Performance Assessment (DeMPA) tool, applied in more than 20 low-income countries, and early experience from the technical assistance it, together with the International Monetary Fund (IMF), is providing low-income countries in developing medium-term debt-management strategies (MTDSs).

The chapter is organized as follows. The next section describes the evolution of government debt management in the context of new financing opportunities in more advanced countries in the 1980s to early 1990s and in emerging-market countries in the late 1990s—experiences that were similar to recent experiences in low-income countries. It discusses how this development gave impetus to the establishment of debt management as a separate policy and institutional consolidation. The following section describes the codification of sound practices through the *Guidelines for Public Debt Management* published by the World Bank and the IMF in 2001. The third section summarizes the insights from a World Bank pilot program in public debt management and domestic debt market development that addressed the challenges in moving from principles to an actionable reform program. The fourth section discusses the results from the DeMPA and the technical assistance in developing MTDSs in low-income countries. The last section concludes and discusses the way forward.

Evolution of Government Debt Management as a Separate Policy and Institutional Consolidation

Government debt management as a distinct policy activity with a focus on managing risk developed in the late 1980s in several small member countries of the Organisation for Economic Co-operation and Development (OECD) with high levels of public debt, including Denmark, Ireland, New Zealand, and Sweden. The need to improve government debt management arose from rising debt levels, caused by macroeconomic imbalances in the 1970s and 1980s. During this period, the volatility of exchange rates and interest rates had increased, as a resulting of the ending of the gold standard in the early 1970s, oil shocks, higher inflation, and the resulting policy responses. These countries had debt portfolios with significant shares of foreign currency–denominated debt and exposure to changes in short-term interest rates. As a result, the servicing of public debt imposed large and uncertain demands on government budgets (Anderson 2006).

Around the same time, innovations in financial instruments and deregulation in the financial sector presented new opportunities and risks in the management of government debt portfolios. New ways of managing risk became available with the development of financial futures in the 1970s and swap markets in the early 1980s. Soon after, government borrowers faced a vast array of structured financial products, many of which were difficult to understand.

In a parallel development, responding to the same environment, banks and corporations were reshaping the way they managed financial risk. The modern corporate treasury emerged in the 1970s. Its role is to manage these risks centrally across a company, within well-defined limits and with effective operational controls.

The momentum for reform of government debt management was boosted in the 1990s with the recognition that risky debt structures contributed to financial crises. Debt portfolios with significant proportions of short-term debt and debt denominated in or indexed to foreign currencies caused debt levels to escalate when shocks hit. The high-risk profile of various OECD and emerging-market country debt portfolios led to a redefinition of the mandate and objectives of debt management, from performing passive debt issuance and servicing functions toward systematic management of the risks inherent in the debt structure, in order to avoid jeopardizing the achievement of the fiscal targets and to reduce the vulnerability to economic and financial shocks. The convergence of large, volatile debt portfolios and greater financial choice underscored the need for sound government debt management as a distinct policy, with new objectives and support from a prudent debt-management strategy and reformed institutional arrangements.

Although the push for policy separation may have originated from these developments, policy makers also realized that separating debt management from fiscal and monetary policies reduces the possibility of policy conflict, because, at least in the short run, the pursuit of the three policy objectives involved trade-offs and the assignment of separate policy objectives enhanced the credibility and effectiveness of implementation. For example, where it is responsible for managing both fiscal policy and debt-management policy, the fiscal authority may wish to keep the cost of debt servicing low in order to create fiscal space in the short run. However, this may increase the volatility of future debt servicing, forcing subsequent governments to cut expenditures or raise taxes. Although the fiscal authorities should be concerned with the long-term consequences, they are often subjected to political pressures arising from election cycles that lead them to make myopic policy choices.

Similarly, the core objective of the monetary authority is to control inflation. If it were also responsible for debt management, it might be tempted to hold interest rates low, increasing the possibility of higher inflation in the future. Alternatively, the monetary authority might be tempted to issue inflation-indexed debt to enhance its policy credibility, which could increase debt-service volatility. Separating the management of debt from the management of fiscal and monetary policies can help avoid such conflicts, real or perceived, and improve policy credibility.

Policy separation requires effective policy coordination to ensure that the overall macroeconomic policy mix is consistent and sustainable. For example, central banks rarely pursue a zero-inflation policy, because of the potential damaging consequence for economic activity that could reduce tax revenues and force large public expenditure cuts for the fiscal authorities and impose prohibitive financing costs on the debt manager. Because of these policy trade-offs, a coordinated policy response that is consistent with long-term sustainability and that reduces the risk of policy conflicts is central to ensuring a credible policy mix. Policy separation has forced transparent coordination to make informed trade-offs rather than risk the conflicts in policy implementation outlined above.

The credibility of policy separation is supported by institutional arrangements that provide for a clear accountability framework in the respective areas. In principle, it should matter little whether debt-management functions are dispersed among multiple entities, provided that debt-management objectives are clearly defined and conveyed and coordination between the different entities is effective. In practice, organizational dispersion often reflects the lack of a common and coherent debt-management objective or strategy and the presence of bureaucratic rivalry across different departments, which result in poor coordination. There is now growing consensus that consolidating debt-management functions into one office is one of the most important steps that can be taken to improve the overall quality of debt management.

Guidelines for Public Debt Management

Prompted by the financial crises of the 1990s in emerging markets, which drew attention to the quality of public debt management and to the role that deeper and more efficient domestic debt markets can play in reducing financial vulnerability, the World Bank and the IMF published the *Guidelines for Public Debt Management* (2001) and the *Handbook on Developing Government Bond Markets* (2001), which codified sound practices in the areas of public debt management and the development of domestic debt markets.[1]

The *Guidelines* cover domestic public debt, external public debt, and management of explicit guarantees. They identify areas in which there is broad agreement on what constitutes sound practice in public debt management (box 12.1).[2] They focus on principles applicable to a wide range of countries at different stages of development and with various institutional structures for government debt management. They are not intended as a set of binding practices or as a rigid prescription. The *Guidelines* recognize that countries' capacity-building needs in government debt management differ. A country's needs should be shaped by the capital market constraints it faces, its exchange rate regime, the quality of its macroeconomic and regulatory policies, its institutional capacity to design and implement reforms, its credit standing, and its objectives for public debt management. The building of capacity and technical assistance must therefore be tailored to meet stated policy goals while recognizing the policy settings, institutional framework, technology, and human and financial resources a country faces.

Insights from the Pilot Program for Government Debt Management and Development of the Domestic Debt Market

The process of moving from a set of general principles to a concrete program of reform and capacity building in a particular country is not straightforward. Recognizing this, in 2002 the World Bank initiated a pilot program covering 12 countries, with the objective of helping them design and implement reform programs in public debt management and the development of domestic government debt markets (see World Bank 2007a, 2007b).[3]

The results of the pilot program suggest that a broad-based diagnostic is more likely to lead to a sound reform program than one focused only on debt management, because it both analyzes the main building blocks of debt management and identifies the interrelationships with macroeconomic policies, the overall governance environment, and the level of development of the domestic government debt market. Analysis of these interactions

---

Box 12.1 Principles of Sound Practice in Public Debt
Management

According to the World Bank and the IMF, the following principles should
govern the management of public debt:

1. Debt management objectives and coordination:
   • Ensure that the government's financing needs and payment obliga-
     tions are met at the lowest possible cost consistent with a prudent
     degree of risk.
   • Develop a common understanding of debt management, monetary,
     and fiscal policy objectives.
2. Transparency and accountability:
   • Publicly disclose the objectives of public debt management, the rele-
     vant measures of cost and risk, and the allocation of responsibilities.
3. Institutional framework:
   • Clarify the legal authority to borrow and issue new debt, invest, and
     undertake other transactions on the government's behalf.
   • Ensure clear roles and responsibilities.
   • Develop accurate and comprehensive debt data.
4. Debt-management strategy:
   • Monitor, evaluate, and manage the risk structure of public debt.
   • Implement cost-effective cash management policies that minimize
     government liquidity and repayment risk.
5. Risk-management framework:
   • Manage the trade-offs between the cost of and the risk of govern-
     ment debt.
   • Consider the impact of contingent liabilities on the government's
     financial position.
6. Development and maintenance of an efficient market for government
   securities:
   • Ensure that policies and operations are consistent with the develop-
     ment of an efficient government securities market.

Source: World Bank and IMF 2001a.

---

helps identify the trade-offs across different policies, priorities for reform,
and the possible consequences of reform of only some areas.

The pilot results indicated that a thorough understanding of the macroeconomic situation and the relationship with debt management is crucial,
because debt-management reforms tend to be more effective if a credible
macroeconomic framework is in place and stability has been achieved or is
progressing. An analysis focused narrowly on debt management that does

not take into account or is inconsistent with the overall macroeconomic framework may lead to unrealistic recommendations. Presentation to the authorities of the broader policy context provides a realistic assessment of what could be achieved by public debt-management reform.

Among the pilot countries with high debt levels and negative debt dynamics, fiscal consolidation was a priority. In countries in which debt levels had become unsustainable, more drastic action was necessary, including debt forgiveness, debt renegotiation with creditors, and voluntary action by the international community to reduce the debt burden. High public debt levels and the associated interest costs sharpened the trade-off between reducing costs in the short run and managing the financial risks in the medium term. For this reason, poor fiscal management can result in riskier debt portfolios and increase vulnerability to shocks.

High and volatile inflation had to be reduced before significant progress could be made in reducing risk in the domestic debt portfolio. Most countries achieved reasonable inflation outcomes before the pilot program and were seeking to establish policy credibility over the medium term. Although policy makers recognized that separating debt management from monetary policy implementation enhanced central bank credibility, doing so proved to be a challenge, particularly in countries in which the central bank also issued significant debt in its own name and capacity in the finance ministry was weak. In countries in which the central bank issued significant debt in its own name, recapitalizing the central bank or transferring its liabilities to the government was necessary before the central bank could stop issuing significant debt. Given the impact on the governments' debt-servicing costs, recapitalization or liability transfer was likely to occur slowly, something the development of reform options had to take into account.

Debt managers in the pilot countries had a general understanding of the key risks in their debt portfolios, but decisions about government borrowing were shaped by unstated or implicit strategies based on these views. Although such an approach has been reasonable in many cases, the lack of an explicit strategy based on thorough analysis of cost-risk trade-offs was limiting. It meant that there was only a partial understanding of the trade-offs being made in terms of possible cost outcomes; it allowed for inconsistencies in the management of different parts of the debt portfolio, resulting in actions to reduce risk or costs of one subportfolio conflicting with those of another; it allowed choices about borrowing to be inconsistent over time; and it allowed short-term fiscal expediency or the priorities of monetary policy implementation to be too readily accepted.

Weaknesses in the institutional arrangements also explained implicit rather than formal debt-management strategies. Where debt-management responsibilities were scattered across institutions, the possibility of inconsistent strategies and inefficiencies arising from the duplication of functions was high. However, consolidation of debt-management functions into one unit without regard to the institutional capacity or the necessary authority to conduct its business also undermined the reform effort and did not guarantee the development of a formal debt-management strategy. A narrower approach, perhaps focused on improving the management of one type of debt (domestic borrowing, for example), might increase organizational fragmentation.

The level of development of the domestic debt market also had a crucial impact on debt management. Issues such as the lack of a predictable and transparent primary market, the dominance of commercial banks as investors in government securities, poor risk management by banks, inadequate development of contractual savings, and the lack of large and liquid benchmark issues and active trading in the secondary market all had implications for the management of domestic debt. A comprehensive diagnostic that examined these interrelationships helped identify a realistic debt-management strategy. Development of a related set of reforms might diminish the impact of these constraints and allow governments to reduce costs and better manage risks in the public debt portfolio.

The pilot program included not only diagnostics but also formulation and implementation of a reform plan. Many countries that took part in the pilot program developed reform plans of some type.

Elements in the design process correlated with success in moving from the diagnostic to the implementation stage. In particular, reform programs that took account of country-specific priorities, the prevailing political climate, the level of technical difficulty, and capacity constraints resulted in greater incremental progress than those that laid out first-best solutions that were impractical to implement. These reforms are best characterized as "good fit" rather than "best practice." In addition, reform plans that incorporated medium-term institutional development and capacity building while taking into account immediate constraints helped keep the bigger picture in sight, allowing governments to identify opportunities to move forward as circumstances permit.

Few generalizations can be made about the sequencing of public debt-management reforms. The basic building blocks that must come first are building capacity in the back office and establishing reliable debt-recording systems, so that accurate and frequent reporting can be produced and debt can be serviced in a timely manner without relying on lenders' notifications.

Comprehensive institutional and legal reforms were not a prerequisite for developing an overall debt-management strategy across institutional boundaries. Indeed, several pilot countries demonstrated that significant progress can be made without such reform. Their experience suggests that much can be achieved by forming a working group or coordination committee or by establishing islands of excellence with special budget and technical support to conduct analysis.

Experience also suggests, however, that such partial solutions, usually not first best, have risks and that their longer-term consequences should be carefully considered. For example, a coordination committee to develop a debt-management strategy could stop meeting if it depends on key members who resign from the ministry of finance or the central bank. If there is no institutional framework to maintain capacity, the departure of trained staff can result not only in the loss of capacity but also in heightened operational risk. Similarly, where legal reforms are difficult to implement, use of secondary legislation could prove useful for avoiding delays in implementing reforms, but such an arrangement could add to the already complicated and fragmented legal frameworks.

Finally, thorough analysis of existing shortcomings is a critical step in the design of a reform plan. Implementation of a public financial management system with a debt-management module without prior study of the users' functional requirements proved highly costly in several countries. Neither the vendor nor the government knew what a debt-management system should look like, and each had different expectations of the contributions of the other. Along with long delays and budgetary overruns, operational risk continued to increase from the aging of the old debt-management system (which did not meet the evolving needs of the debt manager) and the lack of system support.

Government Debt Management in Low-Income Countries

The World Bank's DeMPA (Debt Management Performance Assessment) tool is a comprehensive methodology for assessing debt-management performance. It provides a standard by which to measure performance by assessing the strengths and weaknesses in a country's debt-management operations. This assessment can form the basis for the design of an actionable reform program, thereby helping harmonize donor support in this area. It also permits country authorities, international donors, and creditors to monitor progress in strengthening public debt-management operations in a country over time.

DeMPA covers six core functions of public debt management: governance and strategy development, coordination with macroeconomic policies, borrowing and related financing activities, cash-flow forecasting and cash-balance management, operational risk management, and debt records and reporting. Its scope is the management of public debt by the central government and closely related functions, such as issuance of loan guarantees,

Table 12.1 Debt Management Performance Assessment Indicators

Indicator	Description
Governance and strategy development	
DPI–1	Legal framework
DPI–2	Managerial structure
DPI–3	Debt-management strategy
DPI–4	Evaluation of debt-management operations
DPI–5	Audit
Coordination with macroeconomic policies	
DPI–6	Coordination with fiscal policy
DPI–7	Coordination with monetary policy
Borrowing and related financing activities	
DPI–8	Domestic borrowing
DPI–9	External borrowing
DPI–10	Loan guarantees, onlending, and derivatives
Cash-flow forecasting and cash-balance management	
DPI–11	Cash-flow forecasting and cash-balance management
Operational risk management	
DPI–12	Debt administration and data security
DPI–13	Segregation of duties, staff capacity, and business continuity
Debt records and reporting	
DPI–14	Debt records
DPI–15	Debt reporting

Source: World Bank 2008.

onlending, and cash-flow forecasting and cash-balance management. The six functions are in turn disaggregated into 15 indicators (table 12.1). Public debt-management operations are scored across several dimensions under each indicator, with an emphasis on meeting a minimum requirement that is considered a necessary condition for effective performance (that is, achieving a C score for a specific dimension). Failure to meet that minimum requirement signals a serious deficiency in performance, indicating a priority area for reform. The dimensions of each indicator provide a level of detail that can form the basis for the design of an actionable reform plan.

Early results from DeMPAs confirm similarities in the results obtained in the 12-country pilot program (figure 12.1). In particular, few low-income countries have formal debt-management strategies. Although countries

Figure 12.1 Early Results from the DeMPA Tool: Core Functions and Debt Management

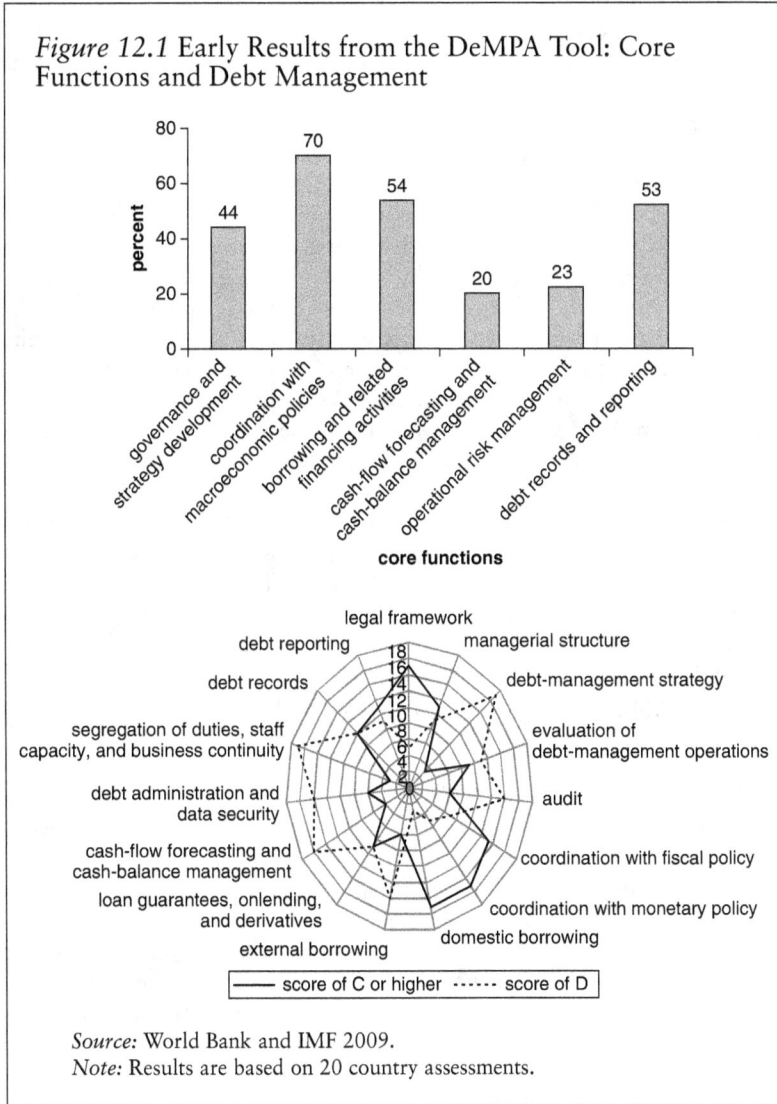

Source: World Bank and IMF 2009.
Note: Results are based on 20 country assessments.

followed some form of strategy, it was generally unpublished, did not have approval of the highest-level policy makers, and was not supported by a decision-making process that would ensure its regular production and updating. In addition, the treatment of the debt portfolio was not comprehensive, with external and domestic debt dealt with separately. In several cases, the authorities faced conflicts between the objective of reducing the stock of domestic debt and that of developing the domestic debt market. Overall, strategies lacked a firm analytical underpinning.

This has resulted in weakness in external borrowing, characterized by a low degree of assessment of the most beneficial (cost-effective) borrowing terms and conditions, and a general absence of documented procedures for borrowing in foreign markets. Weaknesses in cash-flow forecasting and management have also been identified as important, with long-term domestic borrowing often used to manage short-term cash-flow needs.

Weaknesses in the governance structure manifested themselves in scattered organizational structures, with multiple departments and institutions responsible for managing the debt, often operating without an explicit agency agreement. Low-income countries were also characterized by weak operational risk management, with countries lacking business continuity planning, strong operational controls, and well-articulated responsibilities for staff. Accountability frameworks were also weak, as evidenced by the lack of regular performance audits. These weaknesses outweigh the fact that the majority of countries have effective legal frameworks that underpin borrowing.

Another tool, developed by the World Bank and the IMF, is the MTDS (medium-term debt-management strategy) Toolkit, a framework for formulating and implementing a debt-management strategy that raises the required amount of funding while achieving the government's risk and cost objectives, consistent with maintaining debt sustainability (World Bank and IMF 2009). It consists of a Guidance Note that provides practical guidance on the process of developing an effective MTDS, describing each step involved in detail (box 12.2), and a spreadsheet-based analytical tool.

Using the process set out in the Guidance Note, policy makers can evaluate the cost-risk trade-off of different borrowing strategies within a medium-term context. Setting clear medium-term strategic goals helps debt managers make informed choices and avoid decisions made solely on the basis of cost or short-term expediency. The process helps them identify, monitor, and manage key financial risks. It also explicitly requires coordination with fiscal and monetary management, helping identify the constraints that limit the debt manager's choices as well as the steps to ease those constraints. Finally, by encouraging transparency, this approach can help facilitate the relationship with external investors, rating agencies, and others in the financial markets and, consequently, support the development of domestic debt markets.

Box 12.2 Steps in Establishing an Effective MTDS

The key steps involved in establishing an effective MTDS include the following:

1. Identify the objectives for public debt management and the scope of the MTDS.
2. Identify the current debt-management strategy, and analyze the costs and risks of the existing debt.
3. Identify and analyze potential funding sources, including cost and risk characteristics.
4. Identify baseline projections and risks in key policy areas: fiscal, monetary, external, and market.
5. Review key longer-term structural factors.
6. Identify the cost-risk trade-offs, and assess and rank alternative strategies.
7. Review the implications of candidate debt-management strategies with fiscal and monetary policy authorities and for market conditions.
8. Submit and secure agreement on the MTDS.

Source: World Bank and IMF 2009.

Experience in six countries in which the Bank and the IMF have provided technical assistance in developing an MTDS suggests that the typical informal debt-management strategy followed by low-income countries was to maximize concessional debt. Following that strategy meant that development of a domestic debt market was often neglected; in general, domestic debt was contracted as a residual to fill the financing gap left after external borrowing had been determined. Domestic debt also played the role of a fiscal anchor to control expenditures in order to satisfy the conditions attached to various donor programs. Investment projects often determined the currency composition of the debt, which was driven by donors rather than the strategy. Borrowing decisions were driven by month-to-month financing needs and the taking of whatever financing may have been available at the time. Debt sustainability analysis was often considered synonymous with debt-management-strategy analysis.

As a reflection of these policies, debt portfolios displayed an external debt composition that was dominated by official sector financing, which helped minimize debt-servicing costs. The proportion of external to domestic debt in many countries has shifted toward increased shares of domestic debt, not because of increased domestic issuance but because of reduction in external debt following the HIPC Initiative or MDRI debt relief.

Despite this shift, significant exchange rate risk remains in low-income countries' debt portfolios. The composition of the domestic debt portfolio varies across countries, ranging from those unable to issue debt in their local currency or to do so only at short maturities to those that issue debt in a range of fixed-rate domestic currency instruments with maturities ranging from 3 months to 20 years. In general, domestic debt portfolios tended to be dominated by shorter-term debt and characterized by high refinancing risk. In some countries, the share of floating-rate debt is high (increasing the interest rate risk) or debt is indexed to foreign currency (introducing exchange-rate risk).

Assessment of the vulnerabilities arising from the macroeconomic framework reveals that many low-income countries are subject to external shocks that affect their external balances, including negative terms-of-trade shocks because of primary commodity export dependence as well as dependence on fuel and food imports. Furthermore, as a consequence of the slowdown in advanced economies, there has been a reduction in remittances, foreign direct investment, and capital inflows, and the gradual reduction in international reserves has exerted pressure on the exchange rate precisely at a time when the budgetary shortfall was increasing and the capacity to service the debt had weakened.

On the fiscal front, in the short term, new pressures arising from declining revenues and pressing expenditure needs caused by the economic slowdown are likely to widen financing gaps in many low-income countries. In addition, weather-related supply shocks, including droughts and hurricanes, as well as the potential realization of explicit and implicit contingent liabilities, can require unplanned budgetary expenditures. In the medium term, massive social and infrastructure needs will continue to demand additional sources of financing. For this reason, special attention must be paid to ensure that low-income countries do not reaccumulate unsustainable debt and that the debt structure does not create additional vulnerabilities.

Monetary policy has been a challenge. Large capital inflows before 2008 required intervention to sterilize the excess liquidity in the domestic banking system. Spikes in food and fuel prices led to a rapid increase in headline inflation in most low-income countries. Combined with high fiscal deficits, some central banks have been unable to anchor inflation expectations, causing them to maintain high interest rates despite the drying up of excess liquidity. Others have been able to accommodate liquidity needs in the wake of rapid capital outflow and reduced domestic liquidity.

The short-term outlook for financing will continue to be challenging. However, over time liquidity conditions can be expected to return to normalcy, and renewed risk appetite will reverse the direction of capital flows. Furthermore, several low-income countries, such as Kenya and

Nigeria, are finding that heightened risk aversion by domestic investors has allowed them to finance their deficits; they have identified a window of opportunity to develop their domestic debt market amidst the global financial crisis.

Although reliance on official sources has served low-income countries well in the past, governments in some of these countries have sought alternative sources of financing to accommodate higher infrastructure expenditures and reduce their dependence on donor financing. For some, such opportunities can be a welcome development, particularly if concessional financing is insufficient or may no longer be as forthcoming as it once was given the severity of the financial crisis in donor countries.

Experience in developing the MTDS in six countries suggests that low-income countries would benefit from quantitative assessments of the cost and risk performance of alternative debt-management strategies under different interest and exchange rate scenarios. Such an exercise provides the authorities with a good understanding of the feasible set of strategies as well as the cost and risk consequence of a particular strategy choice. Domestic debt will almost always imply higher interest costs, shorter maturities, and higher refinancing risk than external debt (concessional or nonconcessional), but it eliminates exchange rate risk. Whether it is preferable to external debt will depend on the country and its characteristics, as well as the nature of the shock scenarios applied. The choice of strategy must be evaluated within the context of the government's overall risk tolerance, taking into account its desire to develop the domestic debt market.

Conclusions and the Way Forward

The volatile and changing outlook for debt markets, creditors, and donors has highlighted the importance of developing and maintaining a diverse range of financing sources, including the development of the domestic debt market, and the urgent need to strengthen debt-management frameworks in low-income countries. Progress in these areas would help promote long-term debt sustainability that is robust to changing macroeconomic and market circumstances.

Countries need to move away from donor-driven debt composition and the practice of financing the funding gap on a month-to-month basis or reprogramming expenditures. Instead, they should move toward a practice guided by a medium-term strategic plan for financing the budget deficit and investment programs, including contingency plans for financing unexpected increases in financing needs. Cost-risk analysis forces discipline in thinking through questions such as the following:

- How rapidly can the domestic debt market be developed, how much longer-term debt can the market absorb without crowding out the private sector, and what are the interest cost implications for the budget?

- What consequences does developing a domestic debt market have for a country's financing cost as it approaches middle-income status?
- At what spreads over U.S. Treasury securities does it make sense to return to borrowing in the international capital markets?
- If a country issues debt in the international capital markets, how likely is it that it will be denied access to traditional concessional lending by the International Development Agency and the African Development Bank?

Adopting a formal debt-management strategy helps prevent situations in which the government makes expensive mistakes. The systematic approach ensures that key issues are addressed and links to macroeconomic policies are taken into account. This helps ensure that domestic debt-market objectives are fully considered and that overall policy consistency is maintained. Adoption of a systematic approach should be the cornerstone for establishing a separate debt-management policy, and it should help guide a more detailed annual borrowing plan.

To support development of a debt-management strategy, policy makers must strengthen governance and institutional reform, to ensure that capacity can be built on a sustainable basis. The main prerequisites for success that emerged from the 12 pilot-country case studies—such as the importance of macroeconomic stability and a reliable and timely database—continue to be binding constraints in many low-income countries. Reforms must prioritize addressing these binding constraints. This is not to say that countries that do not have the necessary preconditions should not develop an MTDS: all countries should develop a strategy to provide discipline to their policy actions. Where good data are not available, however, a more heuristic approach to strategy development may be appropriate.

The development of reform programs in capacity-constrained low-income countries is likely to require tighter focus than in other settings, with sharper identification of priorities and sequencing of action plans.[4] Parallel work to develop the domestic debt market is of paramount importance if the government is to have access to a more secure and robust source of financing over the medium term.

Notes

1. The *Guidelines*, published in March 2001 and updated in November 2003, and the *Handbook*, published in July 2001, were followed by the *Guidelines for Public Debt Management: Accompanying Document and Selected Case Studies* (2003). It contains 18 case studies written by country authorities on how they implemented public debt management based on sound principles.

2. Government debt managers from some 30 countries commented on the initial draft of the *Guidelines*, and more than 300 representatives from 122 countries attended five conferences and provided feedback before the *Guidelines* were finalized.

3. The 12 countries in the pilot program—Bulgaria, Colombia, Costa Rica, Croatia, Indonesia, Kenya, Lebanon, Nicaragua, Pakistan, Sri Lanka, Tunisia, and Zambia—are geographically diverse and at different stages of economic and financial development. Since completion of the pilot, the Bank has continued this work, mostly in middle-income countries, carrying out needs assessment in more than 40 countries.

4. The World Bank has developed a program to help low-income countries design reform programs. The program has been implemented in Albania, Bangladesh, and Ghana.

References

Anderson, Phillip. 2006. "Should Public Debt Be Managed by a Separate Agency?" In *Government Debt Management: New Trends and Challenges*, ed. Mike Williams, 79–92. London: Central Banking Publications.

World Bank. 2007a. *Developing the Domestic Government Debt Market: From Diagnostics to Reform Implementation*. Washington, DC: World Bank.

———. 2007b. *Managing Public Debt: From Diagnostics to Reform Implementation*. Washington, DC: World Bank.

———. 2008. *Debt Management Performance Assessment Tool*. Washington, DC: World Bank.

World Bank and IMF (International Monetary Fund). 2001a. *Guidelines for Public Debt Management*. Washington, DC: World Bank and IMF.

———. 2001b. *Developing Government Bond Markets: A Handbook*. Washington, DC: World Bank and IMF.

———. 2003. *Guidelines for Public Debt Management: Accompanying Document and Selected Case Studies*. Washington, DC: World Bank and IMF.

———. 2009. *Managing Public Debt: Formulating Strategies and Strengthening Institutional Capacity*. Washington, DC: World Bank and IMF.

13

Debut Sovereign Bond Issues: Strategic Considerations and Determinants of Characteristics

Udaibir S. Das, Michael G. Papaioannou, and Magdalena Polan

The improved domestic macroeconomic conditions—including debt sustainability and enhancements in debt-management frameworks—ample international financial liquidity, and strong investor appetite for new asset classes and higher-risk instruments that characterized the past decade allowed many debut sovereign bond issuers to tap international financial markets for larger volumes and at lower coupon rates than did those of earlier debut issuers (Klassen 2004). The proceeds of these bonds have been used for a variety of purposes, including funding infrastructure development projects (Bahrain and Sri Lanka); easing budget financing pressures (Ecuador and the Arab Republic Egypt); and financing some of the repayment of existing debt (Gabon, Indonesia, Poland, and Ukraine).

The main benefit of international bond issuance is that it augments domestic savings. When bond issuance is undertaken in the context of a sustainable debt framework, it can significantly enhance a country's available resources and, hence, its prospects for sustainable growth and prosperity. Other benefits include the additional incentive to increase macroeconomic discipline and move forward with structural reforms as a result of the intense scrutiny of the domestic economy by international market participants; establishment of the sovereign's presence in international capital markets, which may also allow local corporates to access international markets in the future; and substantial broadening of the country's investor base (Agenor 2001; Dittmar and Yuan 2007).

International bond issuance also entails risks, however. The key challenge for all sovereign bond issuers is to maintain sound macroeconomic policies, especially fiscal sustainability. Such policies are needed to ensure sovereign creditworthiness, as international investors' confidence in many emerging-market and low-income countries is often fragile and quickly reversible. Other risks include the sovereign's foreign currency risk exposure from an international bond issue, possible refinancing needs (especially in periods of tight international financial liquidity conditions), and adverse terms-of-trade shocks.

To reduce the risk of unfavorable developments related to a debut issue, sovereigns need to make appropriate preparations before accessing the markets. In past successful cases, most countries focused on issuing and using the proceeds of a debut bond without compromising their creditworthiness. Before issuing debut bonds, they conducted appropriate analysis to examine the balance sheet implications within a medium-term macroeconomic framework. Such analysis was conducted to ensure that additional fiscal and debt-related vulnerabilities, as well as adverse effects on international reserve dynamics, did not arise (Steneri 2004). In this process, the sovereign also had to make strategic decisions about the specific elements of a debut issue, including its size, maturity, terms, and currency of denomination. Tactical issues, including the choice of legal and financial advisers, underwriters, and jurisdiction of issuance, were of paramount importance as well.

This chapter addresses critical aspects of the decision process governing sovereign international bond issuance during noncrisis periods. It is organized as follows. The first section presents recent trends in debut bond issuance by emerging-market and low-income countries, including some empirical results on the determinants of debut bond size and costs. The second section analyzes the main advantages and risks of international bond issuance. The third section identifies strategic and tactical considerations issuers need to address before issuing external bonds. The fourth section outlines some common mistakes first-time sovereign issuers make. The last section offers concluding remarks on some additional considerations and identifies future directions for research.

Recent Trends in Sovereign Bond Issuance by Emerging-Market and Low-Income Countries

Twenty-one emerging-market and low-income countries—in Africa, Asia, Europe, and the Middle East—issued international bonds for the first time after a long absence from international markets between late 1996 and 2008 (table 13.1 and figure 13.1).[1] The most recent debut issuers were Ghana ($750 million, September 2007), Sri Lanka ($500 million, October 2007), Gabon ($1 billion, December 2007), and Georgia ($500 million, April 2008). Ghana's issue was the first by a Sub-Saharan African country

Table 13.1 Debut Issues by Emerging-Market and Low-Income Countries, 1996–2008

Country	Date	Size (US$ millions)	Size (percentage of GDP in issue year)	Coupon (percent)	Price (currency of issuance)	Spread (basis points)	Maturity (years)	Composite rating
Bahrain	Jan-03	500	5.15	4.00	99.311	75[a]	5	Not rated
Bulgaria	Mar-02	510	3.27	8.25	93.681	369	13	BBB
Bulgaria	Mar-02	738	4.73	7.50	96.617	275	11	BBB
Chile	Apr-99	500	0.68	6.875	99.864	175	10	A
Costa Rica	Apr-98	200	1.42	8.00	100.000	250	5	BB
Croatia	Dec-96	60	0.06	12.50	98.500	—	2	—
Croatia	Feb-97	300	1.49	7.00	99.917	80	5	BBB
Dominican Republic	Sep-01	500	2.03	9.50	100.000	566	5	B–
Ecuador	Dec-05	650	1.75	9.375	91.692	623	10	B–
Egypt, Arab Rep. of	Jun-01	500	0.55	7.625	99.631	275	5	BB+
Egypt, Arab Rep. of	Jun-01	1,000	1.11	8.75	99.881	335	10	BB+
Egypt, Arab Rep. of	Jul-07	1,000	0.14	8.75	99.504	—	5	—
El Salvador	Aug-99	150	1.20	9.50	92.196	500	7	BB+
Fiji	Sep-06	150	4.74	7.00	99.480	225	5	B+

(continued)

315

Table 13.1 (continued)

Country	Date	Size (US$ millions)	Size (percentage of GDP in issue year)	Coupon (percent)	Price (currency of issuance)	Spread (basis points)	Maturity (years)	Composite rating
Gabon	Dec-07	1,000	9.80	8.2	100.000	426	10	BB–
Georgia	Apr-08	500	3.88	7.50	100.000	474	5	B+
Ghana	Sep-07	750	4.99	8.50	100.000	387	10	B+
Indonesia	Mar-04	1,000	0.39	6.75	99.285	277	10	BB–
Latvia	May-99	159	2.18	6.25	98.750	330	5	BBB
Pakistan	Feb-04	500	0.52	6.75	100.000	370	5	B+
Peru	Feb-02	500	0.88	9.125	97.732	455	10	BB–
Peru[b]	Feb-02	930	1.64	9.125	97.732	455	10	BB–
Qatar	May-99	1,000	8.07	9.50	99.936	395	10	AA–
Seychelles	Sep-06	200	20.67[c]	9.125	99.508	470	5	B (S&P)
Sri Lanka	Oct-07	500	1.55	8.25	100.000	397	5	BB–
Vietnam	Oct-05	750	1.42	6.875	98.223	256	10	BB–

Source: Authors' compilation based on Bloomberg and Dealogic.

Note: The Bulgarian, second Croatian, and Latvian issues were in euros. The first Croatian issue was in kunas, and the third Egyptian issue was in Egyptian pounds. All other issues were in U.S. dollars. — Not available. S&P = Standard & Poor's.

a. Priced over midrate swaps.

b. Issued in exchange for older Brady bonds.

c. The government reopened the bond by issuing an additional $30 million of bonds in 2007.

Figure 13.1 Characteristics of Debut Issues by Emerging-Market and Low-Income Countries, 1996–2008

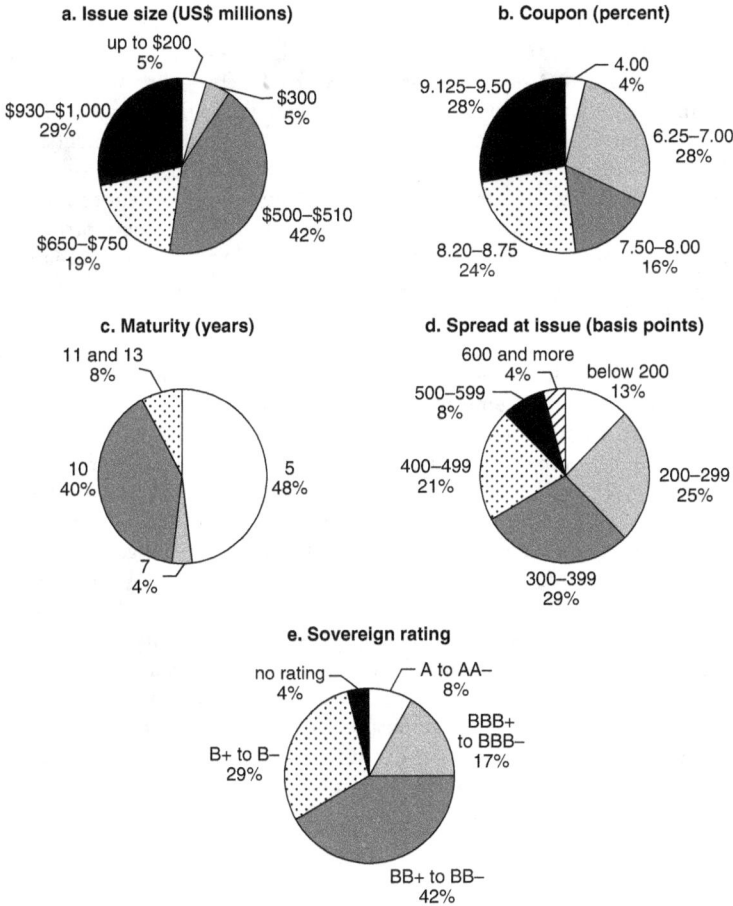

a. Issue size (US$ millions)

- up to $200 5%
- $300 5%
- $500–$510 42%
- $650–$750 19%
- $930–$1,000 29%

b. Coupon (percent)

- 4.00 4%
- 6.25–7.00 28%
- 7.50–8.00 16%
- 8.20–8.75 24%
- 9.125–9.50 28%

c. Maturity (years)

- 11 and 13 8%
- 10 40%
- 7 4%
- 5 48%

d. Spread at issue (basis points)

- 600 and more 4%
- below 200 13%
- 500–599 8%
- 400–499 21%
- 300–399 29%
- 200–299 25%

e. Sovereign rating

- no rating 4%
- A to AA– 8%
- BBB+ to BBB– 17%
- B+ to B– 29%
- BB+ to BB– 42%

Source: Authors' compilation based on Bloomberg and Dealogic.

other than South Africa. In addition, several other emerging-market and low-income countries—including Azerbaijan, Cameroon, Kenya, Mongolia, and Uganda—have expressed their intention to access international capital markets with debut issues.

Recent sovereign debut issues were the latest manifestation of a more general move away from concessional financing toward nonconcessional and nontraditional sources (box 13.1); and also reflected issuers'

Box 13.1 IMF Policy on Nonconcessional External
Debt Financing to HIPCs

The International Monetary Fund (IMF) maintains that concessional
financing is generally the best source for all low-income countries and
imposes limits on nonconcessional external debt—both market and
nonmarket—in the context of IMF arrangements. In the case of nonpro-
gram countries and countries not using policy support instruments, the
IMF provides advice on the appropriate level of concessionality in the
context of its regular surveillance. The objective is to prevent the buildup of external debt to levels that might lead to debt-servicing problems
in the medium term; ensure that restraint on domestic demand is not
threatened by unanticipated recourse to external financing; and reduce
a country's external vulnerability. Nonconcessional borrowing in IMF
programs (and possibly policy support instruments) is usually limited. In
countries with a low risk of debt distress, a declining debt level, improving expenditure management, and increasing debt-management capacity,
such a ban is not critical

For countries that received debt relief, the IMF's policy, reaffirmed by
its Executive Board in the discussion of the debt sustainability framework
for low-income countries post–debt relief, is that grants and concessional
borrowing remain the most appropriate forms of financing. Exceptions
can be considered, on a case-by-case basis, if concessional financing is
not available. Criteria for exceptions include the impact on debt sustainability, the overall strength of the country's policies and institutions, and
the quality of the investment to be financed, as well as that of the overall
public expenditure program. For example, exceptions can be made if the
nonconcessional borrowing supports a financially viable project that otherwise would not be undertaken or if borrowing helps avoid immediate
social hardship. However, exceptions must not affect debt sustainability,
as determined by the Debt Sustainability Framework.

---

increased "borrowing space" as a result of improved debt sustainability.
This trend has been particularly notable in countries that benefited from
debt relief, such as that provided by the Heavily Indebted Poor Countries (HIPC) Initiative. Nonconcessional sources tapped by emerging-
market and low-income countries included the official sector (regional
development banks, bilateral creditors), the private sector (banks),
and bond investors. The trend in non–HIPCs has been the opposite
(figure 13.2).[2]

Most debut issuers accessed international markets under generally
favorable external conditions. There was ample liquidity and strong risk
appetite on the part of international investors, as measured by the VIX

Figure 13.2 Concessional and Nonconcessional Financing in Sub-Saharan Africa, 1990–2004

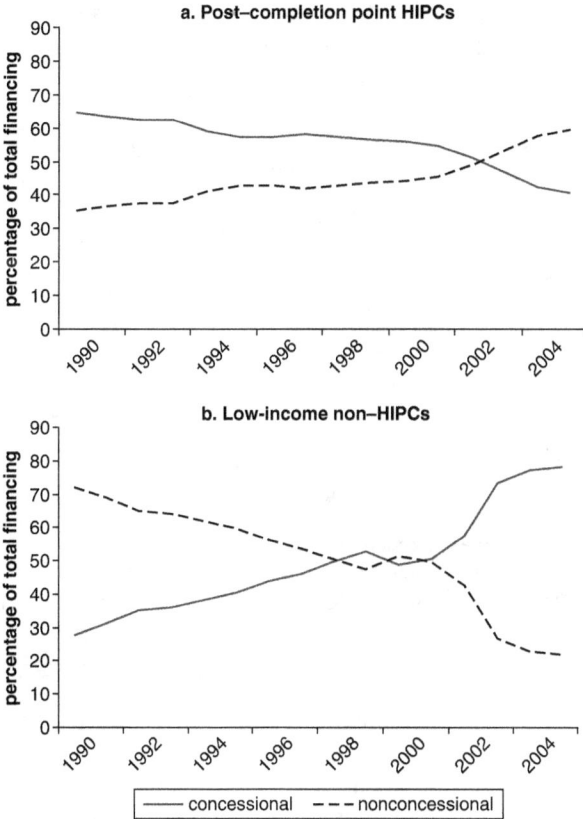

a. Post–completion point HIPCs

b. Low-income non–HIPCs

——— concessional   – – – nonconcessional

Source: World Bank various years.

Note: The figure includes the 18 Sub-Saharan African countries that had reached the HIPC completion point as of December 4, 2007. Loans from major regional development banks, the IMF, and the World Bank are classified as concessional according to each institution's classification. Other concessional flows are as defined by the Development Assistance Committee of the Organisation for Economic Co-operation and Development. HIPCs = heavily indebted poor countries.

Index (figure 13.3).[3] In particular, then-prevailing low interest rates led many investors to search for higher yield and diversification opportunities for their portfolios.[4] Investor demand for new sovereign debt was also high because of the decrease in the supply of sovereign external debt by

Figure 13.3 Spreads and Risk Level of Debut Bonds Issued 1997–2008

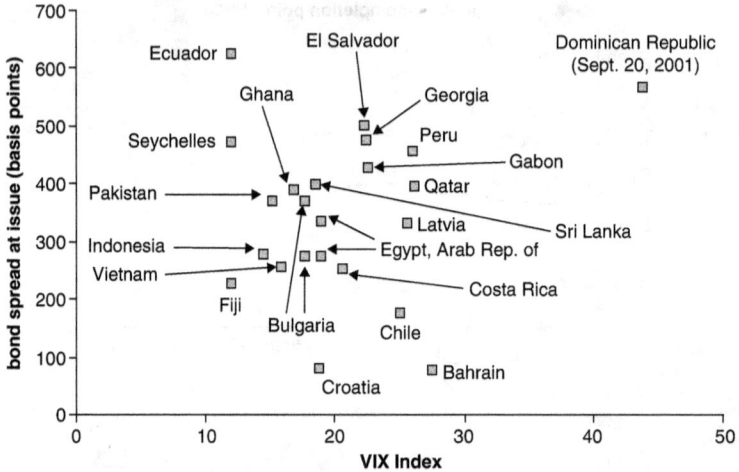

Source: Authors' compilation based on Bloomberg and Dealogic.

Note: The country selection mirrors that in table 13.1. The Dominican Republic can be considered an outlier, because the country issued its debut bond on September 20, 2001, during a period of very high volatility following the September 11 attacks. VIX = volatility index.

many advanced emerging-market countries that were replacing external debt with domestic currency issues. On the real side, the global growth outlook was positive, and prices of commodities—often major exports of debut issuers—were high.

On the domestic front, most of these countries had fulfilled a number of preconditions considered necessary to attract investors to debut international issues. These preconditions, which allowed most of them to obtain the best possible credit ratings well in advance of their planned issues, included the following:

• Building a record of good economic performance over the preceding few years, maintaining a positive medium-term outlook, and demonstrating that their debut issues were part of their debt-management framework and did not adversely affect debt sustainability

• Maintaining robust growth, keeping inflation under control, and ensuring that international reserves were adequate and the external current account deficit was being financed without difficulty

- Adopting prudent fiscal stances and servicing existing public debt without any difficulty (in some countries, public debt had been reduced to sustainable levels following substantial debt-relief packages)
- Making progress in disseminating data and ensuring transparency in the conduct of macroeconomic policies and structural reforms
- Having a political situation that was supportive of the pursuit of appropriate economic policies.

In addition, many emerging-market debut issuers had improved their public debt-management capabilities before accessing international capital markets. In particular, they had strengthened the institutional capacity for debt management by developing a comprehensive risk-management framework, often with the help of external advisers (IMF and World Bank 2007). Within this framework, priority had been given to the hiring and training of personnel at debt-management offices and to investment in information technology. Enhancement of debt-management capabilities reflected realization of the need to carefully evaluate and monitor these bond issues, which can have significant impact on a country's debt indicators and debt sustainability (IMF 2003).

Although the size of the initial bonds varied widely across first-time issuers, other characteristics of debut bonds tended to be similar. The majority of emerging-market sovereigns issued at least $500 million, the minimum size for a bond to be included in a bond index (such as the J.P. Morgan Emerging Markets Bond Index [EMBI] Global) (see table 13.1 and box 13.2). In addition, almost all recent first-time sovereign issuers placed fixed-coupon bullet bonds with maturities of 5–10 years. Most initial bond issues were denominated in U.S. dollars and offered relatively high coupons. They also included collective action clauses and were privately placed or issued as Eurobonds rather than global bonds (Grigorian 2003).[5]

Advantages and Risks of International Issuance

The issuance of sovereign bonds on international markets has advantages for low-income countries, but it also increases risks. This section examines both.

Advantages of International Issuance

External issuance can benefit the issuer in many ways. First, as with other forms of external borrowing, international issuance supplements domestic savings. It can reduce the risk of crowding out domestic private sector borrowers in the domestic market, thereby supporting domestic investment and growth, and it can help develop the local capital market (Feldstein and Horioka 1980). Second, raising financing in capital markets helps

Box 13.2 Determinants of the Size and Cost of Debut
Bond Issues

Using cross-section equations that regress debut bond size and the cost of
issue against a number of macroeconomic and market variables, we find
several commonalities across debut bond issues.

1. *The issue size depends more on market conventions than on mac-*
roeconomic variables.
   Our results indicate that the absolute debut issue size is associated
with international reserves but not with real growth, inflation, the fiscal
deficit, or the country's credit rating. Also, the coefficient of the three-
month LIBOR (London interbank offered rate) (which approximates
global liquidity, or the cost of investors' financing) is negative, but it
is significant only at the 11 percent level. Expressed as a percentage of
GDP, the size of the debut issue does not appear correlated with any
macroeconomic or market variable; this result may depend on the sample
selection, however.
   The size of recent debut bonds seems to be determined more by market
conventions than by strictly economic considerations. As recent experience
has shown, despite differences in their economies and market conditions
at the time of issuance, most countries have issued bonds of $500 million–
$1 billion. Moreover, except in small economies, the issue represented less
than 5 percent of GDP, suggesting a certain upper limit.
   The regression results of the equations used in determining issue size are

$$Size_i = \alpha_0 + \alpha_1 Rating_i + \alpha_2 Reserves_i + \alpha_3 Growth_i + \alpha_4 Inflation_i + \alpha_5 Deficit_i + \varepsilon_i^{size1}$$

and

$$Size_i = \beta_0 + \beta_1 VIX_i + \beta_2 Libor3M_i + \varepsilon_i^{size2},$$

where the subscript i is a country index for the corresponding variable at
the time of issue.

Macroeconomic and Financial Market Determinants of Size of Debut Issue

Variable	US$ millions		Percentage of GDP	
	Coefficient	Probability	Coefficient	Probability
Macroeconomic conditions				
Constant	360	0.2355	0.3283	0.9518
Rating (index)	6.7281	0.7769	0.4136	0.3457
Reserves				
(US$ millions)	0.0155	0.0530	−0.000137	0.1468
Growth (percent)	11.80	0.6896	0.0911	0.8656

Box 13.2 (continued)

Macroeconomic and Financial Market Determinants of Size
of Debut Issue *(continued)*

| | US$ millions | | Percentage of GDP | |
Variable	Coefficient	Probability	Coefficient	Probability
Inflation (percent)	4.4852	0.8710	−0.4147	0.1495
Deficit (percentage of GDP)	24.1234	0.1640	−0.3730	0.2351
R^2		0.28		0.29
Financial market conditions				
Constant	808	0.0044	3.6443	0.4471
VIX Index	−0.8066	0.9282	−0.1342	0.4231
3-month LIBOR (percent)	−60.3945	0.1114	0.7349	0.2883
R^2		0.12		0.095

Source: Authors.

Note: The probability value indicates the probability that the actual value of the parameter is zero. The number of observations is 24. VIX = volatility index.

2. The cost of the issue (spread and coupon) depends on the country's credit rating and on global market conditions.

When regressed against certain macroeconomic and market variables, the spread at issue is strongly and significantly dependent on the credit rating—the lower the rating, the higher the spread—and on the overall EMBI Global spread. A one-notch move in the rating (for example, from BB to BB+) leads to a decline in the debut issue spread of 50 basis points (controlling for the EMBI Global). Similarly, the coupon rate depends on the credit rating and the overall EMBI Global spread: a one-notch move in the rating corresponds to a reduction in the coupon rate of 0.4 percent. This result clearly indicates that to reduce the cost of borrowed funds, debut issuers should wait to access the markets until after they have obtained the highest possible credit rating (see figures 13.4 and 13.5).

The regression results of the equations used in determining the cost of issue are

$$Spread_i = \delta_0 + \delta_1 Rating_i + \delta_2 Reserves_i + \delta_3 EMBIG_i + \varepsilon_i^{spread}$$

and

$$Coupon_i = \phi_0 + \phi_1 Rating_i + \phi_2 Reserves_i + \phi_3 EMBIG_i + \varepsilon_i^{coupon},$$

where the subscript i is a country index for the corresponding variable at the time of issue.

(continued)

Box 13.2 (continued)

Determinants of Cost of Debut Issue

Variable	Dependent variable: Spread at issue (basis points)		Dependent variable: Coupon rate (percent)	
	Coefficient	Probability	Coefficient	Probability
Constant	−396	0.0075	0.4328	1.4164
Rating (index)	49.22	0.0000	0.0010	0.4033
Reserves (US$ millions)	−0.0037	0.0882	0.2318	0.0000344
EMBI Global spread (basis points)	0.2835	0.0013	0.0138	0.0027
R^2	0.70	0.47		

Source: Authors.
Note: The probability value indicates the probability that the actual value of the parameter is zero. EMBI Global = [J.P. Morgan's] Emerging Markets Bond Index Global.

Figure 13.4 Bond Spreads and Composite Credit Ratings of Debut Sovereign Issuers, 1996–2008

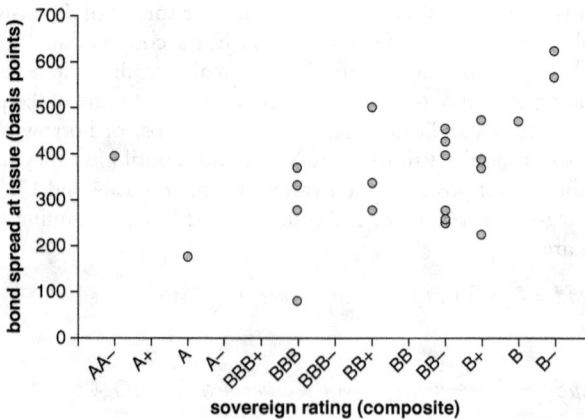

Source: Authors' compilation based on Bloomberg and Dealogic.

Figure 13.5 Spread of Debut Issues over EMBI Global Spread on Day of Issuance

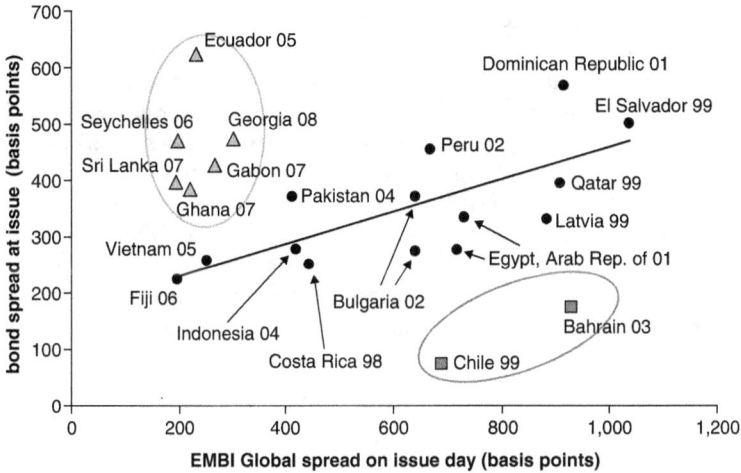

Source: Authors' compilation based on Bloomberg and Dealogic.

Note: The country selection mirrors that in table 13.1 but excludes external issues in domestic currencies (Croatia 1996 and Egypt 2007). The upward-sloping line shows a relatively strong positive relationship between the bond spread at issue and the EMBI Global spread on the issue day. The circled data points in the upper left-hand side represent recent entrants to the international financial markets with possibly inadequate preparation; those in the lower right-hand side represent countries with appropriate preparation, high credit ratings, or both. EMBI Global = [J.P. Morgan's] Emerging Markets Bond Index Global.

governments diversify their sources of capital and reduce their reliance on bank financing from abroad and official financing, often associated with conditionality. Third, in principle, external market financing can help strengthen incentives for maintaining macroeconomic discipline (IMF 2003).

External issuance may also improve the risk profile of the government debt portfolio and help corporate issuers and parastatals access external markets. Especially for first-time issuers that issue in foreign currency, debt raised in international markets usually carries a lower coupon and has a longer maturity than domestic debt.[6] This is the case because of the lower risk (especially foreign exchange and political risk), stronger investor protection, and more reliable depository and settlement systems available to international investors, as well as lower currency and inflation risks of, say, euro- or U.S. dollar–denominated debt.[7] By issuing abroad, a government may also establish an interest rate benchmark, against which corporate issues can be priced. This can facilitate the access of corporate issuers to international markets. The experience of a number of emerging-market countries (for example, Brazil and Nigeria), however, shows that the existence of a sovereign benchmark is neither necessary nor sufficient for successful corporate issuance abroad.[8]

An important but less quantifiable benefit of international issuance is the increase in transparency and closer market monitoring that come with it. The prospectus or the offering memorandum of a bond issue requires disclosure of a substantial amount of data, allowing investors a close look at the current economic situation of the issuing country and its prospects for successfully meeting its debt-service payments. The successful issue of an international bond gives a signal of approval of current and planned economic policies. It may help maintain a steady momentum in maintaining prudent macroeconomic policies and carrying out critical structural reforms, especially because markets subject issuers to close scrutiny and monitor economic developments on a regular basis.

Risks of International Issuance

Notwithstanding its numerous benefits, the issuance of external debt may considerably increase foreign currency risks. As in the case of other forms of external borrowing, external issuance may exacerbate the currency mismatch of government liabilities and revenues, increasing the risk of a depreciation of the currency and leading to high ex post debt-servicing costs. Issuance of external debt may also leave the sovereign more vulnerable to abrupt changes in international financial conditions. Should global financial liquidity decrease, for example, interest rates in the country of placement may change, the exchange rate between the issuing country and that of placement may move substantially, and international investors' perceptions about the performance of the economy may deteriorate.

Negative or inaccurate international market perceptions about a sovereign issuer's economy may develop because of a lack of comprehensive and timely information on the pursuit of appropriate policies, fears of instability stemming from political developments, and unfavorable interpretations of economic or political pronouncements. The issuer may also fall victim to contagion or panic that could affect all emerging-market or low-income countries, regardless of their performance and ability to service debt. These factors can undermine the sovereign's ability to secure access to international capital markets on a sustained basis, significantly increasing refinancing risk.

These risks tend to pose particularly serious problems for small economies or economies subject to swings in their terms of trade. If, for example, a small economy issues a relatively large bullet bond, it may experience difficulty in repaying or refinancing the face value at maturity after adverse changes in its exchange rate or international market conditions. A country subject to swings in its terms of trade—as is often the case for commodity-dependent developing economies—may face similar debt-servicing problems.

Strategic Considerations for Sovereign Debut Issuers

In planning for an initial international bond issue, a country needs to make a number of decisions at various points in the process. Broader and more strategic issues can best be addressed in the context of an asset-liability management framework and a medium-term debt-management strategy. These decisions should be made first, because they affect the servicing and repayment of the bond. Other decisions are primarily tactical and related to the execution of the issue. These issues may be no less important, because they can affect the pricing and potential future liability of management operations associated with the issue. Laying the groundwork early improves the chances of meeting the objectives of the issue, lowers its costs, and helps achieve a more stable investor base (IMF 2003; IMF and World Bank 2007).

Debt Sustainability Aspects of Issuance

Three sets of factors affect the sustainability of debt issued on global capital markets. The first includes the size of the issue and use to which its proceeds are put. The second includes the maturity, repayment structure, and currency of denomination. The third includes asset and liability management implications.

Size of Issue and Use of Proceeds. In principle, the key factor in determining the size of a debut international bond issue is whether it endangers the country's debt sustainability. Issuers must ensure that the size of the first-time issue does not push the net present value of the public-external-debt-to-GDP ratio above the sustainable levels indicated in its Debt Sustainability Framework (DSF).[9] The issue's debt-service payments should be assessed to ensure that they do not create budgetary difficulties. In this regard, to attract investors in a relatively large issue, the debut issuer may need to consider various ways to reduce the risk premium associated with higher repayment risk, including agreement with the IMF on a policy support instrument. Such a step would offer investors reassurance that the country's macroeconomic policies remain sound, thus reducing repayment risk.

Principal consideration must be given to the volume of funds that need to be raised from markets over the next few years and whether that sum should be raised in a single bond issue or multiple bond issues. When proceeds are to be used only slowly, or the initial bond issue is insufficient for its intended purpose, the issuer can reopen the issue in the future or issue one or more bonds later in order to build a yield curve and minimize the negative carrying costs. In this context, it is advisable that the issuer think about raising funds as a dynamic process, not a static event. These matters are often decided within the framework of a comprehensive debt-management strategy.

The issue needs to be large enough to ensure market liquidity, especially if the issuer plans to either establish the issue as a benchmark (minimum $200–$250 million) and avoid the illiquidity premium or include it in a bond index (minimum $500 million). Higher liquidity and participation in an index are both generally attractive to investors and can result in better pricing for the issuer.[10] In determining the size, the issuer should also take into account demand conditions in international capital markets. In particular, favorable demand for bonds from emerging-market or low-income countries and reduced volatility in mature markets can positively affect potential demand for new bonds.

However, a larger issue tends to increase the risk and cost of the issue. It can increase the rollover or repayment risk, because the issuer has to raise more funds before the maturity date under uncertain future market conditions.[11] Issues in excess of immediate financing needs can also add to the government's costs, because funds that are not needed in the near term are held in international reserves that yield less than the interest rate on the new bonds.[12] Moreover, if the size of the initial issue is perceived as too large relative to the issuer's economy—raising questions about future debt sustainability—markets could charge a penalty rate that could cancel out possible liquidity benefits. A very small economy may not be able to issue an international bond of minimum size without drastically increasing its debt-to-GDP ratio, which could adversely affect its debt-related vulnerabilities.

Maturity, Repayment Structure, and Currency of Denomination. Choosing the repayment profile of a bond involves setting both the date of final payment (final maturity) and the amounts of any intermediate principal repayments before that date (IMF 2003). Generally, debut bonds have shorter maturities than outstanding bonds issued by countries that have regularly borrowed externally. Markets prefer a rather short final maturity (five to seven years) because of insufficient knowledge about the country and an unproven repayment history.[13] Debut issuers also often prefer issuing relatively short maturities, because they often expect their credit spreads (country risk premia) to decline before refinancing is needed, as economic performance improves and a record in servicing external debt is established (table 13.2). Issuing shorter-term debt thus reduces the risk of locking in higher interest rates (Mauro, Sussman, and Yafeh 2006). However, depending on the use of proceeds and market conditions, it may be feasible and advantageous for the issuer to consider a longer maturity,

Table 13.2 Credit Ratings and EMBI Global Spreads for Selected Emerging-Market Countries, 2008

| Country | Rating | | Spread (basis points) | | |
	Moody's	Standard & Poor's	Average in August 2008	Average in September 2008	At debut
Argentina	B3	B	668	792	—
Belize	Caa1	B	729	755	—
Brazil	Ba1	BBB-	235	290	—
Bulgaria	Baa3	BBB+	233	259	369 (dollars), 275 (euros)
Chile	A2	A+	173	187	175
China	A1	A+	151	172	—
Colombia	Ba1	BB+	222	271	—
Croatia	Baa3	BBB	—	—	80
Dominican Republic	B2	B+	509	537	566
Ecuador	B3	B-	700	880	623
Egypt, Arab Rep. of	Ba1	BB+	221	279	275 (5 year) and 335 (10 year)
El Salvador	Baa3	BB+	0	0	500
Fiji	Ba1	B	312	342	225
Gabon	Not rated	BB-	394	454	426
Ghana	Not rated	B+	466	558	387
Hungary	A2	BBB+	158	157	—
Indonesia	Ba3	BB-	350	395	277
Latvia	A2	BBB+	0	0	330

(continued)

Table 13.2 (continued)

Country	Rating		Spread (basis points)		
	Moody's	Standard & Poor's	Average in August 2008	Average in September 2008	At debut
Lebanon	B3	B–	477	503	—
Mexico	Baa1	BBB+	199	242	—
Pakistan	B2	B	883	1240	370
Panama	Baa1	BB+	220	262	—
Peru	Baa1	BBB–	195	255	455
Philippines	B1	BB–	263	292	—
Poland	A2	A–	133	136	—
Qatar	Aa2	AA–	0	0	395
Russian Federation	Baa1	BBB+	211	308	—
Serbia	Not rated	BB–	342	453	—
Seychelles	Not rated	SD	—	—	470
South Africa	Baa1	BBB+	235	295	—
Sri Lanka	Not rated	B+	0	0	397
Tunisia	Baa2	BBB	225	273	—
Turkey	Ba3	BB–	307	346	—
Ukraine	B1	B+	551	666	—
Uruguay	B1	BB–	321	366	—
Venezuela, R. B. de	B2	BB–	681	817	—
Vietnam	Ba3	BB	368	388	256
EMBI Global			321	382	

Source: Authors' compilation based on Bloomberg, EMBI Global spreads, and credit ratings as of September 30, 2008.
Note: — Not available.

even if the coupon rate is slightly higher. Especially if the proceeds are used to finance projects, repayment should preferably start only after the projects are expected to begin generating returns.

Another important choice a new issuer has to make is whether to issue a bullet bond or an amortizing bond. Bullet bonds tend to increase the rollover risk for the issuer, because they create a "hump" in the debt-repayment profile. Reopening such a bond at a later date only increases the size of the payment due on the maturity date, and debt-management operations to smoothen debt-service humps (for example, prefunding or debt buybacks and debt exchanges) are often costly and not always easy to conduct.

In particular, small countries and issuers that expect to be going to the markets relatively infrequently should very carefully weigh the advantages of an amortizing structure rather than the more common bullet bond. Amortizing bonds smooth the repayment profile, make reopening easier (the issuer can reopen the bond and avoid a substantial increase in the bullet payment), and decrease information asymmetry between the issuer and investors. Regular payments help investors monitor the issuer and reassure them that the issuer is able to honor the payments. This approach can lead to a more rapid reduction in risk spreads. Amortizing bonds also have shorter durations than bullet bonds, making them less risky and, in turn, less expensive. Moreover, there is no evidence that issuers pay a yield or liquidity premium for issuing amortizing bonds. Callable bonds, an alternative, are generally less preferred, because of the difficulty in pricing them and the relative aversion of investors toward these bonds.

The issuer may also consider including a sinking-fund provision, in which it systematically commits funds that, depending on market conditions, are used to repay part of the outstanding debt. These funds can be used to service debt (if prices are above par) or to buy back outstanding bonds (if prices are below par).[14] In general, it is advisable to issue bonds with simple features and to avoid bonds with complicated enhancements, including various forms of options.

An additional consideration is the currency denomination of the issue. The currency of denomination of a new issue should be decided only after it has been carefully discussed with both the country's financial advisers and the potential investors in predeal roadshows. Generally, first-time bond issues have been denominated in U.S. dollars, because the market for U.S. dollar–denominated fixed-income instruments is the deepest and most liquid. However, the choice can be affected by sovereign asset-liability management factors, such as a currency mismatch between government revenue and liabilities or the currency composition of the country's foreign trade and debt, the use of the proceeds, the investor base targeted, and the issuer's borrowing costs. If the objective is to establish a sovereign benchmark in a foreign currency that would support private issuance, the government also needs to take into account investor preferences and the currency composition of the government balance sheet. In principle, there should be no need to issue in currencies other than the U.S. dollar or the euro, because governments and private issuers can use swaps to manage currency risk.

A few emerging-market countries (for example, Brazil, Colombia, Egypt, and Turkey) have recently issued external debt in their domestic currency for the first time. This type of issuance has developed as investors have been willing to take on more foreign exchange risk in return for the extra yield typically offered by emerging-market countries, especially when the currency appears to be appreciating (as in the case, for example, of Colombia during 2004–06 or Egypt in 2007). The potential benefits to the country include reduced balance sheet risks, which include foreign exchange risk. The disadvantages of "purchasing" such insurance are higher domestic yields and potentially a smaller supply of government debt domestically, which could adversely affect development of the local debt market.

Asset and Liability Management Implications. Before issuance, it is imperative that a country carefully assess the implications of an international bond issue on the assets and liabilities of its balance sheet. The decision to access international capital markets should be consistent with the country's asset and liability management objectives, as well as with its plans to develop domestic capital markets. Assessment of an international bond issue should determine whether the foreign exchange proceeds will augment the country's foreign exchange reserves and warrant sterilization. The assessment should also consider longer-term implications—that is, the requirements that the issuance imposes on the size, volatility, and currency structure of reserves for servicing and repaying the bond.

From the debt-management perspective, an international bond issue is best assessed within a country's debt-strategy framework. Such an assessment entails evaluation of the constraints it places on the country's debt structure, management, and sustainability. In particular, the size and terms of an issue should be consistent with the country's medium-term fiscal policy objectives and debt sustainability. Especially for developing countries, it is imperative that the public debt burden and the risk of external debt distress be kept low by avoiding excessive increases in external debt servicing. The issuer also needs to determine how an international bond issue affects interest rate and currency mismatches in the sovereign's asset and liability structures.

For many emerging-market and low-income countries, an international bond issue may not be the best source of funds to finance planned projects; alternative sources of financing should be considered. In particular, when financing needs for projects are spread over a long time period, repayment options are uncertain, and the servicing of an international bond issue is expensive given the country's current credit rating, the authorities may need to resort to financing that is more flexible and, to the extent possible, less costly. Alternatives include the use of the resources of sovereign wealth or development funds, external concessional financing that is priced significantly below external commercial borrowing, and issuance in domestic capital markets. Some emerging-market and low-income countries may also opt for private sector financing of the intended project by, for example, attracting foreign direct investment or entering into partnerships with the private sector.

Practical and Operational Aspects of Issuance

The execution of the issue and its technical aspects are determined by the issuer's strategic choices, including future issuance plans, preferred investor base, and intended role for the lead managers. These choices should support the main objectives of the debut issue, such as establishing a presence in international markets or creating a sovereign benchmark. At the execution stage, the issuer needs to focus on reaching preferred investors, building demand for the new bond, establishing the legal characteristics of the bond, and selecting lead managers.

Investor Relations and the Building of Demand. The issuer needs to determine the proper balance in targeting potential classes of investors. The choice of target investors will in turn influence the choice of certain characteristics of the debut issue. In particular, the issuer must decide whether to focus on global investors or investors in one region (who may already be familiar with the country) or on institutional or retail investors (including immigrants willing to invest in their home country). It must also decide whether there should be any initial sales to local financial institutions, which often have high demand for high-yielding, low-risk weighted foreign currency assets. These decisions are best made in consultation with financial advisers.

Regardless of the investor base chosen, it is best to take time to build potential demand by properly introducing the country to international investors. One important way to do this is to obtain a rating well before issuance, preferably from two credit rating agencies, and to maintain public Web sites with adequate economic statistics and appropriate data transparency. Demand can also be built through roadshows, which can be conducted before or during the issue. In both predeal and deal roadshows, senior officials from the country attempt to inform potential investors about the country's economic performance, stability, and creditworthiness. Financial advisers, including potential lead managers, can help prepare materials for the credit rating agencies and organize predeal roadshows.

Legal Issues and Documentation. The issuer needs to decide on the legal terms of the new bond, particularly the law that will govern the bond and the market in which it will be issued. The choice depends largely on the target investor group, the currency of denomination, demand of investors, and other strategic objectives of the issuer. An issuer may choose to issue a global bond under New York law, a eurobond under British law, or an exotic bond (such as an Islamic Sukuk bond). It also selects the modalities of the issuance (for example, a public offering or a private placement, in which the bond is sold to a narrow group of qualified institutional investors) (IMF 2003).

The issuer must keep in mind that different types of bonds imply different costs and requirements regarding data disclosure and transparency. Global bonds are the most expensive to issue and require the most disclosure, but they can reach the widest group of investors. For this reason, sovereign bonds are frequently issued under New York law, albeit with some restrictions limiting their sale to retail investors.

The issuer makes decisions about additional legal terms as well. For example, it must determine whether to include collective action clauses and call options and whether to use a trust structure or fiscal agency structure to intermediate between the issuer and investors during the life of the bonds.[15]

Selection of Legal Advisers and Lead Managers. Most debut issuers require extensive legal advice in the early stages of the bond-issuing process. It is therefore crucial that they engage a legal adviser very early in the process. The legal adviser (for example, a law firm) should have a strong presence in the major jurisdictions, such as the United States and the United Kingdom, and a thorough knowledge of the relevant laws (for example, New York or British law). It should also have solid experience in advising on sovereign bond issuance and other aspects of sovereign debt management.

The issuer also needs to hire a lead manager (or managers), usually an investment bank, with international and domestic financial experience. Investors tend to be more comfortable when the lead manager has an established presence in the issuing country or is able to provide research and information about the issuer on a regular basis. Smaller countries may decide to work with only one lead manager.

The choice of a lead manager can be made once the country has decided on its debt and basic issuance strategy. At an earlier stage, first-time issuers may find it beneficial to hire independent financial advisers (who would not earn fees from the sale of the new bonds) to help develop the issuance strategy; obtain credit ratings; and select, through competitive offers, the lead manager.

In selecting the lead manager, issuers should consider both cost and important factors other than cost. These factors include the way in which the lead manager will market the issue (including whether post-issue marketing support will be provided) and whether it will prepare a specific distribution plan of the new bond to investors. Although post-issue support may increase fees, it may decrease the cost of servicing and managing debt in the longer term and prove extremely valuable if markets experience a downturn.[16] The extra fee for these services may be worth spending, because experience shows that a bond issued with relatively low administrative costs may be sold at a discount (that is, priced at a yield higher than the relevant one from the benchmark yield curve), resulting in a higher debt-service cost for the issuer.

With respect to fees, the issuer and lead manager need to decide whether the issuer will pay for the manager's "best efforts" to place the bond and create a market for the instrument, partial underwriting, or full underwriting. Each of these options is progressively more expensive. Paying for full underwriting may turn out to be an unnecessary and costly choice. Under favorable market conditions, paying for best efforts should be sufficient.

Summary

Debut issuers must make many decisions before successfully issuing debt on the international capital marks. These considerations can be summarized as follows:

- *Size of the issue.* Countries should determine the size of the issue by using the Debt Sustainability Analysis framework. In general, sovereigns should not place bonds larger than they require for liquidity purposes, because larger bond issues entail payment of higher "carrying" costs and higher exchange rate and repayment risks.
- *Use of the proceeds.* The intended use of the bond proceeds should be publicly announced, especially if the purpose of the issuance is to fund infrastructure projects or buy back expensive government debt. In general, investors tend to offer better terms for such bond issues.
- *Repayment structure.* The maturity and repayment structure should minimize refinancing and rollover risks. Small countries and infrequent sovereign issuers may consider an amortizing structure rather than a bullet bond to ensure a smoother debt-repayment profile.
- *Currency of denomination of the issue.* In recent years, U.S. dollar–denominated debut bond issues have been placed more easily than bonds issued in other currencies, because U.S. dollar fixed-income markets are the deepest and most liquid.
- *Asset and liability management implications.* Issuers should evaluate the issue in terms of its implications for the sovereign's balance sheet. In general, the issue should be consistent with the country's asset and liability management objectives.
- *Jurisdiction and law.* The issuer needs to select the legal jurisdiction in which the debut bond will be issued. This decision depends mainly on the target investor base and the currency of denomination.
- *Building of demand.* Sovereigns need to pay particular attention to the establishment of strong investor relations and the building of demand well before issuance. Doing so may entail introducing the country to

international investors through predeal roadshows and obtaining a credit rating, preferably from more than one credit rating agency.

- *Selection of financial and legal advisers.* In the design and execution of debut issues, sovereigns need to employ financial and legal advisers from the very beginning. Financial advisers help sovereigns obtain a credit rating and prepare economic and financial reports. Legal advisers help them work out legal issues (for example, the laws that will govern the bond, the inclusion of collective action clauses, and the creation of a trust structure), decide on the type of bond to be issued (for example, global bond versus eurobond), and handle documentation. Reputation and experience should matter more than cost in their selection.

- *Hiring of a lead manager (or managers).* Lead managers should be selected independently of financial advisers. They should primarily help first-time sovereign issuers with the execution of the issue. In principle, lead managers should be hired after decisions have been made regarding the level of debt and the basic issuance strategy. Lead managers should be chosen competitively and on the basis of the services they will offer to the issuer, such as marketing and distribution of the debut bond and commitment to provide market support after issuance.

Pitfalls of First-Time Sovereign Issuance

Many issuers have succeeded in placing their debut bonds in the international markets and achieving their goals in recent years. Some have encountered significant difficulties and may not have fully attained their objectives. As a result of inadequate preparation or mistakes in execution, some debut issuers did not choose an efficient balance between the costs and benefits of the issue, worsened their debt profiles, were unable to establish a benchmark, or could not stimulate corporate issuance. To avoid common mistakes, prospective issuers must learn from the experience of others.

The three most common mistakes have included the following:

- *The size of the issue was too large relative to the intended use of the proceeds.* The issues were large enough to support liquidity but larger than they needed to be to meet the sovereign's near-term needs (see box 13.2). This resulted in high carrying costs, because the unused portion of the funds produced returns that were lower than their costs (for example, they were invested in external government bonds with yields lower than those of the new bond). Several issues have also been very large in comparison with the size of the economy, sometimes representing more than 20 percent of a country's GDP, resulting in high levels of risk and cost for the country, including risks to debt sustainability.

- *Bullet bonds were issued.* In small economies, the repayment and rollover risks were magnified by the bullet structure of bonds. These risks could have been reduced by using an amortizing bond.
- *Preparations were inadequate.* A number of first-time issuers could have achieved better pricing by preparing more thoroughly and providing more precise information on the intended use of the proceeds. A few issuers have come to market without strong fundamentals, during periods of unfavorable market conditions, or without predeal roadshows—in some cases, without any roadshows—shortly after obtaining a credit rating. This resulted in higher-cost funds than could have been achieved through more careful fulfillment of economic preconditions for debut issuance, concerted efforts to obtain a better rating, and more patient building of investor demand (figures 13.4 and 13.5).[17] A number of new issues have specified only "general governmental use" as the intended use of proceeds, when in fact proceeds were used to pay down expensive debt or to fund investment projects or other expenses that did not increase the issuer's ability to repay debt. This possibly led to underpricing of the debut bonds.[18]

In several cases, the inappropriate choice of lead manager and the failure to solicit independent opinion raised the cost of the issue and led to poor initial pricing, high volatility, and low liquidity in the secondary market. In a few countries, the lead manager was not selected through a competitive process. This resulted in higher fees than necessary, prevented the government from getting the benefit of a wider set of opinions, and perhaps led to higher debt-service costs. Selecting a lead manager on the basis of fees only and issuing "on the cheap" led to poor initial pricing and additional volatility in and a lower volume of secondary trading in some cases, hindering establishment of a sovereign benchmark.[19]

To avoid these problems, debut issuers should seek independent opinions before accessing the markets. In the early stages of preparation, issuers have benefited from advice on maintaining debt sustainability, formulating a debt strategy, and creating capacity to manage new types of risks associated with the issuance of international bonds. Most first-time issuers who have sought the opinion of independent financial advisers or international financial institutions in addition to their lead managers have enjoyed better-structured bonds and better deal execution.

Concluding Remarks

Countries contemplating debut issues need to carefully consider the benefits and risks associated with doing so and to prepare well ahead of the issuance before attempting to raise funds in international markets. To maximize the benefits and minimize the risks of an international bond issue, governments should consider a number of factors, ranging from broad macroeconomic considerations to narrow market-access mechanics. In particular, governments need to plan their actions within a timeframe that extends beyond the date of first-time market access, contemplating a bond issue within a medium-term debt sustainability framework. Issuers should view market access as a multifaceted process, not a single event. Doing so is especially important for low-income countries, given the small size of their economies and possibly less sophisticated fiscal and debt-management capacity.

If the debut issuer wants to establish its presence in international markets or to create a sovereign benchmark, it is advisable that it opt for issuing bonds with characteristics that ensure a large investor base, liquidity in the secondary market, and if possible, inclusion in at least one of the major bond indexes used by investors and asset managers. This can be achieved if the country issues a standard instrument (a global bond or eurobond), without enhancements or complex options, targeted to a wide range of institutional investors. To attract investors, the debut issuer should also specify the use of the proceeds and provide returns that are sufficiently high to guarantee timely service of the bond. To ensure a low coupon rate, the issuer should try to enter the international financial markets with the best possible credit rating and at periods of high international liquidity. To improve liquidity in the secondary markets, the issuer should contract its lead managers to provide post-issue support.

If economic conditions in emerging-market and low-income countries continue to improve and if the global liquidity squeeze and reduced appetite for high-yield assets that developed in the second half of 2007 give way to more favorable investment conditions, then these countries will become increasingly attractive options for international investors. Under favorable conditions, many countries in Africa, Asia, and Europe—including Azerbaijan, Belarus, Botswana, Georgia, Kenya, Mongolia, Romania, and Zambia—are expected to become debut issuers in international capital markets in the next few years.

If international investors' risk aversion continues to grow, however, sovereign bond issuers with unfamiliar profiles or lower credit ratings will likely face increased scrutiny and possibly less-attractive issuance terms (smaller sizes and higher spreads, if not a total inability to access the markets). In such circumstances, prospective first-time sovereign bond issuers will need to persevere with prudent macroeconomic financial policies and necessary preparations, such as setting up appropriate debt-management systems, in order to raise the international community's confidence in their economies and increase the likelihood of quick access to international capital markets when international financial conditions improve.

Notes

Udaibir S. Das, Michael G. Papaioannou, and Magdalena Polan are staff members of the International Monetary Fund (IMF). The views expressed in this chapter are those of the authors and do not necessarily reflect the views of national authorities, the IMF, or IMF Executive Directors. This chapter is an extended version of Das, Papaioannou, and Polan (2008).

1. The countries are Bahrain, Bulgaria, the Czech Republic, the Arab Republic of Egypt, Gabon, Georgia, Ghana, Hungary, Indonesia, Kazakhstan, Poland, Sri Lanka, Vietnam, and Ukraine.

2. African countries are used because 18 of the 22 post–completion point HIPCs over the 1990–2004 period were in Sub-Saharan Africa. These countries had several financing options, including nontraditional creditors with concessional (sometimes not full concessional) finance, project financing, securitized financing of some infrastructure, public-private partnerships, and sovereign issues.

3. Studies by the IMF (2004a, 2004b) suggest that the VIX Index is strongly correlated with emerging-market spreads, with lower indexes (higher risk appetite) correlated with lower spreads.

4. The correlation between debt markets in the more advanced emerging-market countries and debt markets in mature economies has increased substantially over the past years. Debut issuers and "frontier" markets are relatively disconnected from other markets, offering a chance for greater diversification of investors' portfolios.

5. Collective action clauses in bond contracts consist of the majority enforcement provisions and the majority restructuring provision. The majority enforcement provisions (including acceleration and deacceleration clauses) are designed to limit the ability of a minority of bondholders to disrupt the restructuring process by enforcing their claims after a default but before a restructuring agreement. The majority restructuring provision allows a qualified majority of bondholders of an issuance to bind all holders of that issuance to the financial terms of a restructuring, either before or after a default.

6. Some emerging-market sovereign issuers cannot issue long-term domestic bonds (for example, beyond a 10-year maturity) or pay a high premium on their domestic debt (even correcting for expected exchange rate appreciation).

7. Stronger investor protection stems largely from the fact that external bonds are issued under foreign law (for instance, New York, British, or Luxembourg law). This approach ensures that the issuing government cannot, for example, forcibly restructure the bond or declare it illegal or change the bond contract without the consent of investors without legal consequences.

8. Factors other than the existence of a sovereign benchmark that may also be important include legal and tax frameworks, market conditions (for example, international demand for corporate debt), and domestic liquidity. The opposite may also hold true: that is, sovereign international bond issuance may follow international private sector bond issuance.

9. The DSF includes indicative thresholds for various debt ratios, which are used in the debt sustainability analysis of low-income countries. There are no debt thresholds for assessing the sustainability of middle-income countries. Several academic studies consider public external debt sustainable if the ratio of total general government external debt to GDP is below a certain level. For emerging-market and developing countries, some studies set this threshold at 50 percent for countries without debt crises and at 15–30 percent for countries in which debt crises emerge frequently (Reinhart, Rogoff, and Savastano 2003). Other studies maintain a limit of 40 percent (Manasse, Roubini, and Schimmelpfenning 2003).

10. Because institutional investors usually track indexes, participation in the index guarantees interest and long-term holdings by this group of investors. Investors who do not track the index may also become interested in a debut issue if they know that the bond will be held by a stable group of investors.

11. This presupposes that reopening(s) of a bond issue will not be frequent enough to cause similar rollover risks.

12. This is referred to as "negative carry." Some issuers may prefer to pay a negative carry if funding costs may be higher in the future. In this case, the negative carry is viewed as an up-front insurance premium that the issuer is willing to pay against future higher borrowing costs or the risk of not being able to easily access external markets.

13. Ghana's debut issue of a 10-year bond in 2007 indicates that investors can be interested in even longer maturities, especially when the supply of external sovereign debt is relatively low and demand for debt from emerging-market or low-income countries is high.

14. Countries can also issue bullet bonds and simultaneously commit to set aside resources annually in a sinking fund to meet the principal repayment. This structure is analytically equivalent to an amortizing bond.

15. Under a trust structure, the right of individual bondholders to initiate litigation is effectively delegated to the trustee, who is required to act only if, among other things, it is requested to do so by bondholders holding a requisite percentage of outstanding principal. The terms of the trust deed also ensure that the proceeds of any litigation are distributed by the trustee on a pro rata basis among all bondholders. In contrast, under a fiscal agency structure, individual bondholders have the right to initiate legal proceedings against the issuer following a default and to keep any recoveries from such proceedings.

16. If, for example, the lead manager maintains post-issue support by providing market-making services or enhancing liquidity, it could be easier for the issuer to engage in debt buybacks or swaps at a later date.

17. Figure 13.4 indicates that, although spreads correspond to different issuance periods, bond spreads at issue tend to increase with the deterioration of the issuer's credit rating. This is consistent with the literature, which finds that credit ratings—used as proxies for macroeconomic fundamentals and credit quality—are significant and strong determinants of spreads (IMF 2004a, 2004b).

18. Lack of specific knowledge by creditors about the use of funds often leads to an adverse selection premium on an issue.

19. In some cases (Brazil, for example), corporate issuers accessed the markets ahead of the sovereign. In other countries, corporate issuance did not increase following the issuance of a benchmark bond.

References

Agenor, Pierre-Richard. 2001. "Benefits and Costs of International Financial Integration: Theory and Facts." Working Paper in International Economics, Trade and Capital Flows 2699, World Bank, Washington, DC.

Das, Udaibir S., Michael G. Papaioannou, and Magdalena Polan. 2008. "Strategic Considerations for First-Time Sovereign Bond Issuers." IMF Working Paper 08/261, International Monetary Fund, Washington, DC.

Dittmar, Robert F., and Kathy Yuan. 2007. "Do Sovereign Bonds Benefit Corporate Bonds in Emerging Markets?" Working Paper, University of Michigan, Stephen M. Ross School of Business, Ann Arbor.

Feldstein, Martin, and Charles Horioka. 1980. "Domestic Saving and International Capital Flows." *Economic Journal* 90 (358): 314–29.

Grigorian, David. 2003. "On the Determinants of First-Time Sovereign Bond Issues." IMF Working Paper 03/184, International Monetary Fund, Washington, DC.

IMF (International Monetary Fund). 2003. *Access to International Capital Markets for First-Time Sovereign Issuers: Country Cases.* November 17. Washington, DC: IMF.

——— 2004a. *Global Financial Stability Report.* April. Washington, DC: IMF.

——— 2004b. *Global Financial Stability Report.* September. Washington, DC: IMF.

IMF (International Monetary Fund) and World Bank. 2007. *Strengthening Debt Management Practices: Lessons from Country Experiences and Issues Going Forward.* March. Washington, DC: IMF and World Bank.

Klassen, S. 2004. "Asian Government Issuance 2004." January 15. JPMorgan.

Manasse, Paolo, Nouriel Roubini, and Axel Schimmelpfenning. 2003. "Predicting Sovereign Debt Crises." IMF Working Paper 03/221, International Monetary Fund, Washington, DC.

Mauro, Paolo, Nathan Sussman, and Yishay Yafeh. 2006. *Emerging Markets and Financial Globalization: Sovereign Bond Spreads in 1870–1913 and Today.* Oxford, U.K.: Oxford University Press.

Reinhart, Carmen M., Kenneth S. Rogoff, and Miguel A. Savastano. 2003. "Debt Intolerance." *Brookings Papers on Economic Activity* 1: 1–74.

Steneri, Carlos. 2004. "Uruguay Debt Reprofiling: Lessons from Experience." *Georgetown Journal of International Law* 35 (July 1): 795.

World Bank. Various years. *Global Development Finance.* Washington, DC: World Bank.

14

Subnational Debt Management by Low-Income Countries in Transition to Market Access

Lili Liu, Abha Prasad, Francis Rowe, and Signe Zeikate

Subnational debt management is emerging as an important public policy agenda for low-income countries, for several reasons.[1] First, the financial landscape facing these countries has been undergoing a significant change since the start of the millennium. Macroeconomic fundamentals had improved up to mid-2008, reflecting the reduction in heavy public sector indebtedness, the increase in foreign exchange reserves, and more balanced external accounts. In tandem, new creditors and new sources of financing, particularly the rise of domestic and international nonconcessional financing, expanded opportunities for low-income countries to access market financing at both the national and the subnational level. Reflective of this trend, an increasing number of low-income countries are being rated by international rating agencies. These developments provide opportunities for low-income countries to become market-access countries in the medium to long term.[2]

These positive developments in macroeconomic fundamentals and new sources of financing are being challenged by the ongoing global financial crisis, which underscores the importance of sound regulatory frameworks and strategies for managing subnational borrowing and debt. The uncertain macroeconomic environment requires a careful approach to expanding subnational borrowing, because deteriorating macroeconomic fundamentals could negatively affect the debt structure of subnational governments, which in turn could exacerbate macroeconomic fundamentals. Moreover, slower economic growth and revenue shortfalls of national governments are likely to reduce fiscal transfers from national to subnational governments. This is a cause for concern, because fiscal transfers account for the majority share of subnational finance in many developing countries, a situation that is likely to be exacerbated by shortfalls in subnational governments' own-source revenues.[3] States and municipalities in the United States are struggling financially, and there are signs of stress threatening the fiscal and debt sustainability of subnational governments in a growing number of developing countries.

Second, many low-income countries, including Ethiopia, Nigeria, Tanzania, and others, are continuing to decentralize. As the experiences in middle-income countries suggest, decentralization significantly increases the share of subnational finance in the consolidated public finances. With sovereign access to markets, subnational governments are likely to push for access as well, particularly given growing regional and subnational political power, a driving force behind decentralization. Such access needs to be managed carefully, with proper regulatory frameworks, prudent debt-management strategies, and strengthened fiscal-management capacity. Moreover, off-budget activities (special-purpose vehicles and public utility companies) are already a problem in many low-income countries. The off-budget borrowing by the companies affiliated with subnational governments poses a special risk.

Although it offers numerous benefits, unregulated subnational borrowing entails risks that threaten service delivery and the stability of a country's macroeconomic and financial systems. Widespread financial distress at the subnational level in several major middle-income countries, including newly decentralizing countries, has led to profound legal and institutional reforms for sound subnational debt management.

This chapter makes recommendations on the legal, regulatory, and institutional frameworks that should be in place before subnational governments access market-based borrowing.[4] It is organized as follows. The first section describes the changing financial landscape and the decentralization trend in low-income countries and examines how these two broad developments, together with the current uncertain macroeconomic environment, call for prudent management of subnational debt. The second section, drawing from Liu and Waibel (2008a, 2008b), shows the benefits and risks of subnational borrowing and discusses ways to enforce borrowing discipline given the moral hazard problem posed by potential bailouts from the national government. The third section discusses how subnational debt management differs from sovereign borrowing and highlights the choices and constraints facing subnational governments as they seek to achieve debt sustainability. The last section summarizes the chapter's main conclusions and proposes areas for future research.

The Changing Financial Landscape and Decentralization in Low-Income Countries

Two important trends are increasing the need for better management of debt. This section describes both the changing financial landscape in low-income countries and the trend toward decentralizing both authority and responsibility for service provision.

The Changing Financial Landscape in Low-Income Countries

The financial landscape facing low-income countries has been undergoing a significant change since the start of the millennium. Until mid-2008, macroeconomic fundamentals had strengthened, with marked improvements in debt dynamics, significant reductions in public indebtedness, and improvement in countries' external positions, as reflected by increased foreign exchange reserves and improvements in the balance of payments. Starting in the mid-1990s, the aggregate public debt level in low-income countries fell across all regions except South Asia, which recorded a modest increase over the period.

The downward trend can be attributed to several factors. Among the most significant are debt-relief initiatives, particularly the Heavily Indebted Poor Countries (HIPC) Initiative and the Multilateral Debt Relief Initiative (MDRI)[5] (figure 14.1).

Figure 14.1 External Debt of and Debt Relief to Low- and Middle-Income Countries, 1990–2007

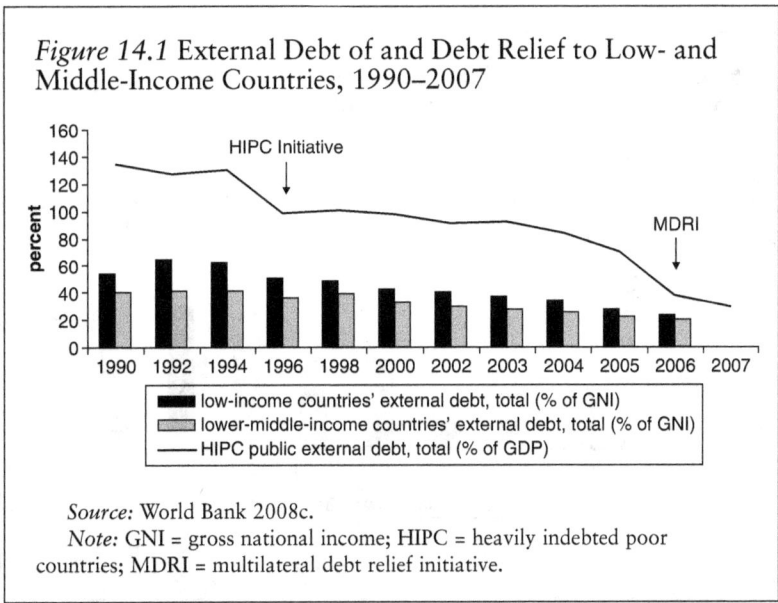

Source: World Bank 2008c.
Note: GNI = gross national income; HIPC = heavily indebted poor countries; MDRI = multilateral debt relief initiative.

Stronger macroeconomic outcomes—especially the lower external debt-burden indicators and, until recently, the favorable global financial environment—led to the emergence of new creditors, new sources of financing, and expanded opportunities for accessing market financing. At the beginning of this decade, official development assistance (ODA) flows were larger than private external flows. Private external flows reached about the same level as ODA flows in 2004 (figure 14.2). In 2007, private capital flows were about twice as large as ODA flows. In addition, some low-income countries tapped international capital markets, and an increasing number of low-income countries were rated by Moody's and Standard & Poor's (figure 14.3).

Some of these positive developments have now been put on hold, as foreign investors retrench from low- and middle-income countries during the global financial crisis. Experience from advanced and middle-income countries shows that the risks from unregulated subnational borrowing are exacerbated during periods of macroeconomic uncertainty. For low-income countries, the timing is right to undertake reforms and prepare the sound regulatory frameworks and strategies for managing subnational borrowing and debt, which are only likely to grow in importance.

Decentralization and Subnational Borrowing in Low-Income Countries

The ongoing decentralization in low-income countries is an important driver behind the emerging importance of subnational debt management.

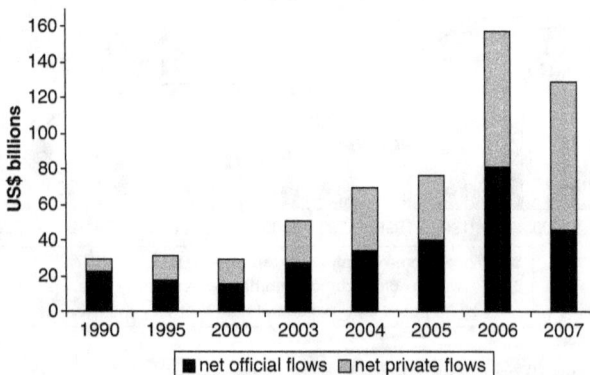

Figure 14.2 Net Official and Private Capital Flows to Low-Income Countries, 1990–2007

Source: World Bank 2008c.

Figure 14.3 Number of Low-Income Countries Rated by
Moody's and Standard & Poor's, 1998–2007

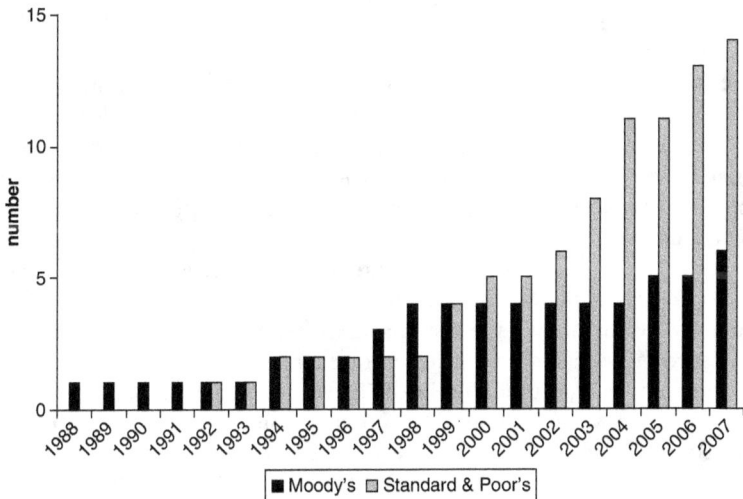

Source: Authors' estimates.

In a number of low-income countries, subnational governments have either
issued bonds or used off-budget debt financing (examples include Nigeria,
Vietnam, and Zimbabwe) or started to explore the potential to access the
market (examples include Ethiopia, Pakistan, and Uganda).[6] Even without
accessing the market explicitly, central governments have onlent to subnational governments. Subnational governments have also accessed domestic
bank financing through arrangements with or approval from the central
government. Regardless of the sources of financing, as long as subnational
governments have accumulated debt obligations, the management of such
debt obligations—be it implicit, explicit, or contingent—ought to become
a part of the framework for consolidated public debt management.[7]

As in many middle-income countries, decentralization in low-income
countries gathered momentum in the 1990s. The trend is continuing.
Ethiopia, Ghana, Mali, Namibia, Nigeria, Senegal, and Uganda have constitutions that are explicitly prodecentralization and formally recognize
the existence of local governments. In these countries, the devolution of
power was often viewed as a natural process of dispersing political power
more widely or as a more effective way of delivering services.[8]

The early wave of decentralization, in the 1990s, focused largely on
political decentralization. Since the start of this decade, low-income countries have been undergoing a second wave of decentralization focusing

on fiscal decentralization. A World Bank study (2003) of 30 Sub-Saharan African countries finds that about 30 percent of these countries had a high degree of political decentralization, with another 20 percent moderately decentralized.[9] The same study finds that only four Sub-Saharan African countries scored high on the level of administrative and fiscal decentralization (table 14.1).[10]

Studies of Ethiopia, Pakistan, and low-income countries in East Asia also find limited fiscal and administrative autonomy.[11] Fiscal decentralization since the start of the decade has focused on increasing subnational financial autonomy, widening the own-source revenue base, and increasing performance-oriented grants to strengthen local accountability (see World Bank 2008d).

As a result of these developments, the share of subnational finance in consolidated public finance has increased. Although comprehensive data are not available, the rising share of subnational finance has been observed in a range of countries.[12] For example, the share of subnational government budget spending in the consolidated public budget doubled in Nigeria between 1999 and 2005, rising from 23 percent to 46 percent (World Bank 2007). In Uganda, this share increased nearly threefold during the same period (Steffensen 2006). In Vietnam, the share doubled between 1992 and 2002, to 48 percent of the consolidated public budget (World Bank 2005b). Across a range of selected countries, the median

Table 14.1 Decentralization in Selected Sub-Saharan African Countries

Administrative decentralization	Fiscal decentralization		
	High	*Moderate*	*Low*
High	Kenya, Nigeria, Uganda, Zimbabwe	Ghana, Rwanda, Tanzania	
Moderate	Côte d'Ivoire	Democratic Republic of Congo, Ethiopia, Guinea, Senegal	Angola, Benin, Burkina Faso, Eritrea, Madagascar, Mali, Mozambique, Namibia, Zambia
Low		Burundi, Cameroon, Malawi	Central African Republic, Chad, Niger, Sierra Leone

Source: World Bank 2003.

value of subnationals' expenditures in the consolidated public budget is about one-third (figure 14.4).

A main explanation for the rising share of subnational finance in the consolidated public finance across developing countries is the increasing decentralization of key social and infrastructure services. Together with the private sector, subnational governments are the main investors in infrastructure in an increasing number of middle-income countries (figure 14.5).

This pattern is similar to that in more advanced countries, such as the countries of the European Union, where subnational governments contribute two-thirds of gross national capital formation.[13] Although on average national governments still dominate infrastructure provision in low-income countries,[14] local governments have started to play a more influential role in infrastructure decisions.

As subnational governments take on more infrastructure investment responsibilities, they seek out capital markets for infrastructure financing, a trend similar to that observed in developed countries and middle-income countries. Subnational governments in Bolivia, Nigeria, and Vietnam have already issued bonds or contracted loans for subnational capital projects.

Figure 14.4 Subnational Government Expenditure in Selected Low- and Middle-Income Countries, Various Years
(percentage of total national government expenditure)

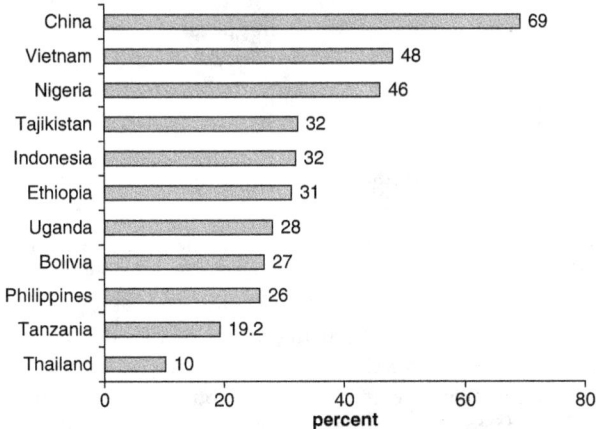

Source: Authors' compilation based on data from IDB 2000, Steffensen and Tideman 2004, Steffensen 2006, Freinkman 2007, and World Bank 2007.

Note: Data for the Philippines, Tajikistan, and Thailand are for 2001; data for China, Indonesia, and Vietnam are for 2002; data for Nigeria and Uganda are for 2005.

Figure 14.5 Share of Total Annual Investment in
Infrastructure by Investing Entity in Selected
Middle-Income Countries

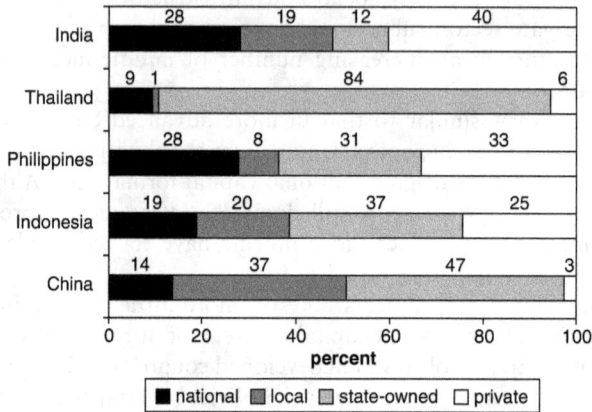

Source: Asian Development Bank 2007.
Note: Data are for the most recent year available for each country, and they are rounded up.

For example, the municipality of La Paz in Bolivia issued subnational bonds in foreign currency at the end of the 1990s. The bond issuance did not carry an explicit central government guarantee, but it was secured by a revenue stream from a portion of property and automotive taxes. These bonds were earmarked for infrastructure improvements; the municipality even specified in its public offer the cost breakdown for the eight public infrastructure projects (IDB 2000).

State governments in Nigeria are allowed to issue debt in domestic markets by contracting loans and issuing securities and are allowed to provide guarantees.[15] Provincial governments in Vietnam have also borrowed domestically by issuing bonds and contracting loans.[16] By the end of 2006, 3 of 64 provinces (Ho Chi Minh City, Hanoi, and Dong Nai) had issued municipal bonds, together mobilizing about $614 million (7 percent of total public bond issues in Vietnam) (IFC 2007). The level of subnational debt in Vietnam has been relatively modest, but given the serious deficiencies in and needs for infrastructure investment at the subnational level across the country, the government expects this level of debt to increase (World Bank 2005b).

In sum, the changing financial landscape and the process of decentralization in low-income countries have brought into sharp focus the management of subnational borrowing and debt. Lessons from the experience of middle-income countries are valuable in understanding the causes of subnational debt crises. One important lesson is that unregulated subnational borrowing is particularly risky in an uncertain macroeconomic environment. Open market access by subnational borrowers, especially in speculative and unregulated financial markets, can outpace the development of an effective regulatory framework. Important lessons can also be learned from the ways in which middle-income countries responded to the subnational debt crisis in the 1990s by developing regulatory and institutional frameworks. The purpose of these regulatory frameworks was not to limit or prohibit subnational access to the capital market but to enhance subnational fiscal discipline, ensure debt sustainability, reduce the cost of borrowing, and promote sustainable infrastructure finance.

Regulatory Frameworks for Subnational Borrowing

Access to financial markets offers subnational governments an opportunity to finance their infrastructure and promote fiscal transparency. Such benefits can be realized, however, only when the risks of subnational borrowing are managed through regulatory frameworks. Such frameworks help mitigate the risks of default, establish credibility about the subsovereign government among market participants, and help reduce borrowing costs.

Benefits and Risks of Subnational Borrowing

Borrowing by subnational governments expands the financial resources needed to finance infrastructure. Pressing demands for infrastructure—particularly urban infrastructure—will continue to rise as cities strive to be successful conduits for innovation and growth while absorbing massive influxes of people from rural areas. The unprecedented scale of urbanization in developing countries requires large-scale infrastructure financing. Many infrastructure investment responsibilities have been decentralized to subnational governments.[17]

Borrowing enables local government to capture the benefits of major capital investments immediately, rather than having to wait until sufficient savings from current income can be accumulated to finance them. Financing infrastructure through debt instruments allows borrowers to match the maturity of the debt with the economic life of the assets the debt is financing. Because infrastructure investment benefits future generations, they too should bear their cost. Matching asset life to maturity is sound public policy, because these infrastructure services can be paid for by the beneficiaries of the services.[18]

Given the limited fiscal resources from own-revenues and fiscal transfers from the national government, subnational governments in middle-income countries are increasingly tapping the financial market to finance infrastructure. With the long-term objective of developing competitive financial markets in developing countries, a subnational credit market with numerous buyers and sellers and financial options can encourage competition and reduce borrowing costs.[19] Over time, prime-rated subnational bond issues may become the dominant points of reference for establishing a yield curve for other subnational issuers. Developing a diversified and competitive subnational credit market has been a policy objective since the ending of the apartheid regime in South Africa, for example (see Liu and Waibel 2008b).

Notwithstanding these benefits, there are substantial risks to subnational borrowing in the absence of an effective regulatory framework. Low-income countries can benefit from lessons from recent subnational debt crises in middle-income countries such as Argentina, Brazil, Mexico, and the Russian Federation. Although India, for instance, has not yet experienced explicit and systemic subnational insolvency,[20] the subnational fiscal stresses and contingent liabilities Indian states faced in the late 1990s can also be instructive.[21] Understanding the root causes of fiscal stress and debt crisis helps policy makers develop regulatory frameworks that directly address these causes.

Subnational borrowing behavior is strongly influenced by the design of the intergovernmental fiscal system and the structure of financial markets. Soft budget constraints, a key aspect of fiscal incentives, allow subnational governments to live beyond their means, weakening competitive incentives and fostering corruption and rent-seeking.[22] According to Webb (2004), subnational debt markets have three important agency problems: subnational borrowers as agents have an incentive not to repay their lenders as principals if they anticipate bailouts; subnational borrowers have an incentive not to reveal certain characteristics about themselves to lenders, resulting in adverse selection;[23] and although they are entrusted to maintain the nation's payment system and creditworthiness, banks often abuse this trust by lending to uncreditworthy subnational governments with the expectation of bailouts by the national government in case of trouble. The incidence of these agency problems varies considerably depending on the structure of each country's subnational debt market.

These risks apply not only to the borrowing of subnational governments and their quasi-fiscal entities from the financial market but also to onlending from the central government to subnational governments. Regardless of the sources of borrowing, a soft budget constraint undermines the sustainability of subnational fiscal policy and leads to contingent liabilities for the central government.

Although imbalances between expenditures and revenues may cause fiscal stress, the regulatory framework for borrowing profoundly affects the debt sustainability of subnational governments, because accumulation of fiscal deficits is feasible only if they are financed.[24] Unregulated subnational borrowing grew rapidly in countries such as Hungary and

Russia in the 1990s, contributing to subnational debt overhang. Borrowing by subnational governments in these countries was also facilitated by decentralization, which granted substantial autonomy in debt financing to subnational governments but failed to impose hard budget constraints. In Zimbabwe, for example, poorly regulated subnational borrowing resulted in accumulated liabilities for the central government and significant financial losses for investors (White and Glasser 2004). Unregulated borrowing is particularly risky in an uncertain macroeconomic environment, as illustrated by the subnational debt crises in Russia.

The fiscal deficit itself may not be a problem if borrowing finances capital investment and economic growth, but borrowing to finance operating deficits leads to an unsustainable debt path.[25] A major cause of subnational debt crisis in Hungary, India, Russia, and other countries was the use of borrowing to finance operating deficits.[26] In India much of the growth in fiscal deficits of states in the late 1990s was driven by borrowing to finance revenue deficits. At the height of the crisis, for example, in some states more than 70 percent of new borrowing was used to refinance existing debt.[27]

Furthermore, like national debt profiles, subnational debt profiles can experience rollover risks, which are exacerbated by macroeconomic and financial shocks. Before the macroeconomic crisis in Mexico in the mid-1990s and in Russia in the late 1990s, for example, subnational governments there had risky debt profiles—short maturities, high debt-service ratios, and variable interest rates. The macroeconomic crisis exposed the vulnerability of the subnational governments' fiscal positions and triggered widespread subnational debt crises.[28]

Finally, several sources of implicit borrowing by subnational governments can contribute to the deterioration of fiscal position and insolvency. Subnational governments can circumvent borrowing limitations imposed by the national government through a variety of channels, such as establishing off-budget companies; providing guarantees to the borrowing of public enterprises that do not have the credit strength to borrow on their own; establishing public-private partnership arrangements; borrowing from pension funds; and accumulating arrears to wages, pension payments, and suppliers. Among Indian states in the late 1990s, special-purpose vehicles became a convenient way of circumventing tight budgets. Guarantees by states to support market borrowing of loss-making public sector undertakings, a contingent liability, grew rapidly.

All major international rating agencies include the borrowing of subnational quasi-fiscal entities as part of subnational government debt profile. They include subnational debt from all public sector enterprises and other implicit and contingent obligations, such as public-private partnerships; bailouts of private companies; off-balance-sheet project financing; lease obligations; debt guarantees; and equity interests and liabilities in utilities, businesses, and banks.[29]

Rationale for Regulatory Frameworks and Debt Management

The development of regulatory frameworks for subnational borrowing in middle-income countries since the late 1990s is the direct result of, and response to, subnational fiscal stress and debt crises. Some middle-income countries, such as Peru, developed regulatory frameworks for subnational borrowing at the beginning of the decentralization process, in order to preempt systemic subnational debt crises. Benefiting from middle-income countries' reform experience, low-income countries should consider policy options before opening up a subnational debt market.

Regulatory frameworks for subnational borrowing should contain two parts: (a) ex ante control, regulation of borrowing, and monitoring of the subnational fiscal position and (b) ex post debt restructuring (to be used if subnational governments become insolvent). The regulatory frameworks in many countries are still evolving, and the pace of putting together a full range of regulatory elements varies.[30] Regulatory frameworks are inseparable from the reform of intergovernmental fiscal systems and financial markets, because they profoundly shape incentives for subnational governments to pursue sustainable fiscal and debt policies and for creditors to price returns and risks appropriately.

Legislation on subnational borrowing functions as a commitment device that allows subnational governments to access the financial market within a common framework. Inherent incentives exist for a subnational government to free-ride, because it bears only part of the cost and all of the benefits of unsustainable fiscal policies. Realizing these benefits depends on good fiscal behavior by most of the other subnational governments. For this reason, governments benefit collectively from a system of rules to discourage such defection and free-riding. The commitment device controls and coordinates subnational governments across space in various localities and across time to commit future governments to a common borrowing framework (Webb 2004).

Ex ante regulations are unlikely to foster commitment in the absence of an ex post insolvency mechanism.[31] A well-designed insolvency mechanism helps enforce the commitment device and hard budget constraints on subnational governments.[32] Pressures for ad hoc political intervention decrease as restructurings become more institutionalized. Equally important, insolvency procedures help an insolvent subnational government maintain essential services while restructuring its debts. Because subnational governments perform public functions, they cannot be liquidated and dissolved like private corporations; reorganization is the essence of insolvency for public entities. Ultimately, subnational governments need to reenter the financial market. Insolvency proceedings need to balance the interests of creditors and the debtor.

Together with triggering events, each country's political, economic, legal, and historical context motivate it to develop a regulatory framework. These differences affect the entry point for reform, the framework's design, and the framework's relation to subnational borrowing legislation.

For example, the U.S. municipal bankruptcy framework has influenced the design of insolvency proceedings in some middle-income countries,[33] but it cannot be copied by low-income or other middle-income countries without care. Chapter 9 of the U.S. bankruptcy code was conceived with the narrow objective of resolving the holdout problem, against the background of a mature intergovernmental fiscal system and a market-oriented financial system. In developing countries, development of a subnational insolvency mechanism must be sequenced with other reforms, and it must reflect the country's institutional capacity. The unique federal structure of the United States also profoundly affected the design of Chapter 9 (with respect to the role of federal courts in the debt adjustment plan of insolvent municipalities, for example). Because a country's subnational insolvency mechanism must define the respective role of different branches and tiers of government, the political and economic history of a country plays a key role in shaping the design of an insolvency system.

Frameworks for Subnational Borrowing

The two basic parts of regulatory frameworks—ex ante control and ex post debt restructuring in the event that subnational governments become insolvent—are closely related. By increasing the pain of circumventing ex ante regulation for lenders and subnational borrowers, insolvency mechanisms enhance the effectiveness of preventive rules.

Ex Ante Regulation. Ex ante regulation deals with the control of borrowing and the monitoring of the subnational fiscal position. Widespread subnational debt crises in the 1990s in countries such as Brazil and Mexico and prevalent subnational fiscal stress in countries such as Colombia and India motivated these countries to develop or strengthen ex ante regulation to help prevent future systemic stress and crises. In countries such as Peru, where decentralization has recently started, the government has emphasized the importance of fiscal sustainability and the need to reduce the risks of decentralization.

Several middle-income countries have developed ex ante fiscal rules for subnational governments. Brazil's Fiscal Responsibility Law (2000), which applies to all levels of government, consolidated various pieces of legislation passed since 1997 into one unifying framework. Colombia's Fiscal Transparency and Responsibility Law (2003) consolidated legislation passed since 1997. India's 12th Finance Commission put forward recommendations on fiscal rules and provided incentives for states to comply with them.[34] Mexico's new borrowing framework was developed in response to the subnational debt crisis triggered by the financial crisis of the mid-1990s. Peru developed a subnational borrowing framework from 2003 to 2005 while embarking on decentralization, in order to avoid the mistakes of unregulated subnational borrowing while decentralizing.

These countries' ex ante regulation shares several common elements that low-income countries may want to consider (Liu and Waibel 2008a). First, borrowing is allowed only for long-term public capital investments (the "golden rule"). (Short-term borrowing for working capital is allowed, but provisions should be built in to prevent governments from using roll-over borrowing to cover operating deficits.) Middle-income countries including Brazil, Colombia, India, Peru, Russia, and South Africa have recently adopted this rule.[35]

Second, the frameworks specify limits on key fiscal variables, such as fiscal deficit, primary deficit, debt-service ratios, and ceilings on guarantees issued. In Brazil, the debt-restructuring agreements between the federal government and the states established a comprehensive list of fiscal targets—debt-to-revenue ratio, primary balance, personnel spending as share of total spending, own-source revenue growth, and investment ceilings—as well as a list of state-owned enterprises or banks to be privatized or concessioned.

Colombia sought to limit subnational debt to payment capacity (through Law 358 in 1997 and the Fiscal Transparency and Responsibility Law in 2003). A traffic-light system was established to regulate subnational borrowing. Subnational governments rated in the red-light zone are prohibited from borrowing; those in the green-light zone are permitted to borrow. A state in the red-light zone is defined as one in which the ratio of interest to operational savings exceeds 40 percent and the ratio of debt stock over current revenues exceeds 80 percent.[36]

In India, a state with a debt-service ratio exceeding 20 percent of revenues is classified as having debt-stress status, triggering the central government's close monitoring of additional borrowing by the state.[37] Following the recommendations of the 12th Finance Commission and responding to incentives of greater resource flows, all states have enacted fiscal responsibility legislation. These laws include commitments to eliminate revenue deficits and a time path for reducing the fiscal deficit to 3 percent of gross state domestic product.

Third, several legal frameworks, such as those in Brazil, Colombia, and Peru, include procedural requirements that subnational governments establish a medium-term fiscal framework and a transparent budgetary process. This requirement is intended to ensure that fiscal accounts move within a sustainable debt path and that fiscal adjustment takes a medium-term approach, in order to better respond to shocks and differing trajectories for key macroeconomic variables that affect subnational finance. The transparent budgetary process facilitates debates by executive and legislative branches on spending priorities, funding sources, and required fiscal adjustments. Peru's Fiscal Decentralization Law (2004) requires regional and local governments to prepare detailed multiyear budgetary frameworks that are consistent with the national government's multiyear budget framework.

Fiscal transparency is increasingly becoming an integrated part of fiscal frameworks. Transparency includes having an independent audit of subnational financial accounts, making periodic public disclosures of key fiscal data, exposing hidden liabilities, and moving off-budget liabilities on budget. In Brazil, the accrual accounting method for all levels of government eliminates an important source of hidden liabilities: arrears. Article 48 of Brazil's Fiscal Responsibility Law (2000) enshrines fiscal transparency as a key component of the new framework. Proposals, laws, and accounts are to be widely distributed, including through the use of electronic media (all reports are made available on the Web site of the Ministry of the Treasury). Article 54 requires that all levels of governments publish a quarterly fiscal management report that contains the major fiscal variables and indicates compliance (or lack of compliance) with fiscal targets. This report must be certified by the audit courts. In India, several reforming states have started to move off-budget liabilities onto the budget and have established a measure of consolidated fiscal deficit beyond the conventional cash deficit; the reported fiscal deficit does not capture the financing deficit of large public sector undertakings, which implicitly are states' liabilities.

Ex ante regulation need not be purely on the borrower side. In Colombia, the Fiscal Transparency and Responsibility Law (2003) tightened the regulations on the supply side. Lending to subnationals by financial institutions and territorial development institutions must meet the conditions and limits of various regulations, such as Law 617 and Law 817. If they do not, the credit contract is invalid and borrowed funds must be restituted promptly, without interest or any other charges. To improve fiscal transparency in Mexico, policy makers there introduced a credit rating system for subnational governments. Although subnational participation in the credit rating is voluntary, the requirements of the capital-risk weighting of bank loans (introduced in 2000) and of loss provisions (introduced in 2004) aim at imposing subnational fiscal discipline through the market pricing of subnational credit.

Ex Post Insolvency Mechanisms. Ex ante regulation reduces the risk of defaults, but it cannot prevent all defaults. Ex post regulations—that is, subnational insolvency mechanisms—deal with insolvent subnational governments.[38] Defaults may arise from a subnational's fiscal mismanagement or from macroeconomic or exogenous shocks.

Several design considerations arise concerning insolvency procedures. They include the fundamental differences between public and private insolvency, the choices between judicial or administrative approaches, and the operation of the insolvency procedure itself. The central question is the resolution of the interests of creditors and the insolvent subnational borrower.

The public nature of the services provided by governments explains the fundamental difference between public insolvency and the bankruptcy of a private corporation. This difference leads to the basic tension between protecting creditors' rights and maintaining essential public services. Creditors' remedies against defaulting subnationals are narrower than the remedies they can take against defaulting corporations, leading to greater moral hazard (strategic defaults). Whereas a corporation is able to self-dissolve, this route is barred for subnational governments. When a private corporation goes bankrupt, all of its assets are potentially subject to attachment. By contrast, the ability of creditors to attach the assets of subnational governments is greatly restrained in many countries. In the case of subnational insolvency, the insolvency mechanism is generally reorganization, not liquidation of all assets.

Mechanisms for resolving subnational financial distress are either administrative or judicial in nature, although various hybrids also exist. The choice depends on several factors. In administrative interventions, a higher level of government temporarily takes over financial management of the subnational entity. Provided the courts are independent, the judicial approach can reduce political interference during the restructuring and thus provide greater assurances to creditors. When Hungary introduced a subnational insolvency framework in 1996, it chose a judicial system for this reason. It thereby insulated the procedure from strong political pressure to bail out subnational governments, increasing the credibility of its no-bailout policy.

The power and legitimacy of the courts to render decisions with respect to expenditures and revenues is limited, however; leaving a wide margin of discretion to elected officials is critical. In the United States, judicial and administrative approaches coexist. At the federal level, Chapter 9 provides procedural machinery under which a debt-restructuring plan acceptable to a majority of creditors can become binding on a dissenting minority. This procedure grants substantial leeway to the debtor in terms of policy choices and budget priorities. However, states need to consent to their municipalities filing for Chapter 9. Several states employ additional administrative procedures for resolving municipal financial distress.

Key elements of subnational insolvency procedures include defining when a subnational entity is insolvent, undertaking fiscal adjustment to close the gap between expenditures and revenues, and restructuring debt to bridge any remaining shortfall in payment capacity. Fiscal adjustment and consolidation are preconditions for financial workouts. Often a subnational government's own fiscal mismanagement is the root cause of insolvency. Even when subnational insolvency is triggered by macroeconomic shocks, such as a sharp rise in real interest rates through a currency crisis, fiscal adjustment is inherent to any insolvency procedure.

The maturity of the legal system influences the choice of procedure. Implementation of insolvency procedures—in the corporate and subnational contexts—rests on the shoulders of insolvency experts and on institutions (courts) that resist political influence and corruption. In many developing countries (both middle- and low-income countries), limited judicial and administrative capacity may be a binding constraint. The first step should be to develop institutional ingredients and train bankruptcy professionals. In countries in which the judicial system is embryonic, formal procedural guidelines can be a stepping stone to a fully developed mechanism. This interim solution can be used to build institutional and professional capacity in substantive restructuring (Gitlin and Watkins 1999).

Framework for Subnational Debt Management

In addition to the broad regulatory framework for subnational borrowing and insolvency, subnational debt management is essential to prudent fiscal and debt management, thereby reducing the probability of default. Subnational insolvency can result from any of the following factors: mismanagement of a subnational's fiscal accounts, such as a mismatch between borrowing and debt-service capacity; macroeconomic or exogenous shocks; and a risky profile of debt composition, such as one that includes short maturity, currency risks, and variable interest rates.

Strategy for Managing Subnational Debt

Like national debt management, subnational debt management is the process of establishing and implementing a strategy for prudently managing the entity's debt to meet its financing needs in a way that meets its risk objectives and any other goals it may have set. The stock of debt, and new borrowings arising from budget and off-budget sources, should be managed in a manner that is consistent with the subnational government's cost and risk preferences. Doing so entails using the following four-pillar framework, based on the World Bank's Debt Management Performance Assessment Tool (World Bank 2007) and cross-country experiences drawn from countries such as Brazil and Colombia:

- *Governance and strategy development.* A sound governance framework refers to the legal and managerial structure that directs the operations of government debt managers. It includes legislation that defines goals and accountabilities; embodies the management framework; and covers the formulation and implementation of strategy, operational procedures, quality assurance practices, and reporting responsibilities (Wheeler 2004). The strategy outlines the path by which the subnational's debt-management objectives are operationalized in the medium term. Under this pillar, the subnational government establishes clear debt-management objectives that are supported by a sound governance framework, a prudent cost–risk management strategy, an efficient organizational structure, appropriate management information systems, and a strong in-house risk management culture.

- *Coordination of borrowing with macro policies.* Coordinating borrowing with macro policies helps ensure that all portfolio-related transactions are consistent with the government's fiscal and debt-sustainability strategy and are executed in an effective manner. Fiscal sustainability implies the government's ability to maintain a certain set of fiscal and central government monetary policies without becoming insolvent. It also means that a government's intertemporal budget constraint holds without explicit default on its debt. For policy purposes, it is useful to disentangle the growth and inflation effects on indebtedness as shown in equation (14.1):[39]

$$b_t - b_{t-1} = i_t - x_t - \frac{g_t}{(1+g_t)(1+\pi_t)}b_{t-1} - \frac{\pi_t}{(1+\pi_t)}b_{t-1}, \qquad (14.1)$$

where b_t, i_t, and x_t are the outstanding public state debt, interest payments, and primary balance, respectively, as shares of gross subnational domestic product in period t; g_t is the real annual growth rate; and π_t is the annual inflation rate. Under different scenarios, debt sustainability is assessed using

$$b_t = \frac{(1+r_t)}{(1+g_t)}b_{t-1} - x_t, \qquad (14.2)$$

where r_t is the real interest rate, defined as $r_t = [(n_t + 1)/(\pi_t + 1)] - 1$.

- *Borrowing and related activities.* Well-developed local capital markets are important because they provide stable funding sources in domestic currency for subnationals and allow liabilities to be more closely matched to the revenues that will service them. Well-developed domestic markets also enhance the efficiency and stability of financial intermediation, provide a broader range of assets, and facilitate better risk management. To the extent possible, debt issuance by subnationals should use market-based mechanisms (including competitive auctions) and syndications. Engaging in domestic borrowing activities that are transparent and predictable will provide the government with a mechanism with which to finance its expenditures in a cost-effective manner while minimizing risks.[40] All borrowing activities should be in accordance with the government's debt strategy (World Bank 2008b).

- *Evaluation, debt recording, and reporting.* Sound practice requires comprehensive debt management systems to record, monitor, settle, and account effectively for all subnational government debt and debt-related transactions. The subnational government should report total debt outstanding to foster transparency and accountability.

Cross-country experiences show that subnational entities range from those that are "regulated and monitored" by the federal government (for example, Brazil and Colombia) to those in which subnational entities have more autonomy (for example, Canada and the United States) in meeting their borrowing requirements. The degree of independence from the center affects how regulatory oversight and compliance with budgetary rules are enforced, which in turn determines the regulatory and debt-management frameworks that can be applied in such countries. Any strategy for subnational debt management must be mindful of different channels of subnational borrowing (box 14.1).

Box 14.1 Autonomy and Regulation in Issuing Subnational Debt in India

An important factor affecting subnational regulation and debt management is the degree and extent to which the federal government monitors and controls such debt. Variants range from onlending by the federal government to accessing of debt through wholesale markets or by issuance of retail debt at fixed rates of interest. The federal government (or the center) exercises control by determining either the quantity of borrowings the subnational can assume or the rate at which it can borrow (in extreme cases, it determines both) The debt-management arrangements and the regulatory frameworks are then determined by the degree of operational independence the subnational exercises in sourcing its financing requirements.

In India, 40 percent of state government debt is wholesale debt for which the central government determines the level of debt to be contracted in a year. Wholesale debt (loans from banks and financial institutions, loans from the domestic market, and external loans from multilateral development agencies) is monitored and regulated by the center, which derives this power from Article 293 of India's constitution. Article 293 mandates that if a state government is indebted to the central government, it requires the consent of the central government to raise loans or offer guarantees.

A large component of total debt (more than 60 percent) is retail debt, which has an exogenous accumulation mechanism and thus lies outside the regulatory ambit of the federal government. This debt, which is at above-market rates, results in higher costs to the subnational governments, dilutes overall fiscal discipline, compromises budgetary constraints, and could result in building unsustainable debts. Retail debt is contracted through public accounts and small saving instruments. In 2007, India's 12th Finance Commission recommended reforming this system. Reforms would strengthen subnational fiscal discipline.

Source: Prasad, Goyal, and Prakash 2004.

Differences between National and Subnational Debt Management

Although the dynamics of national and subnational debt are similar, critical differences exist. A debt-management strategy for subnational governments must be developed in the context of these differences.

One important difference is the inability of subnational governments to issue their own currency. Seigniorage plays no role in subnational government finance. Just as in a Ricardian regime,[41] the state government's lifetime budget constraint suggests that for debt to be sustainable, the outstanding stock of debt should not exceed the present value of all current and future primary surpluses:

$$B_{-1} = \sum_{i=0}^{\infty} D_{0t} X_t, \tag{14.3}$$

where B_{-1} is the stock of initial total public debt of the state and $D_{0t} = (1 + n_0)^{-1} \ldots (1 + n_t)^{-1}$.

The present value approach incorporates creditors' incentives in determining the financing options facing the government. Under this approach, creditors lend to the government only if they consider government policies sustainable. As long as credit risk plays a role in the subnational financing system, additional borrowing will dry up if policies are perceived as unsustainable; only by reducing debt or adjusting the policy stance (that is, by ensuring that past and current primary deficits imply future primary surpluses in present value terms) will the government be able to borrow again.

Because monetary policy is under the purview of the central government in almost all countries, the nominal interest rate is arguably outside the influence of a single subnational government, as long as the subnational entity is small. Although the subnational government cannot set the interest rate at which it borrows (at least not in a competitive bond market), the spread it pays over the central government's rate is presumably linked to its own creditworthiness.

Another key difference between subnational and national debt is that foreign exchange risk may not directly affect subnational finance. In China, Kazakhstan, Peru, and Vietnam, for example, subnational governments are prohibited from external borrowing, and all external borrowing needs approval and guarantee from the national government.[42] In cases in which subnational entities are allowed to borrow in foreign currency, the analysis of such risks is important, as illustrated by the debt crises in Brazil in 1990 and Russia in 1998. Even if subnationals are prohibited from borrowing externally, currency risks can indirectly affect their sustainability through real interest rate shocks, as they did in Mexico in 1994–95.

Legal constraints set by the constitutions and laws of subnational governments limit their ability to raise their own revenue, a key determinant of the primary balance. For example, there are no subnational taxes in Vietnam, where the central government controls tax bases and rates and the Department of Tax Administration collects all nontrade revenues (World Bank 2007). In India, the constitution limits the power of states in setting tax policy for major categories of taxation. In countries in which the legal framework for fiscal decentralization is still evolving, the ability of subnational governments to raise their own revenue can change over time. For example, whereas before 2005 Chinese provinces levied and retained personal income tax, personal income tax is now shared equally by China's central government and the provinces.[43]

Transfers from the central government (or higher levels of government in multitier structures) are an important source of subnational revenues, although the dependency of subnational governments on fiscal transfers varies significantly across countries. On average, fiscal transfers represent just under 40 percent of states' revenues in India (World Bank 2005a), 50 percent in Ethiopia except for Addis Ababa (World Bank 2008a), 85–95 percent in Mexico (Webb 2004), and 85 percent in Uganda (Mayanja and Mayengo 2007).

The predictability of transfers—an important consideration in a fiscal-sustainability analysis—depends on how the transfer system is set up. India and Vietnam use a formula-based approach that enhances transparency and fosters predictability.[44] Nigeria's constitution provides that all revenues collected by the federal government be paid into one distributable pool, called the Federation Account.[45]

The central government affects the fiscal balance and the growth prospects of the subnational economy in other ways as well. In some countries (such as Brazil, Cambodia, India, Thailand, and Vietnam),[46] the center sets or influences policy on wages and pensions. In others (such as Colombia, Indonesia, Mexico, Peru, Russia, and Thailand), it establishes ceilings on debt services and debt stock. In countries such as Nigeria, Uganda, and Vietnam, the center has set ceilings on subnational debt service.

Expected bailouts by the central government affect subnational debt dynamics. Market participants may tolerate unsustainable fiscal policy of a subnational government if history backs their perception that the central government implicitly guarantees the debt service of the subnational government. This situation was apparent in the early 2000s, as evidenced by the market subscription for even highly stressed states in India. Central governments' guarantees for local government bailouts were perceived to be contributing factors for widespread subnational debt stress in Mexico in the mid-1990s and Russia in the late 1990s. Bailouts in Bolivia over the years did not provide an adequate environment for proper subnational debt controls (IMF 2006). The problem of moral hazard is often compounded by lack of market transparency, weak market governance, distortions in the competitive framework among market participants, and inadequate capacity for financial management by subnational entities.

In addition to the differences outlined above (Ianchovichina, Liu, and Nagarajan 2007), debt management at the subnational level can also be affected by the lack of adequate liquidity and the fragmentation of issuances at the subnational level. If supported by an implicit sovereign guarantee, debt issuance at the subnational level implies multiple issuers of securities, with varying claims to sovereign creditworthiness that fragment the market. This is reflected in poor secondary market trading of subnational bonds. In Nigeria, one or two state governments access the domestic markets, creating pools of illiquid paper that is neither traded nor fungible, most of it held to maturity. This type of debt does not contribute to the development of a domestic debt market. Moreover, the multiplicity of subnational issues in a bond market that is still relatively underdeveloped can make the establishment of national benchmarks difficult (World Bank and IMF 2001).

Subnational governments must also overcome adverse perceptions of their debt-related activities. Historically, most subnationals have confronted hard budget constraints set by the central government by either allocating the ceiling amount of borrowings or fixing the rates of interest. Over time, such budget constraints can loosen as a result of subnationals accessing borrowing outside the central allocations and off-budget measures and special-purpose vehicles. The perception of states' credibility and creditworthiness is determined largely by the budgetary position of their parastatals. Debt management at the subnational level is largely constrained by these characteristics. To gain market acceptance and overcome such shortcomings, subnational governments must impose greater transparency and market-governance mechanisms

These differences call for greater intergovernmental coordination and policy dialogue about reform. Both national and subnational governments in a range of countries have been experimenting with and strengthening their strategies and capacity in implementing the four-pillar debt management framework outlined above. Brazil and Colombia closely monitor their subnational debt profile through a series of indicators.[47] Several states in India focused on the first pillar for governance by enacting fiscal responsibility legislations. Mexico introduced a credit rating system for subnational governments. Although subnational participation in the credit rating is voluntary, the requirements of the capital risk weighting of bank loans (introduced in 2000) and of loss provisions (introduced in 2004) aim to impose subnational fiscal discipline through the market pricing of subnational credit.

Conclusion

Subnational debt management is emerging as an important public policy agenda for low-income countries. Coupled with decentralization, the changing financial landscape presents both opportunities and challenges for subnational governments in low-income countries in transition to market access. Experience from middle-income countries suggests that subnational borrowing offers numerous benefits, particularly for facilitating infrastructure financing to match the maturity of debt with asset life for more efficient and equitable financing. But it also suggests that unregulated borrowing by subnational entities creates substantial fiscal risk, principally from borrowing to finance operating deficits, risky debt structures, or large contingent liabilities. Imprudent borrowing not only threatens service delivery at the subnational level, but also produces negative macroeconomic spillovers for the central government and other subnational governments. Middle-income countries' experience also shows that risks are high during the initial stage of fiscal decentralization, the stage in which some low-income countries now find themselves.

These risks are exacerbated if decentralization is accompanied by episodes of macroeconomic instability and unregulated financial markets. The ongoing global financial crisis is putting stress on macroeconomic frameworks and reducing growth prospects in all countries. The structural trend in fiscal decentralization in the midst of macroeconomic uncertainty requires more care in managing subnational borrowing. As middle-income countries' experience in the 1990s shows, decentralization and rapid development of subnational borrowing in the midst of macroeconomic uncertainty can be hazardous.

Although the dynamics of national and subnational debt are similar, critical differences exist. A regulatory framework for subnational borrowing and debt management must be developed in the context of these differences.

In addition, the principal-agent problem is particularly potent for subnational borrowing, and the threat of the soft-budget constraint weakens competitive incentives and fosters corruption and rent-seeking. Bailouts of insolvent subnational governments can undermine the effectiveness of subnational borrowing regulations. Worse, banks may act as implicit agents of the nation by lending to uncreditworthy subnationals with the expectation of bailouts in case of trouble.

For middle- and low-income countries, a well-designed regulatory framework for all subnational borrowing helps preempt soft-budget constraints, strengthens fiscal discipline, better aligns incentives of both borrowers and creditors, supports broader intergovernmental fiscal reforms, and encourages the efficient use of capital. By hardening the budget constraint for fiscal irresponsibility, such regulation helps subnational governments fulfill their broader public responsibilities as self-standing borrowers.

The pace of developing a subnational borrowing framework varies across countries, depending on a country's historical, political, and economic conditions and its entry point for reforms. Other countries' experience cannot be copied without care. An active subnational debt-management strategy highlighting cost-risk trade-offs complements regulatory frameworks. Unlike borrowing by the national government, borrowing at the subnational level can be affected by low liquidity and fragmentation: debt issuance at the sub-national level carrying an implicit sovereign guarantee implies multiple issu-ers of securities with varying claims to sovereign creditworthiness, which may fragment the market and reduce its liquidity and efficiency.

The experience of middle-income countries indicates that the subna-tional borrowing framework needs to be tailored to the evolution of a country's subnational borrowing market, especially its shortcomings. Borrowing and debt-management frameworks should be embedded in a country's political, legal, and intergovernmental system, particularly when the insolvency framework needs to define the respective roles of the legislative, executive, and judicial branches in subnational fiscal and debt adjustment. Institutional and capacity differences can also affect the entry point for reform.

Increasing (or introducing) transparency should be a policy priority. Off-budget liabilities present tremendous fiscal risks. As part of ex ante regula-tions, subnational governments in middle-income countries are increasingly required to develop a medium-term fiscal framework, improve fiscal trans-parency, and strengthen the timely availability and independent audit of fiscal accounts, including implicit and contingent liabilities.

In this rich policy agenda, many topics remain to be explored further. In many low-income countries, for example, onlending from the central government to subnational governments is likely to continue. What are the pros and cons of such activities? What policy frameworks should gov-ern them? How can investors measure the extent of off-budget liabilities associated with quasi-fiscal entities in low-income countries? All of these topics merit further research.

Notes

1. The subnational level of government is defined as the level of government below the central or federal government. Based on the World Bank's July 2008 classification, there are 49 low-income countries, defined as countries with aver-age gross national income (GNI) per capita (calculated using the World Bank Atlas method) of $935 or less. Middle-income countries are divided into two groups: lower-middle-income ($936–$3,705) and upper-middle-income ($3,706–$11,455) countries.

2. For the purpose of this chapter, *market-access countries* are defined as the subset of low- and middle-income economies in which a significant share of debt is issued purely on market terms (for example, nonconcessional commercial debt).

3. According to the World Bank's classification, the term *developing economy/country* includes low- and middle-income economies.

4. This chapter focuses on a subset of issues concerning subnational borrow-ing regulations and debt management. Broader reforms, such as reform of the intergovernmental fiscal system and the development of government security mar-ket, are beyond the chapter's scope. The chapter focuses on the subset of countries that are already decentralizing and exploring subnational government access to financial markets.

5. Launched by the World Bank and the International Monetary Fund (IMF) in 1996, the HIPC Initiative provides debt relief to low-income countries in which the ratio of the net present value of debt to exports exceeds 150 percent or the ratio of the net present value of debt to fiscal revenue exceeds 250 percent. The MDRI provides 100 percent relief to low-income countries on eligible debt from four multilateral institutions: the IMF, the International Development Association of the World Bank, the African Development Fund, and the Inter-American Development Fund.

6. See Werner and David (2007) on Ethiopia; FitchRatings (2008) and DFID (2007) on Nigeria; Kim (2003) on Pakistan; IFC (2007) and World Bank (2007) on Vietnam; Mayanja and Mayengo (2007) on Uganda; and White and Glasser (2004) on Zimbabwe.

7. Countries face two options: onlending funds from the central government to subnational governments or allowing subnationals access to the financial market. The pros and cons of each option relate to the stage of development of their financial markets, the capacity of subnational governments in fiscal and debt management, and the political dimension of decentralization. The focus here is on the conditions that must be established before allowing some creditworthy subnationals access to financial markets.

8. For a more detailed discussion of the reasons behind decentralization in Bolivia, Brazil, China, India, Indonesia, South Africa, and Uganda, see Bardhan and Mukherjee (2006).

9. The study measured the degree of political decentralization by the number of directly elected (versus appointed) levels of local governments and the degree of fairness and freedom of such elections.

10. The study measured administrative decentralization by the clarity of functional assignments and the use of the subsidiarity principle in their distribution across levels of government. It measured fiscal decentralization by the existence of rules for intergovernmental transfers and the level of public expenditures that was under subnational governments' control (at least 5–10 percent).

11. During the second half of the 1990s, the government of Ethiopia, together with development partners, conducted a number of studies to identify the factors that hindered public sector efficiency and accountability (see, for example, World Bank 2008a). These studies reveal that local governments had limited fiscal or administrative autonomy with which to respond to the needs of their constituencies. Findings in other low-income countries, such as Pakistan (World Bank 2004) and those in East Asia (World Bank 2007), are similar.

12. Constructing a comprehensive data set on subnational finance is challenging given the lack of good-quality data at the subnational level in many developing countries and the different ways in which countries classify their subnational expenditure items.

13. In 2005, 63.9 percent of public capital expenditure in Europe was made by local and regional governments. Between 2000 and 2005, local and regional investment rose more rapidly than GDP (Dexia 2006).

14. The national government contributes 88 percent of annual infrastructure investments in Pakistan and 84 percent in Bangladesh, for example (Kim 2003; Asian Development Bank 2007).

15. In 2007, states accounted for 41.8 percent of Nigeria's total external public debt. The federal government guarantees all external debts of states. Over the years, states have amassed large formal and informal debts, including bank loans, credits and long-term debts, pension and salary arrears, and debts to contractors (see DFID 2007).

16. According to the Budget Law (2002), the stock of outstanding subnational debt cannot exceed 30 percent of capital budget in a given budget year.

17. China, for example, has been investing about 10 percent of its GDP annually in infrastructure since the 1990s, with subnational governments accounting for a large share of these investments, particularly in urban infrastructure. The majority of financing comes from proceeds from land leasing and public bank lending securitized on property and land valuation. In contrast, public infrastructure investment by Indian states has remained below 3 percent of their gross state domestic product since the 1990s (Liu 2008). In the United States, subnational infrastructure is financed predominantly by bonds raised in the private capital market.

18. Borrowing to finance infrastructure that is badly planned and managed can burden future generations with debt without yielding corresponding benefits.

19. In establishing a framework for municipal finance borrowing after the fall of apartheid, South Africa clearly understood the benefits of competition in the subnational credit market. Its Intergovernmental Fiscal Review report states, "Active capital markets, with a variety of buyers and sellers, and a variety of financial products, can offer more efficiency than direct lending. First, competition for municipal debt instruments tends to keep borrowing costs down and create structural options for every need. Second, an active market implies liquidity for an investor who may wish to sell. Liquidity reduces risk, increases the pool of potential investors, and thus improves efficiency" (South Africa National Treasury 2001, p. 192).

20. The economics literature approaches insolvency from the perspective of the sustainability of fiscal policies. In a number of countries, specific legal definitions serve as procedural triggers for initiating insolvency procedures. In a legal sense, subnational insolvency refers to the inability to pay debts as they fall due. Details vary across countries (see Liu and Waibel 2008b).

21. For China, see Liu (2008); for India, see Ianchovichina, Liu, and Nagarajan (2007).

22. See Weingast (2007) for a summary of the literature within the context of second-generation fiscal federalism.

23. This is a generic concern, irrespective of whether the borrower is a subnational entity. It can be greater, however, if the borrower is a subnational entity and its system of financial management and reporting is not transparent.

24. Such finance can take multiple forms, including direct borrowing and the running of arrears.

25. This statement assumes that economic growth translates into increased capacity to service debt. This may not happen if a subnational government is unable to exploit its growing tax base. In this case, borrowing can provoke a fiscal crisis even if the proceeds have been put to good use.

26. Prasad, Goyal, and Prakash (2004) and Ianchovichina, Liu, and Nagarajan (2007) analyze key factors affecting subnational fiscal sustainability.

27. A revenue deficit is the amount of current expenditure (such as wages, pension outlays, subsidies, transfers, and operation and maintenance) net of total revenues. For a discussion of the state fiscal crisis in India, see Ianchovichina, Liu, and Nagarajan (2007).

28. From 1998 to 2001, at least 57 of 89 regional governments in Russia defaulted (Popov 2002). In 2001, six years after the peso crisis, 60 percent of subnational governments in Mexico still struggled financially (Schwarcz 2002). One interesting difference is that subnational governments were allowed to borrow overseas in Russia, whereas such borrowing was prohibited in Mexico. Subnational governments in Mexico were not insulated from foreign exchange risks, however, because the risks were transmitted through inflation and interest rates.

29. For a review of subnational credit rating methodologies by major rating agencies, see Liu and Tan (2009).

30. See Ter-Minassian and Craig (1997) for a summary of subnational borrowing control frameworks in more than 50 countries and Liu and Waibel (2008a) for a review of ex ante regulations since the late 1990s in several countries. For comparative experiences of ex post insolvency mechanisms, see Liu and Waibel (2008b).

31. Insolvency mechanisms could be in the form of an administrative type of debt restructuring without a formal bankruptcy law.

32. If a bailout system exists, subnational governments are likely to share the national rating assigned by rating agencies. The subnational governments might thereby have easier and cheaper access to the capital market.

33. Chapter 11, the U.S. bankruptcy law for corporations, has significantly affected other countries. Chapter 9 of the Bankruptcy Code has strongly influenced subnational insolvency frameworks in countries such as Hungary and South Africa.

34. The constitutionally mandated Finance Commission convenes every five years to determine the sharing of revenues between the center and the states. Depending on its terms of reference, it may also recommend measures to improve state finances.

35. Brazil's fiscal responsibility legislation tightly controls current expenditure and aims for a positive primary balance. Colombia's Fiscal Transparency and Responsibility Law (2003) mandates that the primary surplus must exceed debt service. India's 12th Finance Commission mandates that states eliminate revenue deficits (current expenditure exceeding total revenue), which implies that borrowing should be used to finance capital expenditure only. Under Article 24 of Peru's Fiscal Decentralization Law (2004) and Article 51 of its General Debt Law (2005), borrowing can be used solely to finance infrastructure projects. According to the Russian Budget Code (1998), current expenditure by regional governments may not exceed total revenues, and their borrowing may be used only to finance investment expenditures. The South African constitution prohibits borrowing for consumption expenditure (South Africa National Treasury 2001).

36. The rating system established under Law 358, passed in 1997, established indebtedness alert signals, based on a liquidity indicator (interest payment/operational savings) and a solvency indicator (debt/current revenue). Subnational governments were classified into one of three zones. Governments in the red-light zone were not allowed to borrow, governments in the green-light zone were allowed to borrow, and governments in the yellow-light zone were allowed to borrow with the permission of the central government. Law 795, passed in 2003, eliminated the yellow-light category. Law 617, passed in 2000, established a ceiling for the ratio of discretionary current expenditure to nonearmarked current revenues. The implementing rules for Law 819, passed in 2003, added a third indicator to the traffic-light system, by relating the primary surplus to debt service.

37. The debt-service ratio measures the capacity to service debt. Many national governments monitor the debt-service ratio of subnational entities, although they define payment capacity differently. Brazil's Fiscal Responsibility Law defines it as the share of current revenue net of transfers. Colombia's Law 358 of 1997 records it as the share of operational savings. India defines it as the ratio of debt-service payments over total revenues. In a 2003 law amending its Fiscal Prudence and Transparency Law, Peru treats it as the share of current income including transfers. Russia's Budget Code denotes it as the share of total budgetary expenditures.

38. The boundary between ex ante regulation and ex post insolvency is not clear cut. Fiscal responsibility regulation, for example, may incorporate elements of ex post consequences. For example, India's 12th Finance Commission mandates that states enact fiscal responsibility legislation and meet specific fiscal targets, such as eliminating the revenue deficit. The commission also provides incentives to states, such as swapping high-cost debt with lower-cost debt to meet fiscal targets.

Such incentives can be interpreted as ex post consequences. Webb (2004) includes transfer intercepts and lender control mechanisms as part of ex post consequences. The focus here is on the insolvency proceedings themselves.

39. For countries allowing subnational governments to access external financing, equation (14.2) must be amended to include the exchange-rate effect.

40. International practice has shown that sovereigns can benefit by providing market participants and investors with details of borrowing plans and other market activities well in advance and then acting consistently when issuing new treasury bonds or undertaking other activities. Doing so leads to lower costs by providing investors with greater certainty, increasing liquidity, broadening the investor base, and creating a level playing field for investors.

41. In a Ricardian regime, the government issues debt to cover deficits but never issues money.

42. In India, the 12th Finance Commission recommended that the center directly pass through all external borrowings to the states at the same terms (currency, maturity, and interest rates) it pays.

43. See IMF (2006) for a discussion of subnational tax policy limitations in Bolivia.

44. India's constitutionally mandated Finance Commission convenes every five years to determine the sharing of revenues between the center and the states on the basis of a formula using weights, which could be changed, for relevant factors (such as population, income disparity, area, tax effort, and fiscal discipline). In Vietnam, intergovernmental transfers are distributed on the basis of formulas that remain unchanged for three to five years.

45. The Federation Account excludes personal income tax on members of the armed forces, police force, the Ministry of Foreign Affairs, and residents of the Federal Capital Territory.

46. Subnational governments in Cambodia, Thailand, and Vietnam prepare their own budgets, subject to certain central mandates and strict civil service regulations (World Bank 2007). This practice is now being phased out in Vietnam, allowing for greater subnational autonomy.

47. Brazil's Fiscal Responsibility Law (2000) provides a framework for regulating and monitoring government fiscal and debt performance, including those of subnational governments. In Colombia, four entities manage Bogota's public debt and risk. The Risk Policy Committee establishes guidelines and policies, and it defines and approves the operational guidelines for implementing risk-control strategies. The Office of Risk Control updates and monitors guidelines and methodologies for the control of the liability portfolio. The Directorate of Public Credit administers the debt portfolio, distributes the resources, and manages the risks. The debt-risk management guidelines spell out rules. The rule on liquidity specifies that maximum annual amortization should be 15 percent of total debt, with a deviation of up to 18 percent and a minimum average life of 4.15 years. The rules on foreign exchange and interest rates specify a maximum of 20 percent of debt with exposure to a foreign currency and a maximum of 70 percent in variable-rate instruments.

References

Asian Development Bank. 2007. *Market Survey of Subnational Finance in Asia and the Pacific*. Manila: Asian Development Bank.

Bardhan, Pranab, and Dilip Mukherjee. 2006. *Decentralization and Local Governance in Developing Countries: A Comparative Perspective*. Cambridge, MA: MIT Press.

Dexia. 2006. "Subnational Public Finance in the European Union: Subnational Governments—European Leaders in Public Investment." *Economic Outlook* November 2006. Paris.

DFID (Department for International Development). 2007. "Nigeria: Assessment of Sub-national Debt." Final Report. Phase 2 of Support for the Debt Management Office, vol. 1. London.

Fitch Ratings. 2008. *Federal Republic of Nigeria: International Credit Analysis.* London.

Freinkman, Lev. 2007. *Inter-Governmental Relations in Nigeria: Improving Service Delivery in Core Sectors.* Washington, DC: World Bank.

Gitlin, Richard A., and Brian N. Watkins. 1999. "Institutional Alternatives to Insolvency for Developing Countries." Paper presented at the conference "Building Effective Insolvency Systems," World Bank, Washington, DC, September 29–30.

Ianchovichina, Elena, Lili Liu, and Mohan Nagarajan. 2007. "Subnational Fiscal Sustainability Analysis: What Can We Learn from Tamil Nadu?" *Economic and Political Weekly* 42 (52): 111–19

IDB (Inter-American Development Bank). 2000. "Subnational Investment Needs and Financial Market Response." Regional Operations Dept. 1 Sector Study, Washington, DC.

IFC (International Finance Corporation). 2007. *Vietnam: Capital Market Diagnostic Review.* Washington, DC: IFC.

IMF (International Monetary Fund). 2006. "Bolivia: Selected Issues." Washington, DC.

Kim, Yun-Hwan. 2003. *Local Government Finance and Bond Market: Pakistan.* Manila: Asia Development Bank.

Liu, Lili. 2008. "Creating a Regulatory Framework for Managing Subnational Borrowing." In *Public Finance in China: Reform and Growth for a Harmonious Society*, ed. Jiwei Lou and Shuilin Wang, 171–90. Washington, DC: World Bank.

Liu, Lili, and Kim Song Tan. 2009. "Subnational Credit Ratings: A Comparative Review." Policy Research Working Paper 5013, World Bank, Washington, DC.

Liu, Lili, and Michael Waibel. 2008a. "Subnational Borrowing, Insolvency and Regulation." In *Macro Federalism and Local Finance*, ed. Anwar Shah, 215–41. Washington, DC: World Bank.

———. 2008b. "Subnational Insolvency: Cross-Country Experiences and Lessons." Policy Research Working Paper 4496, World Bank, Washington, DC.

Mayanja, Abubaker, and Israel Mayengo. 2007. "Municipal Bonds for Financing Development of Infrastructure: A Way Forward for KCC and Local Governments in Uganda." Economic Policy Research Centre, Kampala, Uganda.

Popov, Dimitri. 2002. "Subsovereign Defaults in Russia." Moody's Investors Service, New York.

Prasad, Abha, Rajan Goyal, and Anupam Prakash. 2004. "States' Debt and Debt Relief." *Economic and Political Weekly*, June 26.

Ribot, Jesse. 2002. "Africa Decentralizes: Local Actors, Powers and Accountability." Democracy, Governance, and Human Rights Paper 8, United Nations, Geneva.

Schwarcz, Steven L. 2002. "Global Decentralization and the Subnational Debt Problem." *Duke Law Journal* 51 (4): 1179–250.

South Africa National Treasury. 2001. *Inter-Governmental Fiscal Review.* Pretoria.

Steffensen, Jesper. 2006. "Local Government Organization and Finance: Uganda." In *Local Governance in Developing Countries,* ed. Anwar Shah, 93–136. Washington, DC: World Bank.

Steffensen, Jesper, and Per Tideman. 2004. *A Comparative Analysis of Decentralization in Kenya, Tanzania and Uganda.* Copenhagen: Nordic Consulting Group.

Ter-Minassian, Teresa, and Jon Craig. 1997. "Control of Subnational Government Borrowing." In *Fiscal Federalism in Theory and Practice,* ed. Teresa Ter-Minassian, 156–72. Washington, DC: International Monetary Fund.

Webb, Stephen B. 2004. "Fiscal Responsibility Laws for Subnational Discipline: The Latin American Experiences." Policy Research Working Paper 3309, World Bank, Washington, DC.

Weingast, Barry R. 2007. "Second Generation Fiscal Federalism: Implications for Development." Department of Political Science, Stanford University, Stanford, CA.

Werner, Jan, and Nguyen-Thanh David. 2007. "Municipal Infrastructure Delivery in Ethiopia: A Bottomless Pit or an Option to Reach the Millennium Development Goals?" Institute of Local Public Finance, Langen, Germany.

Wheeler, Graeme. 2004. *Sound Practice in Government Debt Management.* Washington, DC: World Bank.

White, Roland, and Matthew Glasser. 2004. "Sub-Saharan Africa: Zimbabwe." In *Subnational Capital Markets in Developing Countries: From Theory to Practice,* ed. Mila Freire and John Petersen, 337–54. Washington, DC: World Bank.

World Bank. 2003. "Decentralization in Africa: Emerging Trends and Progress." *Public Sector Reform and Capacity Building* 229. Washington, DC.

———. 2004. *Subnational Capital Markets in Developing Countries: From Theory to Practice.* Washington, DC: World Bank.

———. 2005a. *State Fiscal Reforms in India.* Washington, DC: World Bank.

———. 2005b. *Vietnam: Public Expenditure Review and Integrated Financial Accountability Report.* Washington, DC: World Bank.

———. 2007. *East Asia Decentralizes: Making Local Governments Work.* Washington, DC: World Bank.

———. 2008a. "Achieving Better Service Delivery through Decentralization in Ethiopia." Working Paper 131, World Bank, Washington, DC.

———. 2008b. "Debt Management Performance Assessment Tool." Economic Policy and Debt Department and Banking and Debt Management Department, World Bank, Washington, DC.

———. 2008c. *Global Development Finance 2008: The Role of International Banking.* Washington, DC: World Bank.

———. 2008d. "An Overview of Experience from Performance-Based Grant Systems in Systems in Africa." Internal document, World Bank, Washington, DC.

World Bank, and IMF (International Monetary Fund). 2001. *Developing a Government Bond Market: A Handbook.* Washington, DC: World Bank and IMF.

15

Managing Volatility: Fiscal Policy, Debt Management, and Oil Revenues in the Republic of Congo

Nina Budina, Sweder van Wijnbergen, and Ying Li

Resource-rich countries have witnessed stagnating growth, deindustrialization, low savings, lagging human and physical capital accumulation, and stagnating or declining productivity. Recent turmoil in commodity markets has highlighted an important factor behind such performance problems: the volatility of what for most resource-rich countries is the dominant source of export earnings. Managing volatility may well be the prime challenge facing resource-rich countries, superseding traditional concerns about competitiveness of nonresource sectors.

"Debt overhang"—when arrears on old debt deter new lenders, blocking the country's access to capital markets—has been cited in the literature as a potential explanation for the negative macroeconomic experiences of many resource-rich countries. In Nigeria, for example, debt-overhang problems have magnified expenditure volatility, contributing to a hostile climate for private sector development.

Many countries have been classified as heavily indebted notwithstanding their resource wealth. High levels of external debt left many of these countries vulnerable to resource-wealth volatility. Several commodity exporters have gone through external debt crises and long periods of depression (Mexico and Nigeria are well-known examples). Public indebtedness also tends to be high in oil-exporting countries, a substantial number of which have run into debt problems, most often when oil prices were in decline but sometimes even in boom periods (see Sengupta 2008). This evidence suggests that the design of fiscal policy should pay special attention to downside risk in international capital markets, as debt-overhang problems imply that world capital markets become inaccessible at precisely the moment they are needed most.

This chapter focuses on the role of fiscal and debt-management policies in managing resource-wealth volatility and its implications for debt and development. The case study selected for assessment is the oil-rich Republic of Congo (countries with other natural resources, such as copper, would present similar problems). It presents a new framework for assessing fiscal sustainability and vulnerability to debt-overhang problems applicable to oil-rich countries and applies it to such problems in the Republic of Congo.

The Republic of Congo is rapidly building up its production and export capacity, and it can expect to become a substantial energy producer for several decades to come. But the country's oil reserves are smaller than those of many other oil producers. If the country's oil wealth is to prove a resource blessing rather than a resource curse, policy makers must manage a short-lived oil windfall in a way that ensures fiscal sustainability when that windfall is gone.

This chapter analyzes the effects of uncertainty through stochastic analysis allowing for value-at-risk assessments. It provides an example of how fiscal policy can be used to actively manage debt, in this particular case to reduce its volatility. Implementing a fiscal policy rule, which implies tightening fiscal policy whenever negative debt shocks occur, can greatly reduce the variance of future debt outcomes, reducing the riskiness of the economic environment without on average increasing the expected burden of fiscal policy.

The chapter is organized as follows. The next section describes the country's poor growth record despite its oil wealth. The following section examines the challenge of managing oil revenue volatility. The third section uses the new framework to assess fiscal sustainability and suggests options for managing debt and its volatility. The last section summarizes the chapter's main conclusions.

Oil Wealth and the Poor Growth Record

The Republic of Congo began exploiting its petroleum reserves in the late 1950s. In 2007, oil accounted for 90 percent of exports and 80 percent of government revenues. In 2005, the country was the sixth-largest oil producer in Sub-Saharan Africa, after Nigeria, Angola, Sudan, Equatorial Guinea, and Gabon. The Republic of Congo gained $57 billion in oil exports between 1970 and 2007, or 7.4 times 2007 GDP expressed in constant 2007 dollars. This sizable oil windfall created wealth and thus additional spending room, but it also complicated macroeconomic management and led to an extreme dependency on oil, a highly volatile source of income.

The many years of oil money have not brought an end to poverty or, at least not until recently, allowed the economy to break out of perennial stagnation in the nonoil economy. The Republic of Congo once ranked as a lower-middle-income country. During the 1970s and 1980s, per capita GDP closely tracked oil sector developments, increasing substantially during the first and the second oil price shocks and declining steadily in the late 1980s, when oil prices collapsed (figure 15.1). The decline in per capita GDP continued through the 1990s, when low oil prices were exacerbated by the effects of the war that ravaged the country. Armed conflicts have exacted a heavy toll on the country's infrastructure; the poverty rate remains very high (close to 50 percent in 2005), after peaking at close to 70 percent in the period immediately following the conflicts; and unemployment among the active population is estimated at close to 50 percent.

Real per capita GDP has been increasing since 2000 (figure 15.2). The adoption of a new constitution and a peace agreement between the government and all remaining rebel groups in 2003 have boosted economic activity and contributed to macroeconomic stability. Nonoil sector growth remained robust, growing at an annual rate of about 8 percent between 2000 and 2007. Oil sector performance during the same period was much weaker, largely because of a huge decline in production, caused by an accident in May 2007. Oil production is expected to rise through 2011, as new fields come onstream. Without any new oil discoveries, oil revenues

Figure 15.1 Oil Revenues as a Percentage of GDP and Total Exports, 1970–2007

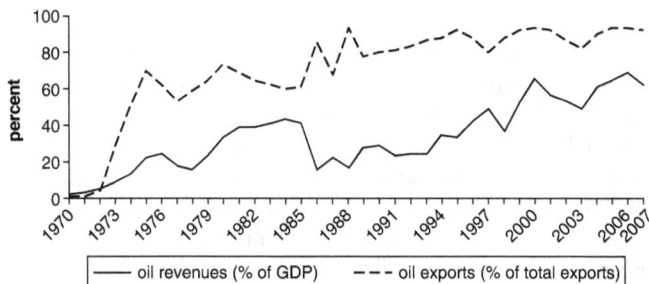

Source: Authors' calculations based on data from Comtrade and World Bank.

Figure 15.2 Total and Nonoil per Capita Income,
1970–2007

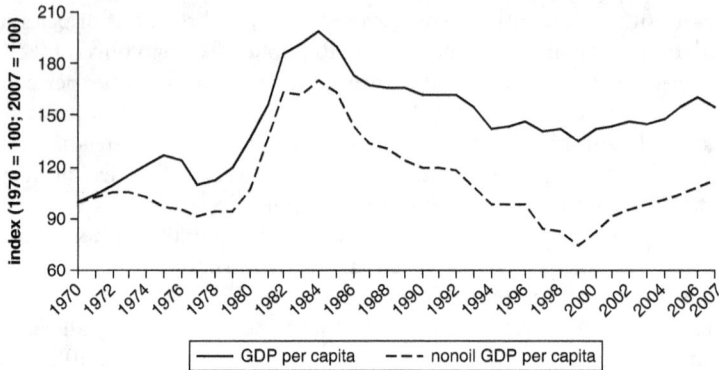

Source: Authors' calculations based on data from Comtrade and World
Bank.

are projected to decline quickly, returning to their 2007 level by 2016,
dropping to about a third of their 2007 level by 2028, and falling to zero
by 2045 (IMF 2008).

Managing this windfall is a major challenge in the Republic of Congo.
Are there lessons it can learn from its poor record in the past that could
help ensure that current favorable developments become structural and
will last beyond the end of the current windfall gains?

The Challenge of Managing Oil Revenue Volatility

Oil income is highly volatile even when quantities are relatively easy to predict, because oil price volatility is high (figure 15.3a). High spending out of
oil income therefore translates income volatility into expenditure volatility,
with potentially serious negative macroeconomic consequences (see Devlin
and Lewin 2005 on managing booms and busts in developing countries).

Volatility can be seen as a tax on investment. Investment requires
irreversible decisions, because once installed, capital cannot be moved
to other sectors. Highly volatile relative prices discourage the irreversible commitments to specific sectors that capital investment implies (van
Wijnbergen 1985). Aghion and others (2006) show empirically that high
volatility slows productivity growth by a substantial margin in countries
with relatively underdeveloped financial sectors, such as the Republic of

Congo. In their sample, a 50 percent increase in volatility slows productivity growth by 33 percent on average. Fiscal policy has clearly exacerbated the volatility stemming from variable oil prices; the government itself has become a source of macroeconomic volatility (figure 15.3b).

Like many oil-rich countries, the Republic of Congo also faces another problem: debt overhang. When oil prices decline unexpectedly, it is often

Figure 15.3 Oil Price, Fiscal Policy, and Output Volatility

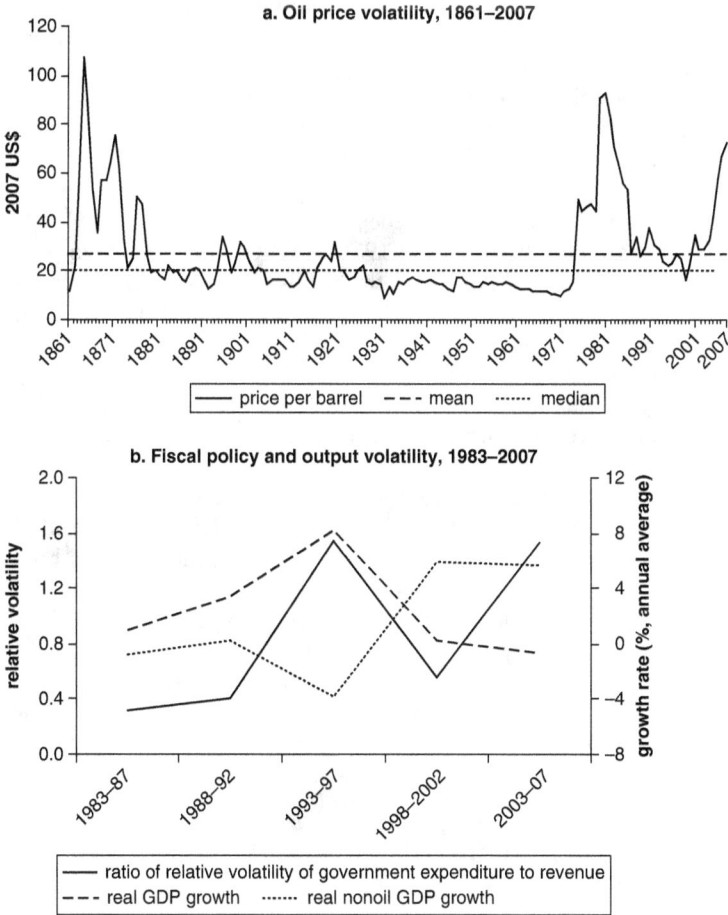

Source: Authors' calculations based on World Bank data.

difficult and costly to adjust expenditure downward, although the need to do so may be greater than the actual decline in income that triggered the need for adjustment to begin with. This is so because oil-rich countries, particularly the Republic of Congo, have a peculiar problem concerning capital market access: when oil prices are low, the need to borrow rises and access to capital falls. The value of their de facto collateral—oil wealth—also peaks when prices are high and drops when they are low. Thus, their borrowing capacity is inversely related to their borrowing need. This perverse link between income shortfalls, declining collateral values, and reduced resource inflows is a recipe for debt-overhang problems. Without adequate collateral, new lenders fear that too much of their money will be diverted to service old debt, thereby reducing the value of their claims even if projects financed by the new borrowing have a sufficiently high rate of return to service new debt in the absence of old claims outstanding. Manzano and Rigobon (2001) suggest a link between debt problems and slow growth in resource-rich countries.[1] High public indebtedness in oil-exporting countries suggests that the design of fiscal policy should pay special attention to the downside risk in international capital markets associated with the fact that world capital markets become inaccessible at precisely the moment they are needed most.

Following the oil boom of the 1970s, the Republic of Congo pursued highly procyclical fiscal policies in the 1980s. Together with the civil war, these policies resulted in growing deficits and a rapid rise in public spending during the oil boom years of the early 1980s. The late 1980s and early 1990s were characterized by large macroeconomic imbalances (figure 15.4). The decline in oil prices of the late 1980s resulted in significant decline in oil revenues, cuts in government investment spending, and limited structural reforms.

In addition, 1994 saw a 50 percent devaluation of the CFA franc—decided at the CFA franc zone level—to restore competitiveness and boost exports (figure 15.5). Together with the civil war, these factors brought external public debt and the associated debt-service burden to unsustainable levels (figure 15.6). Successive economic programs supported by the International Monetary Fund (IMF) went off track, because of political instability, weak fiscal discipline, and insufficient resolve to implement structural reforms, especially in the oil sector. As a result, the economy stagnated, fiscal and external imbalances widened markedly, and large domestic and external payment arrears accumulated.

Maintaining Fiscal Sustainability and Managing Oil Price Uncertainty

Assessing fiscal sustainability and vulnerability to debt-overhang problems for oil-rich countries requires distinguishing between oil and nonoil

Figure 15.4 Oil Revenue and Public Spending as a
Percentage of GDP, 1971–2005

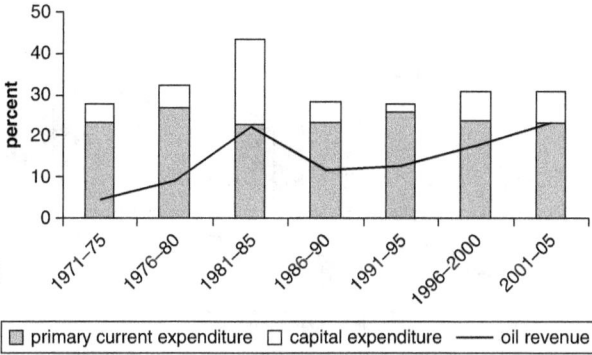

Source: IMF 2007; Carcillo, Leigh, and Villafuerte 2007.

Figure 15.5 Real Effective Exchange Rate, 1978–2007

Source: International Financial Statistics database.

primary deficits (see Davis, Ossowski, and Fedelino 2003; World Bank
2006). Such a distinction is warranted because of the nature of oil-related
fiscal revenue. Fiscal revenues from oil extraction result from (natural)
asset decumulation. This means that oil revenue is more like a financing
item than a source of current revenue. More rapid oil depletion today
means less oil revenue for future generations, unless part of the oil revenue
is reinvested in other forms of capital.

Figure 15.6 External Public and Publicly Guaranteed Debt and the Price of Oil, 1971–2005

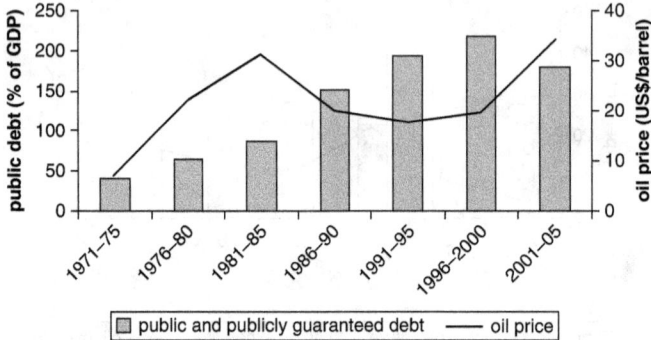

Source: Carcillo, Leigh, and Villafuerte 2007.

We use a model based on simulation methods to forecast the distribution and evolution of net public debt and assets, accounting for various rules governing oil fund allocations, the nonoil primary deficit, and foreign debt accumulation (figure 15.7).[2] The model consolidates the government's fiscal accounts with the Oil Stabilization Fund (similar to Norway's Oil Fund or Chile's Copper Stablization Fund) and the central bank's foreign currency reserves. Fiscal policy is captured by restrictions on the size of the nonoil primary deficit of the public sector plus the rule for allocating current oil revenues from the Oil Stabilization Fund to the budget. Fiscal sustainability analysis then means examining the impact of the nonoil primary fiscal deficit and Oil Stabilization Fund allocation rules on net debt levels, including money saved in the fund under various scenarios for the oil price. It allows for explicit analysis of the effects of uncertainty, not just through scenario analysis but also through full stochastic analysis.

The Value of Oil Wealth and Sustainable Spending

Three strategic questions frame the challenge the Republic of Congo faces in managing its oil windfall: How should the government manage an oil windfall that is likely to be short-lived? How much oil revenue should be saved and spent every year to ensure fiscal sustainability when that windfall is gone? How can the government assess the impact of uncertainty and manage the volatility in oil revenue?

Figure 15.7 Fiscal Sustainability Framework for Oil-Rich Countries

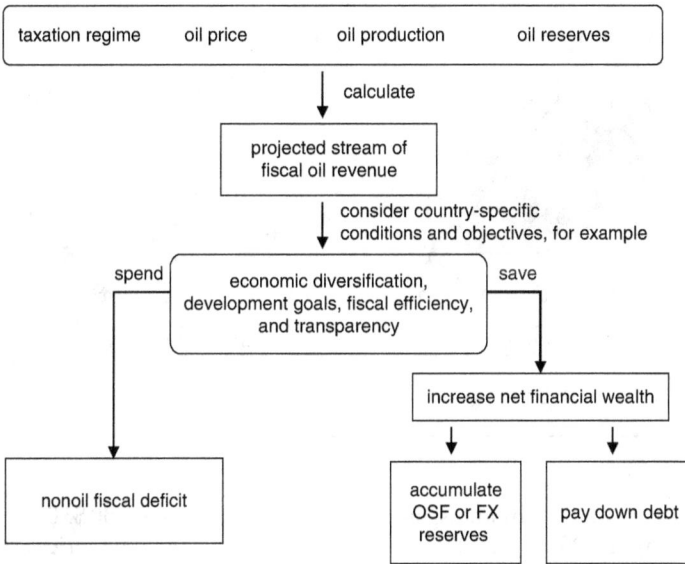

| taxation regime | oil price | oil production | oil reserves |

calculate

projected stream of fiscal oil revenue

consider country-specific conditions and objectives, for example

spend — economic diversification, development goals, fiscal efficiency, and transparency — save

increase net financial wealth

nonoil fiscal deficit

accumulate OSF or FX reserves

pay down debt

Source: Authors.
Note: FX = foreign exchange; OSF = Oil Stabilization Fund.

Below, we sketch answers to these questions. All calculations and scenarios should be considered illustrative; they need to be updated on the basis of new information and fine-tuning of key parameters in the framework.

The first set of inputs concerns the oil sector. The Republic of Congo's oil reserves are estimated at 1.6 billion barrels (IMF 2007). Oil production has been going up steadily and is expected to rise substantially until 2010, when new offshore fields come onstream and new extraction technologies are applied to extract more oil from maturing fields (figure 15.8). The government oil model assumes that, barring new oil discoveries, oil production will decline after 2010 and growth will depend increasingly on the nonoil sector.

The second critical input concerns oil price projections. In view of the high level of uncertainty surrounding long-term oil prices, we use three sets of projections in order to check the sensitivity of the results to different assumptions: (a) the official World Bank oil price forecast as of

Figure 15.8 Projected Oil Extraction, 2007–45

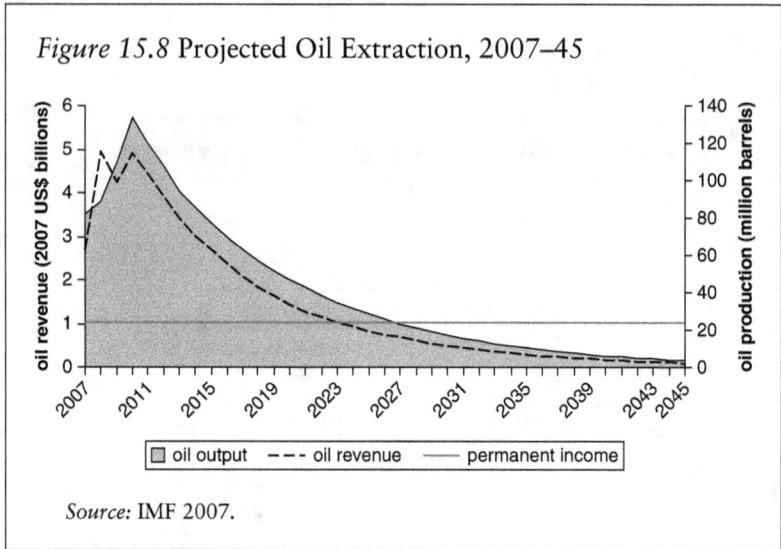

oil output   – – – oil revenue   —— permanent income

Source: IMF 2007.

October 7, 2008; (b) an assumption of a constant price of $50 a barrel in and after 2009; and (c) a low oil-price scenario, in which prices return to their long-term (since 1861) mean in 2009 (estimated at about $28 a barrel in 2009 dollars) and remain at this level thereafter (see British Petroleum 2008) (figure 15.9; see annex A).

As a result of the global financial turmoil and fears of a global recession, average oil prices fell more than $100 a barrel from their peak in July 2008 (figure 15.10a). Oil price volatility was high and increasing throughout 2008 (figure 15.10b), suggesting the importance of capturing the sensitivity of the Republic of Congo's fiscal position to relatively large changes in oil prices.

The revenue projections are derived from a framework that includes production forecasts of different fields and accounts for profit sharing and government charge schemes. By changing price assumptions, this framework produces the corresponding revenue profile (see figure 15.8). Under the official World Bank oil price assumptions, the Republic of Congo will experience a very steep increase in oil fiscal revenues during 2008–11. Without any new oil discoveries, oil revenues are projected to decline quickly, returning to their 2007 level by 2016, dropping to about a third of their 2007 level by 2028, and falling to zero by 2045.

To estimate the net present value of the projected stream of oil-related fiscal revenues, we discount the future income back to 2007 (table 15.1). We assume a safe real rate of interest of 3 percent, a long-term U.S. inflation projection of 2.4 percent, and a risk premium of 3 percent, the current academic consensus on the equity premium, based on the assumption that

Figure 15.9 Projected Oil Revenues, 2007–28

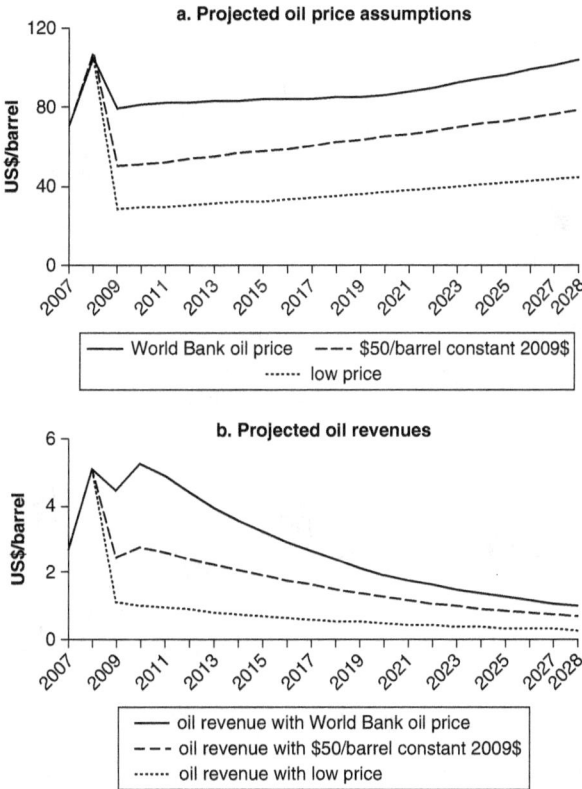

a. Projected oil price assumptions

US$/barrel

120
80
40
0

2007 2009 2011 2013 2015 2017 2019 2021 2023 2025 2027 2028

——— World Bank oil price   – – – $50/barrel constant 2009$
······· low price

b. Projected oil revenues

US$/barrel

6
4
2
0

2007 2009 2011 2013 2015 2017 2019 2021 2023 2025 2027 2028

——— oil revenue with World Bank oil price
– – – oil revenue with $50/barrel constant 2009$
······· oil revenue with low price

Source: Authors' calculations based on data from the World Bank
Development Economics Prospects Group.
Note: Oil price projections are as of October 2008.

oil shocks are largely demand driven and thus highly and positively correlated with stock markets. Under the World Bank oil price projections,
oil wealth equals about four times 2007 GDP and at least 11 times 2007
nonoil GDP. Under a more realistic price assumption of $50 a barrel, oil
wealth falls by about a third; it falls by another third if oil prices collapse
to their historical average.

   We also calculate the permanent-income equivalent of the net present value measure of oil wealth—the amount that can safely be spent
on an annual basis indefinitely, assuming that every generation receives
an equal amount of real wealth. The corresponding permanent-income

Figure 15.10 Average Daily Oil Price and Volatility, 2008

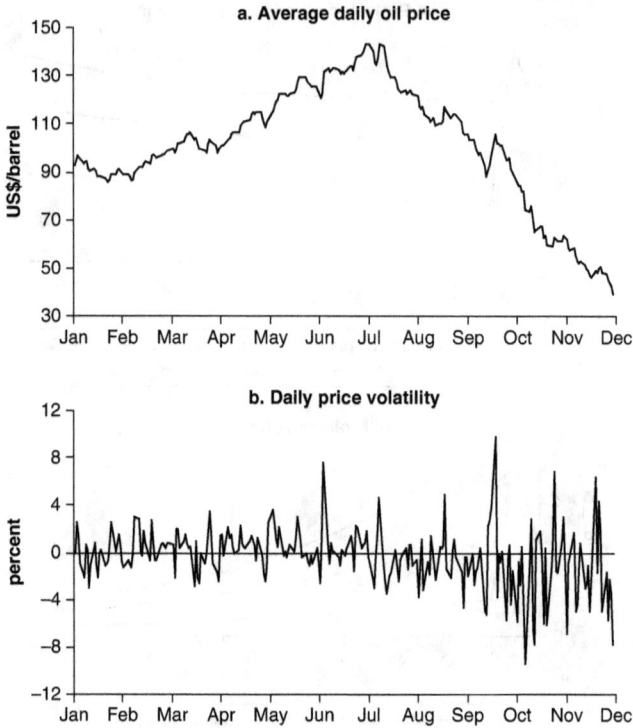

a. Average daily oil price

b. Daily price volatility

Source: Authors' calculations based on data from World Bank 2008.

equivalent is estimated at 35 percent of 2007 nonoil GDP under the World Bank price assumptions, 22 percent under the assumption of constant oil prices of $50 a barrel, and 11 percent under the low oil-price scenario. Annual permanent income in constant 2007 dollars is projected at $1 billion under the World Bank price assumptions, $0.7 billion under the constant oil-price assumption, and $0.3 billion under the low oil-price assumption.

These estimates are less back-loaded than they would be under a constant-share-of-GDP rule. Calculating annual permanent income based on a constant share of GDP would transfer substantially more to future generations, despite their greater nonoil wealth. We consider this feature of a constant-share-of-GDP rule unattractive.

Table 15.1 Present Value of Net Oil Wealth Based on
Permanent-Income Approach

Oil price assumption	Net wealth (2007 US$ billions)	Net oil wealth as percentage of 2007 GDP	Net oil wealth as percentage of 2007 nonoil GDP	Annuity (2007 US$ billions)	Permanent income as percentage of 2007 nonoil GDP
World Bank oil price (October 7, 2008)	34.1	445.0	1,171.7	1.0	35.2
$50/barrel in constant 2009 dollars	21.7	283.4	746.1	0.7	22.4
Historical average oil price ($29/ barrel in constant 2009 dollars)	11.1	145.0	381.8	0.3	11.5

Source: Authors' projections.
   Note: These calculations assume a safe real interest rate of 3 percent, a risk premium of 3 percent, and foreign inflation (U.S. inflation projection) of 2–4 percent a year.

Fiscal Sustainability under Uncertainty

This section examines fiscal sustainability under uncertainty in two ways. The first part of the section presents the results of scenario analysis. The second part of the section presents the results of Monte Carlo analysis.

Scenario Analysis. These permanent-income estimations should be compared with the nonoil primary deficit, which represents the net claim on nonoil resources, to be covered by the permanent-income amount (figure 15.11). Using this rule, the Republic of Congo will need to save substantial shares of its oil revenues over the next 20 years. Current levels of expenditure, which are increasing rapidly, have been well above the permanent-income equivalent level in 2007, even under optimistic oil price assumptions.

   These permanent-income estimates were used with other macro assumptions to obtain illustrative simulations for the likely trajectory of the net debt-to-GDP ratio. A permanent-income-based fiscal strategy assumes that nonoil deficits are bounded by the level of the permanent income from oil. This income is constant in real terms, which implies that it will decline

Figure 15.11 Projected Oil Revenue, Permanent Income, and Nonoil Primary Deficit

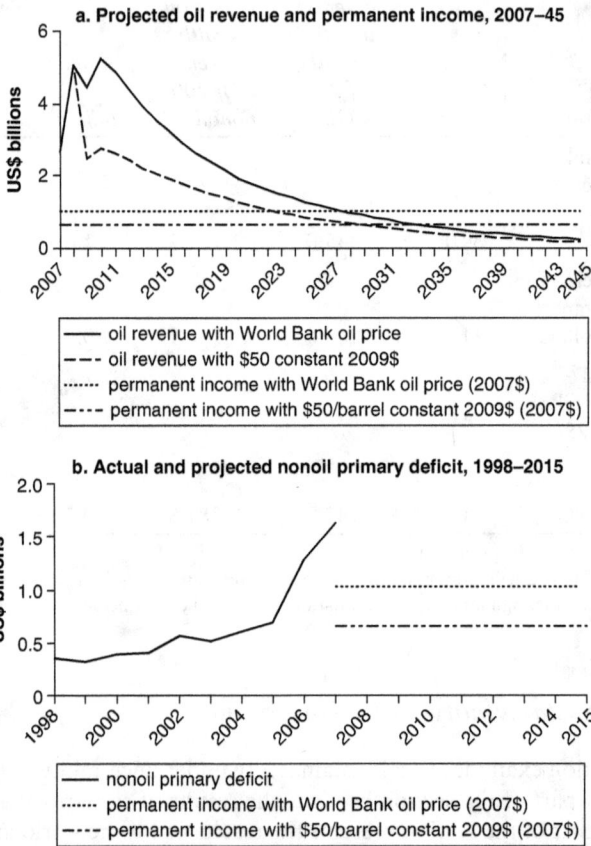

a. Projected oil revenue and permanent income, 2007–45

oil revenue with World Bank oil price
--- oil revenue with $50 constant 2009$
...... permanent income with World Bank oil price (2007$)
---- permanent income with $50/barrel constant 2009$ (2007$)

b. Actual and projected nonoil primary deficit, 1998–2015

nonoil primary deficit
...... permanent income with World Bank oil price (2007$)
---- permanent income with $50/barrel constant 2009$ (2007$)

Source: Authors' calculations based on World Bank data.

as a share of GDP (as long as the economy is growing). This is a reasonable sharing rule, because overall GDP growth is projected to be based not on population growth but on capital accumulation and productivity growth.

We also assess the impact of three illustrative fiscal strategies on fiscal sustainability: (a) a drastic adjustment of the nonoil primary deficit to its permanent-income equivalent at the beginning of projection period,[3] (b) gradual fiscal adjustment to permanent income, and (c) gradual fiscal adjustment to permanent income assuming that all the spending in excess of the permanent-income strategy is invested in public capital (figure 15.12). Assessing the impact of various fiscal strategies on fiscal sustainability involves forward-looking simulations of the net debt-to-GDP ratio over a longer time horizon. We choose until 2040 in order to check sustainability and robustness of various fiscal strategies during the post-oil period.[4] To check the sensitivity of these simulations to oil prices, we use various oil price assumptions.

Figure 15.12 Illustrative Fiscal Strategies for Managing Oil Windfall, 2007–40

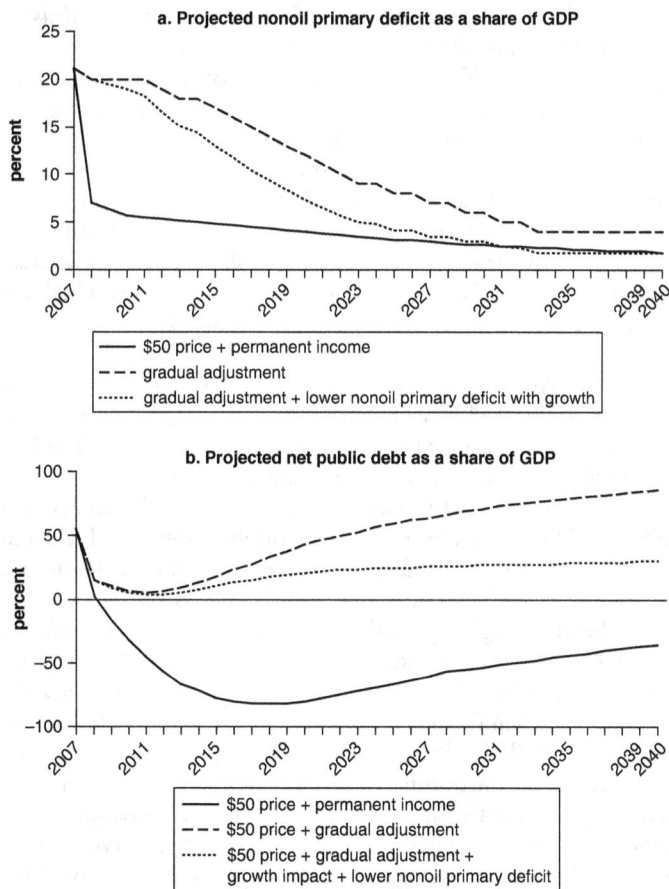

a. Projected nonoil primary deficit as a share of GDP

— $50 price + permanent income
--- gradual adjustment
······ gradual adjustment + lower nonoil primary deficit with growth

b. Projected net public debt as a share of GDP

— $50 price + permanent income
--- $50 price + gradual adjustment
······ $50 price + gradual adjustment +
growth impact + lower nonoil primary deficit

Source: Authors' projections.

Under the permanent-income scenario, sustainability is not threatened, because the strategy is explicitly designed as sustainable: the net asset position remains strong and basically unchanged over the projection horizon. Because of the hump-shaped profile of oil extraction, initial net savings are positive, as oil revenues exceed the permanent-income transfer and the nonoil primary deficit is limited to the value of the permanent-income transfer. Later, net savings stop, but the overall net asset position remains essentially stable. Given that the 2007 nonoil primary deficit is already substantially above the permanent-income equivalent spending out of oil wealth, such a strategy implies drastic fiscal adjustment during the next few years.

There may be legitimate reasons for spending more during the initial years than implied by the permanent-income approach. In particular, improving both the quantity and the quality of the country's infrastructure may require more financing than indicated under the permanent-income approach. This will add to upward pressure on the exchange rate and thus reduce competitiveness in the short run, but it may improve future competitiveness and therefore growth. Such a scenario is purely illustrative and assumes that the nonoil primary deficit over 2008–11 will remain close to its 2007 level and then decline, albeit much more gradually than the nonoil primary deficit levels implied by the permanent-income approach. This scenario assumes that all public spending in excess of its permanent-income equivalent is invested in infrastructure, which contributes to higher capital accumulation and therefore higher nonoil growth (see annex B).

What is the overall impact of such a growth scenario on fiscal sustainability? Initially (2008–13), when oil production is high, the corresponding fiscal revenues will be larger than the nonoil primary deficit. The Republic of Congo will therefore reach a near balanced net asset position. Beyond that period, gaps will start to emerge, because oil production is projected to decline rapidly in the absence of new oil discoveries and fiscal adjustment will be much more gradual. If, however, public spending in excess of the permanent-income equivalent contributes to higher public investment and therefore higher growth, it will have a dampening effect on the speed of public debt accumulation. As a result, the net public-debt-to-GDP ratio will increase initially but then stabilize at about 30 percent. Caution is advisable when financing domestic infrastructure, however: sudden oil wealth may easily lead to wasteful spending, corruption, and binding absorptive capacity constraints. To avoid such a scenario, countries should not allow expenditure to rise too rapidly. Institutional investments in anticorruption measures and project evaluation capacity deserve high priority.

To check the robustness of such a scenario to the risks of debt overhang, we assess fiscal sustainability of such a gradual adjustment strategy without the growth dividend. Given the steep increase in oil revenue and its high level during 2008–13, the Republic of Congo will reach a near balanced net asset position; beyond then, massive gaps are likely to emerge. Without any growth dividend, oil revenues start declining rapidly and the net debt will grow, reaching 85 percent of GDP in 2040. Unlike the permanent-income scenario, this scenario is not robust to negative oil price shocks. This simulation shows that if the price of oil were to drop to the historical long-run average, then the Republic of Congo would again become a major debtor.

Monte Carlo Simulations. Because fiscal revenues from oil account for the bulk of the government's revenues, oil price volatility—and the volatility of variables such as the real interest rate, the growth rate, and the real exchange rate—creates significant risks for the country's fiscal position. To assess the extent to which volatility of these driving variables translates in volatility of the country's future debt-output ratio, we performed 5,000 random simulations using the historical volatility of oil prices, the real exchange rate, the real growth rate, and the real interest rate to derive the distribution of future debt stocks. The results for the debt-to-GDP ratio are presented in a fan chart (Celasun, Debrun, and Ostry 2005; see also Budina and van Wijnbergen 2008b).

To assess the riskiness of the permanent-income-based fiscal strategy, we run two sets of simulations: one using historical variances for all the variables being simulated (figure 15.13a) and one in which the variance of the real exchange rate is reduced by 50 percent, reflecting the fact that this run has a more stable expenditure policy and should therefore have much less real exchange rate volatility (figure 15.13b). The simulations show that reducing the variance of the real exchange rate helps: the maximum possible loss at 97.5 percent probability falls from 50 percent to 20 percent of GDP. In the second scenario, the Republic of Congo stays out of debt with about 90 percent certainty during the entire horizon. These results suggest that the permanent-income scenario provides the country with a much safer environment.

Debt Management and Fiscal Policy

All simulations presented so far assume a fixed nonoil primary deficit rule (for example, a nonoil primary deficit equal to the ex ante calculated permanent-income level of oil revenues). The lack of any ex post response to adverse shocks then leads to a great deal of uncertainty about future debt stocks; even the use of a fixed permanent-income rule is not enough to obtain manageable levels of debt variance. This matters a great deal: default risk premia depend on the likelihood that debt levels are larger than a threshold level beyond which political problems will block debt service (see Schabert and van Wijnbergen 2008). Although we do not know what these thresholds are, for any given value, greater uncertainty about future debt levels implies a greater probability of future crises.

Figure 15.13 Distribution of Future Public Debt Stocks under Permanent-Income-Based Fiscal Strategy, 2007–40

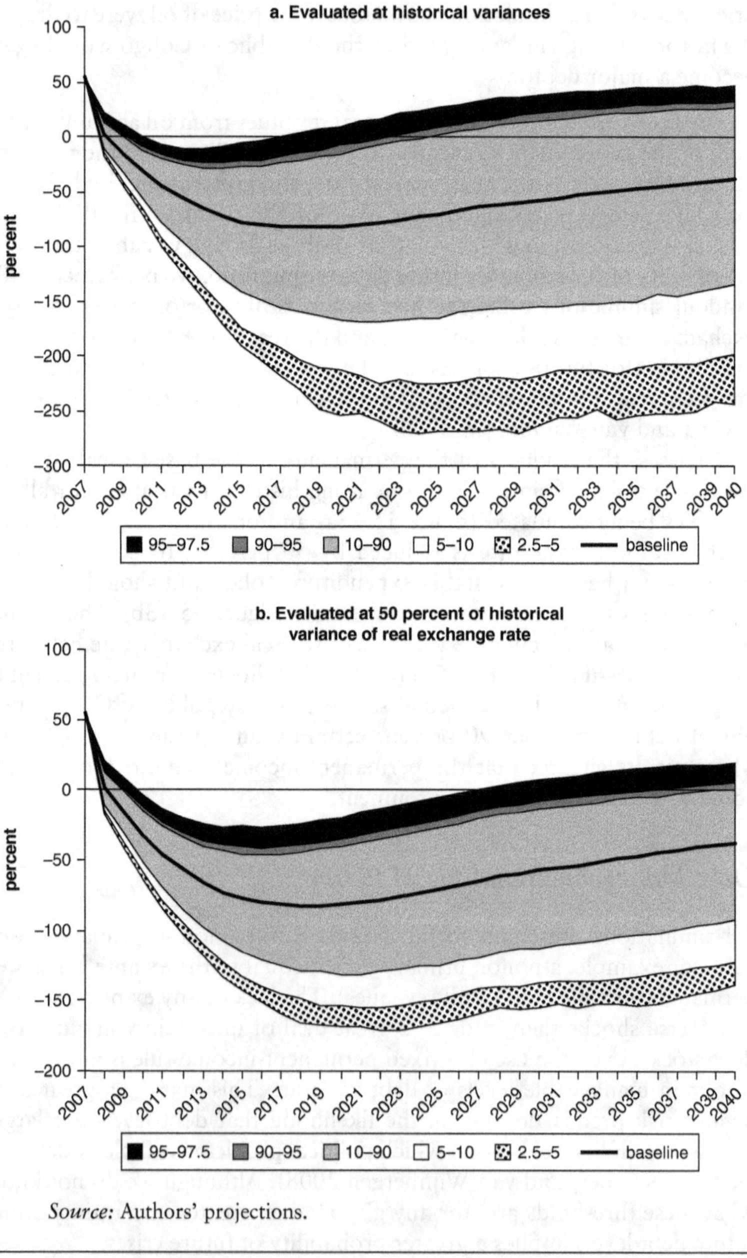
a. Evaluated at historical variances
percent
100
50
0
–50
–100
–150
–200
–250
–300
2007
2009
2011
2013
2015
2017
2019
2021
2023
2025
2027
2029
2031
2033
2035
2037
2039
2040
95–97.5
90–95
10–90
5–10
2.5–5
baseline
b. Evaluated at 50 percent of historical variance of real exchange rate
percent
100
50
0
–50
–100
–150
–200
2007
2009
2011
2013
2015
2017
2019
2021
2023
2025
2027
2029
2031
2033
2035
2037
2039
2040
95–97.5
90–95
10–90
5–10
2.5–5
baseline

Source: Authors' projections.

Using an active debt-feedback rule—tightening fiscal policy whenever negative debt shocks occur—can greatly reduce the variance of future debt outcomes. Doing so reduces the riskiness of the economic environment without on average increasing the expected burden of fiscal policy. Such a debt-feedback rule is an example of how fiscal policy can be used to actively manage debt, in this case to reduce its volatility.

In what follows, we apply this rule to a permanent-income-based scenario to reduce the volatility of future net debt. In figure 15.13b, we assume that the nonoil primary deficit equals the permanent-income value (as currently estimated) of oil revenues and that the increased stability of spending reduces the variance of the real exchange rate by 50 percent. Although there is 90 percent certainty the Republic of Congo will stay out of net debt, there is a very wide range of expectations about future debt stocks.

Next we assume a feedback rule from higher-than-anticipated debt stocks to a stricter fiscal policy. In particular, we assume a simple linear feedback rule in which a fixed percentage, α, of the previous year's excess debt (higher than projected in the base run for given nonoil primary deficit assumptions) is offset by a lower nonoil primary deficit. Adding such a feedback rule (assuming a coefficient of 5 percent) to the simulations in figure 15.13 yields the results summarized in figure 15.14.

The simulations show a dramatically improved outlook. Although the expected value of future debt stocks is not affected, the distribution around the baseline narrows substantially. The 95 percent worst-outcome line now stays at a positive net assets position of 40 percent of GDP instead of touching zero, and the range between the 95 percent worst outcome and the 95 percent best outcome narrows to about 100 percentage points in 2040, down from a high of 220 percent of GDP.

These results suggest that it is advisable to complement the fiscal deficit strategy (nonoil deficits equal to the permanent-income level of future oil revenues) by a target level for net debt, with a rule that any excess over that target level will result in a smaller nonoil primary deficit (of, for example, 5 percent of that excess). Such a policy should have a strong impact on confidence; although it does not affect the average spending level of the government, it will greatly reduce the variance of debt outcomes, thereby lowering crisis expectations. A fiscal policy reaction should translate in lower costs of debt servicing and less volatility in the capital account.

Assessing the Riskiness of a Growth-Oriented Fiscal Strategy

Next we assess the riskiness of a hypothetical scenario of a gradual fiscal adjustment to permanent income. This scenario assumes that all public spending in excess of its permanent-income equivalent is invested in infrastructure, which contributes to higher capital accumulation and therefore

Figure 15.14 Distribution of Future Public Debt Stocks under Permanent-Income-Based Fiscal Strategy with Debt Feedback, 2007–40

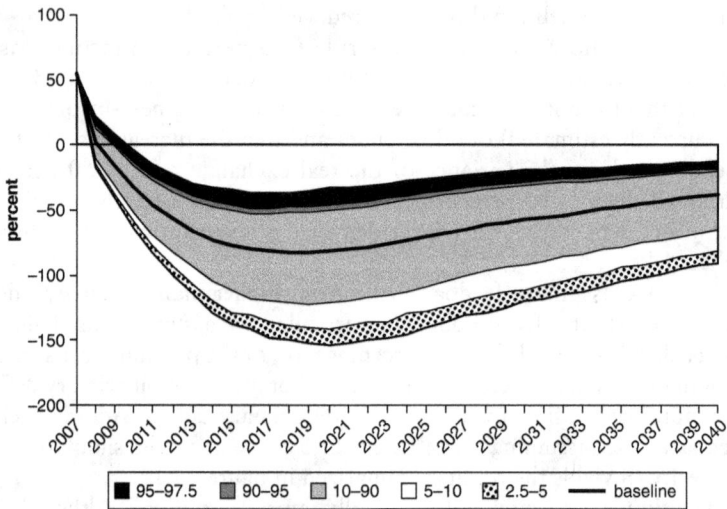

Source: Authors' projections.

Note: The figure shows feedback from debt surprises to primary surplus, $\alpha = 0.05$, historical variance for oil prices and at 50 percent of historical variance for real exchange rate.

results in higher future nonoil growth. In the absence of shocks and if one assumes constant oil prices of $50 a barrel during the projection period, the Republic of Congo will reach a near balanced net asset position between 2008 and 2013, largely as a result of sizable fiscal revenues caused by rapid expansion of the oil sector. Beyond that period, the net public-debt-to-GDP ratio will increase initially before stabilizing at about 30 percent.

Such a strategy introduces considerable uncertainty in the sense that the resulting distributions become very wide: there is a 50 percent chance that the net debt-to-GDP ratio will be higher than 30 percent of GDP and a 97.5 percent probability that the maximum net debt will be 53 percent of GDP by 2040. Therefore, according to historical variances and the complete lack of any feedback of rising debt levels on fiscal policy, the net debt position can become very large over the next three decades. This indicates that the risk of major debt problems is very real under this strategy (figure 15.15a).

Figure 15.15 Distribution of Future Debt Stocks under a
Growth-Oriented Fiscal Strategy, 2007–40

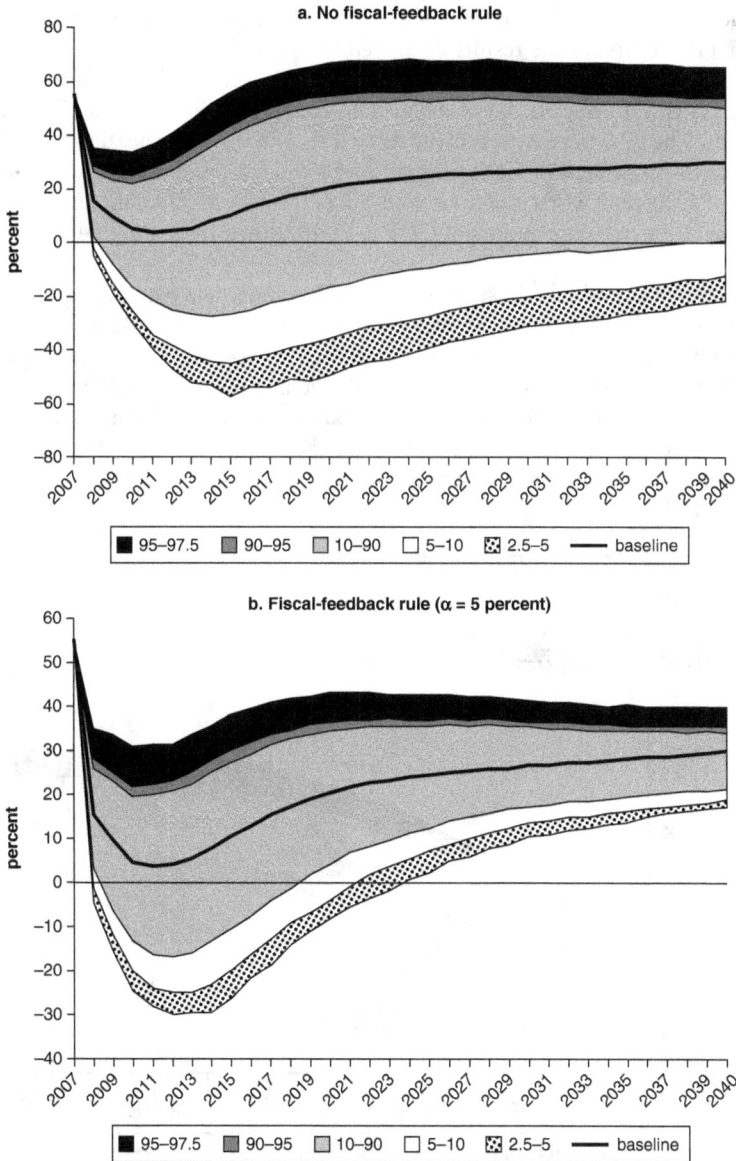

a. No fiscal-feedback rule

Legend: 95–97.5 | 90–95 | 10–90 | 5–10 | 2.5–5 | baseline

b. Fiscal-feedback rule (α = 5 percent)

Legend: 95–97.5 | 90–95 | 10–90 | 5–10 | 2.5–5 | baseline

Source: Authors' projections.

Using an active debt feedback rule—tightening fiscal policy whenever negative debt shocks occur—can greatly reduce the variance of future debt outcomes. We apply this rule to the hypothetical growth-oriented scenario in order to reduce the volatility of future net debt. We add a debt feedback rule (assuming a coefficient of 5 percent) to the simulations of figure 15.11b, to obtain the results displayed in figure 15.15b.

The simulations show that although the expected value of future debt stocks is not affected, the distribution around that line narrows substantially. The 97.5 percent worst-outcome line now stays at a net debt-to-GDP ratio of 40 percent of GDP (instead of 53 percent), and the range between the 95 percent worst outcome and 95 percent best outcome narrows to about 23 percentage points of GDP in 2040 (down from a high 49 percent of GDP).

If such a gradual adjustment strategy does not yield a growth dividend, the net asset position evaporates over time (figure 15.16). As a result, the Republic of Congo is expected to become a major net debtor once again, with the net debt-to-GDP ratio in 2040 reaching nearly 90 percent of GDP. In addition, a fiscal-feedback rule introduces considerable uncertainty, in the sense that the resulting distributions become very wide: there is a 50 percent chance that net debt will exceed 90 percent of GDP.

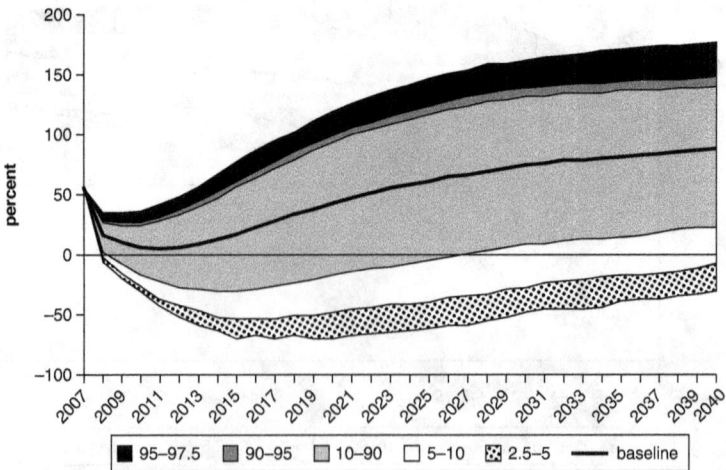

Figure 15.16 Projected Public Sector Debt under Gradual Adjustment to Permanent Income without Growth Dividend, 2007–40

Source: Authors' projections.

Conclusions

The Republic of Congo faces a major challenge in managing its high but temporary and volatile oil wealth. Because of the temporary nature of this windfall, intergenerational fairness is a major issue, as are concerns about post-oil economic performance. The highly volatile nature of oil revenues is the most pressing immediate concern. If income volatility translates into volatile spending levels—and thus increases the volatility of the real exchange rate—an effective tax on private investment will result, with negative consequences for economic growth.

Explicitly adopting a permanent-income approach to the decision of how much to spend from oil revenues is advisable. The illustrative simulations, in which the nonoil primary deficit is initially at close to its 2007 level but then gradually declines with lower levels of expenditure, shows the reemergence of the Republic of Congo as a net debtor once oil revenues start declining. If spending levels remain at current levels, unsustainable levels of net debt will emerge once the oil windfall is gone. Limiting the net claim on resources by the public sector (the nonoil primary deficit) to the permanent-income equivalent of the country's oil wealth will result in sustainable spending programs, in which the Republic of Congo is not expected to run into a net debt position at any time during the projection period.

Stochastic simulations deriving the entire distribution of future debt stocks based on historical variances of the simulated driving variables reveal that future debt levels are characterized by a very wide distribution as uncertainty accumulates. This matters a great deal: projections of crises will depend on the likelihood that critical debt levels are exceeded, so the wider the distribution of future debt stocks around a given baseline, the greater the associated estimates of crisis probabilities, even if the baseline remains below any crisis trigger level. Under the gradual fiscal adjustment to permanent income, in a variant on the value-at-risk approach, the maximum debt level that can be expected with 90 percent confidence reaches as high as 100 percent. Under the scenario in which the nonoil primary deficit equals its current level, debt is unsustainable given the declining production profile. These scenarios expose the country to considerable risk. The permanent-income approach reduces that risk a great deal. If we also assume a decline in the variance of the real exchange rate in response to more stable expenditure patterns, we can say with 95 percent certainty that the Republic of Congo will remain out of debt for the entire simulation horizon, substantially reducing crisis probabilities.

These results are particularly important in countries with large infrastructure gaps, where investing in (public) infrastructure may yield higher returns than elsewhere and help meet development objectives. Caution is advisable when financing domestic infrastructure, however: sudden oil wealth may easily lead to wasteful spending, corruption, and binding absorptive capacity constraints. To prevent waste caused by absorptive capacity constraints, care should be taken not to let expenditure rise too rapidly if oil money is used for public investment. Institutional investments in anticorruption measures and project evaluation capacity deserve high priority.

This chapter illustrates how fiscal policy can be used to actively manage debt. Use of an active debt feedback rule—in which fiscal policy is tightened whenever negative debt shocks occur—greatly reduces the variance of future debt outcome. Under an active feedback loop, targets for deficits are extended by targets for debt; any excess of debt over that target path results in a deficit reduction equal to a given percentage of the excess debt stock of the previous year. With a correction coefficient of 5 percent, we show that such a feedback policy leads to a dramatic narrowing of the range within which future debt stocks will fall. In particular, the debt level stays widely negative under the permanent-income scenario: with 95 percent certainty, net assets will remain at 20 percent of GDP or higher. Such a debt feedback rule will not raise the average burden of fiscal policy, but it will greatly reduce the probabilities of estimated crisis by reducing variance in the economy.

Annex A: Oil Price and Revenue Projections

Table 15A.1 Oil Price and Revenue Projections, 2007–28

Item	2007	2008	2009	2010	2011	2012	2013	2014	2015	2016	2017
World Bank oil price	71	105	79	81	82	82	83	83	84	84	85
Constant $50/barrel (in constant 2009 dollars)	71	107	50	51	52	54	55	56	58	59	60
Historical average oil price ($29/barrel in constant 2009 dollars)	71	105	28	29	30	30	31	32	32	33	34
World Bank oil revenue (billion CFAF)	1,284	2,189	1,953	2,289	2,114	1,895	1,692	1,531	1,386	1,253	1,131
Oil revenue with constant price of $50/barrel	1,284	2,189	1,077	1,195	1,133	1,041	951	881	816	755	699
Oil revenue with historical average oil price ($29/barrel)	1,284	2,189	483	436	416	381	345	316	289	267	249

(continued)

Table 15A.1 (continued)

	2018	2019	2020	2021	2022	2023	2024	2025	2026	2027	2028
World Bank oil price	71	105	79	81	82	82	83	83	84	84	85
Constant $50 (in constant 2009 dollars)	62	63	65	66	68	70	71	73	75	77	78
Historical average oil price ($29/barrel in constant 2009 dollars)	35	36	37	37	38	39	40	41	42	43	44
World Bank oil revenue (billion CFAF)	1,021	920	828	762	702	647	595	547	501	464	430
Oil revenue with constant price of $50/barrel	645	595	548	505	464	428	398	370	344	319	296
Oil revenue with historical average oil price ($29/barrel)	232	217	203	191	179	167	156	146	136	126	117

Source: Authors' projections.

Annex B: Public Debt Dynamics

Increases in net public debt (that is, debt net of net foreign assets, public debt holdings of the central bank, and oil fund assets) can be decomposed into various contributing factors, which in turn can be linked to macroeconomic projections. Public debt dynamics can be broken down into several components as percentages of GDP: the primary fiscal deficit net of seigniorage revenues; growth-adjusted real interest rate payments on domestic debt; the real cost of external borrowing, including capital gains and losses on net external debt caused by changes in the real exchange rate; and other factors. Debt can be expressed as follows:

$$\dot{d} = (pd - \sigma) + (r - g)b + (r^* + \hat{e} - g)(b^* - nfa^*)e + OF, \qquad (15A.1)$$

where d is the net public-debt-to-GDP ratio (net of net foreign assets, public debt holdings of the central bank, and oil fund assets); pd is the overall primary deficit as a share of GDP; g is the real GDP growth rate; r is the real interest rate on domestic debt; r^* is the real interest rate on external debt; e is the real exchange rate; and OF is other factors.[5] The variable OF collects residuals from cross-product terms arising from the use of discrete time data (see Budina, van Wijnbergen, and Bandiera 2009 for explicit discrete time formulas) and the impact of debt-increasing factors that in a perfect accounting world would be included in deficit measures but in the real world are not. Examples are contingent liabilities that actually materialize, such as the fiscal consequences of a bank bailout, and one-off privatization revenues. Of course, if countries borrow in more than one foreign currency, more than one foreign debt stock should be kept track of in an analogous manner. Note that in this single-equation exercise, debt levels are generated but all other variables are exogenous (that is, feedbacks from shocks to debt levels are not incorporated).

Given the special features of oil revenue—in particular, its exhaustibility and volatility— the next step requires the incorporation of various nonoil deficit rules in the public debt-dynamics equation. We break the overall primary balance into two components: the nonoil primary balance f, which measures the true fiscal effort in an oil-producing country, and the projected oil fiscal revenues $Roil$, (revenue projected using the World Bank's World Economic Outlook/Development Prospects Group oil price projections), which reflects the fact that oil windfall caused by high prices or more rapid oil extraction results in a much lower primary deficit. Isolating oil revenue also allows us to assess the impact of oil shocks on the overall net debt/net asset position:

$$pd = f - Roil. \qquad (15A.2)$$

After expressing pd in equation (15A.2) in terms of the nonoil primary deficit, we obtain:

$$\dot{d} = (f - \sigma) + (r - g)b + (r^* + \hat{e} - g)(b^* - nfa^*)e - Roil + OF. \quad (15A.3)$$

The public debt-dynamics equation (equation 15A.3) reveals the fact that net public debt could increase because of the higher nonoil primary deficit and decrease because of higher oil revenues caused by high prices or more rapid oil extraction. Isolating oil revenue also allows us to assess the impact of oil shocks on the overall net debt/net asset position.

Given oil price uncertainty and the possibility of volatility clustering, many oil-rich countries have introduced rules that aim at stabilizing the oil revenue flow to the budget. Some countries use a conservative budget reference price of oil. In what follows, all revenues stemming from actual prices in excess of this reference price are diverted to an oil fund (revenue shortfalls caused by prices falling short of the reference price can be met from the oil fund). Implementation of such a price stabilization rule is especially relevant for mature oil producers with a relatively constant extraction profile, for which the price of oil is the main source of volatility.

Such an oil fund rule needs to be modified for countries with new oil discoveries (such as Azerbaijan), which may find that they can suddenly and substantially raise the nonoil deficit. Whereas the same considerations—absorptive capacity, impact on the real exchange rate and the nonoil economy, and intergenerational equity—apply, the emphasis would be different, with absorptive capacity becoming much more important. For countries in which oil is running out (such as Yemen), the emphasis on the nonoil economy and diversification should receive more prominence.

To be meaningful at all, any oil fund accumulation rule should be complemented with targets for the nonoil deficit. Putting money aside with one hand but borrowing on the side with the other obviously would make the oil fund rule ineffective.

To assess the fiscal sustainability implications of oil fund/nonoil deficit rules, we break oil fiscal revenues, $Roil$, into two parts: oil revenue flow to the budget $Roil_{sb}$ and net inflow into the oil fund (or the difference between total oil revenue and oil revenue flow to the budget, $Roil - Roil_{sb}$). By subtracting and adding the oil revenue flow to the budget, $Roil_{sb}$, on the right-hand side of equation (15A.4), we express the public debt–dynamics equation in terms of these two components of total oil fiscal revenue:

$$\dot{d} = (f - Roil_{sb} - \sigma) + (r - g)b + (r^* + \hat{e} - g)(b^* - nfa^*)$$
$$e - (r^* + \hat{e} - g)oa^*e \, (Roil - Roil_{sb}) + OF. \quad (15A.4)$$

We assume that oil revenue above the oil revenue flow to the budget and interest earned on the stock of oil fund assets is saved in a ring-fenced oil fund:

$$\dot{oa}^* - (r^* + \hat{e} - g)oa^*e\ (Roil - Roil_{sb}). \tag{15A.5}$$

The change in the net public-debt-to-GDP ratio now also accounts for the accumulation of assets in a ring-fenced oil fund, oa^* – dot.

$$d = (f - Roil_{sb} - \sigma) + (r - g)b + (r^* + \hat{e} - g)(b^* - nfa^*) \\ e - \dot{oa}^*e + OF. \tag{15A.6}$$

The modified public debt-dynamics equation (15A.6) isolates the impact of oil on public finances in several ways. First, it reveals the fact that a substantial share of fiscal revenues is derived from oil; the primary fiscal deficit (noninterest spending minus revenues) is replaced with the nonoil primary deficit, isolating net oil revenues evaluated at reference price as a financing flow, $Roil_{sb}$. Second, the change in the net debt-to-GDP ratio now also accounts for fiscal savings out of oil, accumulated in a ring-fenced oil fund, oa^* – dot.[6] Third, given the higher volatility of oil fiscal revenue, uncertainty about the net debt trajectory for oil-rich countries is likely to be much greater. For this reason, a great deal of attention should be paid to uncertainty and risk in the fiscal sustainability assessment.

Notes

1. Budina, Pang, and van Wijnbergen (2007) provide empirical evidence of this problem for Nigeria.
2. See Budina and van Wijnbergen (2008a) for the use of this model in Nigeria. See Budina, van Wijnbergen, and Bandiera (2009) for fiscal sustainability under uncertainty in Azerbaijan.
3. For the derivation of such a strategy of a gradual adjustment to permanent income equivalent, see IMF (2007).
4. For more information and details on the methodology, see Budina, van Wijnbegren, and Bandiaera (2009).
5. To simplify the exposition, we present a continuous time formula. See Budina, van Wijnbergen, and Bandiera (2009) for a discrete derivation of formulas for public debt dynamics. World Bank (2005) uses a similar debt decomposition formula.
6. Ring-fenced oil funds can be successful only if complemented with a rule that limits the nonoil deficit or public debt. Absent such a rule, the government will accumulate assets in the oil fund while borrowing; the net asset position may even deteriorate, because the cost of borrowing is typically higher than the interest earned on oil fund assets.

References

Aghion P., P. Bacchetta, R. Ranciere, and K. Rogoff. 2006. "Exchange Rate Volatility and Productivity Growth: The Role of Financial Development." NBER Working Paper 12117, National Bureau of Economic Research, Cambridge, MA.

British Petroleum. 2008. "British Petroleum Statistical Review." http:\\www.bp .com\productlanding.do?categoryld=6929&contentld=7044622.

Budina, N., G. Pang, and S. van Wijnbergen. 2007. "Nigeria's Growth Record: Dutch Disease or Debt Overhang?" Policy Research Working Paper 4256, World Bank, Washington, DC.

Budina, N., and S. van Wijnbergen. 2008a. "Managing Oil Revenue Volatility in Nigeria: The Role of Fiscal Policy." In *Africa at a Turning Point? Growth, Aid and External Shocks*, ed. D. Go and J. Page, 427–59. Washington, DC: World Bank.

———. 2008b. "Quantitative Approaches to Fiscal Sustainability Analysis: A Case Study of Turkey since the Crisis of 2001." *World Bank Economic Review* 23 (1): 119–40.

Budina, N., S. van Wijnbergen, and L. Bandiera. 2009. "'How to' of Fiscal Sustainability in Oil-Rich Countries: The Case of Azerbaijan." *Proceedings of the Workshop on Fiscal Sustainability*, Bank of Italy, Rome.

Carcillo, S., D. Leigh, and M. Villafuerte. 2007. "Catch-up Growth, Habits, Oil Depletion, and Fiscal Policy: Lessons from the Republic of Congo." International Monetary Fund, Washington, DC.

Celasun, O., X. Debrun, and J. Ostry. 2005. "Primary Surplus Behavior and Risks to Fiscal Sustainability in Emerging Markets: A Fan-Chart Approach." International Monetary Fund, Washington, DC.

Davis, J. M., R. Ossowski, and A. Fedelino, eds. 2003. *Fiscal Policy Formulation and Implementation in Oil-Producing Countries*. Washington, DC: International Monetary Fund.

Devlin, J., and M. Lewin. 2005. "Managing Oil Booms and Busts in Developing Countries." In *Managing Economic Volatility and Crises: A Practitioner's Guide*, ed. J. Aizenman and B. Pinto, 186–209. Cambridge, U.K.: Cambridge University Press.

IMF (International Monetary Fund). 2007. "Republic of Congo: Selected Issues." Country Report 07/206, IMF, Washington, DC.

———. 2008. *Republic of Congo: Staff Report for the First Assessment under the Staff-Monitored Program*. Washington, DC: IMF.

Manzano, O., and R. Rigobon. 2001. "Resource Curse or Debt Overhang?" NBER Working Paper W8390, National Bureau of Economic Research, Cambridge, MA.

Schabert, A., and S. van Wijnbergen. 2008. "Sovereign Default and the Stability of Inflation Targeting Regimes." University of Amsterdam.

Sengupta, R. 2008. "Republic of Congo: A Brief Report." Economic Policy and Debt Department (PRMED), World Bank, Washington, DC.

van Wijnbergen, Sweder. 1985. "Trade Reform, Aggregate Investment, and Capital Flight: On Credibility and the Value of Information." *Economics Letters* 19 (4): 369–72.

————. 2008. "The Permanent Income Approach in Practice: A Policy Guide to Sustainable Fiscal Policy in Azerbaijan." University of Amsterdam.

World Bank. 2005. "Nigeria's Opportunity of a Generation: Meeting the MDGs, Reducing Indebtedness." Anchor report prepared for Africa Region, Poverty Reduction and Economic Management (PREM), World Bank, Washington, DC.

————. 2006. "Debt Sustainability Analysis in Oil-Rich Countries." PRMED Note, Economic Policy and Debt Department, World Bank, Washington, DC.

————. 2007. *World Development Indicators*. Washington, DC: World Bank.

————. 2008. *World Bank Crude Oil Price Projections*. October, Development Prospects Group (DECPG), World Bank, Washington, DC.

16

Debt-Swap Mechanisms Revisited: Lessons from the Chilean Experience of the 1980s

Leonardo Hernández

In the aftermath of the debt crisis of the early 1980s and the severe recession of 1982–83, in which real aggregate output fell by about 17 percent, the Chilean economy was in a critical situation. The country was faced with a large and growing stock of foreign debt, totaling about 90 percent of GDP, which rose to a peak of more than 120 percent of GDP in 1985.

Chile's indebtedness was the result of excess borrowing by the country's private sector for several years before the crisis. Such borrowing was possible because of foreign banks' lax lending policies, lax national banking regulations, and high liquidity in the international capital markets during the second part of the 1970s. Faced with severe indebtedness and exclusion from the international capital markets, which caused a severe scarcity of foreign exchange, in May 1985 the economic authorities created two special mechanisms to convert or swap foreign debt for Chilean assets in the form of either new domestic debt or equity. By 1991, these mechanisms had helped reduce foreign debt by about $6.9 billion—equivalent to 35 percent of the debt stock outstanding in December 1984.

This chapter reviews the Chilean experience with debt-swap mechanisms during the 1980s. It highlights their main features, drawbacks, and achievements, with the aim of drawing lessons for other heavily indebted countries. It examines this particular experience because it may be valuable to countries seeking reduction in their external debt beyond that attained by debt-relief mechanisms. Additional debt reductions would enhance the benefits that result from lower indebtedness, such as increased access to private capital markets, increased school enroll-ment rates, and others discussed in this volume. Debt-swap mechanisms complement rather than substitute for debt-relief efforts. As such, they could be pursued by countries that fulfill minimum institutional, legal, and macro policy framework requirements and are interested in resolving their debt-overhang problem.

The chapter is organized as follows. The first section examines the factors that led to Chile's overindebtedness. The second section briefly describes the two mechanisms put in place by the Chilean authorities in the second half of the 1980s and presents their results. The third section discusses their economic rationale. It analyzes the advantage of the two mechanisms relative to others and identifies and discusses the main pros and cons put forward by supporters and opponents of the mechanisms at the time. The fourth section examines the conditions countries must meet before they can introduce and expect a positive outcome for debt swaps. The concluding section summarizes the most important issues policy makers need to consider when evaluating the use of debt-swap mechanisms.

What Led to Overindebtedness?

Beginning in 1974, the Chilean economy underwent a significant struc-tural transformation, in which the old development model of import sub-stitution cum government intervention was replaced by a competitive open market economy. Stringent fiscal and monetary reforms introduced to reduce inflation and cut the fiscal deficit, at a time when the country faced severe external constraints, brought on a sharp recession in 1975, followed by a period of rapid economic growth in 1976. Real GDP con-tracted about 13 percent in 1975; between 1977 and 1980, the economy grew at an average annual rate of 8.5 percent. At the same time, the rate of consumer price inflation fell steadily, from 376 percent in 1974 to less than 10 percent in 1981, while the fiscal balance improved, with the deficit falling from 24 percent in 1973 to less than 3 percent of GDP in 1976 and a small surplus appearing in 1979. All this occurred during a period in which the terms of trade were half the average of the previous decade and fairly stable (see annex tables 16A.1 and 16A.2).

Although the recovery from the 1975 recession can explain some of this rapid economic growth, the principal impetus was the profound eco-nomic transformation that was under way. This transformation included the opening of the trade account;[1] a large privatization program for banks and state-owned enterprises; financial liberalization; partial lib-eralization of the capital account, including the granting of special legal status to foreign direct investment (FDI);[2] introduction of the value added tax; abolition of multiple exchange rates; and, in 1979, the pegging of the nominal exchange rate to the dollar. Until then, a crawling peg had been used with the aim of attaining a depreciated real exchange rate to boost exports and reducing domestic inflation. The reforms brought on a period of very rapid growth, led initially by the export sector and later by the rapid increase in aggregate demand and imports.

But this was not the end of the story. Rapid economic growth led to high expectations, which in turn led firms and households to borrow heavily. In the presence of lax banking regulations and easy access to syndicated loans offered by foreign banks to their Chilean counterparts, overborrowing and connected lending grew unchecked, increasing financial fragility. As a result, total foreign debt more than tripled between 1975 and 1982, from $5.5 billion to $17.3 billion. This staggering increase—from 214 percent of the country's exports in 1977 to 370 percent in 1982–83—occurred despite the rapid growth of Chilean exports, which grew at an annual rate of more than 15 percent a year in the second half of the 1970s. More important, because the government had been reducing its deficit, the share of private debt in total debt increased from 19 percent in 1976 to 65 percent in 1981, whereas that of the public sector (comprising the central government, the central bank, and public enterprises) fell from 81 percent to 35 percent. Meanwhile, the current account deficit grew unchecked, to a maximum of more than 14 percent of GDP in 1981, the year before the crisis.

At this critical stage of mounting internal and external fragility, the tightening of monetary policy in the United States (with the corresponding appreciation of the U.S. dollar, in which most of Chile's foreign debt was denominated)[3] and the sharp deterioration of the country's terms of trade (by about 20 percent between 1980 and 1982) were all that was needed to precipitate a major balance of payments crisis. The crisis forced Chile to abandon the nominal peg, increasing the burden of servicing foreign debt and pushing the country into a deep recession and financial crisis.

The magnitude of the financial crisis is evidenced by the government's action in taking over or intervening in about 60 percent of the banking industry, at the time privately owned and managed, for future liquidation or recapitalization and posterior privatization. Action was taken through the central bank, which offered soft loans and took on bad bank assets as collateral. These developments brought many private corporations into bankruptcy; the government had to provide rescue packages and offer soft loans to make them viable. Cleaning up the corporate and banking sectors took until the end of the decade—and much longer for a few emblematic cases (resolving the so-called subordinated debt of some large private banks took well beyond 1990; in one case, repayment is still ongoing).

A distinctive feature of the Chilean experience is that foreign debt was originated by the private sector but had to be guaranteed or assumed by the government at a later stage in the crisis. This occurred because, given the severity of the crisis and the fact that Chile—like most developing countries at the time—was unable to access international capital markets, the country needed to renegotiate and reschedule the payment of interest and principal. As a condition of renegotiating and offering soft new loans ("fresh money"), which would allow the country to resume normal foreign trade, foreign banks demanded that the government guarantee the stock of outstanding debt.

In general, in the years after the crisis, private foreign debt began to be substituted for sovereign debt with the multilateral financial institutions or foreign banks. Because Chile was unable to service its debt and interest payments were being capitalized, total indebtedness did not decrease. In fact, foreign debt increased by another $3 billion between 1982 and 1985, from 71 percent to 124 percent of GDP, reaching 440 percent of the country's exports in 1984–85. By 1985, the share of the private sector in total foreign debt was only 38 percent (34 percent in 1986), down from more than 60 percent only four years earlier.

In sum, by 1985, with a stock of foreign debt above 120 percent of GDP, Chile was facing a severe external constraint and was unable to service its debt without seriously jeopardizing its capacity to grow at a sustainable rate. Although this situation was common to many developing countries, Chile's position was more precarious than that of the Latin American and Caribbean region as a whole, where the average debt-to-GDP ratio in 1985, at almost 60 percent, was less than half that of Chile. In 1985, Chile's interest payments represented 44 percent of exports, about 9 percentage points more than the region's average; at almost 440 percent, the total debt-to-exports ratio stood about 100 percentage points above the region's average. Chile's trade balance represented only 26 percent of the country's interest payments, significantly lower than in many other Latin American countries (see annex table 16A.1).

Debt-Swap Mechanisms in Chile

By 1984, the economic authorities had reinstated capital controls and increased import tariffs to 35 percent, in an effort to increase government revenues and ameliorate the scarcity of foreign exchange.[4] After the debt crisis, all foreign transactions had to occur through and be registered by the commercial banking system; they were settled at the official exchange rate set by the central bank. At the same time, an unofficial parallel foreign exchange market developed, made up of small exchange bureaus in which retail transactions occurred. Though unofficial and unregulated, the parallel market was not illegal at the time. In this market, agents could buy or sell foreign exchange in small amounts for travel and other small-scale transactions.

In a further effort to reduce Chile's debt overhang and regain access to the international capital markets more quickly, in May 1985 the authorities introduced new mechanisms to allow domestic and foreign residents to swap foreign debt for Chilean assets in the form of newly issued local debt or equity. The two mechanisms were known by the corresponding chapters that established and regulated them in the central bank's Compendium of Foreign Exchange Rules. The first, Chapter XVIII, governed the debt-swap operations that domestic residents were allowed to undertake; the second, Chapter XIX, governed transactions permitted by foreign residents. Both mechanisms were designed to attract investors who would benefit from buying Chile's foreign debt at a significant discount in the secondary market and exchanging it for new securities payable in local currency at the official exchange rate and issued at (or near) par value.

The main difference between the two mechanisms, and the reason why they were put in separate chapters in the Compendium, was that future access to the official or formal foreign exchange market—which operated through the banking system—was granted only to foreigners, who were expected to repatriate capital and profits at some date in the future. Chileans were denied access to this mechanism because they were supposed to invest and stay in the country rather than repatriate profits and principal in the future.

Chapter XVIII

Chapter XVIII allowed domestic residents to buy foreign Chilean debt at a discount in the secondary market and exchange it for new debt or equity issued by the original debtor and payable in local currency. Except for the exchange rate applicable to the transaction, which was the official rate at the time of the swap, the parties involved had to agree ex ante to the conversion terms of the debt swap (that is, how many U.S. dollars' worth of new debt or equity would be issued for each dollar of old debt), because this was not regulated. The parties approached the central bank to register the swap only after they had agreed on the terms of the transaction, which had to be executed by a commercial bank. The commercial bank charged a fee for locating the discounted instruments to be bought as part of the transaction and for representing the interested parties before the central bank.

When the original debtor was the central bank (that is, when the original foreign debt securities used in the operation had been issued by the central bank), the conversion terms of the swap were preannounced and nonnegotiable. The central bank paid for its old debt with new debt instruments issued below par and at a floating interest rate, so investors received less than the nominal value of the debt they exchanged.[5] The discount

Figure 16.1 Basic Cash Flows in a Debt-for-Equity
(or Debt-for-Debt) Swap

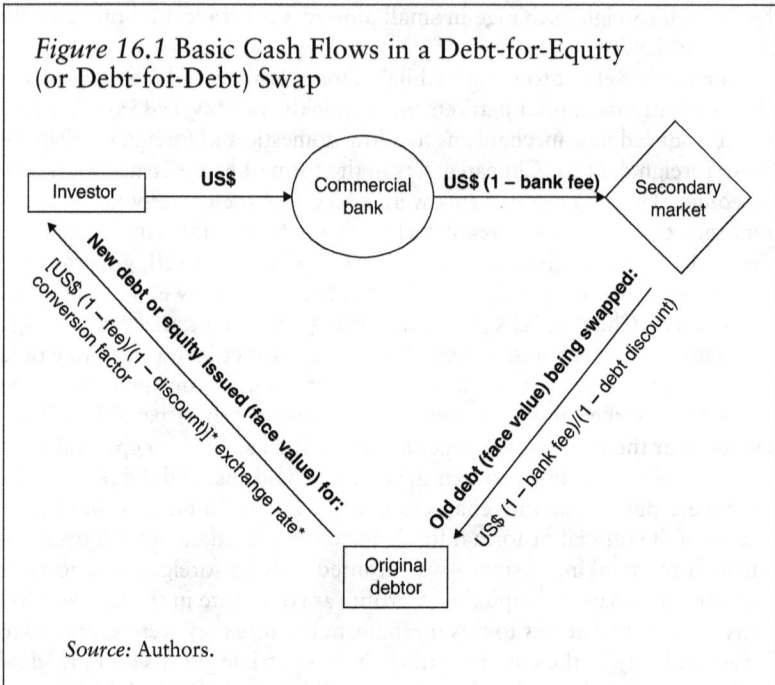

Source: Authors.

from par value of the new debt was regulated by the central bank, which charged a negative premium by setting the interest rate below market rates (figure 16.1).

Investors had to pay for the discounted instruments in the secondary market abroad with their own foreign exchange, because they were not allowed to access the official foreign exchange market to carry out the debt swap. The fact that the debt swapping was executed at the official exchange rate meant that investors incurred an additional loss—the difference between the official exchange rate and the one existing in the unofficial parallel market. By directly accessing the parallel market, investors could have sold their holdings of foreign exchange (if they had such holdings) to obtain local currency. Alternatively, if their initial capital was in local currency, they had to access the parallel market to obtain foreign currency in order to be able to buy discounted Chilean foreign debt abroad.

Concerned about potential adverse redistributive effects, as well as effects on the parallel exchange rate and the level of domestic interest rates if large numbers of debt swaps were to materialize, the authorities decided to cap the monthly volume of Chapter XVIII operations authorized.[6] This was done through monthly auctions, in which investors bid for Chapter XVIII quotas. The bids were a percentage of the nominal value to be swapped; the proceeds from the auctions were kept by the central bank.

The gross return in Chilean pesos for a domestic resident investing in Chilean assets under Chapter XVIII is thus given by

$$\text{Gross Return} = [1 / (1 - \text{Debt Discount})] \times [\text{ER}^{\text{Official}} / \text{ER}^{\text{Parallel}}]$$
$$\times \tau \times (1 - \delta) \times (1 - \text{Bank Fee}),$$

where Debt Discount is the percentage discount of the Chilean foreign debt in the secondary markets; $\text{ER}^{\text{Official}} / \text{ER}^{\text{Parallel}}$ is the ratio between the official and parallel foreign exchange rates; τ is the conversion rate, the amount of new debt or equity issued for each $1 of old debt, expressed in foreign currency; δ is the fee paid to the central bank during the auction (a percentage of the nominal value of the swap); and Bank Fee is commercial bank fees as a percentage of the nominal value of the swap.[7]

Domestic debtors were not allowed to buy back their own debt at a discount and then apply for Chapter XVIII, because allowing them to do so would have violated the sharing clause, under which a debtor cannot prepay a debt with a particular creditor unless the same offer is made to all creditors. (This was the reason why the operation had to be carried out through a commercial bank.) Furthermore, after the debt swap was completed, domestic investors were not required to keep their investments in the firm whose debt had been swapped; they were allowed to sell the securities they had received to other investors or use them to capitalize other national firms or banks.

Chapter XIX

Chapter XIX functioned very much like Chapter XVIII, with three main differences:

- The investment was granted FDI status, guaranteeing the investor access to the official foreign exchange market for the repatriation of dividends (profits) and principal in the future; principal and profits resulting from the investment were subject to minimum stay periods before they could be repatriated (10 years and 4 years, respectively).
- Swap operations under Chapter XIX were approved on a case-by-case basis, to make sure that they meant actual investment and not just the reinvestment of profits resulting from previous FDI or the round-tripping of other available funds; the resources collected from the debt swap could be used only for the authorized investment; and the central bank could accept, reject, or impose additional requirements before approving swap applications.
- Because of (b), the investments were not subject to the auctioning of quotas, allowing investors to retain a larger share of the profitable swap operation.

The Results

Debt-swap operations were authorized in 1985 and abolished in 1995. During this period, 359 transactions were authorized under Chapter XIX, from a pool of 600 applications (an approval rate of 60 percent). Authorized debt-to-equity swap operations under Chapter XIX amounted to about $3.7 billion over this period. The bulk of the transactions took place in the first five and a half years, with 98 percent of the total volume swapped occurring between 1985 and 1990 (table 16.1). A similar pattern is observed for Chapter XVIII. In both cases, the last operation occurred in October 1991.

Debt swaps decreased after 1990, mainly because as the economy began growing, the discount in the secondary market for Chilean debt instruments fell significantly, making it less attractive to use Chapters XVIII and XIX to invest in Chile. The decline was slightly more rapid for Chapter XVIII, because investors lost interest as the profits reaped from buying the discounted debt abroad were arbitraged away by the quota auctioning conducted by the central bank. During the years when most of the transactions occurred, the discount of Chilean debt in international capital markets fluctuated between about 30 percent and 40 percent of its nominal value (table 16.2). By June 1991, the discount had fallen to about 10 percent, from about 35 percent only 16 months earlier (in February 1990).

During the period when the bulk of the debt-swap operations occurred, Chapter XVIII and Chapter XIX together accounted for about

Table 16.1 Chapter XIX Transactions, 1985–95

Applications/year	Number	US$ millions[a]	Percent
1985	—	32	0.9
1986	—	246	6.7
1987	—	953	26.0
1988	—	1,839	50.2
1989	—	3,160	86.3
1990	—	3,578	97.7
1991	—	3,600	98.3
Total	600	6,802[b]	100
Approved	359	3,664	54
Rejected	241	3,138	46

Source: Central Bank of Chile various years.
Note: — Not available.
a. Figures show total authorized cumulative values.
b. Figure is total applications (authorized and unauthorized values).

Table 16.2 Average Monthly Market Price of Foreign Debt Notes in Selected Latin American Countries, 1985–88
(par value = 100)

Country	1985	1986	1987	1988
Argentina	62	64	48	24
Brazil	78	74	53	47
Chile	67	67	62	58
Colombia	82	81	79	63
Ecuador	67	65	44	23
Mexico	81	58	54	48
Peru	47	20	11	5
Venezuela, R. B. de	82	75	64	50

Source: French-Davis 1985, 1987, 1989.
Note: Values for 1985 are as of June. Values for other years are as of December.

Table 16.3 Value of Debt Swaps and Other Capitalization Mechanisms in Chile, 1985–1991
(US$ millions)

Year	Capitalization under FDI law	Chapter XVIII	Chapter XIX	Direct portfolio swaps and other mechanisms	Total
1985	53.0	115.2	32.3	129.7	330.2
1986	56.3	410.6	213.5	303.1	983.5
1987	124.6	695.8	707.3	451.0	1,978.7
1988	51.5	909.3	885.9	1,093.6	2,940.3
1989	2.4	410.3	1,321.4	1,033.2	2,767.3
1990	15.9	591.6	417.5	70.7	1,095.7
1991	—	147.0	21.6	658.9	827.5
Total	303.7	3,279.8	3,599.5	3,740.2	10,923.2

Source: Central Bank of Chile various years.
Note: — Not available.

63 percent of all Chilean debt conversion, with a cumulative volume of $6.9 billion. This percentage increases to 67 percent if 1990—the last year when transactions were significant—is taken as the cutoff point (table 16.3). Considering the stock of outstanding debt at the start of the swap program—about $20 billion—Chapters XVIII and XIX accounted for a debt reduction of about one-third of the initial stock.

Rationale for Debt Swaps in a Heavily Indebted Country

Chapters XVIII and XIX played a significant role in reducing or converting debt, but this does not necessarily mean that these official swap mechanisms were the most efficient ways of resolving the debt-overhang problem or improving welfare. What alternatives were available? What might have happened in Chile had the mechanisms not been created?

Debt swaps cannot be analyzed in isolation; they must be understood as part of a program aimed at relieving overindebtedness. At the time it adopted Chapters XVIII and XIX, Chile was facing a severe foreign exchange constraint and was unable to service its foreign obligations. Following the 1982–83 recession, the authorities were struggling to regain access to the capital markets and obtain new lending to finance the trade account and allow the economy to recover sustainable growth. Doing so did not seem feasible at a time when both debt interest and principal were being capitalized or kept in arrears. Taking into account the context in which these mechanisms were introduced is necessary for understanding some of the arguments raised at the time for and against such mechanisms (table 16.4).

All of the arguments advanced in table 16.4 are based on a partial equilibrium analysis; they are valid only to the extent that market imperfections exist. In other words, because debt-swap mechanisms are nothing but the restructuring of a country's net foreign liabilities, there is no value added by the government creating special mechanisms to restructure a country's liabilities in an economy with complete markets, clear allocation of property rights, and no information asymmetries. Any government intervention will be redundant, because similar private solutions would arise endogenously through market forces that would arbitrage away all possible opportunities for profitable investment. In a general equilibrium setting without market imperfections, some of the arguments in table 16.4 can be dismissed as follows:

- "Con" argument 1 is incorrect, because the higher cost of the new debt (or equity) compensates for the benefit obtained when buying the old debt at a discount (in the case of equity, the higher cost goes hand in hand with the greater risk-sharing component with respect to debt).
- "Pro" argument 3 is incorrect, because the higher or lower procyclicality of remittances will be priced through a lower or higher discount rate (a positive or negative risk premium), so the country will end up paying a price for it.
- "Pro" argument 4 is incorrect, because higher taxes imply that the country will have to pay a higher dividend yield on FDI (because investors care about after-tax rather than pretax returns).
- "Pro" argument 5 is incorrect, because the reduction in country risk would occur in tandem with an increase in the price of debt in the

Table 16.4 Pros and Cons of Debt-Swap Mechanisms

Pros	Cons
1. Reduce capital flight and permit more rapid repatriation of offshore capital held by residents abroad (increase repatriation of capital that fled the country in previous years)	1. Substitute cheap foreign debt for more expensive domestic debt or equity
2. Provide benefits usually associated with FDI flows, including the transfer of new technologies, easier access to foreign markets for exports, and improvements in management	2. May end up substituting for "new money" if investment would have taken place anyhow
3. Increase the procyclicality of transfers abroad, because debt-related payments are stable over time and do not fluctuate with the cycle (or are less procyclical than profit remittances)	3. May push exchange rate up or, if capital controls exist, encourage the emergence of a clandestine foreign exchange market, with all the well-known undesirable consequences, such as underinvoicing of exports and overinvoicing of imports
4. Increase tax revenues, because FDI profits are (were at the time) taxed at a higher rate (flat 40 percent) than debt interest	4. May end up creating inflationary pressures (if paid for by printing money) or raising domestic interest rates (if paid for by issuing new domestic debt)
5. To the extent that markets are not perfect—that is, not every risk is priced and reflected in an interest rate differential—reduction in foreign debt through swaps reduces country risk and therefore the country's cost of capital	5. Exchanging foreign debt for domestic assets in the aftermath of a crisis, when assets are undervalued and markets depressed, means "selling assets too cheap" (fire sale argument)

Source: Authors.

    secondary market (that is, a lower discount from face value), so that the country would not benefit from it on a net basis.
- The fire sale argument ("con" argument 5) is valid only to the extent that one believes that the true intrinsic value of assets is higher than what the market is willing to pay for them (that is, because of some market imperfection, market prices do not fully reflect the true value of assets).[8]

If the arguments in table 16.4 are valid only to the extent that market imperfections exist, what is the value added of a government creating special debt restructuring mechanisms? What imperfections exist that prevent market forces from providing such restructuring mechanisms privately, so that government intervention is justified? Three market imperfections that may justify intervention are coordination problems, incomplete markets, and information asymmetries.

Coordination Problems

Government intervention may be justified if it resolves a market coordination problem—that is, if it allows for an orderly workout, such as bankruptcy proceedings or deposit insurance (to avoid bank runs arising from a crisis of confidence). Debt-swap mechanisms of the type used in Chile may add value in resolving a debt-overhang problem if they allow for a coordinated solution to the problem of allocating losses (a zero-sum game in which a better solution for one creditor is necessarily detrimental to others and thus leads to unstable equilibria).

Market Completion

Government intervention may be justified if it creates a market that would not arise on its own. It is usually argued, for example, that a private long-term debt market will not develop until the government or a public entity such as the central bank starts issuing its own long-term debt because a benchmark is needed before private transactions can start. This argument can be extended to include cases in which official intervention is required because a proper institutional or regulatory framework is lacking (for example, property rights are unclear) or artificial restrictions need to be removed.

Information Asymmetries

Government action may also be justified on the grounds that the market is misinformed or misled with respect to the true value of the country's debt. Thus, if the authorities believe that the country's true repayment capacity is greater than what the market estimates, foreign debt will be undervalued, and the country can profit by buying its debt at a discount. The belief that the market has not correctly valued a country's debt may arise, for instance, if the economic authorities have a poor track record, so that their announcement of a fiscal and monetary stabilization program, however genuine their commitment, is not fully credible.[9] It makes sense to intervene only if the market discount is larger than the discount the debtor's real creditworthiness or risk rating would warrant. This argument is similar to the "leaning against the wind" argument for intervening in the foreign exchange market when the authorities believe that the price of the currency is misaligned in relation to the country's fundamentals.

The Case of Chile

To what extent did these arguments apply in Chile? It can be argued that the two mechanisms created by the central bank, especially Chapter XVIII, served as an efficient coordination mechanism for allocating losses. Both mechanisms were market friendly: they relied on market prices to determine the value of the debt being exchanged, and no investor was precluded from buying or selling Chilean debt. The measures thus respected the sharing clause and relied on market forces to allocate losses, reducing the possibilities for arbitrary decision making favoring one participant over others.[10] The central bank quota auctioning for Chapter XVIII swaps also reduced the likelihood of unfair treatment. The same logic applied to the international secondary market for debt. Indeed, as Edwards and Larraín (1989) argue, for debt swaps to work, investors need a deep enough secondary debt market, one in which prices (discounts) are competitive and investors and creditors are not left unprotected or subject to market squeezes or other uncompetitive practices.[11]

But that is not all. In Chile, where the majority of the debt originated in the private sector and was later assumed by the public sector, the coordination mechanism for debt resolution needed to make sure that the proceeds from the debt swap would not benefit the original borrowers. For countries in which much of the foreign debt originates in the public sector, this may be less of a problem.

Chapter XIX overcame this difficulty by its case-by-case approval mechanism for transactions, in which the applicant's investment proposal as well as personal history and references were scrutinized. For Chapter XVIII operations, the problem was surmounted by precluding agents from buying their own debt and by the central bank's quota auctioning, which provided the added advantage that part of the debt-swap benefits accrued to the central bank (which had assumed part of the private debt after the crisis). The compulsory undertaking of all swap operations through commercial banks (which charged fees) permitted the domestic banks to receive some of the benefits, allowing them to rebuild their eroded capital base. Because the government had taken over banks that were in distress and near default during the crisis, forcing management and owners out, the swap-related earnings benefited the new owners (either the state or the stockholders who bought stock after privatization).

The market completion rationale is also tenable for Chile. Indeed, there is anecdotal evidence that the mechanisms were created after a Saudi Arabian banker approached a central bank official in 1984, expressing his interest in undertaking a debt capitalization in Chile (Garcés 1987). Before these formal debt-conversion mechanisms were introduced in Chile and other Latin American countries, an embryonic secondary market for debt swaps (called by some observers "a bazaar"[12]) already existed, which probably needed the encouragement of a consistent legal and regulatory framework before it could become truly effective. The lack of a proper institutional and legal setting had apparently held down the development of the secondary debt market and its swapping for new securities. Significantly, only 3 percent of the total debt swaps undertaken during 1985–95 were private sector debt; 97 percent involved securities issued or guaranteed by the public sector (of which 59 percent was debt originally issued by the private sector but later guaranteed or underwritten by the public sector). This result is consistent with the view that the exchange of public or publicly guaranteed debt was supported by clearer rules and subject to less arbitrary bargaining with the debtor than was private debt.[13]

The argument based on information asymmetries would justify government or central bank intervention to the extent that the country (the government, the central bank, or domestic residents) captures the discount on the debt. However, given the severe shortage of foreign exchange, which prevents the country from financing its current account or buying back its discounted debt, it may be necessary to transfer some of this benefit to foreigners in order to attract new investment. This transfer can be achieved by swapping the debt at par in local currency or, more generally, at a lower discount than that being offered in foreign markets. In Chile, the economic benefits of the debt swaps were shared by the central bank (when auctioning swap quotas), commercial banks (which urgently needed to recapitalize), other private domestic agents undertaking Chapter XVIII operations, and foreigners undertaking Chapter XIX operations.

The benefits of Chapter XVIII swaps were reaped entirely by domestic agents.[14] In contrast, Chapter XIX swaps benefited foreigners. Why, then, did the government introduce Chapter XIX? One reason why it did so is the standard benefits associated with FDI noted in table 16.4. Another is the need to attract foreign exchange to finance the current account (both Chapter XVIII and Chapter XIX operations were expected to reduce the shortage of foreign exchange). Because Chapter XVIII investors were excluded from the official foreign exchange market and not allowed to repatriate the principal and future profits, these operations were not expected to exacerbate the shortage of foreign exchange. To the contrary, because foreign debt was exchanged for domestic debt or equity, net demand for foreign exchange was expected to fall, because there was no need to service the debt being swapped.

The minimum stay restrictions on Chapter XIX operations for the repatriation of principal and dividends (10 years for principal, 4 years for dividends); the case-by-case approval system; and tight capital controls reduced the chances of round-tripping and undesirable effects such as the overinvoicing of imports and underinvoicing of exports. Case-by-case approval implied that often extra conditions—for instance, additional new investments—were imposed in the interests of increasing welfare. All were used to help contain the pressure on the foreign exchange rate in the case of Chapter XIX operations.

Applicability of Debt Swaps in Other Countries

Our analysis suggests that the two central bank–supported mechanisms used in Chile were effective and important in helping resolve the debt-overhang problem and ease the shortage of foreign exchange faced in 1984–85. The swap mechanisms allowed for a conversion of debt that amounted to about one-third of the total outstanding debt at the time of their inception. It is unlikely that these mechanisms simply substituted for other potential private arrangements, crowding out other sources of foreign exchange, because the mechanisms helped overcome important problems impeding the emergence of alternative private solutions. These problems included coordination problems, market completion, asymmetric information, and other market imperfections.

Our conclusion does not imply that the mechanisms worked perfectly or that they did not create some second-order (undesirable) effects, especially for the distribution of the benefits and the final burden of the crisis. We believe, however, that for the country as a whole, the benefits of the mechanisms outweighed their costs.

How applicable is the Chilean experience to other countries? Does the positive outcome for Chile imply that similar debt-swap mechanisms could be implemented successfully elsewhere? We conclude only that the mechanisms were effective in Chile, where some preconditions were in place before the mechanisms were launched. Principal among these preconditions were a strong legal, regulatory, and supervisory framework; a strict adjustment program aimed at attaining macro stability and sustained high economic growth; a commitment to take into account any redistribution consequences; and a domestic capital market deep enough to intermediate the necessary savings to finance the program. If these prerequisites are not met, debt swaps are not likely to lead to desirable outcomes, as described below.

Rule of Law and Enforceable Regulations

Debt-swap mechanisms of the type put in place by Chile in 1985 could be exploited to enrich some groups at the expense of taxpayers. This will occur, for instance, if there is massive underinvoicing of exports or overinvoicing of imports; if the proceeds from the debt swaps provide the financing for capital flight; if investors can easily round-trip funds; or if investors declare their intention to undertake an investment project in the future that never materializes (and the proceeds from the swap leave the country through some other channel). The larger the discount of foreign debt and the higher the value paid domestically by the government (the higher the conversion rate of public or publicly guaranteed debt), the greater the likelihood that investors looking for private profits will try to elude the capital controls applicable to debt swaps or engage in simple fraud. To ensure that debt swaps do not become the source of major fraud, countries must therefore have in place an institutional setting that is capable of exerting tight and effective monitoring of capital controls and other regulations. This may be a critical issue for developing countries in which institutional development remains weak.

This was not a serious problem in Chile, where the central bank has historically been able to exert tight control over the banking system through the use of capital controls and other regulations. Thus, capital flight was not a major source of indebtedness in the years surrounding the debt crisis: at about $1 billion between 1976 and 1985, total capital flight in Chile accounted for just 6.4 percent of the increase in the country's debt (Edwards and Larraín 1989), a figure significantly smaller than that of other Latin American countries, where capital flight accounted for 60 percent or more of the country's additional debt during the same period. Similarly, in the 1990s, when Chile imposed a reserve requirement (*encaje*) on capital inflows, the central bank was able to exert tight control over banks and other intermediaries, and there was minimal evasion. More evidence of the tight control exerted by the central bank is the fact that about 90 percent of the intended investments foreign companies declared under Chapter XIX operations were subject to *in situ* inspections in the years after their approval and subject to fines and legal sanctions when it was discovered that they had not taken place.

Structural Programs for Macro Stabilization and Growth

Without a sound and consistent macro policy framework, the economy will not be able to regain a high and sustainable rate of growth; the country will not be able to attract and retain new investment; recovery will be short-lived; and capital flight, balance of payments crises, high inflation, and related malaises will recur. With the consequent erosion of credibility, the cost of borrowing will continue to rise, and the authorities will have an even harder road to climb the next time they try to resolve the debt overhang. Ultimately, if the country does not truly improve its repayment capacity, the benefits from buying back its debt at a discount will not materialize.

Distribution Effects

The distribution of income and wealth is a matter of concern for many countries, both developing and developed; it should be the province of policy tools designed to improve income and wealth distribution. Nevertheless, debt-conversion programs, in which smart investors can potentially reap huge gains at the expense of taxpayers, should pay special attention to potentially undesirable redistribution effects. In particular, when designing mechanisms, policy makers should ensure that swap profits do not reward those who were partly responsible for the country's overindebtedness. This was a serious concern for Chile, because the bulk of its debt was originally private. Special provisions prohibited some groups from benefiting from the swap program (unless they used the proceeds to recapitalize and pay their debts in full). Furthermore, the institutional and legal framework allowed the authorities to seize the assets of those involved in the original borrowing, with the government taking full control and ownership of all corporations and banks that went bankrupt after the crisis and whose debt was in the end assumed by the public sector. In addition, several managers and owners of bankrupt banks and corporations were investigated and prosecuted.

These distributional aspects matter not only because of fairness or equity reasons but also because, if unattended, they will erode public support for the debt-conversion program, creating a politically unstable situation that could jeopardize the entire program along with the macro stabilization effort. Ideally, the benefits from the debt swaps should accrue to taxpayers, either directly or indirectly. In the case of Chile, taxpayers benefited because they were given the option of buying stocks in companies and banks that were rescued by the government in a large-scale privatization program that started a few years after the crisis. The option of buying stocks was proportional to the individual taxes paid in previous years.

Proper Financing

As in any other debt-restructuring exercise (except debt forgiveness), debt swaps substitute foreign debt (which, at best, is being partly serviced) for new domestic debt or equity. Unless all the new securities issued after the swap are kept by foreigners, debt swaps raise domestic interest rates, the inflation rate (if the government is unable to cut expenditures or increase tax revenues to service its new obligations), or both. For a debt-swap program to be successful, the volume of debt being swapped must be consistent with the financing capacity of the country (that is, with the government balance and the savings intermediation capacity of the domestic capital market).

In Chile, the economy as a whole was able to swap a relatively large volume of foreign debt because the domestic capital market was growing rapidly, largely as a result of the 1981 pension reform, which replaced a (bankrupt) pay-as-you-go system with a fully funded capitalization system. This meant that a large volume of long-term savings was being intermediated by the domestic capital market every year. Sound fiscal management made sure that these savings were not used by the government to fund its deficit. Other countries considering implementing a debt-swap program similar to Chile's should make sure that the domestic economy has the capacity to generate enough savings and government revenues to finance it. Not being able to fulfill the new debt obligations will lead to higher inflation and interest rates, with all the associated negative effects.

Conclusion

In using debt-swap mechanisms to reduce a country's overindebtedness, policy makers can take a variety of steps to increase the chances of success. They can be summarized as follows:

- To avoid undesirable outcomes such as capital flight, round-tripping, overinvoicing of imports and underinvoicing of exports, and mere fraud, policy makers must be sure that a strong institutional and legal framework is in place.
- To ensure public support, they must pay close attention to distributional effects. In particular, policy makers must make sure that the benefits of the debt swaps do not accrue to those responsible for the overindebtedness.
- They must provide incentives for attracting new investment (larger inflows), delaying the payment of interest and capital (smaller outflows), or both. It may be necessary, for instance, to impose restrictions on flow remittances (that is, to prohibit remittances of profits and principal until a certain number of years have elapsed); require additional investments for the approval of swap transactions; or both. The government can compensate investors for committing their funds for a longer period by providing them with a larger share of the discount on the debt (the share could be proportional to the time horizon of the investment).
- To reduce the scope for discretionary outcomes and help reestablish investors' confidence, they must use market-friendly mechanisms where possible to allocate losses and benefits.

Annex: Selected Macroeconomic Indicators in Chile, 1970–90

Table 16A.1 Selected Macroeconomic Indicators in Chile, 1970–90

Year	Change in GDP (percent)	December to December inflation rate (percent)	Current account balance (US$ billions)	Current account balance (percentage of GDP)	Total reserves minus gold (US$ billions)	Imports of goods and services (US$ billions)	Total reserves minus gold (months of imports)	Exports of goods and services (US$ billions)	Terms of trade 1978 = 100
1970	2.1	34.9	−102.9	−1.15	342	1,212	3.4	1,298	220.8
1971	9.0	22.1	−205.5	−1.92	170	1,289	1.6	1,128	209.2
1972	−1.2	163.4	−404.8	−3.51	97	1,642	0.7	1,232	205.7
1973	−5.6	508.1	−294.6	−1.80	122	1,643	0.9	1,444	225.1
1974	1.0	375.9	−210.8	−1.36	41	2,182	0.2	2,256	186.8
1975	−12.9	340.7	−491.3	−6.80	56	1,980	0.3	1,838	100.4
1976	3.5	174.3	147.9	1.50	405	2,049	2.4	2,476	109.7
1977	9.9	63.5	−551.4	−4.13	426	2,996	1.7	2,755	101.1
1978	8.2	30.3	−1,088.0	−7.06	1,090	3,685	3.5	3,170	100.0
1979	8.3	38.9	−1,189.0	−5.74	1,938	5,413	4.3	4,826	111.4
1980	7.9	31.2	−1,970.6	−7.15	3,123	7,438	5.0	6,292	114.3
1981	6.2	9.5	−4,732.6	−14.50	3,213	8,734	4.4	5,360	105.3
1982	−13.6	20.7	−2,304.2	−9.47	1,815	5,173	4.2	4,712	91.5
1983	−2.8	23.1	−1,117.3	−5.65	2,036	4,215	5.8	4,771	97.3
1984	5.9	23.0	−2,110.5	−10.97	2,303	4,651	5.9	4,477	87.6
1985	2.0	26.4	−1,413.0	−8.57	2,450	4,152	7.1	4,649	84.1
1986	5.6	17.4	−1,191.2	−6.72	2,351	4,613	6.1	5,155	84.2
1987	6.6	21.5	−735.0	−3.52	2,504	5,670	5.3	6,264	92.6
1988	7.3	12.7	−231.2	−0.94	3,161	6,668	5.7	8,349	106.3
1989	10.6	21.4	−689.9	−2.43	3,629	8,609	5.1	9,885	105.2
1990	3.7	27.3	−484.8	−1.54	6,068	9,506	7.7	10,498	98.7

Source: Authors' compilation based on data from Central Bank of Chile various issues; World Bank various years; and Wagner, Jofré, and Lüders 2000.

Table 16A.2 Selected Macroeconomic Indicators in Chile, 1970–90

Year	Real effective exchange rate index (1978 = 100)	Total external debt (US$ billions)	Short-term debt (US$ billions)	Medium- and long-term debt (US$ billions)	Total debt as percentage of total exports	Total short-term debt as percentage of total exports	Total short-term debt as percentage of GDP	Total debt as percentage of GDP	Fiscal deficit as percentage of GDP
1970	39.6	2,977	409	2,568	229	31.5	4.6	33.1	2.86
1971	36.9	3,048	431	2,617	270	38.2	4.0	28.5	9.50
1972	34.0	3,540	493	3,047	287	40.0	4.3	30.7	12.46
1973	51.2	3,855	581	3,273	267	40.3	3.5	23.5	24.02
1974	77.6	5,243	722	4,521	232	32.0	4.6	33.7	9.32
1975	101.1	5,519	758	4,761	300	41.2	10.5	76.4	3.39
1976	91.0	5,620	772	4,848	227	31.2	7.8	57.0	2.31
1977	81.7	5,883	864	5,019	214	31.4	6.5	44.0	1.67
1978	98.7	7,374	1,101	6,273	233	34.7	7.1	47.9	0.83
1979	99.6	9,361	1,635	7,726	194	33.9	7.9	45.2	-1.65
1980	87.7	12,081	2,560	9,521	192	40.7	9.3	43.8	-3.01
1981	75.4	15,664	2,989	12,675	292	55.8	9.2	48.0	-1.72
1982	87.8	17,315	3,338	13,977	367	70.8	13.7	71.1	2.42
1983	106.4	17,928	2,599	15,329	376	54.5	13.1	90.7	3.90
1984	109.9	19,737	1,914	17,823	441	42.7	10.0	102.6	4.42
1985	139.4	20,384	1,668	18,716	438	35.9	10.1	123.6	6.52
1986	149.4	21,144	1,689	19,455	410	32.8	9.5	119.3	3.09
1987	155.9	21,489	2,017	19,472	343	32.2	9.6	102.8	0.50
1988	166.1	19,582	2,202	17,380	235	26.4	8.9	79.5	1.79
1989	162.1	18,032	2,973	15,059	182	30.1	10.5	63.5	1.20
1990	168.3	19,226	3,382	15,844	183	32.2	10.7	60.9	1.16

Source: Authors' compilation based on data from Central Bank of Chile various issues; World Bank various years; and Wagner, Jofré, and Lüders 2000.

Notes

This chapter was written while the author was affiliated with the Central Bank of Chile. The author is extremely grateful to Ángel Salinas for providing very valuable data and relevant hindsight.

1. Reforms consisted of lifting all administrative restrictions on trade, abolishing import quotas, and unilaterally reducing tariffs to a 10 percent flat rate (except on a few luxury items, such as jewelry, fur, and cars).

2. Restrictions were maintained only for short-term capital flows; they were gradually abolished for medium- and long-term inflows.

3. About 85 percent of Chile's foreign debt was dollar denominated (Fontaine 1989).

4. After the crisis, the government balance moved swiftly into deficit, because of the cost incurred in bailing out the banking, corporate, and household sectors.

5. The conversion rate was initially set at $0.91 per dollar. It was later changed several times.

6. The move was motivated by two sources of initial uncertainty surrounding the debt-swap operations. First, it was not clear ex ante how much pressure would be exerted on the parallel exchange rate (because investors would turn to that market to obtain foreign currency to make the swap) or domestic interest rates (because foreign debt was being swapped for domestic debt denominated in local currency). Second, there was considerable uncertainty about potential adverse effects on the distribution of benefits.

7. Exchange rates are expressed in local currency per US$ 1.

8. Such market distortion occurs when policy makers, or the domestic community at large, believe that a negative externality arises if specific groups (usually foreigners) own the country's assets. Such arguments are usually advanced to limit the foreign ownership of domestic firms (in many countries, foreigners are allowed only a minority participation in the stock of traded firms) or the flow of FDI to exploit natural resources.

9. Conversely, if the debtor country believes there is a smaller chance that its debt will be serviced than do creditors, it will not buy back the debt even at a discount. If the market discount is fair—that is, if it reflects the country's true repayment capacity—the country will be indifferent between buying the debt back and not buying the debt back.

10. This is not entirely true to the extent that the conversion rate of the debt had to be negotiated directly with the original debtor. This unresolved coordination problem may be the reason why 97 percent of the debt swaps comprised debt issued or guaranteed by the central bank, whose conversion rate was nonnegotiable and preannounced by the central bank.

11. According to Edwards and Larraín (1989), these conditions were met only after the 1985 Baker Plan.

12. This observation is attributed to the deputy comptroller of the currency at the time, Mr. Bench (Garcés 1987).

13. This is also consistent with the previous (complementary) argument based on the resolution of coordination problems (see note 10).

14. Internal redistribution toward specific groups may be an undesirable second-order effect of Chapter XVIII operations, but this problem should probably be dealt with by other policies, not those designed to overcome a debt-overhang (macro) problem.

References

Central Bank of Chile. Various issues. *Boletin Mensual.* Santiago

———. Various years. *Chilean External Debt.* Santiago.

Edwards, S., and F. Larraín. 1989. "Debt, Adjustment, and Recovery in Latin America: An Introduction." In *Debt, Adjustment and Recovery*, ed. S. Edwards and F. Larraín, 1–27. London: Basil Blackwell.

Fontaine, J.A. 1989. "The Chilean Economy in the Eighties: Adjustment and Recovery." In *Debt, Adjustment and Recovery*, ed. S. Edwards and F. Larraín, 208–40. London: Basil Blackwell.

French-Davis, R. 1985. "La economía Chilena y la deuda externa: Después de la renegociación de 1985." Apuntes CIEPLAN 9 (Noviembre), Santiago

———. 1987. "Conversión de pagarés de la deuda externa en Chile." Estudio 129, Colección Estudios CIEPLAN 22 (Diciembre): Corporación de Estudios para Latinoamérica, Santiago

———. 1989. "Debt-Equity Swaps in Chile." Notas Técnicas CIEPLAN 129 (Mayo), Corporación de Estudios para Latinoamérica, Santiago

Garcés, F. 1987. "Foreign Debt Conversion in Chile." Central Bank of Chile, Santiago.

Wagner, G., J. Jofré, and R. Lüders. 2000. "Economía Chilena 1810–1995: Cuentas fiscales." Documento de Trabajo 188, Instituto de Economía, Universidad Católica de Chile, Santiago.

World Bank. Various years. *World Development Indicators.* Washington, DC: World Bank.

Index

Boxes, figures, notes, and tables are indicated by b, f, n, and t, respectively.

ECO-AUDIT
Environmental Benefits Statement

The World Bank is committed to preserving endangered forests and natural resources. The Office of the Publisher has chosen to print *Debt Relief and Beyond: Lessons Learned and Challenges Ahead* on recycled paper with 30 percent postconsumer fiber, in accordance with the recommended standards for paper usage set by the Green Press Initiative, a nonprofit program supporting publishers in using fiber that is not sourced from endangered forests. For more information, visit www.greenpressinitiative.org.

Saved:
- 8 trees
- 3 million Btu of total energy
- 808 lb. of net greenhouse gases
- 3,892 gal. of waste water
- 236 lb. of solid waste

g green press INITIATIVE

www.ingramcontent.com/pod-product-compliance
Lightning Source LLC
Chambersburg PA
CBHW071948270326
41928CB00009B/1384